All American History

Volume II

Uniting America's Story, Piece by Piece

The Civil War to the 21st Century

Teacher's Guide & Answer Key

A full year's curriculum in 32 weekly lessons

CELESTE W. RAKES

Bright Ideas PRESS

Dover, DE

All American History, Volume II: Uniting America's Story, Piece by Piece;
The Civil War to the 21st Century — Teacher's Guide & Answer Key
by Celeste W. Rakes
Vol. II of the All American History series

Published by Bright Ideas Press
P.O. Box 333, Cheswold, DE 19936
www.BrightIdeasPress.com

Cover and interior design by Pneuma Books, LLC. Visit www.pneumabooks.com for more information.
The publisher wishes to thank Melissa E. Craig for compiling the unit book lists.

ISBN-13: 978-1-892427-43-4 (Softcover Teacher's Guide & Answer Key)
ISBN-10: 1-892427-43-5 (Softcover Teacher's Guide & Answer Key)

Publisher's Cataloging-In-Publication Data
(Prepared by The Donohue Group, Inc.)

Rakes, Celeste W.
 All American history. Teacher's guide : uniting America's story, piece by piece / Celeste W. Rakes.

 2 v. : ill., maps ; cm.

 Title from v.1 t.p.
 "A full year's curriculum in 32 weekly lessons."
 Contents: v. 1. The explorers to the Jacksonians — v. 2. The Civil War to the 21st century
 Includes bibliographical references.
 ISBN-13: 978-1-892427-10-6 (v. 1)
 ISBN-10: 1-892427-10-9 (v. 1)
 ISBN-13: 978-1-892427-43-4 (v. 2)
 ISBN-10: 1-892427-43-5 (v. 2)

 1. United States—History. 2. United States—History—Study and teaching. 3. United States—History—Problems, exercises, etc. I. Title. II. Title: All American history. Teacher's guide & answer key : uniting America's story, piece by piece

E178.1 .R274 2006   2008922020
973

PRINTED IN THE UNITED STATES OF AMERICA
∞
17 16 15 14 13 12 11 10 09 08   01 02 03 04 05 06 07 08 09 10

TABLE OF CONTENTS

Section One

HOW TO USE
ALL AMERICAN
HISTORY
VOL. II

How Do I Get the Most from This Curriculum?

Introduction

All American History, Volume II, is organized into thirty-two lessons, each of which is designed to provide a week's worth of instruction. However, the lessons on World War I and World War II are longer than the other thirty lessons; you may want to spend an extra week on one or both of those lessons or set aside more time for history during the week that you are working on those lessons. An additional four weeks (one at the end of each unit) can be devoted to unit reviews, field trips, and/or completion of special projects.

Both volumes of *All American History* have been designed with the following unique features:

- Adaptability for both younger students and high school students
- Both hands-on activities and strong, challenging content
- Emphasis on social *and* cultural history
- Interactive forms to be used while reading and teaching the lessons
- Context for each lesson provided in the Atmosphere section of each lesson
- Weekly summation of the important points of each lesson

How Do I Use the Student Reader?

The *Student Reader* is designed to be used in tandem with the *Student Activity Book*. Whether the student reads the lesson in the reader independently or has the material taught or explained to him by a teacher, he should be encouraged to work on that lesson's corresponding *forms* (not the For Review or For Further Study questions) in the *Student Activity Book* as he processes the information in the reader. Completing these forms while being introduced to the material in the *Student Reader* provides practice in "note-taking" and helps the student analyze and retain the material better. In the section "How Do I Use This Curriculum with My Co-op?" below, you will find more details concerning how to present the lessons in the reader to students with auditory and kinesthetic learning styles. A strong reader should not struggle with mastering the information in the *Student Reader* and the accompanying pages in the *Student Activity Book*.

How Do I Use the Student Activity Book?

The *Student Activity Book* is not optional. Filling out the forms designed for each lesson will not only improve the student's understanding and retention of the material he has read (or been taught), but it will also provide him with additional information not found in the *Student Reader*. The For Review questions for each lesson (found after the forms in the *Student Activity Book*) were also carefully crafted to ensure that the student has mastered the important information for that lesson.

At the end of each of the thirty-two lessons, the *Student Activity Book* lists four For Further Study questions. In the Section Four answer keys of this *Teacher's Guide*, you will find a great deal of information related to these projects — in other words, the answers! Even if you do not assign these projects to your student, plan on reading the information in Section Four, under "For Further Study Questions and Answers," for each lesson. *A wealth of interesting historical details is contained in this section, much of which you could share quickly and easily with your child if he is not attempting to research the For Further Study Questions on his own.*

How Do I Use the Teacher's Guide?

 This *Teacher's Guide* is a tremendous resource, and the wealth of ideas that make this curriculum complete, memorable, and fun can ONLY be found in this *Teacher's Guide*.

Section Two, Teaching Resources, contains the following information, broken down unit by unit:

- Project Possibilities that can be ongoing for the entire eight weeks
- Book List Reminder
- Timeline Dates
- Mapmaking Reminder
- Review Games
- Family Activities
- Checklists

Section Three is filled with annotated book lists of both fiction and nonfiction reading for the primary, middle, and secondary levels. This section is also divided into four units.

Section Four consists of the answers to the For Further Study questions in the *Student Activity Book*, as well as suggestions for adapting these questions for younger students.

Section Five provides the answers to the *Student Activity Book* forms and maps and the For Review questions.

Section Six has eleven optional, reproducible forms that your students can use to guide them into further research about significant topics.

Section Seven contains all the reproducible images needed for the *Student Activity Book* forms. These images may also be used for your timelines or review games, or for making other projects/notebooks.

How Do I Use This Curriculum with Sixth – Eighth Grade Students?

 This curriculum was created to be used with middle school/junior high students (sixth–eighth graders). However, students in these grades possess a wide range of abilities and a variety of learning styles. The older and more capable the student, the more you should expect in terms of comprehension and retention of the information in the *Student Reader*, degree of completion of the *Student Activity Book* pages, and tackling of the For Further Study questions. Many students in this grade range have become excellent independent readers, but others still struggle with reading on their own and become easily discouraged without verbal interaction and/or hands-on activities. *All American History* was developed to offer learning opportunities to visual, auditory, and kinesthetic learners. Please remember that this is also a high school level course; therefore, be discerning in how much you assign to your sixth–eighth grade student.

How Do I Use This Curriculum with High School Students?

All American History, Volume II, is a rich, in-depth course for high school students. For your student to earn an American History high school credit, my recommendations would be to:

- Assign the majority of the For Further Study questions in the *Student Activity Book* (found at the end of each lesson)
- Accomplish some of the Project Possibilities listed in this *Teacher's Guide*
- Require the use of some of the optional forms in the *Student Activity Book*
- Compile the For Review questions (or selections from those questions) in the *Student Activity Book* to use for tests

How Do I Use This Curriculum with Younger Students?

Even though *All American History, Volume II*, was designed with middle school/junior high students in mind, a homeschooling family should find many activities and projects for younger students in the *Teacher's Guide*, as well as fun learning experiences for the entire family. It is important for you to re-alize that the *Student Reader* was not designed to be read word-for-word to younger children (unless they are gifted and working above grade level). However, much of the information in the reader lessons *will be* very interesting to them if shared in a simple storytelling fashion. The teacher or an older child can re-tell or narrate the lesson to younger students, concentrating on the important people and events and showing them the pictures in the *Student Reader* for that lesson.

You may decide, however, not to narrate the *Student Reader* to your younger students. Rather, you may choose to have them read books related to the topics in the *Student Reader*, while their older sibling(s) are studying the *Student Reader*. For each of the four units, you will find in this *Teacher's Guide* lists of individuals for whom you can find biographies. You will also find annotated reading lists for younger, middle, and high school students. If your younger child enjoys reading or being read to, you should easily be able to locate more than enough books from the library to keep him and/or you busy for the eight weeks of each unit. Don't worry about covering all the peo-ple and events found in the *Student Reader* and don't worry about whether your reading is perfectly chronological. Just concentrate on making learning history enjoyable; awaken your younger student's appetite for further study of American history in the years ahead.

If a younger child likes to write or do things with his hands, he may enjoy cutting out the images and flags in the *Student Activity Book* and placing them on the correct forms while an older sibling completes the forms. (Section Seven of this *Teacher's Guide* has all the images for the forms, so you could easily copy some for a younger student.) The younger child doesn't have to fill in all the blanks on the form —just a few of the more important ones. Many younger children would enjoy using colored pencils to draw on the maps found on the back of many of the forms or using a children's atlas to find major places mentioned in the lessons.

Section Four of this *Teacher's Guide* also has lesson-by-lesson suggestions on how to adapt the For Further Study questions for use with younger children. Your older students may enjoy sharing with their younger siblings some of the information that they are learning in these projects. Each lesson also has at least one suggested Family Activity. All of these were designed particularly with the younger members of the family in mind.

How Do I Use This Curriculum with My Family?

The first day or two of each lesson should be spent digesting the information found on the week's topic in the *Student Reader*. Older students will probably be able to read and understand the information and complete the corresponding forms in the *Student Activity Book* on their own. These forms were intended to be used as the student is reading/hearing the information from the *Student Reader*. (If younger children in the family are included in the unit study, the parent should read carefully the previous section on how to use this curriculum with younger students.)

Following the completion of the lesson's required forms, the student can check to see how well he has mastered the material by tackling the lesson's For Review questions. You will probably also want to add the Timeline Dates (which can be found for each unit in Section Two of this *Teacher's Guide*) to your family timeline.

If your state requires a portfolio, a notebook containing the required forms as well as any additional maps, timelines, and your student's Native American and African American notebooks would make excellent portfolio additions.

The remainder of the week should be devoted to other projects chosen by the student and/or parent. Each of the thirty-two lessons in the *Student Activity Book* contains four For Further Study questions related to that week's topic. Some of these projects are research-oriented, whereas others are more hands-on activities. Choose which projects you wish to pursue each week. Providing your junior high student with an opportunity to try his hand at some historical research would be of great benefit to him. If you have younger students, you may choose to use the adaptations of the For Further Study questions created just for them. A high school student should usually do all four of the For Further Study questions every week. To make your job easier, the information that should be gained from working on these questions is included in the For Further Study answers in Section Four of this *Teacher's Guide*. If time does not allow for completion of all four of the For Further Study questions, your student would certainly profit from hearing or reading the brief account of the historical details contained in these For Further Study answers.

The *Teacher's Guide* also contains Project Possibilities that span the entire eight weeks of each unit. If you have children who love to read, supply them with a stack of biographies or historical fiction for each time period. My daughter, who is a voracious reader, read biographies of all the presidents and many other important American historical figures. You might also pick a family read-aloud book for each of the units. Even if your child is not a big reader, try to get him to read at least several books for each eight-week unit. He doesn't have to pick large volumes; I have learned many fascinating historical facts from short biographies and works of nonfiction, and the illustrations and photographs in such books are usually wonderful.

If you have younger children or children who enjoy hands-on learning, look specifically at Lessons 15, 16, 31, and 32 and plan opportunities for them to do some cooking, to listen to music, or to look at paintings. There are also a number of hands-on activities scattered throughout the For Further Study questions in each unit. Don't be afraid to let them write a play or videotape a news report or come up with some other creative way to use the information that they are learning. Some of our most precious homeschooling memories as a family resulted from such attempts.

At the end of each unit you may choose to insert a *bonus* week before beginning the next unit's lessons. This ninth week could be used for field trips, watching related movies, and finishing projects or adding to notebooks. Planning for this *bonus* week is a wonderful stress reducer and provides *catch-up* time if there has been any sickness or other reasons why your student might be behind.

How Do I Use This Curriculum with My Co-op?

The co-op class for which I developed this curriculum met once a week for an hour. During that time period, I shared with the students most of the information found in the *Student Reader* for that week's lesson. I did not read it to them word-for-word. Rather, I attempted to share it with them in a storytelling fashion. Although I didn't memorize the facts of the lesson, I was familiar enough with them that I could tell the story in my own words.

I also tried to make my presentation interactive. Instead of doing all the talking, I came up with questions to get the students involved in discovering some of the information on their own and in forming opinions about what they were learning. I also had them working on their *Student Activity Book* forms in class.

As I talked about a president, students were cutting and pasting his picture to his form and filling in the information about him. I discovered that I didn't need to be afraid to let my students do something with their hands while I was telling the story. This multi-sensory approach really seemed to solidify their understanding of the information that I was sharing. Years later, my son can remember almost everything he learned using this hands-on approach.

During our class time, I also brought in many pictures and photographs to make what we were discussing more real to my students. If I had been teaching just my own child at home, I might not have gone to the trouble of doing that. However, for a classroom of students, I made the effort—and it was well worth it. Looking at the visual depictions of the material that we were studying always raised further questions or provoked other insights, and I ended up learning from my student's reactions to the images. We also did map and timeline work in class.

In some of my co-op classes, we did the For Review questions in the *Student Activity Book* together as a class. One group in particular loved doing this. With other groups, I assigned the For Review questions for them to do at home, and then we went over them as a review at the beginning of the next class period. I have also used the unit Review Games found in the *Teacher's Guide*—sometimes with teams, depending on the size of the group, and sometimes with the opportunity to earn little treats. This is always a big hit!

During the four days that my co-op students were at home, they were encouraged to choose at least a couple of related projects to work on (either from the lesson's For Further Study questions or from the Project Possibilities listed for the unit in the *Teacher's Guide*). In the co-op situation in which I taught, the responsibility for monitoring the students' progress in their work at home was left with their parents. However, I always encouraged my students to bring to class any of their projects that they would like to show me, and I occasionally offered some kind of reward for them to do so. I also planned a special co-op field trip or activity for each of the units.

How Do I Use This Curriculum with My Classroom?

 Most of what I shared concerning the co-op classes that I taught would apply in this context as well. The major difference is that you (the classroom teacher) will be supervising the projects that your students work on, rather than their parents at home. You will also have to come up with a means of grading their work. The following are some of the decisions that you will have to make.

- Will you require your students to do any reading other than that from the *Student Reader*? If so, will you require biographies, historical fiction, nonfiction, or a combination? How much reading will you require them to do, and how much choice will you give them in what they pick to read? How will you hold them accountable for what they read—will you have them write a report, give an oral presentation, do a poster, or create some sort of art project?
- Will you require your students to construct any of the suggested notebooks—Native American or African American? If so, which ones? Will you assign any creative writing projects? Will they work on these individually or in groups?
- Will you require your students to do any of the For Further Study questions? If so, how many? Will it be the same number for each lesson?
- Will you assign the same project(s) to the entire class or will you allow the students to individually choose which of the Project Possibilities they would like to do?
- Will you plan review games for the class, or does your schedule allow for field trips or special historical days —complete with food and other hands-on activities?
- Will you give tests on the material? If you desire to do so or are required to do so, the review activities in the *Student Activity Book* would provide a rich resource for test questions.

There are dozens of possible combinations of projects and activities that you could choose for your classes. As their teacher, you'll be the best one to determine which activities are chosen and in what order they are accomplished. That said, here are two *possible* schedules:

Option One

(for classes that meet five days a week)

- Monday — Students read to themselves from the *Student Reader* and/or participate in teacher-led discussion of the information contained in the *Student Reader* along with work on the corresponding forms (including maps) in the *Student Activity Book*
- Tuesday — Timeline Dates and the For Review questions
- Wednesday — Reading day (allowing them time to read supplemental books relating to the time period for that unit or lesson)
- Thursday — For Further Study questions and Review Games
- Friday — Testing day (if you are required to test) and/or more supplemental reading time

Option Two

(for classes that meet three days a week)

- Monday — Students read to themselves from the *Student Reader* and/or participate in teacher-led discussion of the information contained in the *Student Reader* along with work on the corresponding forms (including maps) in the *Student Activity Book* and adding Timeline Dates
- Wednesday — For Review questions, additional reading, begin For Further Study questions
- Friday — Finish For Further Study questions, additional reading, and/or Review Games, testing day (if required)

Detailed Instructions

Forms

This curriculum was developed with the intention of having the students complete the forms in the *Student Activity Book* while reading and studying the lessons in the *Student Reader*. All the information that I have requested from the students for these forms is included in the lessons of the *Student Reader*. If the information is not included in the *Student Reader* or is not specific in the text of the *Student Reader*, then that space on the form is filled in for the student. *These forms are NOT intended to be used as quizzes or tests, only as multi-sensory reinforcement of the information from the lessons.* They are also great practice for note-taking.

Optional Forms

In Section Six of this *Teacher's Guide* as well as in the *Student Activity Book*, there are eleven additional forms that may be photocopied repeatedly. Filling in the Notebook Timeline form is one option for your student to use in creating a timeline. The other forms can guide your student in doing additional research and/or creating notebooks. The Optional Forms include:

- Notebook Timeline
- Native American Tribe
- Native American
- African American
- United States President
- Civil War Battle
- World War I Battle
- World War II European Battle
- World War II Pacific Battle
- Korean War Battle
- Vietnam War Battle

Images and Flags

The *Student Activity Book* forms were designed to allow removal of the pages from the binding and placement in a three-ring binder, if so desired. The images and flags to be glued onto these forms are all included in the back of each *Student Activity Book*. For ease of cutting, I have placed the images and flags in order, starting at the bottom right-hand corner and moving up each column, right to left. These images are in the exact order that they will be used, and some students will begin to recognize this pattern. You will also notice a thin, black line in the space between a few of the images. This line indicates the last of the images for one unit and the first of the next unit.

A majority of the images included in both the *Student Reader* and the *Student Activity Book* were obtained from either the Library of Congress or the National Archives. I have included the reproduction numbers or call numbers in the credit lines of each of these images. If you are interested in doing further research on these topics, both the Library of Congress and the National Archives contain a vast array of visual resources (many of which are available online) that can be searched topically or by these reproduction or call numbers.

All the images and flags have also been included in the back of this book for your use. Feel free to photocopy them before cutting and use them for review games, flashcards, or replacements for your students. Please note that I have chosen to use current flags to represent the countries that were involved in wars and not historical flags of those countries, unless no current flag exists. This was done solely for ease of visual identification.

Maps

There is a map on the back of most of the required *Student Activity Book* forms. Some of these maps are to be completed to match the corresponding maps in the *Student Reader*. However, maps on the back of the president forms, the states and capitals review maps, and the presidents review maps are to be completed using different directions, which can be found on each individual map.

A legend box has been included on each of the maps so that your student can choose colors and/or patterns to express information as desired. Additional blank maps might be helpful for reviewing the location of cities and countries, states and capitals practice, and illustrations for optional For Further Study questions. Blank maps are also handy for younger students who enjoy coloring, for kinesthetic or visual learners, and for students desiring to do more hands-on projects.

Book Lists

Books can really make history come to life for students of all ages! We have done the work for you in finding a plethora of books. These extensive, annotated book lists are found in Section Three, listed by unit and then by primary, middle, and secondary grade levels. Enjoy yourself—read aloud with your students as much as is reasonably possible. Make a point of finding attractive, well-illustrated books for your visual learners. Find books-on-tape for the auditory ones. While none of these books are required, they will add depth to your studies.

Timelines

In this *Teacher's Guide*, Timeline Dates are listed, by unit, in Section Two, Teaching Resources. Section Seven, Images for Required Forms, of this book contains many images that are perfect for timelines, as well as for the optional Notebook Timeline form.

Timelines are especially useful for:

- Seeing the events of history in a graphically organized fashion
- Seeing the events of history at a glance
- Seeing relationships between people, places, and events
- Making an abstract concept concrete
- Visual learners
- Kinesthetic learners as they construct their timeline
- Reinforcing the information being studied

There are a number of methods for recording timelines. Here are a few examples:

- On strips of paper along a wall
- On poster board or science project boards
- On a laminated Timeline of World History
- On index cards

Another option (especially appealing to older students) is to have the student create a notebook-style timeline. To that end, we have included in this *Teacher's Guide* a notebook-style timeline form.

An extremely useful website for seeing photos of a variety of timeline styles is www.homeschoolinthewoods.com by Amy Pak, whose illustrations are used in *All American History, Volumes I and II.*

Additional Resources: Atlases, Maps, and Timelines

All the following atlas, map, and timeline resources are recommended by and available from Bright Ideas Press.

Atlases

Choose the ones that are right for your students. Both a world and a USA atlas are necessary.

- *Rand McNally Children's Illustrated Atlas of the World* (grades 4–8)
- *Rand McNally Answer Atlas* (world atlas) (grades 8–12)
- *Rand McNally Premier Atlas* (world and USA) (grades 9 and up)
- *Rand McNally Children's Illustrated Atlas of the United States* (all ages)
- *Rand McNally Historical Atlas of the United States* (optional but highly recommended for grades 7 and up)

Outline Maps

- *Uncle Josh's Outline Map Book* (includes world maps as well as maps of each state)
- *Wonder Maps: Maps for all Ages CD-ROM* (print out maps as you need them)
- Blank, laminated, oversized USA map
- Blank, laminated, oversized world map

Timeline Resources

- *History through the Ages: America's History* timeline figures by Amy Pak — available in both a cardstock version and a CD-ROM version.
- Laminated Timeline of World History

Section Two

TEACHING
RESOURCES

UNIT ONE
Resources

Project Possibilities

1. Have your student(s) choose a biography of one or more of these key figures from the Civil War and Reconstruction period.

   - Henry Clay
   - Harriet Tubman
   - Zachary Taylor
   - Millard Fillmore
   - Franklin Pierce
   - James Buchanan
   - Dred Scott
   - Harriet Beecher Stowe
   - William Lloyd Garrison
   - Frederick Douglass
   - Sojourner Truth
   - John Brown
   - Abraham Lincoln
   - Jefferson Davis
   - Robert E. Lee
   - Ulysses S. Grant
   - Thomas "Stonewall" Jackson
   - Clara Barton
   - J. E. B. Stuart
   - William Tecumseh Sherman
   - Thaddeus Stevens
   - Andrew Johnson

Your student(s) should decide how the key figure's childhood and life experiences prepared that individual for the contributions that he or she made during the Civil War or Reconstruction.

2. Have your student(s) pick one or more works of historical fiction to read from the Unit One Book List.

3. Have your student(s) select one or more creative writing projects related to the information you learn concerning the Civil War and Reconstruction. Projects may include writing a poem about a war leader or a battle, a journal entry from a day in the life of a Union or Confederate soldier, a newspaper article or a script for a TV news report describing a battle, or a drama depicting a significant event that occurred during this period.

   The drama could be performed for an audience or the TV news report could be performed and videotaped.

   Your student(s) can also illustrate the writing project or make a mural depicting one of the battles of the Civil War.

4. Have your student(s) compile a Civil War Battles Notebook. There are forms in the optional forms section of the *Student Activity Book* to use to do this. If possible, plan a trip to visit a Civil War battle site, fort, or prison. Go to a nearby cemetery and look for graves dating back to the Civil War and Reconstruction. Also look for houses or buildings from this period in history. Take a tour if you can.

5. If your student(s) began an African American notebook when studying Volume I (or would

---

like to start one now), add a page to the notebook about Harriet Tubman and Dred Scott when you study Lesson 1, Frederick Douglass and Sojourner Truth when you study Lesson 2, and Hiram Revels when you study Lesson 8.

Book List Reminder

See the annotated bibliography in Section Three.

Timeline Dates

As you study each important event in the Civil War and Reconstruction period, record the dates on your timeline.

- 1849–1850: Zachary Taylor (Lesson 1)
- 1850: Compromise of 1850 (Lesson 1)
- 1850–1853: Millard Fillmore (Lesson 1)
- 1853–1857: Franklin Pierce (Lesson 1)
- 1857–1861: James Buchanan (Lesson 1)
- 1859: John Brown's Raid (Lesson 2)
- 1861–1865: Abraham Lincoln (Lesson 2)
- 1861–1865: Civil War (Lesson 2)
- 1861–1865: Confederacy (Lesson 2)
- 1863: Emancipation Proclamation (Lesson 4)
- 1863: Gettysburg Address (Lesson 5)
- 1865: Freedmen's Bureau Act (Lesson 7)
- 1865: Lincoln's Assassination (Lesson 7)
- 1865: Black Codes (Lesson 7)
- 1865: Ratification of the Thirteenth Amendment (Lesson 7)
- 1868: Ratification of the Fourteenth Amendment (Lesson 7)
- 1865–1869: Andrew Johnson (Lesson 8)
- 1867–1877: Radical Reconstruction (Lesson 8)
- 1868: Impeachment of Andrew Johnson (Lesson 8)
- 1869–1877: Ulysses S. Grant (Lesson 8)
- 1870: Ratification of the Fifteenth Amendment (Lesson 8)

Mapmaking Reminder

Directions for completing the map forms can be found in the introduction to the *Student Activity Book*.

Review Games

For long-term usage and durability, you may wish to either photocopy the images onto cardstock or glue them to a piece of poster board before cutting them out.

1. Begin working on learning the U.S. presidents in order. If you have a copy of *All American History, Volume I*, cut out the pictures of the first eleven presidents — George Washington, John Adams, Thomas Jefferson, James Madison, James Monroe, John Quincy Adams, Andrew Jackson, Martin Van Buren, William Henry Harrison, John Tyler, and James Polk. If not, just write their names on individual cards. Cut out the pictures of Zachary Taylor, Millard Fillmore, Franklin Pierce, James Buchanan, Abraham Lincoln, Andrew Johnson, and Ulysses S. Grant. See if your student(s) can lay out the presidents, one by one, in the order that they served. Then practice saying them in order without their pictures.

2. Locate the descriptions of individuals from the Civil War Hall of Fame in the Unit One Final Review. Make a copy of the descriptions. Cut out the pictures from the Hall of Fame that match the descriptions. Glue the description to one side of an index card. Write the person's name and glue his picture to the other side, and use them as flash cards for review. This review can be done beginning with Lesson 2 of Unit One. Just keep adding pictures of individuals and descriptions to your collection of flash cards as you study them each week.

Family Activities

Lesson 1

- Secret information was passed along the Underground Railroad by fugitive slaves using lyrics from spirituals, such as "Swing Low, Sweet Chariot" or "Wade in de Water." In "Swing Low, Sweet Chariot," a person from the Underground Railroad was "coming for to carry" a fugitive slave "home" to freedom. "Wade in de Water" was used to tell runaway slaves to travel in rivers and streams so that dogs would not be able to track them. Look for the words of these and other African American spirituals and try to listen to a recording of them.

Lesson 2

- Read together what the Bible has to say about slaves and slavery. One southern argument was that slavery was not wrong because the Bible did not say that it was wrong. Do you agree? Why or why not?

- Find the words to the song "John Brown's Body." What other famous Civil War song is sung to the same tune?

Lesson 3

- Listen to a recording of the song "Dixie" and look at its words. This song was played at the inauguration of Confederate President Jefferson Davis and became identified with the Confederacy. However, "Dixie" was written in 1858 by Daniel Emmett, whose parents were strict abolitionists, for a New York (northern) minstrel show. The playing of "Dixie" is controversial in a public setting; talk about whether you think it should be played and why or why not. If you want to do some family "research," look for the different explanations of how the word *Dixie* originated.

Lesson 4

- Clara Barton, remembered for her work as a Civil War nurse, also went on to found the American Red Cross. Visit a local Red Cross center and discover what local, national, and international services the Red Cross provides.

Lesson 5

- See if your extended family has any photographs dating from the Civil War and any other war

memorabilia or stories. If there is a museum with Civil War artifacts in your area, plan a family field trip there. The Internet has many slide shows of photographs taken during the Civil War. Look at one or more of those slide shows together. Pay close attention to the uniforms worn by the soldiers and the clothing worn by civilians, as well as to weapons and other war equipment.

Lesson 6

- "Sutlers" were civilians who sold "extras" to the troops during the Civil War at inflated prices. Some of their prized items for sale included preserved peaches, cans of condensed milk, and molasses cookies. Bake some molasses cookies and eat some peaches, and remember the soldiers who fought so many years ago.

Lesson 7

- Many of the popular songs sung in the Civil War and Reconstruction period are still familiar today. Each side freely adapted the other's music and altered the lyrics. Favorite Union songs were "Tenting Tonight," "Marching through Georgia," and "When Johnny Comes Marching Home Again." Favorite songs of the Confederacy were "Cheer, Boys, Cheer," "The Bonnie Blue Flag," and "The Yellow Rose of Texas." See if you can find words and recordings for several of the songs and listen to them.

Lesson 8

- See if there is an African Methodist Episcopal (AME) church in your community. Find out how an AME church is different from your family's church. Discuss whether you think there should be separate white churches and separate African American churches.

UNIT ONE
Checklist

Please Note:
SR = *Student Reader*
SAB = *Student Activity Book*
TG = *Teacher's Guide*

Required for Lesson 1
- ❏ Lesson 1 (page 5, SR)
- ❏ Corresponding Required Forms (page 1, 3, 5, 7, 17, SAB)
- ❏ Corresponding Maps (page 2, 4, 6, 8, SAB)
- ❏ For Review questions (page 9, SAB)

Optional for Lesson 1
- ❏ For Further Study questions (page 10, SAB)
- ❏ Additional Options for Unit (page 13, TG)

Required for Lesson 2
- ❏ Lesson 2 (page 19, SR)
- ❏ Corresponding Required Forms (page 13, 15, 17, 18, SAB)
- ❏ Corresponding Maps (page 14, 16, SAB)
- ❏ For Review questions (page 19, SAB)

Optional for Lesson 2
- ❏ For Further Study questions (page 21, SAB)
- ❏ Additional Options for Unit (page 13, TG)

Required for Lesson 3
- ❏ Lesson 3 (page 33, SR)
- ❏ Corresponding Required Forms (page 17, 23, 25, SAB)
- ❏ Corresponding Maps (page 26, SAB)
- ❏ For Review questions (page 27, SAB)

Optional for Lesson 3
- ❏ For Further Study questions (page 30, SAB)
- ❏ Additional Options for Unit (page 13, TG)

Required for Lesson 4
- ❏ Lesson 4 (page 47, SR)
- ❏ Corresponding Required Form (page 23, 21, SAB)
- ❏ Corresponding Map (page 32, SAB)
- ❏ For Review questions (page 33, SAB)

Optional for Lesson 4
- ❏ For Further Study questions (page 36, SAB)
- ❏ Additional Options for Unit (page 13, TG)

Required for Lesson 5
- ❏ Lesson 5 (page 61, SR)
- ❏ Corresponding Required Form (page 23, 24, 37, SAB)
- ❏ Corresponding Map (page 38, SAB)
- ❏ For Review questions (page 39, SAB)

Optional for Lesson 5
- ❏ For Further Study questions (page 40, SAB)
- ❏ Additional Options for Unit (page 39, TG)

Required for Lesson 6
- ❏ Lesson 6 (page 75, SR)
- ❏ Corresponding Required Form (page 24, 41, SAB)
- ❏ Corresponding Map (page 42, SAB)
- ❏ For Review questions (page 43, SAB)

Optional for Lesson 6
- ❏ For Further Study questions (page 91, SAB)
- ❏ Additional Options for Unit (page 47, TG)

Required for Lesson 7
- ❑ Lesson 7 (page 91, SR)
- ❑ Corresponding Required Form (page 47, SAB)
- ❑ Corresponding Map (page 48, SAB)
- ❑ For Review questions (page 49, SAB)

Optional for Lesson 7
- ❑ For Further Study questions (page 52, SAB)
- ❑ Additional Options for Unit (page 13, TG)

Required for Lesson 8
- ❑ Lesson 8 (page 105, SR)
- ❑ Corresponding Required Form (page 47, 53, SAB)
- ❑ Corresponding Map (page 54, SAB)
- ❑ For Review questions (page 55, SAB)

Optional for Lesson 8
- ❑ For Further Study questions (page 56, SAB)
- ❑ Additional Options for Unit (page 13, TG)

Required for Unit One
- ❑ Final Review (page 57, SAB)

Additional Options for Unit
- ❑ Project Possibilities (page 13, TG)
- ❑ Timeline Dates (page 14, TG)
- ❑ Review Games (page 14, TG)
- ❑ Additional Reading from Book Lists (page 39, TG)
- ❑ For Further Study Questions/Answers and Younger Student Adaptations (page 66, TG)
- ❑ Family Activity Ideas (page 14, TG)

Teaching Resources — Unit One Checklist
©2008 Bright Ideas Press. All rights reserved.

UNIT TWO
Resources

Project Possibilities

1. Have your student(s) choose a biography of one or more of these key figures from the Gilded Age.

   - Alexander Graham Bell
   - William Jennings Bryan
   - Teddy Roosevelt
   - "Wild Bill" Hickok
   - Sitting Bull
   - George Armstrong Custer
   - Buffalo Bill Cody
   - John D. Rockefeller
   - Andrew Carnegie
   - Cornelius Vanderbilt
   - William Howard Taft
   - Woodrow Wilson
   - Elizabeth Cady Stanton
   - Susan B. Anthony
   - Jane Addams
   - Booker T. Washington
   - W. E. B. Du Bois
   - Dwight L. Moody
   - Fanny Crosby
   - Phineas T. Barnum
   - Thomas Edison
   - John Philip Sousa
   - Scott Joplin
   - Mark Twain

   Your student(s) should decide how the key figure's childhood and life experiences prepared that individual for the contributions that he or she made during the Gilded Age.

2. Have your student(s) pick one or more works of historical fiction to read from the Unit Two Book List.

3. Have your student(s) select one or more creative writing projects related to the information you learn concerning the Gilded Age. Projects may include writing a poem about life on the western frontier, a journal entry from a day in the life of a cowboy on the trail, a newspaper article or a script for a TV news report describing an important event in a president's administration or a battle during the Spanish-American War, or a drama depicting another significant event that occurred during this period.

   The drama could be performed for an audience or the TV news report could be performed and videotaped.

   Your student(s) can also illustrate the writing project or make a mural depicting the battles of the Spanish-American War or one of the presidents' administrations.

4. If your student(s) began a Native American notebook when studying Volume I, add a page when you study Sitting Bull and the Lakota in Lesson 11.

5. If your student(s) began an African American notebook when studying Volume I (or would like to start one now), add pages to the notebook when you study Booker T. Washington and W. E. B. Du Bois in Lesson 15.

Book List Reminder

See the annotated bibliography in Section Three.

Timeline Dates

As you study each important event in the Gilded Age, record the dates on your timeline.

- 1877–1881: Rutherford B. Hayes (Lesson 9)
- 1881: James A. Garfield (Lesson 9)
- 1881–1885: Chester A. Arthur (Lesson 9)
- 1885–1889: Grover Cleveland (Lesson 9)
- 1889–1893: Benjamin Harrison (Lesson 9)
- 1893–1897: Grover Cleveland (Lesson 9)
- 1897–1901: William McKinley (Lesson 9)
- 1898: Spanish-American War (Lesson 10)
- 1865–1885: Era of the Long Cattle Drive (Lesson 11)
- 1876: Custer's Last Stand (Lesson 11)
- 1887: Dawes Act (Lesson 11)
- 1890: End of the Indian Wars (Lesson 11)
- 1881: Founding of the AFL (Lesson 12)
- 1892: Establishment of Ellis Island Immigration Station (Lesson 12)
- 1901–1909: Teddy Roosevelt (Lesson 13)
- 1909–1913: William Howard Taft (Lesson 13)
- 1913–1921: Woodrow Wilson (Lesson 13)
- 1913: Ratification of the Sixteenth and Seventeenth Amendments (Lesson 13)
- 1919: Ratification of the Eighteenth Amendment (Lesson 13)
- 1920: Ratification of the Nineteenth Amendment (Lesson 13)
- 1876: Philadelphia Centennial Exposition (Lesson 16)
- 1893: World's Columbian Exposition (Lesson 16)

Mapmaking Reminder

Directions for completing the map forms can be found in the introduction to the *Student Activity Book*.

Review Games

For long-term usage and durability, you may wish to either photocopy the images onto cardstock or glue them to a piece of poster board before cutting them out.

1. Continue working on learning the presidents in order. Add cards for the presidents studied in Unit Two–Rutherford B. Hayes, James Garfield, Chester Arthur, Grover Cleveland, Benjamin Harrison, William McKinley, Teddy Roosevelt, William Howard Taft, and Woodrow Wilson. See if your student(s) can lay out the presidents, one by one, in the order that they served. Then practice saying them in order without using the cards. By the end of Volume II, the student should be able to recite all the U.S. presidents in order.

2. Review all the states and their capitals that your student(s) has learned thus far. Have him use an unlabeled map of the United States to practice identifying the location of each state and its capital. By the end of Volume II, the student should be able to locate all fifty states on an unlabeled map and identify the capital of each state.

Family Activities

Lesson 9

- A Disney movie, *The One and Only Genuine Original Family Band*, takes place during the time of Benjamin Harrison and Grover Cleveland. See if you can find a copy of the movie and watch it together. Notice the clothing, houses, and other cultural aspects of the Gilded Age depicted.

Lesson 10

- Teddy Roosevelt was an advocate of the "strenuous life." He battled back to health from childhood illness by his vigorous approach to living. Does your family need to find more ways to get physical exercise and keep their bodies strong? Be inspired by Roosevelt's example; encourage one another and hold each other accountable!

Lesson 11

- Watch the Peanuts movie *The Building of the Transcontinental Railroad* (part of the This Is America series).

- Find the words to "Home on the Range" and sing it. Dress like a cowboy.

- Explore the life of the Wilder family (unit studies and activities related to this family are easy to find online) and try recipes from *The Little House Cookbook: Frontier Foods from Laura Ingalls Wilder's Classic Stories*.

Lesson 12
- During the Gilded Age, American railroads and bicycles began to achieve a special place in the nation's music. Sing "I've Been Workin' on the Railroad" and "Daisy Bell" (also known as "Daisy, Daisy" and "A Bicycle Built for Two"), and read the story of Casey Jones. Compare your bicycle to pictures of bicycles from the Gilded Age.

Lesson 13
- Locate all the teddy bears owned by your family. Find out how the teddy bear got its name. Look for pictures of teddy bears from the early years of the twentieth century.

Lesson 14
- Make paper dolls dressed in Gilded Age fashions.

- Try cooking an entire meal from Fanny Farmer's *Boston Cooking-School Cook Book* (see the infor-

mation in the fourth For Further Study question for this lesson in the *Student Activity Book*).

Lesson 15
- Have a Fanny Crosby sing-a-thon. Decide how her songs are different from praise choruses sung today.

- Enjoy some of the recreational activities that were popular or that originated in the Gilded Age — basketball, baseball, croquet, and bicycling — or order a deck of Authors cards and learn to play that game. Take a field trip to the circus the next time that it comes near your home.

Lesson 16
- Ride around your town and see if you can find any houses or other buildings built during the Gilded Age. Can you find "Victorian Gothic" features in these structures? If you live near a mansion built during the Gilded Age, take a field trip to see it.

- Organize a vaudeville show using family members and/or friends.

UNIT TWO
Checklist

Please Note:

SR = *Student Reader*

SAB = *Student Activity Book*

TG = *Teacher's Guide*

Required for Lesson 9
- ❑ Lesson 9 (page 123, SR)
- ❑ Corresponding Required Forms (page 63, 65, 67, 69, 71, 73, SAB)
- ❑ Corresponding Maps (page 64. 66. 68. 70. 72. 74, SAB)
- ❑ For Review questions (page 75, SAB)

Optional for Lesson 9
- ❑ For Further Study questions (page 77, SAB)
- ❑ Additional Options for Unit (page 19, TG)

Required for Lesson 10
- ❑ Lesson 10 (page 139, SR)
- ❑ Corresponding Required Form (page 79, SAB)
- ❑ Corresponding Map (page 80, SAB)
- ❑ For Review questions (page 81, SAB)

Optional for Lesson 10
- ❑ For Further Study questions (page 84, SAB)
- ❑ Additional Options for Unit (page 81, TG)

Required for Lesson 11
- ❑ Lesson 11 (page 155, SR)
- ❑ Corresponding Required Form (page 85, SAB)
- ❑ Corresponding Map (page 86, SAB)
- ❑ For Review questions (page 87, SAB)

Optional for Lesson 11
- ❑ For Further Study questions (page 89, SAB)
- ❑ Additional Options for Unit (page 19, TG)

Required for Lesson 12
- ❑ Lesson 12 (page 169, SR)
- ❑ Corresponding Required Form (page 91, SAB)
- ❑ For Review questions (page 93, SAB)

Optional for Lesson 12
- ❑ For Further Study questions (page 96, SAB)
- ❑ Additional Options for Unit (page 19, TG)

Required for Lesson 13
- ❑ Lesson 13 (page 186, SR)
- ❑ Corresponding Required Forms (page 97, 99, 101, SAB)
- ❑ Corresponding Maps (page 98, 100, 102, SAB)
- ❑ For Review questions (page 103, SAB)

Optional for Lesson 13
- ❑ For Further Study questions (page 105, SAB)
- ❑ Additional Options for Unit (page 19, TG)

Required for Lesson 14
- ❑ Lesson 14 (page 195, SR)
- ❑ Corresponding Required Form (page 107, SAB)
- ❑ For Review questions (page 109, SAB)

Optional for Lesson 14
- ❑ For Further Study questions (page 111, SAB)
- ❑ Additional Options for Unit (page 19, TG)

Required for Lesson 15
- ❑ Lesson 15 (page 207, SR)
- ❑ Corresponding Required Form (page 113, SAB)
- ❑ Corresponding Map (page 114, SAB)
- ❑ For Review questions (page 115, SAB)

Optional for Lesson 15
- ❏ For Further Study questions (page 117, SAB)
- ❏ Additional Options for Unit (page 19, TG)

Required for Lesson 16
- ❏ Lesson 16 (page 219, SR)
- ❏ Corresponding Required Form (page 119, SAB)
- ❏ For Review questions (page 121, SAB)

Optional for Lesson 16
- ❏ For Further Study questions (page 123, SAB)
- ❏ Additional Options for Unit (page 19, TG)

Required for Unit Two
- ❏ Final Review (page 125, SAB)

Additional Options for Unit
- ❏ Project Possibilities (page 19, TG)
- ❏ Timeline Dates (page 20, TG)
- ❏ Review Games (page 20, TG)
- ❏ Additional Reading from Book Lists (page 45, TG)
- ❏ For Further Study Questions/Answers and Younger Student Adaptations (page 85, TG)
- ❏ Family Activity Ideas (page 20, TsG)

UNIT THREE
Resources

Project Possibilities

1. Have your student(s) choose a biography of one or more of these key figures during the period from 1910 to 1945.

   - Warren G. Harding
   - Calvin Coolidge
   - Henry Ford
   - Orville and Wilbur Wright
   - Charles Lindbergh
   - Amelia Earhart
   - Clarence Darrow
   - Alexander Fleming
   - Billy Sunday
   - Babe Ruth
   - Louis Armstrong
   - Frank Lloyd Wright
   - Herbert Hoover
   - Franklin D. Roosevelt
   - Eleanor Roosevelt
   - Shirley Temple
   - Lou Gehrig
   - Jesse Owens
   - George Gershwin
   - Winston Churchill
   - Dwight D. Eisenhower
   - George Patton
   - Douglas MacArthur
   - Albert Einstein

   Your student(s) should decide how the key figure's childhood and life experiences prepared that individual for the contributions that he or she made during this period in history.

2. Have your student(s) pick one or more works of historical fiction to read from the Unit Three Book List.

3. Have your student(s) select one or more creative writing projects related to the information you learn concerning the period from 1910 to 1945. Projects may include writing a poem about the Roaring Twenties, a journal entry from a day in the life of someone living during the Great Depression, a newspaper article or a script for a TV news report describing an important event in a president's administration or a battle during World War I or II, or a drama depicting another significant event that occurred during this period.

   The drama could be performed for an audience or the TV news report could be performed and videotaped.

   Your student(s) can also illustrate the writing project or make a mural depicting the battles of the world wars or one of the presidents' administrations.

4. Have your student compile a World War I and/or World War II Battles Notebook. There are forms in the optional forms section of the *Student Activity Book* to use for this.

5. If your student has been keeping an African American notebook, add pages to the notebook when you do the For Further Study projects on George Washington Carver and African American musicians in Lesson 20.

6. Begin a notebook documenting your family history during the twentieth century. Record family stories from the time of the Roaring Twenties, Great Depression, and World War II. Interview family members still alive who lived during this period and include copies of family photographs from the period.

Book List Reminder

See the annotated bibliography in Section Three.

Timeline Dates

As you study each important event in the period from 1910 to 1945, record the dates on your timeline.

- 1914–1919: World War I (Lesson 17)
- 1917: Russian Revolution (Lesson 17)
- 1920–1929: Roaring Twenties (Lesson 18)
- 1921–1923: Warren G. Harding (Lesson 18)
- 1923–1929: Calvin Coolidge (Lesson 18)
- 1920–1933: Prohibition (Lesson 20)
- 1920: Beginning of the Radio Age (Lesson 20)
- 1929–1933: Herbert Hoover (Lesson 21)
- 1929: Stock Market Crash (Lesson 21)
- 1929–1940: Great Depression (Lesson 21)
- 1933–1945: Franklin D. Roosevelt (Lesson 21)
- 1939–1945: World War II (Lesson 23)
- 1941: U.S. Entry into World War II (Lesson 23)
- 1945: Dropping of the First Atomic Bomb (Lesson 23)
- 1945: Establishment of the United Nations (Lesson 24)

Mapmaking Reminder

Directions for completing the map forms can be found in the introduction to the *Student Activity Book.*

Review Games

For long-term usage and durability, you may wish to either photocopy the images onto cardstock or glue them to a piece of poster board before cutting them out.

1. Continue working on learning the presidents in order. Add cards for the presidents studied in Unit Three — Warren G. Harding, Calvin Coolidge, Herbert Hoover, and Franklin D. Roosevelt. See if your student(s) can lay out the presidents, one by one, in the order that they served. Then practice saying them in order without using the cards. By the end of Volume II, the student should be able to recite all the U.S. presidents in order.

2. Review all the states and their capitals that your student(s) has learned thus far. Have him use an unlabeled map of the United States to practice identifying the location of each state and its capital. By the end of Volume II, the student should be able to locate all fifty states on an unlabeled map and identify the capital of each state.

Family Activities

Lesson 17

- Read some of the Peanuts cartoons involving Snoopy and the Red Baron. Watch a movie set during the World War I period that your family considers appropriate. Some possibilities might be *Sergeant York, All Quiet on the Western Front, The White Cliffs of Dover,* or *On Moonlight Bay.*

Lesson 18

- Pretend to be Calvin Coolidge — spend a whole day not wasting any words.

- Look for photos of Model T's and advertisements for them. What would it be like to ride in a Model T or to work on an assembly line making a Model T? See if there are any "vintage car" shows in your area that you could attend.

- Read comics from the 1920s, such as Mutt and Jeff, Barney Google, Happy Hooligan, and the

Katzenjammer Kids. Was their humor like ours today?

Lesson 19

- Make paper dolls dressed in fashions from the 1920s. There are many websites that have pictures or drawings of clothing from this decade.

- Watch the movie *Singin' in the Rain*, which is set in 1927. Notice the clothing and hairstyles worn by the characters in the movie.

Lesson 20

- Learn the words to "Take Me Out to the Ball Game." Find out more about Babe Ruth. Look for copies of some of his baseball cards.

- Take a field trip to an antique store and see if you can find any toys made during the period from 1900–1930.

- Look for examples of American Foursquare or Craftsman houses in your community.

Lesson 21

- Take a field trip to a stockbroker's office and learn more about investing in the stock market.

Lesson 22

- Toll House cookies were invented during the 1930s. Find out how they got their name. Bake some to enjoy.

Lesson 23

- Watch the movie *The Sound of Music*. Play particular attention to the scenes that occur at the time of the Anschluss. Why does the von Trapp family leave Austria?

- Your family might also want to check out the movie *Tora! Tora! Tora!*, which depicts the story of the Japanese invasion of Pearl Harbor.

Lesson 24

- During World War II, hundreds of female players tried out for the All-American Girls Professional Baseball League, and these teams played to packed stands. Look at their virtual scrapbook online.

- Watch a movie made during World War II (the *Student Reader* has a list) that your family considers appropriate. Notice the clothing and hairstyles worn by the characters in the movie.

UNIT THREE
Checklist

Please Note:

SR = *Student Reader*
SAB = *Student Activity Book*
TG = *Teacher's Guide*

Required for Lesson 17
- ❑ Lesson 17 (page 237, SR)
- ❑ Corresponding Required Forms (page 133, 135, SAB)
- ❑ Corresponding Maps (page 134, 136, SAB)
- ❑ For Review questions (page 137, SAB)

Optional for Lesson 17
- ❑ For Further Study questions (page 138, SAB)
- ❑ Additional Options for Unit (page 25, TG)

Required for Lesson 18
- ❑ Lesson 18 (page 257, SR)
- ❑ Corresponding Required Forms (page 139, 141, SAB)
- ❑ Corresponding Maps (page 140, 142, SAB)
- ❑ For Review questions (page 143, SAB)

Optional for Lesson 18
- ❑ For Further Study questions (page 145, SAB)
- ❑ Additional Options for Unit (page 25, TG)

Required for Lesson 19
- ❑ Lesson 19 (page 271, SR)
- ❑ Corresponding Required Form (page 147, SAB)
- ❑ For Review questions (page 149, SAB)

Optional for Lesson 19
- ❑ For Further Study questions (page 152, SAB)
- ❑ Additional Options for Unit (page 25, TG)

Required for Lesson 20
- ❑ Lesson 20 (page 285, SR)
- ❑ Corresponding Required Form (page 155, SAB)
- ❑ Corresponding Map (page 156, SAB)

- ❑ For Review questions (page 157, SAB)

Optional for Lesson 20
- ❑ For Further Study questions (page 160, SAB)
- ❑ Additional Options for Unit (page 25, TG)

Required for Lesson 21
- ❑ Lesson 21 (page 299, SR)
- ❑ Corresponding Required Forms (page 147, 161, 163, SAB)
- ❑ Corresponding Maps (page 162, 164, SAB)
- ❑ For Review questions (page 165, SAB)

Optional for Lesson 21
- ❑ For Further Study questions (page 167, SAB)
- ❑ Additional Options for Unit (page 25, TG)

Required for Lesson 22
- ❑ Lesson 22 (page 315, SR)
- ❑ Corresponding Required Form (page 169, SAB)
- ❑ For Review questions (page 171, SAB)

Optional for Lesson 22
- ❑ For Further Study questions (page 174, SAB)
- ❑ Additional Options for Unit (page 25, TG)

Required for Lesson 23
- ❑ Lesson 23 (page 329, SR)
- ❑ Corresponding Required Forms (page 175, 177, SAB)
- ❑ Corresponding Maps (page 176, 178, SAB)
- ❑ For Review questions (page 179, SAB)

Optional for Lesson 23

❑ For Further Study questions (page 183, SAB)
❑ Additional Options for Unit (page 25, TG)

Required for Lesson 24

❑ Lesson 24 (page 351, SR)
❑ Corresponding Required Form (page 185, SAB)
❑ Corresponding Map (page 186, SAB)
❑ For Review questions (page 187, SAB)

Optional for Lesson 24

❑ For Further Study questions (page 189, SAB)
❑ Additional Options for Unit (page 25, TG)

Required for Unit Three

❑ Final Review (page 191, SAB)

Additional Options for Unit

❑ Project Possibilities (page 25, TG)
❑ Timeline Dates (page 26, TG)
❑ Review Games (page 26, TG)
❑ Additional Reading from Book Lists (page 51, TG)
❑ For Further Study Questions/Answers and Younger Student Adaptations (page 104, TG)
❑ Family Activity Ideas (page 26, TG)

Teaching Resources — Unit Three Checklist

UNIT FOUR
Resources

Project Possibilities

1. Have your student(s) choose a biography of one or more of these key figures during the period from 1945 to the present.

   - Harry S. Truman
   - George Marshall
   - Dwight D. Eisenhower
   - Douglas MacArthur
   - Jonas Salk
   - Joseph McCarthy
   - Rosa Parks
   - Martin Luther King, Jr.
   - Billy Graham
   - Jackie Robinson
   - Hank Aaron
   - Wilma Rudolph
   - John F. Kennedy
   - Lyndon B. Johnson
   - Richard M. Nixon
   - Gerald R. Ford
   - Jimmy Carter
   - John Glenn
   - Neil Armstrong
   - Bill Gates
   - James Meredith
   - Ronald W. Reagan
   - George H. W. Bush
   - William J. Clinton
   - George W. Bush
   - Norman Schwarzkopf
   - Sally Ride
   - Christa McAuliffe

   Your student(s) should decide how the key figure's childhood and life experiences prepared that individual for the contributions that he or she made during this period in history.

2. Have your student(s) pick one or more works of historical fiction to read from the Unit Four Book List.

3. Have your student(s) select one or more creative writing projects related to the information you learn concerning the period from 1945 to the present. Projects may include writing a poem about the 1960s, a journal entry from a day in the life of someone living during the 1970s, a newspaper article or a script for a TV news report describing an important event in a president's administration or a significant development in the Korean, Vietnam, or Iraq wars, or a drama depicting another significant event that occurred during the 1980s or 1990s.

   The drama could be performed for an audience or the TV news report could be performed and videotaped.

   Your student(s) can also illustrate the writing project or make a mural depicting an important event from this era or from one of the presidents' administrations.

4. If your student has been keeping an African American notebook, add pages to the notebook when you do the For Further Study projects on Elizabeth Eckford and Linda Brown in Lesson 26;

Martin Luther King, Jr., Ralph Abernathy, and Coretta King in Lesson 27; Thurgood Marshall and Medgar Evers in Lesson 30; and Ben Carson in Lesson 32.

5. Continue your notebook documenting your family history during the twentieth century. Record family stories from 1945 to the present—this is your parents' period in history and your period in history. Interview your parents, aunts and uncles, and anyone else you think might share interesting stories, and include copies of family photographs from the period.

 Book List Reminder
See the annotated bibliography in Section Three.

 Timeline Dates
As you study each important event in the period from 1945 to the present, record the dates on your timeline.

- 1945–1953: Harry S. Truman (Lesson 25)
- 1953–1961: Dwight D. Eisenhower (Lesson 25)
- 1948–1949: Berlin Airlift (Lesson 25)
- 1949: Establishment of NATO (Lesson 25)
- 1950–1953: Korean War (Lesson 25)
- 1945–1964: Baby Boom (Lesson 26)
- 1954: *Brown v. Board of Education of Topeka* (Lesson 26)
- 1955–1956: Montgomery Bus Boycott (Lesson 27)
- 1950: Beginning of the Television Age (Lesson 27)
- 1961–1963: John F. Kennedy (Lesson 28)
- 1963–1969: Lyndon B. Johnson (Lesson 28)
- 1969–1974: Richard M. Nixon (Lesson 28)
- 1974–1977: Gerald R. Ford (Lesson 28)
- 1977–1981: James E. Carter (Lesson 28)
- 1961: First American in Space (Lesson 29)
- 1969: First Men on the Moon (Lesson 29)
- 1963: March on Washington (Lesson 30)
- 1981–1989: Ronald W. Reagan (Lesson 31)
- 1989–1993: George H. W. Bush (Lesson 31)
- 1993–2001: William J. Clinton (Lesson 31)
- 2001– : George W. Bush (Lesson 31)
- 1989: Fall of the Berlin Wall (Lesson 31)

- 1991: Operation Desert Storm (Lesson 31)
- September 11, 2001 (Lesson 31)
- 2003– : Operation Iraqi Freedom (Lesson 31)

 Mapmaking Reminder
Directions for completing the map forms can be found in the introduction to the *Student Activity Book.*

 Review Games
For long-term usage and durability, you may wish to either photocopy the images onto cardstock or glue them to a piece of poster board before cutting them out.

1. Continue working on learning the presidents in order. Add cards for the presidents studied in Unit Three — Harry S. Truman, Dwight D. Eisenhower, John F. Kennedy, Lyndon B. Johnson, Richard Nixon, Gerald Ford, Jimmy Carter, Ronald Reagan, George H. W. Bush, Bill Clinton, and George W. Bush. See if your student(s) can lay out the presidents, one by one, in the order that they served. Then practice saying them in order without using the cards. By the end of Volume II, the student should be able to recite all the U.S. presidents in order.

2. Review all the states and their capitals that your student(s) has learned thus far. Have him use an unlabeled map of the United States to practice identifying the location of each state and its capital. By the end of Volume II, the student should be able to locate all fifty states on an unlabeled map and identify the capital of each state.

 Family Activities

Lesson 25
- Practice a duck and cover drill. Imagine what it would be like to have to stay in an air-raid shelter. What would you want to have with you?

Lesson 26
- Cook a casserole that originated in the 1950s (such as green bean casserole or tuna noodle casserole) or eat a Swanson's TV dinner on a TV

tray while watching TV. See if you can find a cookbook from this era.

- The first McDonald's opened in San Bernardino, California, in 1955. Ray Kroc would turn this small drive-in restaurant chain into a fast-food powerhouse. Eat at a McDonald's and find out more about its history.

Lesson 27

- Listen to one of Billy Graham's sermons. See if you can find a video clip from one of his crusades.

- Look at episodes from a television show produced in the 1950s, and see what you can learn about the era—its family life, home furnishings, clothing, and schools.

- Play some of the music from the era, and look at some of the art (which your family considers appropriate). Make a poodle skirt.

Lesson 28

- Take a field trip to the Kennedy Space Center (Cape Canaveral, Florida), the Marshall Space Flight Center (Huntsville, Alabama), the Smithsonian National Air and Space Museum (Washington, D.C.), or the Johnson Space Center (Houston, Texas). If you can't visit one of these sites in person, take a virtual tour online.

- Have a debate about whether Ford should have pardoned Nixon and/or whether the United States should have fought the Vietnam War.

Lesson 29

- Can you find pictures of relatives wearing clothes of this era, such as bell-bottom pants or leisure suits? What about men with long hair and side-

burns or women with a Dorothy Hamill or Farrah Fawcett haircut? Make paper dolls dressed in fashions from the 1960s and 1970s.

Lesson 30

- View episodes from some of the television shows of the 1960s and 1970s. How do these shows compare to the television shows of the 1950s? Did your parents save any of their childhood toys and games? How do they compare to yours? Play some of the music from the era, and find some of Andy Warhol's pop art.

Lesson 31

- Debate whether or not Clinton should have been impeached and whether or not the Iraq War was justified.

- Read a book together about September 11, such as Lisa Beamer's *Let's Roll!*, or look through the news archives from September 11 and the days that followed.

Lesson 32

- Compare today's cars with the cars of the 1980s and 1990s. What new innovations have been made?

- Play some vinyl records (if you have a record player), cassettes, and CDs, and compare the quality of sound. Then listen to an MP3 or use an iPod. What do you think the future holds for listening to music? Look at record album covers from the 1970s and early 1980s. Play a videotape and then a DVD, and compare the experience.

- Look at some examples of modern art that your family considers appropriate.

UNIT FOUR
Checklist

Please Note:

SR = *Student Reader*

SAB = *Student Activity Book*

TG = *Teacher's Guide*

Required for Lesson 25
- ❑ Lesson 25 (page 369, SR)
- ❑ Corresponding Required Forms (page 199, 201, SAB)
- ❑ Corresponding Maps (page 200, 202, SAB)
- ❑ For Review questions (page 203, SAB)

Optional for Lesson 25
- ❑ For Further Study questions (page 206, SAB)
- ❑ Additional Options for Unit (page 31, TG)

Required for Lesson 26
- ❑ Lesson 26 (page 385, SR)
- ❑ Corresponding Required Form (page 207, SAB)
- ❑ Corresponding Map (page 208, SAB)
- ❑ For Review questions (page 209, SAB)

Optional for Lesson 26
- ❑ For Further Study questions (page 210, SAB)
- ❑ Additional Options for Unit (page 31, TG)

Required for Lesson 27
- ❑ Lesson 27 (page 397, SR)
- ❑ Corresponding Required Form (page 211, SAB)
- ❑ For Review questions (page 213, SAB)

Optional for Lesson 27
- ❑ For Further Study questions (page 215, SAB)
- ❑ Additional Options for Unit (page 31, TG)

Required for Lesson 28
- ❑ Lesson 28 (page 417, SR)
- ❑ Corresponding Required Forms (page 207, 217, 219, 221, 223, 225, SAB)
- ❑ Corresponding Maps (page 208, SAB)
- ❑ For Review questions (page 227, SAB)

Optional for Lesson 28
- ❑ For Further Study questions (page 232, SAB)
- ❑ Additional Options for Unit (page 31, TG)

Required for Lesson 29
- ❑ Lesson 29 (page 437, SR)
- ❑ Corresponding Required Form (page 233, SAB)
- ❑ Corresponding Map (page 234, SAB)
- ❑ For Review questions (page 235, SAB)

Optional for Lesson 29
- ❑ For Further Study questions (page 238, SAB)
- ❑ Additional Options for Unit (page 31, TG)

Required for Lesson 30
- ❑ Lesson 30 (page 449, SR)
- ❑ Corresponding Required Form (page 239, SAB)
- ❑ For Review questions (page 241, SAB)

Optional for Lesson 30
- ❑ For Further Study questions (page 243, SAB)
- ❑ Additional Options for Unit (page 31, TG)

Required for Lesson 31
- ❑ Lesson 31 (page 463, SR)
- ❑ Corresponding Required Forms (page 239, 245, 247, 249, 251, SAB)
- ❑ For Review questions (page 253, SAB)

Optional for Lesson 31
- ❏ For Further Study questions (page 255, SAB)
- ❏ Additional Options for Unit (page 31, TG)

Required for Lesson 32
- ❏ Lesson 32 (page 483, SR)
- ❏ Corresponding Required Form (page 257, SAB)
- ❏ For Review questions (page 259, SAB)

Optional for Lesson 32
- ❏ For Further Study questions (page 263, SAB)
- ❏ Additional Options for Unit (page 31, TG)

Required for Unit Four
- ❏ Final Review (page 265, SAB)

Additional Options for Unit
- ❏ Project Posibilities (page 31, TG)
- ❏ Timeline Dates (page 32, TG)
- ❏ Review Games (page 32, TG)
- ❏ Additional Reading from Book Lists (page 59, TG)
- ❏ For Further Study Questions/Answers and Younger Student Adaptations (page 122, TG)
- ❏ Family Activity Ideas (page 32, TG)

Section Three

BOOK LISTS

by Melissa E. Craig

UNIT ONE
Book List

Note that entries preceded by a cross are Christian in nature.

 **Primary (K–4)**

Abe Lincoln: Log Cabin to White House by Sterling North. A Landmark Books biography of this important man. 184 pp.

Allen Jay and the Underground Railroad by Marlene Targ Brill. A picture book based on an event found in Jay's autobiography. 47 pp.

Follow the Drinking Gourd by Jeanette Winter. A family escapes slavery in the South. This tale describes the family's fears and the way a folksong helped them and other slaves escape. 48 pp.

Just a Few Words, Mr. Lincoln by Jean Fritz. This easy reader focuses on Lincoln's famous Gettysburg Address. Including several period photos, the book explains Lincoln's role in freeing the slaves and winning the Civil War. 48 pp.

The Long Way to a New Land by Joan Sandin. An easy reader that tells the story of a family emigrating from Sweden to America in 1868. 64 pp.

The Long Way Westward by Joan Sandin. The sequel to *The Long Way to a New Land*, this book follows the same Swedish family's journey to the West, where many Swedish immigrants were seeking a new life. 64 pp.

Mr. Lincoln's Drummer by G. Clifton Wisler. Recounts the courageous exploits of Willie Johnston, an eleven-year-old Civil War drummer who became the youngest recipient of the Congressional Medal of Honor. 144 pp.

Sounder by William Armstrong. 1970 Newbery Medal Winner. While focusing on a dog named Sounder, this tale takes readers to the postwar South where sharecroppers are common and race relations are poor. A compelling story—classic children's literature. 128 pp.

Sweet Clara and the Freedom Quilt by Deborah Hopkinson. A courageous slave girl plays an unusual part in the Underground Railroad. 40 pp.

A Voice from the Wilderness: The Story of Anna Howard Shaw by Don Brown. Known best for her work as a suffragette, Anna Howard Shaw, who came to the United States in 1851, later becomes a teacher, minister and doctor! 32 pp.

The Dear America books chronicle the stories of fictional American girls through their diaries. They span a wide range of experiences, places, and time periods, and many are written by well-known, award-winning authors. Published by Scholastic. Titles for this time period:

The Girl Who Chased Away Sorrow: The Diary of Sarah Nita, a Navajo Girl, New Mexico, 1864 (Dear America) by Ann Turner. 208 pp.

The Great Railroad Race: The Diary of Libby West, Utah Territory, 1868 (Dear America) by Kristiana Gregory. 204 pp.

I Thought My Soul Would Rise and Fly: The Diary of Patsy, a Freed Girl, Mars Bluff, South Carolina, 1865 (Dear America) by Joyce Hansen. 208 pp.

Land of the Buffalo Bones: The Diary of Mary Elizabeth Rodgers, an English Girl in Minnesota, New Yeovil, Minnesota, 1873 (Dear America) by Marion Dane Bauer. 221 pp.

A Light in the Storm: The Civil War Diary of Amelia Martin, Fenwick Island, Delaware, 1861 (Dear America) by Karen Hesse. 174 pp.

A Picture of Freedom: The Diary of Clotee, a Slave Girl, Belmont Plantation, Virginia, 1859 (Dear America) by Patricia McKissak. 192 pp.

When Will This Cruel War Be Over? The Civil War Diary of Emma Simpson, Gordonsville, Virginia, 1864 (Dear America) by Barry Denenberg. 160 pp.

The If You... series is full of factual information and is written in a way that enables students to put themselves in different time periods or historical situations. Titles for this time period:

If You Lived at the Time of the Civil War by Kay Moore. 64 pp.

If You Lived When There Was Slavery in America by Anne Kamma. 80 pp.

If You Traveled on the Underground Railroad by Ellen Levine. 64 pp.

If You Traveled West on a Covered Wagon by Ellen Levine. 80 pp.

The My America books are journals of fictitious young Americans. Instead of just one journal per character, they tend to be written in trilogies, so the reader can follow the character through different periods of his or her life within a historical setting. Published by Scholastic. Titles for this time period:

After the Rain: Virginia's Civil War Diary, Book Two, Washington, DC, 1864 (My America) by Mary Pope Osborne. 112 pp.

As Far As I Can See: Meg's Prairie Diary, Book One, St. Louis to the Kansas Territory, 1856 (My America) by Kate McMullan. 112 pp.

A Fine Start: Meg's Prairie Diary, Book Three, 1857 (My America) by Kate McMullan. 112 pp.

Flying Free: Corey's Underground Railroad Diary, Book Two, 1857 (My America) by Sharon Dennis Wyeth. 112 pp.

For This Land: Meg's Prairie Diary, Book Two, 1856 (My America) by Kate McMullan. 112 pp.

Freedom's Wings: Corey's Underground Railroad Diary, Book One, 1857 (My America) by Sharon Dennis Wyeth. 112 pp.

Message in the Sky: Corey's Underground Railroad Diary, Book Three, 1857 (My America) by Sharon Dennis Wyeth. 112 pp.

My Brother's Keeper: Virginia's Civil War Diary, Book One, Gettysburg, 1863 (My America) by Mary Pope Osborne. 112 pp.

The My Name Is America series is similar to the Dear America series, except that the title characters are boys, rather than girls. Follow their stories to better understand the trials faced by those who made our country great. Published by Scholastic. Titles for this time period:

The Journal of Brian Doyle, a Greenhorn on an Alaskan Whaling Ship, the Florence, 1874 (My Name Is America) by Jim Murphy. 192 pp.

The Journal of James Edmond Pease, a Civil War Union Soldier, Virginia, 1863 (My Name Is America) by Jim Murphy. 176 pp.

The Journal of Joshua Loper, a Black Cowboy, the Chisholm Trail, 1871 (My Name Is America) by Walter Dean Myers. 160 pp.

The Journal of Rufus Rowe, a Witness to the Battle of Fredericksburg, Bowling Green, Virginia, 1862 (My Name Is America) by Sid Hite. 144 pp.

The Journal of Sean Sullivan, a Transcontinental Railroad Worker, Nebraska and Points West, 1867 (My Name Is America) by William Durbin. 192 pp.

The Journal of Wong Ming-Chung, a Chinese Miner, California, 1852 (My Name Is America) by Laurence Yep. 219 pp.

 Middle (5–8)

Across Five Aprils by Irene Hunt. 1965 Newbery Honor Book. Told from the standpoint of an adolescent boy, this tale allows us to see the effect the Civil War has on a small-town area of Illinois. 192 pp.

Be Ever Hopeful, Hannalee by Patricia Beatty. In this sequel to *Turn Homeward, Hannalee*, the family moves to Atlanta where jobs are plentiful in the wake of the Civil War.

Behind Rebel Lines: The Incredible Story of Emma Edmonds, Civil War Spy by Seymour Reit. The true story of a young woman who fights in the Civil War disguised as a man. Ultimately she becomes a spy! Interesting reading. 144 pp.

The Boys' War: Confederate and Union Soldiers Talk About the Civil War by Jim Murphy. The compiled words of boys who served in the Civil War-as soldiers, drummers, buglers, telegraphers. 128 pp.

Bull Run by Paul Fleischman. The first great battle of the Civil War, Bull Run, is told from sixteen points of view, including southern, northern, young, old, black, white, male, and female. 102 pp.

Charley Skedaddle by Patricia Beatty. Tough Charley Quinn joins the Union Army as a drummer boy after his older brother is killed at Gettysburg, but he deserts when he sees war's reality. 186 pp.

Dragon's Gate by Laurence Yep. 1994 Newbery Honor Book. Story of the building of the transcontinental railroad from a different perspective—that of the Chinese workers. 352 pp.

A Family Apart by Joan Lowery Nixon. The Orphan Train Quartet follows the story of the six Kelly children, whose widowed mother sends them west from New York City in 1856 in hopes of a better life for them. 176 pp.

Freedom Train: The Story of Harriet Tubman by Dorothy Sterling. The true story, well told, of a courageous girl who puts her life on the line to help hundreds of others and changes history in the process. 192 pp.

The Great Turkey Walk by Kathleen Karr. Follow young Simon as he drives one thousand turkeys from Missouri to Denver to make his fortune. A fun read, based on real events. 208 pp.

An Island Far from Home by John Donahue. The twelve-year-old son of a Union army doctor killed during the fighting in Fredericksburg comes to understand the meaning of war and the fine line between friends and enemies when he begins corresponding with a young Confederate prisoner of war. In an exciting, climactic ending, and under dangerous circumstances, the boys finally meet. 179 pp.

Lincoln: A Photobiography by Russell Freedman. 1988 Newbery Medal Winner. Well written and enjoyable to look at, this is a wonderful way to learn more about our sixteenth president. 160 pp.

Little Women by Louisa May Alcott. This story takes place during the Civil War. Based on the author's family, it centers around a family with four daughters whose father is fighting in the war. A sweet tale about the culture at the time. 464 pp.

The Long Road to Gettysburg by Jim Murphy. A well-written book that centers around excerpts from the diaries of two soldiers, one from each side of the war. Alternating accounts give the reader an unusual and balanced view. 128 pp.

Old Yeller by Fred Gipson. 1957 Newbery Honor Book. A classic tale about a dog and the boy who comes to love and depend on him in frontier Texas hill country in the late 1860s. 158 pp.

On to Oregon! by Honore Morrow. After the death of his parents, thirteen-year-old John Sager continues on to Oregon with his younger brother and sisters. Based on a true story. (Although it takes many liberties with the book, the film version, *Seven Alone*, is terrific!) 239 pp.

The Perilous Road by William O. Steele. 1959 Newbery Honor Book. Lessons about prejudice and courage emerge in this story about a southern boy whose brother joins the Union forces. 176 pp.

Promises to the Dead by Mary Downing Hahn. Twelve-year-old Jesse leaves his home on Maryland's Eastern Shore to help a young runaway slave find a safe haven in the early days of the Civil War. 202 pp.

✝ *Ransom's Mark* by Wendy Lawton. Christian tale of a thirteen-year-old girl whose family travels west in a wagon train but is massacred. She is ransomed from her captives by a peaceful tribe. (The fourth book in the Daughters of the Faith Series.) 160 pp.

The Red Badge of Courage by Stephen Crane. Civil War classic. A boy dreams of the excitement and heroism he hopes to find on the battlefield. His experience is far different from his expectations. 152 pp.

Rifles for Watie by Harold Keith. 1958 Newbery Medal Winner. Keith interviewed twenty-two soldiers as the basis for this Civil War novel set in Indian country. An uncommon perspective of the war — full of vivid detail. 352 pp.

Sing Down the Moon by Scott O'Dell. 1971 Newbery Honor Book. Story of a teen-aged girl in the Navaho tribe during their forced march to Fort Sumner. Well written. 128 pp.

To Be a Slave by Julius Lester. 1969 Newbery Honor Book. A realistic compilation of the experiences and words of slaves and ex-slaves, spanning the time from their kidnapping in Africa to their emancipation in the Civil War. Very honest. 160 pp.

True North by Kathryn Lasky. Beginning in 1858, this is the story of two girls from different worlds whose paths cross as one travels the Underground Railroad and the other helps her on her way. They continue to correspond for fifty more years. 264 pp.

Underground Man by Milton Meltzer. Set in pre-Civil War Kentucky, a young white man helps escaped slaves on the Underground Railroad. 288 pp.

With Every Drop of Blood: A Novel of the Civil War by James Lincoln Collier. While trying to transport food to Richmond during the Civil War, fourteen-year-old Johnny is captured by a black Union soldier. Historical details are described with trademark Collier accuracy and emotion. 235 pp.

Secondary (9 and up)

Across Five Aprils by Irene Hunt. (See Middle.)

The Battle of Gettysburg: A Soldier's First-Hand Account by Col. Frank A. Haskell. A first-hand document describing this three-day-long battle in a colonel's letter to a relative. 112 pp.

✝ *Boundless Faith: Early American Women's Captivity Narratives*, edited by Henry L. Carrigan, Jr. A compilation of stories about frontier Christian women who lived out their faith in the face of harrowing circumstances and Indian captivity. 224 pp.

✝ *Call of Duty: The Sterling Nobility of Robert E. Lee* (Leaders in Action Series) by J. Steven Wilkins. A biography that exposes readers to the character of a man who was torn between loyalty to his country and loyalty to his state. 352 pp.

Commander in Chief: Abraham Lincoln and the Civil War by Albert Marrin. A beautiful work, filled with pictures and quotations, this book introduces readers to Lincoln in his role as commander in chief while still exposing them to his life from beginning to end. 256 pp.

Dragon's Gate by Laurence Yep. (See Middle.)

Lincoln: A Photobiography by Russell Freedman. (See Middle.)

Little Women by Louisa May Alcott. (See Middle.)

The Long Road to Gettysburg by Jim Murphy. (See Middle.)

The Red Badge of Courage by Stephen Crane. (See Middle.)

Sound the Jubilee by Sandra Forrester. A slave and her family find refuge on Roanoke Island, North Carolina, during the Civil War. Based on a true story. 183 pp.

To Be a Slave by Julius Lester. (See Middle.)

✝ *Uncle Tom's Cabin* by Harriet Beecher Stowe. Classic work written in 1852. Mentioned extensively in the *Student Reader*. 544 pp.

Underground Man by Milton Meltzer. (See Middle.)

UNIT TWO
Book List

Primary (K–4)

The Adventures of Young Buffalo Bill by E. Cody Kimmel. A series of four books that take the reader through Buffalo Bill's exciting youth. Written by a woman who grew up believing she was related to this famous cowboy. Books range from 144 to 192 pp.

The Big Balloon Race by Eleanor Coerr. A fun easy reader about the famous Myers family. Carlotta was a famous aeronaut in the 1880s, and her husband made balloons for her. 62 pp.

Bill Pickett: Rodeo-Ridin' Cowboy by Andrea Davis Pinkney. About the first African American to be inducted into the National Cowboy Hall of Fame. 32 pp.

Black Cowboy, Wild Horses by Julius Lester. Based on a true story in the life of Bob Lemmons, a cowboy and former slave. 32 pp.

Brothers by Yin. This sweet story about a developing friendship between an Irish immigrant boy and a Chinese immigrant boy gives insight into the development of San Francisco's Chinatown. 32 pp.

Buffalo Bill by Ingri and Edgar d'Aulaire. Typical of d'Aulaire quality, this is another lovely biography with exquisite illustrations. 41 pp.

Buffalo Bill and the Pony Express by Eleanor Coerr. Easy reader that relates the adventures of a young Buffalo Bill when he goes to work for the Pony Express. 64 pp.

By the Great Horn Spoon! by Sid Fleischman. Set during the California gold rush, this book is fast-paced and enjoyable. Likeable characters and lots of period information make this a fun way to learn about the gold rush. 193 pp.

Chocolate by Hershey: A Story About Milton S. Hershey by Betty Burford. This biography of a fascinating American entrepreneur tells about his successes and failures and his big heart for orphans. 64 pp.

Cowboys and Cowgirls: Yippee Yay! by Gail Gibbons. Informative book about cowboys in the Old West; talks about cattle drives, roundups, and cowboy clothing. 32 pp.

Helen Keller by Margaret Davidson. Inspiring telling of Helen Keller's life story. 96 pp.

Hitty: Her First Hundred Years by Rachel Field. 1930 Newbery Medal Winner. Follow the adventures of a doll as she experiences the nineteenth and early twentieth centuries. First published in 1929, this book is a jewel! 256 pp.

Little House Books by Laura Ingalls Wilder. This well-known series of books is the tale of the author's childhood, from the time her family moved out west, through her marriage and the birth of her first baby. A wonderful read, full of details of life on the prairie. Five books in this series are Newbery Honor books: *On the Banks of Plum Creek*, 1938; *By the Shores of Silver Lake*, 1940; *The Long Winter*, 1941; *Little Town on the Prairie*, 1942; and *These Happy Golden Years*, 1944.

Mr. Blue Jeans: A Story About Levi Strauss by Maryann Weidt. This is a fascinating story about a Jewish immigrant who founded a famous jeans company. 64 pp.

Mudball by Matt Tavares. In 1903, Andy Oyler hit the only home run of his entire career, but it's the subject of a much-loved baseball legend. 32 pp.

Sitting Bull by Lucille Recht Penner. Easy reader biography of this famous Native American. 48 pp.

Train to Somewhere by Eve Bunting. Also about the Orphan Trains, this is a beautiful picture book for younger readers. 32 pp.

Zayda Was a Cowboy by June Levitt Nislick. The story of a Jewish immigrant from Russia who enters the United States, is sent out west, and becomes a cowboy! An epilogue fills in the historic background. 74 pp.

The Dear America books chronicle the stories of fictional American girls through their diaries. They span a wide range of experiences, places, and time periods, and many are written by well-known, award-winning authors. Published by Scholastic. Titles for this time period:

A Coal Miner's Bride: The Diary of Anetka Kaminska, Lattimer, Pennsylvania, 1896 (Dear America) by Susan Campbell Bartoletti. 221 pp.

Dreams in the Golden Country: The Diary of Zipporah Feldman, A Jewish Immigrant Girl, New York City, 1903 (Dear America) by Kathryn Lasky. 192 pp.

Hear My Sorrow: The Diary of Angela Denoto, a Shirtwaist Worker, New York City, 1909 (Dear America) by Deborah Hopkinson. 190 pp.

My Face to the Wind:. The Diary of Sarah Jane Price, a Prairie Teacher, Broken Bow, Nebraska, 1881 (Dear America) by Jim Murphy. 188 pp.

My Heart Is on the Ground: The Diary of Nannie Little Rose, a Sioux Girl, Carlisle Indian School, Pennsylvania, 1880 (Dear America) by Ann Rinaldi. 206 pp.

West to a Land of Plenty: The Diary of Teresa Angelino Viscardi, New York to Idaho Territory, 1883 (Dear America) by Jim Murphy. 208 pp.

The If You... series is full of factual information and is written in a way that enables students to put themselves in different time periods or historical situations. Title for this time period:

If Your Name Was Changed at Ellis Island by Ellen Levine. This book uses a question-and-answer style to explain to readers what it was like to immigrate to the United States through Ellis Island. 85 pp.

The My America books are journals of fictitious young Americans. Instead of just one journal per character, they tend to be written in trilogies, so the reader can follow the character through different periods of his or her life within a historical setting. Published by Scholastic. Titles for this time period:

An American Spring: Sofia's Immigrant Diary, Book Three, 1903 (My America) by Kathryn Lasky. 112 pp.

Home at Last: Sofia's Immigrant Diary, Book Two, 1903 (My America) by Kathryn Lasky. 112 pp.

Hope in My Heart: Sofia's Immigrant Diary, Book One, 1903 (My America) by Kathryn Lasky. 112 pp.

The My Name Is America series is similar to the Dear America series, except that the title characters are boys, rather than girls. Follow their stories to better understand the trials faced by those who made our country great. Published by Scholastic. Titles for this time period:

The Journal of Finn Reardon, a Newsie, New York City, 1899 (My Name Is America) by Susan Campbell Bartoletti. 160 pp.

The Journal of Otto Peltonen, a Finnish Immigrant, Hibbing, Minnesota, 1905 (My Name Is America) by William Durbin. 208 pp.

 Middle (5–8)

The Adventures of Tom Sawyer by Mark Twain. This classic American novel draws the reader into the life of endearing Tom, a regular country boy, growing up on the Mississippi River. 256 pp.

The Adventures of Young Buffalo Bill by E. Cody Kimmel. (See Primary.)

Behave Yourself, Bethany Brant by Patricia Beatty. Bethany's insatiable curiosity and penchant for getting into trouble follow her to Texas when she and her brother go to live with relatives. 172 pp.

Billy the Kid by Theodore Taylor. Fun historical fiction with good insight into the "wild west." The story takes place in 1881 when Billy the Kid is nineteen years old. 224 pp.

The Bite of the Gold Bug: A Story of the Alaskan Gold Rush by Barthe DeClements. In 1898, Bucky and his father must overcome extreme conditions on their one thousand mile trek to prospect for gold in Alaska. 56 pp.

The Bone Wars by Kathryn Lasky. Thaddeus, an American frontier boy, and Julian, son of an English paleontologist, become friends and share a mutual love of hunting dinosaur fossils in the west of the 1870s. 378 pp.

By the Great Horn Spoon! by Sid Fleischman. (See Primary.)

Caddie Woodlawn by Carol Ryrie Brink. 1936 Newbery Medal Winner. Based on the true experiences of the author's grandmother in the Wisconsin wilderness, this is an exciting story about pioneer days. 288 pp.

The Call of the Wild by Jack London. This story, as seen through the eyes of a dog, gives insight into human nature, as well as being based on London's experiences as a gold prospector in the Yukon. 160 pp.

Children of the Fire by Harriette Robinet. In Chicago, a young black girl named Hallelujah lives through the Great Fire of October 8, 1871, and learns courage and resourcefulness. 134 pp.

Chocolate by Hershey: A Story About Milton S. Hershey by Betty Burford. (See Primary.)

Cowboys of the Wild West by Russell Freedman. Full of pictures and carefully researched, this is an excellent read to get a feel for the lives of the cowboys. 112 pp.

The Earth Dragon Awakes: The San Francisco Earthquake of 1906 by Laurence Yep. The author carefully includes the most significant ramifications of this event, seen through the eyes of two young boys, one Chinese, one not. The boys learn what it really means to be a hero. 128 pp.

Five Little Peppers and How They Grew by Margaret Sidney. Originally a serial in an 1880 children's magazine, this story was so popular it was published as a book and eleven more followed! This family survives with love and dignity in the face of poverty and adversity. 352 pp.

Gone-Away Lake by Elizabeth Enright. 1958 Newbery Honor Book. Turn-of-the-century tale about a magical summer spent visiting cousins in the country. 272 pp.

The Great Wheel by Robert Lawson. 1958 Newbery Honor Book. Tells the story of the building of the first Ferris wheel, built for the Chicago World's Fair in 1893. Well told. 192 pp.

The Hebrew Kid and the Apache Maiden by Robert J. Avrech. Well-told story encompassing issues of Jewish immigration and westward expansion. Reader will become familiar with Jewish culture in an 1870s Old West setting. 220 pp.

Helen Keller by Margaret Davidson. (See Primary.)

Hitty: Her First Hundred Years by Rachel Field. (See Primary.)

Jenny of the Tetons by Kristiana Gregory. Carrie hates the Indians for killing her parents and stealing her brothers. But when she is taken in by an Englishman named Beaver Dick to help with his children, Carrie quickly grows to love his Indian wife and their family. Gregory's story is dotted with excerpts from the journal of the real Beaver Dick. 192 pp.

Jim Ugly by Sid Fleischman. In 1894, Jake forms an uneasy alliance with Jim Ugly, his father's devoted half-wolf dog, when Jake's father mysteriously disappears. 130 pp.

Little House Books by Laura Ingalls Wilder. (See Primary.)

Mr. Blue Jeans: A Story About Levi Strauss by Maryann Weidt. (See Primary.)

Orphan Train Rider: One Boy's True Story by Andrea Warren. Between 1854 and 1930, more than two hundred thousand orphaned and abandoned children from the cities of the eastern seaboard were "placed out" to new homes and families in the midwestern and western states. 80 pp.

Our Only May Amelia by Jennifer L. Holm. 2000 Newbery Honor Book. As the only girl in a Finnish American family of seven brothers, May Amelia Jackson resents being expected to act like a lady while growing up in Washington state in 1899. 253 pp.

Roller Skates by Ruth Sawyer. 1937 Newbery Medal Winner. A tale of the adventures of ten-year-old Lucinda, who spends an exciting year exploring New York City in the 1890s. 192 pp.

Shoes for Everyone: A Story About Jan Matzeliger by Barbara Mitchell. A story about the Dutch immigrant who revolutionizes the shoe industry. 63 pp.

Silver Dollar Girl by Katherine Ayres. In 1885, unhappy living with her aunt and uncle in Pittsburgh, Valentine Harper disguises herself as a boy and runs away to Colorado, determined to find her father who has gone there in search of gold. 208 pp.

The Spanish-American War: Imperial Ambitions by Alden R. Carter. Details the ten-week war in 1898 between the United States and Spain over the liberation of Cuba. Maps and photos. 64 pp.

The Story of the Rough Riders (Cornerstones of Freedom) by Zachary Kent. Tells the story of how Teddy Roosevelt formed the Rough Riders at the beginning of the Spanish-American War and led them into battle at San Juan Hill. Many photos. 31 pp.

The Traitor by Laurence Yep. Award-winning author portrays the prejudice between Chinese and American miners in Wyoming Territory in 1885 during one of the worst race riots in history. 320 pp.

The Yearling by Marjorie Kinnan Rawlings. A classic story that takes place in backwoods Florida at the end of the nineteenth century. Beautifully written; a must-read. 416 pp.

Zayda Was a Cowboy by June Levitt Nislick. (See Primary.)

Secondary (9 and up)

The Adventures of Tom Sawyer by Mark Twain. (See Middle.)

The Call of the Wild by Jack London. (See Middle.)

The Colonel and Little Missie: Buffalo Bill, Annie Oakley, and the Beginnings of Superstardom in America by Larry McMurtry. An easily read biography of two strongholds of the Old West. 256 pp.

The Country of the Pointed Firs and Other Stories by Sarah Orne Jewett. Vivid descriptions of Maine fishing villages and local lifestyles take the reader to the Maine coast in the 1890s. 256 pp.

Cowboys of the Wild West by Russell Freedman. (See Middle.)

Five Little Peppers and How They Grew by Margaret Sidney. (See Middle.)

The Hebrew Kid and the Apache Maiden by Robert J. Avrech. (See Middle.)

The Jungle by Upton Sinclair. Sinclair depicts the horrors of the meat-packing industry at the turn of the century. Though he uses the book as a platform for sharing his socialist views, it is a classic choice for portraying many of the problems of the industrial age. 448 pp.

Mother Jones: Fierce Fighter for Workers' Rights by Judith Pinkerton Josephson. This book explains the role "Mother Jones" played in ensuring rights for workers during a time of industrial growth and immigrant exploitation. 128 pp.

Setting the Record Straight: American History in Black and White by David Barton. A unique view of the religious and moral heritage of African Americans that has been expertly intertwined with untold, yet significant stories from our rich African American political history. 192 pp.

The Story of My Life (The Restored Edition) by Helen Keller. This well-written autobiography is a jewel. Helen Keller describes her life and experiences in her own words. 240 pp.

The World I Live In by Helen Keller. A close and personal look into the feelings and imagination of this great American hero through essays and stories she has written. Beautiful. 224 pp.

The Yearling by Marjorie Kinnan Rawlings. (See Middle.)

UNIT THREE
Book List

Note that entries preceded by a cross are Christian in nature.

 Primary (K–4)

✝ *Betty Greene: Wings to Serve* (Christian Heroes, Then and Now) by Janet and Geoff Benge. A veteran of World War II, Betty wants to use her love of flying to spread the Gospel and helps to found Mission Aviation Fellowship. 200 pp.

Christmas in the Trenches by John McCutcheon. True story of Christmas 1914 in the trenches when soldiers on both sides put down their guns and celebrated Christmas in unity. 32 pp.

✝ *Clash with the Newsboys* (American Adventure) by Norma Jean Lutz. This is a well-written story about the "newsies" of the early 1900s. 144 pp.

D-Day Landings: The Story of the Allied Invasion (DK Readers) by Richard Platt. This reader details the strategy and mission of the D-Day invasion. 32 pp.

Don't Forget Winona by Jeanne Whitehouse Peterson. A young girl describes her family's departure from the dust bowl of Oklahoma, traveling on Route 66 during the late 1930s. 32 pp.

First Flight: The Story of the Wright Brothers (DK Readers) by Caryn Jenner. This reader describes the Wright brothers' journey to flight — read about their trials, failures, and ultimate success. 48 pp.

Hero Over Here: A Story of World War I by Kathleen Kudlinski. In 1918, Theodore's father and brother are away fighting in the Great War when the flu epidemic arrives and changes life at home forever. 54 pp.

Homer Price by Robert McCloskey. First published in 1943, these fun stories reflect life in small-town America in the middle of the twentieth century. 149 pp.

The Hundred Dresses by Eleanor Estes. 1945 Newbery Honor Book. Story of an immigrant girl who is teased because she is different. The story, though about a Polish family, rings with truth about the human condition. 96 pp.

The Little Riders by Margaretha Shemin. Johanna, an American girl, is trapped by the invading Nazis while visiting her grandparents in Holland. 80 pp.

A Long Way from Chicago by Richard Peck. 1999 Newbery Honor Book. The story of a boy and his sister who live in Chicago but visit their grandmother in the country. A nice tale that spans the years 1929–1942. 176 pp.

Mailing May by Michael O. Tunnell. In 1914, because her family cannot afford a train ticket, May gets "mailed" and rides the mail train to see her grandmother. Beautifully illustrated and based on a true story! 31 pp.

Marven of the Great North Woods by Kathryn Lasky. Marven, who is ten, is sent by his Jewish parents to a remote lumber camp to escape the influenza epidemic of 1918 in his hometown of Duluth, Minnesota. Amazing story, based on a real event. 45 pp.

My Daddy Was a Soldier: A World War II Story by Deborah Kogan Ray. A girl remembers her childhood during World War II when her father went off to fight. While she and her mother receive letters from him, they experience life on the home front. 40 pp.

Night Flight: Charles Lindbergh's Incredible Adventure by S. A. Kramer. This early reader describes the amazing accomplishment and heart-stopping thrill of Charles Lindbergh's famous flight. 48 pp.

Number the Stars by Lois Lowry. 1990 Newbery Medal Winner. This story uses the fictional experience of a ten-year-old girl to depict the event in which the Danish military and people came together to evacuate seven thousand Jews from the country before they could be detained. 144 pp.

Pearl Harbor by Stephen Krensky, An early reader describing the world-changing importance of this event. This book describes the political climate before and after the attack in ways appropriate to younger readers. Nice pen and ink and pastel illustrations. 42 pp.

Polar, the Titanic Bear by Daisy Corning Stone Spedden and Leighton H. Coleman. Based on a true story written in 1913 by Spedden for her young son, Douglas, after their family survived the sinking of the great ship. Fascinating! 64 pp.

Rascal by Sterling North. 1964 Newbery Honor Book (as *Rascal: A Memoir of a Better Era*). This story takes place in 1918 when a boy befriends a raccoon. Heartwarming. 192 pp.

Roll of Thunder, Hear My Cry by Mildred D. Taylor. 1977 Newbery Medal Winner. Set in the Deep South in the 1930s, Taylor's story realistically depicts the trials of a black family in their struggle against racism. 288 pp.

Sea of Ice: The Wreck of the Endurance (Step into Reading) by Monica Kulling. In 1914, Sir Ernest Shackleton set out with his crew aboard the ship, the *Endurance*. He wanted to sail to Antarctica, but one hundred miles from the South Pole, the *Endurance* became trapped in a sea of ice. Against all odds, Shackleton undertook a journey that led to the rescue of his crew after almost two years of surviving in the incredibly harsh climate. 48 pp.

Sky Boys: How They Built the Empire State Building by Deborah Hopkinson. Through the eyes of a young boy, this book details the construction of this famous building. 48 pp.

Spirit of Endurance: The True Story of the Shackleton Expedition to the Antarctic by Jennifer Armstrong. An excellent telling of the Shackleton expedition, with beautiful artwork, useful diagrams, and many photographs. An excellent read for older students as well. 32 pp.

Strawberry Girl by Lois Lenski. 1946 Newbery Medal Winner. Don't be misled by the bland title of this book! This is an excellent depiction of life on a Florida farm, detailing daily struggles of the time. Fun and exciting. 208 pp.

Tar Beach by Faith Ringgold. A black girl in New York City experiences the Great Depression. Her father, who helped build the George Washington Bridge, finds himself discriminated against by the union. 32 pp.

Waiting for the Evening Star by Rosemary Wells. This beautiful picture book details the lives of two brothers growing up on a Vermont farm during a time when life was slower and more peaceful. The book ends as the older boy, Luke, leaves for France and World War I. 40 pp.

The Dear America books chronicle the stories of fictional American girls through their diaries. They span a wide range of experiences, places, and time periods, and many are written by well-known, award-winning authors. Published by Scholastic. Titles for this time period:

Christmas After All: The Great Depression Diary of Minnie Swift, Indianapolis, Indiana, 1932 (Dear America) by Kathryn Lasky. 190 pp.

Color Me Dark: The Diary of Nellie Lee Love, the Great Migration North, Chicago, Illinois, 1919 (Dear America) by Patricia C. McKissack. 222 pp.

Early Sunday Morning: The Pearl Harbor Diary of Amber Billows, Hawaii, 1941 (Dear America) by Barry Denenberg. 160 pp.

Mirror, Mirror on the Wall: The Diary of Bess Brennan, the Perkins School for the Blind, Watertown, Massachusetts, 1932 (Dear America) by Barry Denenberg. 132 pp.

My Secret War: The World War II Diary of Madeline Beck, Long Island, New York, 1941 (Dear America) by Mary Pope Osborne. 208 pp.

One Eye Laughing, the Other Weeping: The Diary of Julie Weiss, Vienna, Austria to New York, 1938 (Dear America) by Barry Denenberg. 254 pp.

Survival in the Storm: The Dust Bowl Diary of Grace Edwards, Dalhart, Texas, 1935 (Dear America) by Katelan Janke. 190 pp.

A Time For Courage: The Suffragette Diary of Kathleen Bowen, Washington, Delaware, 1917 (Dear America) by Kathryn Lasky. 222 pp.

Voyage on the Great Titanic: The Diary of Margaret Ann Brady, RMS Titanic, 1912 (Dear America) by Ellen Emerson White. 197 pp.

When Christmas Comes Again: The World War I Diary of Simone Spencer, New York City to the Western Front, 1917 (Dear America) by Beth Seidel Levine. 172 pp.

The My Name Is America series is similar to the Dear America series, except that the title characters are boys, rather than girls. Follow their stories to better understand the trials faced by those who made our country great. Published by Scholastic. Titles for this time period:

The Journal of Ben Uchida, Citizen 13559, Mirror Lake Internment Camp, California, 1942 (My Name Is America) by Barry Denenberg. 160 pp.

The Journal of C. J. Jackson, a Dust Bowl Migrant, Oklahoma to California, 1935 (My Name Is America) by William Durbin. 169 pp.

The Journal of Scott Pendleton Collins, a World War II Soldier, Normandy, France, 1944 (My Name Is America) by Walter Dean Myers. 144 pp.

 Middle (5–8)

Al Capone Does My Shirts by Gennifer Choldenko. 2005 Newbery Honor Book. Twelve-year-old Moose Flanagan moves with his family to Alcatraz Island in 1935 so that his father can become a prison guard. Learn what life was like for a family living on the island. 228 pp.

✝ *Betty Greene: Wings to Serve* by Janet and Geoff Benge. (See Primary.)

Bread and Roses, Too by Katherine Paterson. Set in the early 1900s, this book depicts life during the immigrant labor struggle, giving readers an understanding of child labor and tenement living. 288 pp.

Causes of World War I (Road to War: Causes of Conflict) by John Ziff. In this book, Ziff focuses on what started World War I as well as on the political world climate at the time. 72 pp.

The Cay by Theodore Taylor. Amazing adventure story of love and racial reconciliation between eleven-year-old, American-born Phillip and the black man Timothy. Set in the Dutch West Indies during World War II. Don't miss this book! 144 pp.

Christmas in the Trenches by John McCutcheon. (See Primary.)

Christy by Catherine Marshall. Based on the life of the author's mother, this is a story of a young woman who leaves a comfortable life to teach in the Smoky Mountains. 512 pp.

✝ *Clash with the Newsboys* by Norma Jean Lutz. (See Primary.)

The Devil's Arithmetic by Jane Yolen. A young American girl, reluctantly celebrating Passover with relatives, is miraculously "transported" to a Polish village where she and the other Jews are captured and sent to a Nazi concentration camp. Well written! 176 pp.

Don't You Know There's a War On? by Avi. The reminiscences of a boy who recalls his fifth-grade year during the height of the war; weaves fifth-grade life into the daily duress of living during the Second World War. 208 pp.

Dragonwings by Laurence Yep. 1976 Newbery Honor Book. Follows Chinese immigrants in San Francisco who survive the earthquake and build a flying machine — fiction, based on real events. 336 pp.

✝ *Dust of the Earth* by Donna Lynn Hess. Fictional story of a sharecropper's son who overcomes illiteracy in the 1920s. 196 pp.

Earthquake at Dawn by Kristiana Gregory. Based on experiences of real-life photographer Edith Irvine during the San Francisco earthquake. 224 pp.

Eight Mules from Monterey by Patricia Beatty. During the summer of 1916, Fayette's mother takes her children on a trip to establish libraries in isolated villages in the rough country surrounding Monterey, California. 192 pp.

Exploring the Bismarck by Robert D. Ballard, Ph.D. This book presents a fascinating and colorful account of both the sinking and the later discovery of Hitler's greatest battleship. 64 pp.

Exploring the Titanic by Robert D. Ballard, Ph.D. With the aid of graphs, drawings, sketches, and photos, this book explores the first and last voyage of the *Titanic*, as well as the discovery of the remains of the ship. 64 pp.

Farewell to Manzanar by Jeanne Wakatsuki and James D. Houston. This is a true story of the Japanese American experience during and after World War II, based on the recollections of a child who was there. 224 pp.

Flags of our Fathers by James Bradley. When James Bradley's father died, he found boxes of letters and pictures that helped him go back and trace the lives of the six men who raised the flag at Iwo Jima. Abridged for children. 224 pp.

Freckles by Gene Stratton-Porter. A classic chidren's novel from the early twentieth century that really captures the social mood of the era. A prequel to *A Girl of the Limberlost.* 362 pp.

✝ *George Washington Carver: Man's Slave Becomes God's Scientist* by David Collins. Carver overcomes racial prejudice to become one of the greatest scientists of the century. 136 pp.

A Girl of the Limberlost by Gene Stratton-Porter. A classic early twentieth century story that takes place in rural Indiana; sequel to *Freckles.* Well-developed characters and a strong female protagonist make this a compelling read. 479 pp.

The Good Fight: How World War II Was Won by Stephen Ambrose. Tons of photos, along with firsthand accounts and easy-to-understand descriptions, make this a good read for students interested in learning more about this world-changing event. 95 pp.

Hell Fighters: African American Soldiers in World War I by Michael L. Cooper. This book follows a National Guard unit, mostly black, from its formation through its service in France. A unique perspective. 80 pp.

✝ *Hey, Mac! A Combat Infantryman's Story* by William McMurdie. A Christian soldier's perspective of World War II from the trenches. 207 pp.

Homesick: My Own Story by Jean Fritz. Although young Jean lived in China until she was twelve, her parents' memories of home and letters from relatives made her feel that she was an American and homesick for a place she'd never seen. 175 pp.

The House of Sixty Fathers by Meindert DeJong. 1957 Newbery Honor Book. In this book, DeJong tells of China during the Japanese occupation in World War II. A boy whose family finally escapes the Japanese, sleeps in a boat that loses its moorings and floats right back to the enemy but is rescued by an American soldier. 189 pp.

The Hundred Dresses by Eleanor Estes. (See Primary.)

Ida Early Comes Over the Mountain by Robert Burch. Tough times in rural Georgia take a lively turn when Ida Early, an Appalachian Mary Poppins, appears out of nowhere to take care of the motherless Suttons. 145 pp.

Letters from Rifka by Karen Hesse. In a series of letters to her beloved cousin Tovah, left behind in Russia, Rifka records her experiences and thoughts about immigrating to America. 148 pp.

A Long Way from Chicago by Richard Peck. (See Primary.)

Miracles on Maple Hill by Virginia Sorensen. 1957 Newbery Medal Winner. A family affected by the emotional and physical damage their father suffered in World War II goes to the country for renewal. Told from the point of view of one of the children. 256 pp.

Moonshiner's Son by Carolyn Reeder. Gain an appreciation for the cultural atmosphere during prohibition. View both sides — that of a moonshiner's son and that of a prohibitionist preacher. 208 pp.

Nothing to Fear by Jackie French Koller. A boy and his mother survive the father's absence in New York City during the depression. Heartwarming. 288 pp.

Number the Stars by Lois Lowry. (See Primary.)

On Board the Titanic by Shelley Tanaka. The sinking of the *Titanic* told through the eyes of two young survivors and filled with paintings and diagrams. 48 pp.

Rascal by Sterling North. (See Primary.)

Say You Are My Sister by Laurel Brady. Three sisters are orphaned in Georgia during the World War II era. A novel about a small town, racial prejudice, and strong family bonds. 205 pp.

✝ *Sergeant York and the Great War* by Tom Skeyhill. Published by Vision Forum, this is the personal diary of Sergeant York, a humble Christian man from Tennessee who was drafted into World War I. 209 pp.

Spirit of Endurance: The True Story of the Shackleton Expedition to the Antarctic by Jennifer Armstrong. (See Primary.)

Under a War-Torn Sky by L. M. Elliott. An effective tale of a young American pilot shot down over Alsace in World War II. He makes his way home through Nazi-occupied Europe, with the help of the French resistance. Full of the drama of wartime Europe and heroic personalities. 288 pp.

The Victory Garden by Lee Kochenderfer. This story about an eleven-year-old girl takes place during World War II and centers around her neighbor's Victory Garden — a very important part of the war effort. 176 pp.

War Horse by Michael Morpurgo. Read about World War I, as told from the perspective of a horse. A beautiful story, not just for horse lovers! 181 pp.

"Who Was That Masked Man, Anyway?" by Avi. This crazy satire, set in 1945, is written entirely through dialogue, old programs, and commercials. Full of nostalgia and cleverly written. 176 pp.

A Whole New Ball Game: The Story of the All-American Girls Professional Baseball League by Sue Macy. This book explores an interesting piece of history — a girls' professional baseball league established when men of the major leagues were depleted by the war. 160 pp.

World War I (DK Eyewitness Books). Though it looks like a children's book, this one is chock full of interesting information for all ages; told through eyewitness accounts. 72 pp.

World War II (DK Eyewitness Books). This is another great title in DK's Eyewitness series. 72 pp.

A Year Down Yonder by Richard Peck. 2001 Newbery Medal Winner. Grandma Dowell returns in this sequel to *A Long Way from Chicago*. This heartwarming story takes place in 1937 and gives us a sense of the depression through her granddaughter's eyes. 144 pp.

 **Secondary (9 and up)**

Babbit by Sinclair Lewis. This satire was written to expose 1920s middle-class values. 432 pp.

Bread and Roses, Too by Katherine Paterson. (See Middle.)

Children of the Dust Bowl: The True Story of the School at Weedpatch Camp by Jerry Stanley. Well written, this book conveys a feel for the true conditions suffered by Americans during the Dust Bowl, as well as for American prejudice against the poor. 96 pp.

Children of the Great Depression by Russell Freedman. Full of stirring black-and-white photos and quotes from those who lived through the depression, this book helps students relate to this trying time. 112 pp.

The Chosen by Chaim Potok. Two very different young men (one a modern Orthodox Jew and one a Hasidic Jew) forge a friendship and discover the challenges and joys of appreciating one another in the midst of a society that does just the opposite. 304 pp.

Christy by Catherine Marshall. (See Middle.)

Death's Men: Soldiers of the Great War by Denis Winter. This book goes beyond politics and war strategy and focuses on the personal experiences of World War I soldiers. 304 pp.

The Devil's Arithmetic by Jane Yolen. (See Middle.)

Freckles by Gene Stratton-Porter. (See Middle.)

✝ *George Washington Carver: His Life and Faith in His Own Words* by William Federer. The author, enamored with the life and character of Carver since a young boy, writes this biography filled with Carver's own words. 104 pp.

A Girl of the Limberlost by Gene Stratton-Porter. (See Middle.)

Going Solo by Roald Dahl. The second volume of the autobiography of the author of *Charlie and the Chocolate Factory* shares his adventures as a World War II RAF pilot! 224 pp.

The Grapes of Wrath by John Steinbeck. This Pulitzer Prize-winning novel, written in 1939, gives a realistic portrayal of our country in its struggles to overcome the depression. 464 pp.

The Great Gatsby by F. Scott Fitzgerald. This classic gives readers insight into the lifestyle on Long Island in the 1920s, when money was king and extravagance was the norm. 240 pp.

Hell Fighters: African American Soldiers in World War I by Michael L. Cooper. (See Middle.)

✝ *The Hiding Place* by Corrie Ten Boom. In this Christian classic, Ten Boom tells the story of her life as a Christian in occupied Holland. The active faith displayed by the Ten Boom family is a living example of the true Christian life. Not to be missed. 272 pp.

Once There Was a Farm: A Country Childhood Remembered by Virginia Bell Dabney. Based on the author's life, this is a touching remembrance of life on a farm during the depression. 273 pp.

✝ *One Soldier's Story: A Memoir* by Bob Dole. This autobiography reveals how World War II (and the injuries he sustained there) affected Dole's life. 304 pp.

Out of the Dust by Karen Hesse. 1998 Newbery Medal Winner. Using free-verse poetry, Hesse paints a picture of the Oklahoma dust bowl in the 1930s depression era. 240 pp.

✝ *Sergeant York and the Great War* by Tom Skeyhill. (See Middle.)

Silent Night: The Story of the World War I Christmas Truce by Stanley Weintraub. True story of Christmas in the trenches during 1914 when soldiers on both sides put down their guns and celebrated together. 224 pp.

Spirit of Endurance: The True Story of the Shackleton Expedition to the Antarctic by Jennifer Armstrong. (See Primary.)

Their Eyes Were Watching God by Zora Neale Hurston. In this book, Hurston, one of the great female authors of the Harlem Renaissance, gives readers a feel for black culture at this time through the use of very realistic characters and authentic dialect. 240 pp.

To Kill a Mockingbird by Harper Lee. A classic book that deals with race relations in the Deep South during the 1930s. We see the community, its inhabitants, and their idiosyncrasies through the eyes of a child. Beautifully written and compelling — a must read! 336 pp.

Tolkien and the Great War: The Threshold of Middle-earth by John Garth. Great fun for Tolkien lovers, this book chronicles the effect of Tolkien's experience in World War I and its influence on his middle-earth novels. 416 pp.

The Worst Hard Time: The Untold Story of Those Who Survived the Great American Dust Bowl by Timothy Egan. A realistic, sobering depiction of those who stayed in the Dust Bowl after the 1935 dust storm — the greatest on record. 352 pp.

✝ *Out of Time* by Alton Gansky. One of the J. D. Stanton mysteries, this is Christian fiction in which a group of teens encounters a deserted ship from World War I. Full of suspense. 352 pp.

Reagan, In His Own Hand: The Writings of Ronald Reagan That Reveal His Revolutionary Vision for America, edited by Kiron K. Skinner, Annelise Anderson, and Martin Anderson. A compilation of Reagan's writing, in his own hand -- letters he wrote and original manuscripts of his radio addresses. Discover his thoughts on the world at the time, and gain insight into why he was known as "The Great Communicator." 576 pp.

Red Scarf Girl by Ji-li Jiang. This book presents a realistic portrayal of life in China during the cultural revolution. Autobiographical and well told. 320 pp.

When Character Was King: A Story of Ronald Reagan by Peggy Noonan. A portrait of Ronald Reagan, written by his speechwriter. 352 pp.

UNIT FOUR
Book List

Note that entries preceded by a cross are Christian in nature.

 Primary (K–4)

The Bus Ride That Changed History: The Story of Rosa Parks by Pamela Duncan Edwards. Written in a cumulative form like "The House That Jack Built," this is an excellent way to introduce young students to the stand that Rosa Parks took. 32 pp.

Chicken Sunday by Patricia Polacco. Winston and Stewart are young Patricia's best friends, despite their differences in religion, sex, and race, and she considers their grandmother, Miss Eula, hers because her own ``babushka'' died. Don't miss this wonderful, uplifting story about friendship. 32 pp.

The Gold Cadillac by Mildred Taylor. During a family trip from Ohio to Mississippi, Lois and Wilma experience prejudice for the first time in their young lives. 48 pp.

In the Year of the Boar and Jackie Robinson by Bette Bao Lord. In 1947, a Chinese girl emigrates from China to Brooklyn. In the midst of the wonders and struggles of her new home, she discovers baseball. 169 pp.

The Keeping Quilt by Patricia Polacco. Originally made by their immigrant ancestors and creatively passed down through four generations, the Polacco's family quilt is the subject of this true story. 32 pp.

Letters from Korea: A Story of the Korean War by Pat McGrath Avery. In this story, a boy visits his grandmother, and together they go through her sons' letters sent home from the Korean War. Based on the experiences of three Korean War veterans. 48 pp.

Mercedes and the Chocolate Pilot by Margot Theis Raven. This book tells the true story of a sweet pilot and a girl affected by the Berlin Airlift. Poignant pictures and a compelling epilogue. 48 pp.

Moonwalk: The First Trip to the Moon by Judy Donnelly. This book allows young readers to read for themselves the story of *Apollo 11* and the first moonwalk—from the preflight preparations to the final splashdown. 48 pp.

Mrs. Katz and Tush by Patricia Polacco. This is a lovely intergenerational story about an elderly Jewish widow, her young African American neighbor, and the kitten that draws them together. 32 pp.

A New Coat for Anna by Harriet Ziefert. The touching story of a mother's determination to acquire a coat for her daughter during the hard times after World War II. 40 pp.

No Star Nights by Anna Smucker. The story of a young girl growing up in a West Virginia mill town. The book's title refers to the fact that Anna couldn't see the stars because the furnaces glowed red all night long. Autobiographical. 64 pp.

Our 50 States: A Family Adventure Across America by Lynne Cheney. This creative almanac includes everything from song lyrics to historical data in a visually appealing format. 74 pp.

Plain Girl by Virginia Sorensen. First published in 1955, this is the story of an Amish girl in Pennsylvania who is forced by the state to attend the public school. 151 pp.

The School Is Not White! A True Story of the Civil Rights Movement by Doreen Rappaport. The true story of a black Mississippi family who, in 1965, decide to send their seven children to a previously all-white school. 40 pp.

The Wall by Eve Bunting. A boy travels to the Vietnam Veterans Memorial with his father to find his grandfather's name. 32 pp.

A Wall of Names: The Story of the Vietnam Veterans Memorial (Step into Reading) by Judy Donnelly. Here is the dramatic story of how "The Wall" came to be. Includes photos. 48 pp.

The Dear America books chronicle the stories of fictional American girls through their diaries. They span a wide range of experiences, places, and time periods, and many are written by well-known, award-winning authors. Published by Scholastic. Title for this time period:

Where Have All the Flowers Gone? The Diary of Molly MacKenzie Flaherty, Boston, Massachusetts, 1968 (Dear America) by Ellen Emerson White. 190 pp.

The My Name Is America series is similar to the Dear America series, except that the title characters are boys, rather than girls. Follow their stories to better understand the trials faced by those who made our country great. Published by Scholastic. Titles for this time period:

The Journal of Biddy Owens, the Negro Leagues, Birmingham, Alabama, 1948 (My Name Is America) by Walter Dean Myers. 141 pp.

The Journal of Patrick Seamus Flaherty, United States Marine Corps, Khe Sanh, Vietnam, 1968 (My Name Is America) by Ellen Emerson White. 188 pp.

 ## Middle (5–8)

Basher Five-Two by Scott O'Grady. The autobiography of Scott O'Grady, a pilot who was shot down over Bosnia; tells of his experiences as he eluded the enemy and ultimately was rescued. 144 pp.

The Bracelet by Yoshiko Uchida. Emi, a young Japanese American child, is sent with her family to an internment camp during World War II. She loses the bracelet her best friend gave her, but events prove that she does not need a physical reminder of that friendship. During World War II, the author was forced to live in West Coast internment camps. This story is based on her experience. 30 pp.

✝ *Children of the Storm: The Autobiography of Natasha Vins* by Natasha Vins. Set behind the Iron Curtain, this book tells the story of a girl whose father leads an underground church. 135 pp.

Escape from Saigon: How a Vietnam War Orphan Became an American Boy by Andrea Warren. A true story of the 1975 Operation Babylift, as seen through the eyes of an eight-year-old Amerasian boy named Long who was part of the airlift and adopted by a family in Ohio. 128 pp.

The Friends by Rosa Guy. Two very different girls unite as friends in this sweet story about life in Harlem in the 1960s. 192 pp.

Heartbeat: George Bush in His Own Words, compiled and edited by Jim McGrath. Glimpse the private George H. W. Bush through his public words — in easy-to-read snippets. 352 pp.

In the Year of the Boar and Jackie Robinson by Bette Bao Lord. (See Primary.)

Letters from Korea: A Story of the Korean War by Pat McGrath Avery. (See Primary.)

Little Britches: Father and I Were Ranchers by Ralph Moody. This is the first in an autobiographical series. A coming-of-age story about a family's move, infused with character-building examples and strong morals. 260 pp. [Warning—some language]

Maniac Magee by Jerry Spinelli. 1991 Newbery Medal Winner. Racial tension, reconciliation, sports, and one amazing boy make this a story your family won't soon forget. Not to be missed! 180 pp.

Man of the Family by Ralph Moody. Sequel to *Little Britches*, this tells the story of what happens to the Moody family after Ralph's father dies and Ralph must become the "man of the family." 272 pp.

The Story of the Saigon Airlift (Cornerstones of Freedom) by Zachary Kent. This straightforward account of the 1975 Vietnam airlift includes many photos. 31 pp.

Words by Heart by Ouida Sebestyen. In 1910, a young black girl from the only black family in her southwestern town memorizes Bible verses in an effort to impress her white classmates. A novel of unexpected outcomes and forgiveness. 176 pp.

The Year of Miss Agnes by Kirkpatrick Hill. A new teacher comes to a small Alaskan village and reforms the lives of the children in the one-room schoolhouse. A sweet story. 128 pp.

 **Secondary (9 and up)**

America and Vietnam: The Elephant and the Tiger by Albert Marrin. Published by Beautiful Feet, this book tries to give a realistic picture of the war, showing how it affected both sides. 277 pp.

✝ *From Basic to Baghdad: A Soldier Writes Home* by J. B. Hogan. Young homeschooled soldier in the Iraq War writes an avalanche of letters to his mother that reassure her he and his sense of humor are alive and well. 250 pp.

The Boys of Pointe du Hoc: Ronald Reagan, D-Day, and the U.S. Army 2nd Ranger Battalion by Douglas Brinkley. This book gives a unique perspective on World War II and the "Great Communicator" as it chronicles Reagan's research for one of his most famous speeches, and then shows the effect it had on our nation. 288 pp.

✝ *Children of the Storm: The Autobiography of Natasha Vins* by Natasha Vins. (See Middle.)

✝ *The Cross and the Switchblade* by David Wilkerson. A young man heeds God's call to minister to the toughest gangs in New York City. 240 pp.

Darkness at Noon by Arthur Koestler. Set in the Soviet Union during the treason trials of the late 1930s. Well written. 224 pp.

Escape from Saigon: How a Vietnam War Orphan Became an American Boy by Andrea Warren. (See Middle.)

✝ *Escape in Iraq: The Thomas Hamill Story* by Thomas Hamill and Paul T. Brown. Thomas Hamill was a truck driver in Iraq whose convoy was ambushed. He escaped twenty-four days later — here is his story. 304 pp.

Fallen Angels by Walter Dean Myers. A coming-of-age story set in Vietnam. Deals with racism as well as with the Vietnam War issue. 320 pp.

✝ *Four Souls: A Search for Epic Life* by Trey Sklar, Jedd Medefind, Mike Peterson, and Matt Kronberg. Four young American men, recently graduated from college, traverse the world in search of what they call "epic life." A great read! 363 pp.

Heartbeat: George Bush in His Own Words, compiled and edited by Jim McGrath. (See Middle.)

✝ *In the Presence of My Enemies* by Gracia Burnham. A gripping true story of the Burnhams' capture by a Muslim-extremist group with ties to Osama bin Laden.

Burnham shares her story honestly, without sensationalizing grizzly events. 336 pp.

Little Britches: Father and I Were Ranchers by Ralph Moody. (See Middle.)

Man of the Family by Ralph Moody. (See Middle.)

A Matter of Character: Inside the White House of George W. Bush by Ronald Kessler. An independent journalist gains access to the West Wing and discovers the true George Bush — a man of character. 320 pp.

Out of Time by Alton Gansky. One of the J. D. Stanton mysteries, this is Christian fiction in which a group of teens encounters a deserted ship from World War I. Full of suspense. 352 pp.

Reagan, In His Own Hand: The Writings of Ronald Reagan That Reveal His Revolutionary Vision for America, edited by Kiron K. Skinnner, Annelise Anderson, and Martin Anderson. A compilation of Reagan's writing in his own hand — letters he wrote and original manuscripts of his radio addresses. Discover his thoughts on the world at the time and gain insight into why he was known as "The Great Communicator." 576 pp.

Red Scarf Girl by Ji-li Jiang. This book presents a realistic portrayal of life in China during the cultural revolution. Autobiographical and well told. 320 pp.

When Character Was King: A Story of Ronald Reagan by Peggy Noonan. A portrait of Ronald Reagan, written by his speechwriter. 352 pp.

Section Four

ANSWER KEY TO THE
FOR FURTHER STUDY QUESTIONS

and

FOR FURTHER STUDY
YOUNGER STUDENT ADAPTATIONS

Lessons 1 — 32
in the Student Activity Book

UNIT ONE
For Further Study Questions and Answers

Lesson 1: For Further Study Questions and Answers

1. **Research the life of Levi Coffin, a Quaker known as the "president" of the Underground Railroad. How many slaves did he help to escape? See if you can find an excerpt from his book, *Reminiscences of Levi Coffin*, and read it. Where is the National Historic Landmark Levi Coffin House located?**
    Answer: Levi Coffin (1798–1877) was a North Carolina schoolteacher and member of the Society of Friends. In 1821, Levi and a cousin attempted to start a Sunday school for slaves, but the slaves' owners soon forced its closure. Several years later, Coffin joined other family members who had moved to Indiana. There he opened a general merchandise store in Newport, a town located on a "line" of the Underground Railroad. Coffin soon became involved in helping runaway slaves, and eventually three principal "railroad lines" from the South converged at his house. As many as two to three thousand slaves are believed to have used the Coffin home as a principal "depot" in their escape to freedom. Built in 1827, the National Historic Landmark Levi Coffin House is located on Main Street in Fountain City (formerly called Newport), Indiana.

    In 1847, the Coffins moved to Cincinnati, where Levi opened a warehouse that handled goods produced by freed slaves. He and his wife continued to help slaves through the Underground Railroad. Near the end of the Civil War, Coffin traveled to England and worked to establish the Englishman's Freedmen's Aid Society, which contributed money, clothing, and other articles to newly freed slaves. Coffin recounted his activities as president of the Underground Railroad in his book, *Reminiscences of Levi Coffin*.

    You can find excerpts from *Reminiscences of Levi Coffin* by typing that title into an Internet search engine.

2. **Read about the life of Harriet Tubman, the famous conductor on the Underground Railroad. How did she suffer as a slave and when did she escape? Why did she decide to join the Underground Railroad, and how many slaves did she escort to freedom? Record the information about Harriet Tubman on an African American form.**
    Answer: Harriet Ross Tubman (1820?–1913), who became known as the "Moses of her people," was born into slavery on a plantation in Dorchester County, Maryland. At the age of five or six, she began to work as a house servant. By the time she was twelve or thirteen, Harriet was sent out to hard labor in the fields. During her early teen years, she was struck in the head with a two-pound iron weight by an overseer when she attempted to protect another slave. Harriet would suffer blackouts resulting from this injury for the rest of her life.

    When she was approximately twenty-five, Harriet married a free African American named John Tubman. In 1849, fearing she would be sold, Harriet escaped to Philadelphia. There she found work, saved her money, and joined the city's abolitionist group. By 1851, she had begun making trips to Maryland to rescue other members of her family. From that point until the Civil War began, Tubman is believed to have made as many as nineteen trips over the Underground Railroad and conducted approximately three hundred slaves to freedom. In 1857, Harriet led her parents to freedom in Auburn, New York, which also became her home.

As Harriet's reputation as a conductor grew, many southerners became determined to stop her. Rewards for her capture totaled as much as forty thousand dollars. Tubman stated that she was confident God would enable her to protect her passengers and those who aided them. She devised clever techniques to ensure the success of her journeys and threatened to shoot any of her passengers who wanted to turn back. In all her trips, Harriet never lost a passenger. During the Civil War, she served the Union army as a cook, a nurse, a scout, and sometimes as a spy, primarily in South Carolina. After the war ended, Harriet returned to Auburn and worked to improve the lives of former slaves and of women.

3. **Discover what role "Beecher's Bibles" played in "Bleeding Kansas." For whom were the Beecher's Bibles named? How was this individual significant in prewar American society?**
   Answer: "Beecher's Bibles" were named for Henry Ward Beecher (1813–1887), the son of a prominent Congregationalist minister and the brother of Harriet Beecher Stowe. Henry Beecher graduated from Amherst College in 1834 and studied at Lane Theological Seminary before serving two Presbyterian churches in Indiana. In 1847, Beecher moved to the newly organized Congregational Plymouth Church in Brooklyn, New York. There he became known for his dramatic oratory and drew as many as twenty-five hundred people to his church each Sunday. Beecher took a public stand from his pulpit on many of the social issues of the day. He supported abolitionism, women's suffrage, temperance, and the theory of evolution.

   Henry Beecher was also politically active. In 1852, he supported the Free-Soil Party, but by 1860, he had switched to the Republican Party. When the Kansas-Nebraska Act was passed in 1854, Beecher condemned it from the pulpit. He also helped to raise money among his congregation to buy weapons to be used by antislavery forces in those territories. These rifles, which became known as "Beecher's Bibles," were shipped to Kansas in crates labeled "Bibles." During the Civil War, Beecher's congregation raised and equipped a volunteer regiment for the Union army. After the war was over, Beecher supported reconciliation.

4. **Look for information on the Free-Soil and Know-Nothing political parties. How did they get their names?**
   Answer: The Free-Soil Party was a short-lived American political party, established for the primary purpose of opposing the extension of slavery into the territories. The party was formed around debate over the Wilmot Proviso, proposed federal legislation requiring that all territory received after the Mexican War be free from slavery. The Wilmot Proviso failed when New Mexico and Utah were opened to slavery by the Compromise of 1850.

   In August 1848, the Free-Soil Party was officially organized in Buffalo, New York, at a meeting of former members of the abolitionist Liberty Party, extreme antislavery Whigs, and the Barnburners. The Barnburners were a pro-Van Buren faction of the Democratic Party in New York. Martin Van Buren and Charles Adams were chosen as the Free-Soil candidates for president and vice president in 1848.

   Free-Soil candidates ran on a platform of "free soil, free speech, free labor, and free men," which also called for a homestead law and a tariff for revenue only. In the presidential contest, Van Buren received nearly three hundred thousand votes (about 10 percent) and gave New York to the Whigs, an important factor in Zachary Taylor's victory. A small number of Free-Soil candidates were also elected to the U.S. Congress. In the 1852 presidential election, the party's candidate, John Hale, received only 5 percent of the vote. By 1854, the Free-Soil Party had been absorbed into the newly formed Republican Party.

   The Know-Nothing Party was another short-lived American political party that flourished between 1852 and 1856. In the 1840s, an increasing number of Irish Roman Catholic immigrants were entering the United States, and many of them became part of Democratic political machines in large cities in the East. In reaction to this development, various secret nativist societies were formed to combat "foreign" influences. By the early 1850s, a number of these organizations had banded together to form the American Party, which eventually became known as the Know-Nothing Party. When a member was asked about party activities, he was supposed to reply "I know nothing."

Know-Nothings wanted the exclusion of Catholics and foreigners from public office and a substantial increase in the numbers of years of residency required for American citizenship. The party had few well-known leaders and gained national prominence primarily because the Whig Party was collapsing over the question of slavery. Know-Nothing candidates won elections in several major U.S. cities in 1854, as well as carrying the Massachusetts governorship and legislature. However, by 1855–1856, the Know-Nothing Party itself became divided over the slavery issue. Its presidential candidate in 1856, Millard Fillmore, received 21 percent of the popular vote. However, the party rapidly fell apart, and most of its antislavery members joined the newly formed Republican Party.

Lesson 1: Younger Student Adaptations

1. Show your younger students photographs of Levi Coffin and of his house in Fountain City, Indiana. Tell them the story of what Levi and his wife did in that house as part of the Underground Railroad.

2. Have them read (or read to them) a short biography of Harriet Tubman or share details of her life.

3. Explain to your students what "Beecher's Bibles" were. Explore with them whether or not their pastor and church are involved in political causes today, as Henry Beecher and his congregation were in the 1850s.

4. Discuss with them what a "third" party in American politics is. Share with them the primary reason for the formation of the Free-Soil Party and the Know-Nothing Party. Ask them what they think of the causes represented by these parties.

Lesson 2: For Further Study Questions and Answers

1. **Look for information on the life of Angelina Grimke, a southerner who moved to the North to join the abolitionist movement. See if you can find excerpts from her pamphlet,** *An Appeal to the Christian Women of the South.* **Do you agree with what she wrote?**
   Answer: Angelina Grimke (1805–1879) and her sister Sarah were the daughters of a slaveholding judge from Charleston, South Carolina. The two moved to Philadelphia in 1819 and joined the Society of Friends. In 1835, a letter that Angelina wrote against slavery was published by William Lloyd Garrison in his newspaper, *The Liberator.* Angelina then proceeded to write an antislavery pamphlet entitled *An Appeal to the Christian Women of the South,* and Sarah followed her example by publishing *An Epistle to the Clergy of the Southern States.* Both pamphlets were publicly burned by officials in South Carolina, and the Grimke sisters were warned that they would be arrested if they returned to the state.

   Sarah and Angelina moved to New York, where they became the first women to give lectures for the Anti-Slavery Society. These lectures drew criticism from religious leaders because they believed that women should not speak out in public on political issues. When faced with this opposition, the Grimke sisters also began addressing women's rights. In 1838, Angelina married another abolitionist, Theodore Weld, and they moved with Sarah to Belleville, New Jersey, where the sisters established their own school. During the Civil War, Angelina lectured and wrote in support of Abraham Lincoln and continued to work for civil rights and women's suffrage.

   You can find excerpts from *An Appeal to the Christian Women of the South* by typing that title into an Internet search engine.

2. **Research the lives of Frederick Douglass and/or Sojourner Truth. Record the information on an African American form.**

   Answer: Frederick Augustus Washington Bailey (1818?–1895), the son of a slave woman and an unknown white man, was born near the town of Easton, on the Eastern Shore of Maryland. Separated from his mother when he was very young, Frederick lived with his grandmother on a plantation during the early years of his life. There he witnessed firsthand the horrors of slavery. At about the age of eight, he was sent to Baltimore to live with a ship carpenter named Hugh Auld. There he learned to read and spent seven relatively comfortable years.

   When Frederick was approximately fifteen, he was sent back to the Eastern Shore and became a field hand. During this period he personally experienced the cruelty of slavery — he was barely fed, whipped daily, and forced to work under brutal conditions. After one failed attempt to escape, Frederick finally succeeded in 1838 and fled to New York City, where he changed his name to Frederick Douglass. He and his new wife moved on to New Bedford, Massachusetts, where he attended abolitionists' meetings and subscribed to William Lloyd Garrison's newspaper, _The Liberator._

   In 1841, Douglass was asked to give a speech at the Massachusetts Anti-Slavery Society's convention. He impressed William Lloyd Garrison, who arranged for Douglass to become a lecturer for the society. Four years later, the society helped Douglass publish his autobiography, _Narrative of the Life of Frederick Douglass, an American Slave, Written by Himself._ After the book's publication, Frederick became fearful that its information might lead to his recapture, so he traveled to Britain to lecture on slavery. When he returned, Douglass began publishing his own antislavery newspaper, the _North Star,_ out of Rochester, New York. He also participated in the Seneca Falls convention for women's rights in 1848.

   Although Garrison had served as Douglass's mentor, the two eventually diverged in their views. Garrison believed that the Constitution was a proslavery document and that the Union should be dissolved. By the time Douglass had begun publishing his newspaper, he was unwilling to advocate dissolution of the Union and was convinced that the Constitution could be used in behalf of emancipation. Despite the efforts of Harriet Beecher Stowe and others to reconcile the two men, they were estranged for a number of years.

   During the Civil War, Douglass served as a trusted advisor to Abraham Lincoln and recruited northern African Americans (including his own sons) for the Union Army. From 1877 to 1881, he served as U.S. marshal for the District of Columbia, and from 1889 to 1891, as U. S. minister to Haiti. When he died, Frederick Douglass was recognized internationally as an uncompromising and hard-working spokesman for racial equality and women's suffrage.

   Originally named Isabella Baumfree, Sojourner Truth (1797?–1883) was born into slavery in Hurley, New York. While a young child, Sojourner was sold several times. As a teenager, she was bought by John Dumont, who treated her brutally. While owned by Dumont, Sojourner married another slave named Thomas, with whom she had five children. In 1827, Sojourner escaped from Dumont and began working for a Quaker family named Van Wagenen. That same year, New York law emancipated all slaves.

   Sojourner Truth was the first African American woman to win a lawsuit in the United States. While working for the Van Wagenens, Sojourner discovered that one of her children had been sold to an Alabama slave owner. The court ruled that Sojourner's son should be returned to New York because at that time it was illegal to sell slaves out of the state into the South.

   Although Sojourner could not read or write, she became a popular speaker for the abolitionist and women's suffrage movements. Many of her speeches showed a deep love for the Bible. In 1843, she took the name Sojourner Truth because she believed that the Holy Spirit had instructed her to change her name and to travel throughout the country to speak the truth. An extremely tall woman (6 feet), Sojourner became known for her commanding voice and sharp sense of humor. In 1850, her dictated autobiography was published as _The Narrative of Sojourner Truth, A Northern Slave._

During the Civil War, Sojourner Truth gathered food and clothing for African American volunteer regiments. In 1864, she met Abraham Lincoln at the White House and received an appointment to the National Freedman's Relief Association. After the war, Sojourner settled in Washington and continued to preach about racial equality and women's rights. She also attempted to persuade Congress to give emancipated slaves free land in the West.

3. **Find out more about the abolitionist activities of John Brown. What role did he play in "Bleeding Kansas"?**

    Answer: Born in Connecticut and raised in Ohio, John Brown (1800–1859) belonged to a deeply religious family. His father was vehemently opposed to slavery and was an agent for the Underground Railroad. Although John studied for the Congregational ministry in Connecticut, he changed his mind and returned to Ohio. During his lifetime he would work at a variety of jobs — as a tanner, farmer, land surveyor, cattle breeder, and businessman — in Ohio, Pennsylvania, Massachusetts, and New York. Married twice and the father of twenty children, Brown was never financially successful.

    John Brown developed passionate opinions about the evils of slavery and became convinced that it would be necessary to use violence to overthrow this system. He participated in the Underground Railroad and gave land to fugitive slaves, and he and his wife raised an African American youth as one of their own children. In 1847, Brown met Frederick Douglass for the first time in Springfield, Massachusetts, and discussed with Douglass his plan to lead a war to free slaves.

    By 1849, Brown had moved his family to the African American community of North Elba, New York. This community had been established due to the generosity of a prominent abolitionist named Gerrit Smith, who donated tracts of land to African American families willing to clear and farm them. After the passage of the Fugitive Slave Act in 1850, Brown recruited more than forty men for the U.S. League of Gileadites, an organization that worked to protect escaped slaves from slave catchers.

    In 1855, Brown and five of his sons moved to the Kansas territory, where they hoped to help antislavery forces gain control. That same year, they were involved in a fight against proslavery forces who had attacked the antislavery town of Lawrence. A year later, in retribution for another attack, Brown led a group of his followers in the murder of five proslavery men on the banks of the Pottawatomie River. According to Brown, he was being used as an instrument in the hands of God. For the rest of the year, Brown and his sons continued to fight in Kansas and in Missouri. His home was burned, and one of his sons was killed.

    With the support of Gerrit Smith and other abolitionists, John Brown moved to Virginia and established a refuge for runaway slaves. He also raised money for an army of emancipation. On October 16, 1859, Brown led his successful raid on the federal arsenal at Harpers Ferry, Virginia. When the company of U.S. men and militiamen led by Robert E. Lee stormed the arsenal, Brown and a small group of his followers barricaded themselves in an engine house and continued to fight. Two of Brown's sons were killed, and Brown himself was wounded and captured.

    John Brown was tried and convicted of treason, insurrection, and murder and was hanged on December 2, 1859. Six others involved in the raid were also executed. Newspapers reported on the trial, and Brown's passionate address to the court regarding his cause made him a martyr in the eyes of many northerners. The song "John Brown's Body," which commemorated the Harpers Ferry raid, was a popular Union marching song during the Civil War.

4. **Mary Chesnut, whose husband served in the Confederate army, lived in Richmond for much of the Civil War. She knew President and Mrs. Davis and many other important Confederate government officials personally. Mrs. Chesnut kept a diary throughout the war. See if you can find excerpts from her diary to read.**

Answer: Type "Mary Chesnut's diary" into an Internet search engine to find excerpts of her diary to read.

Lesson 2: For Further Study — Younger Student Adaptations

1. Share photographs of Angelina and Sarah Grimke with your students and briefly explain some of the details of their lives. Also, explain the meaning of the word *abolitionist*.

2. Have them read (or read to them) a short biography of Frederick Douglass and/or Sojourner Truth.

3. Discuss with your younger students the view held by John Brown concerning the use of violence to overthrow slavery.

4. Look for a Civil War diary or journal in the children's section of the library, and read it to them. Talk about how a diary is different from other types of literature.

Lesson 3: For Further Study Questions and Answers

1. **There were many names given to the conflict that we know today as the Civil War. What name for the war did most southerners prefer? See how many of these names you can find and decide which side would have preferred each name.**
   Answer: Most southerners preferred the name War Between the States. Other names for the war included:
   - The War for the Union (North)
   - The War Against Northern Aggression (South)
   - The Great Rebellion (North)
   - The War for Constitutional Liberty (South)
   - The War Against Slavery (North)
   - The War to Suppress Yankee Arrogance (South)
   - The Southern Rebellion (North)
   - The Second War for Independence (South)
   - The War for Abolition (North)
   - The War for States' Rights (South)
   - The War of the Rebellion (North)
   - The Yankee Invasion (South)
   - The Lost Cause (North)
   - The War for Southern Rights (South)
   - The Second American Revolution (South)
   - The War for Southern Independence (South)

   Also, the Brothers' War, Mr. Lincoln's War, the War of the Sixties, and the War of the North and South were other names for the Civil War.

2. **Research the history of the Confederate flag. Explain its symbolism. How is this flag controversial today?**
   Answer: The first official flag of the Confederate States of America was the Stars and Bars, which was flown from March 4, 1861, to May of 1863. The original version of the Stars and Bars included seven stars representing the first seven states that seceded from the Union. The final version contained thirteen stars, representing the four

---

additional states that seceded, as well as two states that attempted to secede but failed to do so. The Stars and Bars contained three wide stripes (red, white, and red) and a blue canton (rectangular division of a flag, occupying the upper corner next to the staff) for the white stars. This flag caused confusion on the battlefield because it was similar to the Union Stars and Stripes.

The best-known of all the Confederate flags was the battle flag known as the Southern Cross, which was used in battle from November of 1861 to the end of the war. The Southern Cross was made in various sizes for the different branches of the service. Some of the flags were made square and others rectangular. The Confederate battle flag featured the cross of St. Andrew, the apostle martyred by crucifixion on an x-shaped cross. Many southerners were of Scotch and Scotch-Irish ancestry and thus familiar with St. Andrew, the patron saint of Scotland. The cross was navy, the thirteen stars were white, and the background was red. The Southern Cross was next to impossible to confuse with the Stars and Stripes in battle.

The second official Confederate flag was the Stainless Banner, which was flown from May 1, 1863, to March 1865. The Stainless Banner was white with a Southern Cross battle flag in the canton. The first official use for this flag was as the covering for Stonewall Jackson's casket. It was also used as a battlefield flag. However, because the flag was largely white, it was thought that it might be mistaken for a white flag of surrender. A final version of the Confederate flag, adopted in April of 1865, added a wide red band to the right side of the Stainless Banner to distinguish it from a flag of surrender.

The Confederate battle flag is seen by some as a proud symbol of southern heritage and by others as a shameful symbol of slavery. In past years, several southern states flew the Confederate battle flag, along with the U.S. and state flags, over their statehouses. A couple of southern states actually incorporated the Southern Cross into the design of their state flags. The Confederate battle flag was also used by the Ku Klux Klan and other racist hate organizations.

3. **One of the first accounts of the infamous "rebel yell" came from the First Battle of Bull Run. What was the purpose of this yell? How did it sound and from where did it originate?**

   Answer: Confederate armies used the rebel yell as a battle cry during the Civil War to intimidate their enemy and boost their own morale. The exact sound of the yell is not known and is the subject of much debate. The origin of the yell is also uncertain. Some have traced its origin to rural life in the prewar South, where hunting was enjoyed by many and included screaming and hollering at dogs or other people.

   After the war, a number of Confederate soldiers tried to describe the yell in writing. Here are a few of their attempts:
   - Woh—who—ey! Who—ey! Who—ey! Woh—who—ey! Who-ey!
   - Yai, yai, yi, yai, yi
   - Y-yo you-wo-wo

   The yell has also been described as similar to Native American cries or a rabbit's scream. There may have been several different yells associated with different regiments and geographical regions. Several recordings of rebel yells are in existence.

   Confederate units competed with one another to see who could produce the best yell. Standard orders of the Union army called for the shooting of any Union soldier who gave the yell as a prank.

4. **Many new words came from the Civil War. Three of these were *sideburns*, *chignon*, and *greenbacks*. Look for the origin and definition of these words.**

   Answer: *Sideburns* are whiskers worn on the sides of a man's face, especially when the chin is shaved. The term arose from altering the name of General Ambrose Burnside, who became more famous for his mutton-chop whiskers than for his ability as a Union commander.

A *chignon* was a word of northern origin that referred to a lady's hairstyle in which the hair was wrapped plainly into a knot at the back. This became a popular style for women to wear to show support for the war.

The word *greenback* entered the American vocabulary in 1862 when the federal government began issuing paper money backed not by gold or silver but simply by the full faith and credit of the government. As a precaution against counterfeiting, a patented ink was devised that was difficult to imitate or erase. The ink on the back side of the money was also green instead of black, which led to the bills being called *greenbacks*. The blue or gray Confederate money became known as *bluebacks* and *graybacks*.

Lesson 3: For Further Study Younger Student Adaptations

1. Read to your younger students the list of names for the Civil War and have them guess which were popular in the South and which were popular in the North.

2. Show them color pictures of the different Confederate flags and explain their symbolism. Discuss with them why the use of the Confederate battle flag is controversial today.

3. Explain the purpose of the rebel yell and have your students attempt to reproduce it.

4. Find pictures of sideburns, a chignon, and a greenback. Explain the origins of these words during the Civil War.

Lesson 4: For Further Study Questions and Answers

1. **Read about Belle Boyd (Confederate spy) and Emma Edmonds (Union spy). What spying techniques did they use?**
   Answer: Belle Boyd (1844–1900), one of the most notorious Confederate spies, was born in Martinsburg, Virginia (now West Virginia). At least three other members of her family were also Confederate spies. In July of 1861, Union forces occupied Martinsburg. Belle, who was seventeen years old, shot and killed a drunken Union soldier. At this point, she reportedly began her espionage activities for the Confederacy.

   Belle operated from her father's hotel in Front Royal, Virginia, but she also traveled to enemy camps and battlefields in the Shenandoah Valley. She used her feminine wiles, as well as her eavesdropping and conversational abilities, to gather information. Known as "La Belle Rebelle" and the "Siren of the Shenandoah" by Union forces, Belle Boyd was arrested multiple times and imprisoned at least twice. In 1865, she made her way to England, where she remained for two years writing her memoirs and acting on the stage. When Belle returned to the United States in 1866, she continued her stage career.

   Sarah Emma Edmonds (1842–1898), a native of Nova Scotia, was living in Michigan when the first call for Union enlistments came. She cut her hair, obtained a man's suit of clothing, took the name Frank Thompson, and tried to enlist in the Union army. Although it took her four tries, Emma finally succeeded. On April 26, 1861, Frank Thompson became a male nurse in the 2nd Volunteers of the U.S. Army.

   While stationed in Virginia during McClellan's Peninsula Campaign, Edmonds volunteered for a mission inside Confederate lines at Yorktown. Using silver nitrate to darken her skin and wearing a black minstrel wig, she assumed the identity of an African American man named Cuff. The following day, Edmonds joined slaves working with shovels and picks on fortifications at Yorktown. That evening she persuaded another slave to exchange duties with her.

   For the next two days, Edmonds carried buckets of water around the camp, a job that enabled her to gain much useful information — the size of the army, the weapons available, and the morale of the troops. The evening of her third day inside Confederate lines, Edmonds was sent with a group of slaves to carry supper to the picket lines, which allowed her to escape. Two months later, she once again infiltrated Confederate lines, this time as a fat Irish peddler woman named Bridget O'Shea. Once again she gathered useful information.

When Emma's unit was transferred to the Shenandoah Valley, she continued spying on the Confederacy. At the end of 1862, her unit was sent to join the 9th Corps near Louisville, Kentucky. There she assumed the role of Charles Mayberry, a young man with southern sympathies. When Emma's unit was transferred to Grant's army in preparation for the battle of Vicksburg, she became ill with malaria.

Unable to go to the military hospital because she would be revealed to be a woman, Edmonds checked herself into a private hospital. She intended to return to military life once she was well. However, when she left the hospital, she saw posters that listed Frank Thompson as a deserter and decided not to return to the army. Instead, she boarded a train for Washington, D.C., and spent the rest of war working there as a female nurse in a hospital that cared for wounded soldiers. After the war, Edmonds published her memoirs entitled *Nurse and Spy in the Union Army*, a highly successful book that sold more than 150,000 copies.

2. **Research the life of Dorothea Dix. What position did she hold during the Civil War? Why was she known as "Dragon Dix"? With what had she been involved before the war?**

   Answer: Dorothea Dix (1802–1887) was a well-known social reformer from the early 1840s until well after the Civil War. A self-educated woman, Dorothea became wealthy as a result of a school that she established for girls in Boston. She also wrote books for children. In March of 1841, while serving as a substitute teacher for a Sunday school at the East Cambridge jail, Dorothea discovered that mental patients were being housed with prisoners and confined in cages and pens. When she spoke with Horace Mann about this situation, he replied that repeated attempts to correct the problem had failed.

   Over a period of eighteen months, Dorothea traveled to every jail in Massachusetts and documented the condition of the various facilities. She wrote the following to the Massachusetts legislature, "I call your attention to the present state of Insane Persons confined within this Commonwealth, in cages, closets, cellars, stalls, and pens; chained, naked, beaten with rods, and lashed into obedience." The legislature questioned the authenticity of her report and criticized Dorothea for interfering in state business. However, she succeeded in gaining the support of other social reformers and doctors, and the legislature finally passed a reform law. For the next twenty years, Dorothea Dix worked investigating prison and asylum conditions and campaigning for reform from state to state. In 1841, there were 11 mental hospitals in the United States. By 1880, the number had risen to 123.

   A week after the Confederate attack on Fort Sumter, Dix volunteered her services to the Union. In June 1861, she was named superintendent of Union army nurses. Dix moved to Washington, D.C., and served in this position without pay throughout the war. At first she was forced to overcome opposition from skeptical military officials, who were unaccustomed to female nurses and unconvinced that women could perform the work acceptably. Dix developed an efficient system for taking care of the injured and sick, as well as strict criteria for the selection of nurses — they must be at least thirty years old, plain-looking, and willing to wear drab clothing and no jewelry.

   Even with Dix's requirements, which were relaxed somewhat as the war continued, over three thousand women served as Union army nurses. Some of Dix's assistants, who considered her to be too brusque and high-handed, referred to her as "Dragon Dix." After the war was over, she resumed her lobbying on behalf of the mentally ill, primarily through letter writing. Dix spent the last years of her life as a guest at the New Jersey State Hospital in Trenton.

3. **Read about the life of Mathew Brady, a photographer of the Civil War. Look for photographs that he took. He and other photographers followed the armed forces in wagons that served as traveling darkrooms.**

Answer: The most well-known photographer of the Civil War was Mathew B. Brady (1823?–1896). Born in Warren County, New York, Brady had moved to New York City by the age of seventeen and studied photography under several teachers, including Samuel F. B. Morse. By 1844, Brady had established his own photography studio and soon gained a reputation as one of the greatest portrait photographers of famous Americans. He won many awards for his work.

Eventually, Brady opened a studio in Washington, D.C., so that he might be better able to photograph national leaders and foreign dignitaries. As a result, he became one of the first Americans to use photography to chronicle U.S. history. A supporter of the Republican Party, Brady made more than thirty portraits of Abraham Lincoln during the 1860 campaign.

In July 1861, Brady and an artist who worked for *Harper's Weekly* traveled to Manassas to witness the Battle of Bull Run firsthand. There Brady got so close to the action that he was almost captured by the Confederates. After returning to Washington, he decided to make a photographic record of the Civil War. Despite the financial risks and battlefield dangers, Brady organized a corps of more than twenty photographers to follow the troops. He equipped each of these men with a traveling darkroom so that they would be able to process their photographic plates on the spot.

During the war, Brady spent most of his time in Washington—supervising his photographers, preserving their negatives, and buying negatives from other photographers returning from the fields. When photographs from Brady's collection were published, they were credited with "Photograph by Brady," even though they were the work of many different people. These photographs could not be reproduced in newspapers because the technology to do so had not yet been developed in the 1860s. However, many of the photos in Brady's collection were used as the basis for line engravings in illustrated publications. His 1862 exhibition of graphic photographs from the Battle of Antietam brought home to many Americans the terrible carnage of war.

After the Civil War ended, war-weary Americans were no longer interested in buying photographs of the bloody conflict. Brady had expected the government to buy many of his prints when the war ended, but that did not happen. Instead, he was forced to sell his New York City studio and declare bankruptcy. In 1875, Congress agreed to purchase the entire archive of Brady's war negatives for twenty-five thousand dollars; but he still remained heavily in debt. Brady died a penniless alcoholic in the charity ward of Presbyterian Hospital in New York in 1896.

To view some of Mathew Brady's photographs, type "Mathew Brady photographs" into an Internet search engine.

4. **Find out what famous military song came from the Seven Days' Battles. See if you can find the conflicting stories concerning the origin of this song. Read the words and listen to the music of the song.**
   Answer: "Taps" is the famous military song that came from the Seven Days' battles. One story that has circulated about the origin of "Taps" concerns Union army Captain Robert Ellicombe and his Confederate son. According to this story, Ellicombe heard the moans of a wounded soldier on the field and risked his life to bring the man in for medical treatment. It was then he realized that the soldier was actually a Confederate, that he was dead, and that he was his own son. When the Civil War started, the son had been studying music in the South and had enlisted in the Confederate army. Ellicombe received permission to give his son a full military burial and asked the bugler to play a series of musical notes that had been written on a paper found in a pocket of the son's uniform. The notes were what we know today as the music of "Taps."

   However, historians believe that the Ellicombe story is a myth. Instead, they maintain that "Taps" was written by General Daniel Butterfield to honor his men encamped at Harrison's Landing, Virginia, following the Seven Days' Battles of the 1862 Peninsula Campaign. According to this story, Butterfield felt that the call for Extinguish Lights was too formal and wrote a new melody with the help of the brigade bugler, Oliver Willcox

Norton. The new call was sounded in July of 1862 and soon spread to other units of the Union army. After the war ended, "Taps" was made an official bugle call.

Lesson 4: For Further Study Younger Student Adaptations

1. Look for pictures of Belle Boyd and Emma Edmonds and share their stories. Explain the meaning of the word *espionage*.

2. Show them a picture of Dorothea Dix and explain what mental illness is. Share about Dix's reform and war activities. Ask if they can guess why she became known as "Dragon Dix." You may able to find a short biography of Dix.

3. Share with your younger students some of Mathew Brady's photographs. See if you can find several of his portraits of Abraham Lincoln, as well as of famous military leaders. Also look for photographs that show what life was like for the troops during the Civil War.

4. Play for them a recording of "Taps" and tell them the stories about its origin.

Lesson 5: For Further Study Questions and Answers

1. **Research the role that telegraphs played during the war.**
   Answer: During the Civil War, telegraphs played an important role in the sending of military orders and the receiving of reports. Both the Union and Confederate armies made full use of existing civilian telegraph networks and developed and extended them as the war continued. Journalists also used telegraphy to file stories with their newspapers, which helped to keep public interest in and support of the war high.

   Between 1860 and 1865, the North laid fifteen thousand extra miles of telegraph wire. On both sides, messages were transmitted in Morse code. Only a handful of operators were trusted with coding and decoding messages. In an attempt to gain military intelligence, both the Confederacy and the Union tapped each other's wires, with varying degrees of success. General Lee's telegraph operator entered the Union lines during the siege of Petersburg, connected to the Union telegraph, and intercepted all Union messages sent for six weeks.

2. **What was the most popular newspaper during the Civil War? Look for examples of newspaper reporting during the war.**
   Answer: Large numbers of American and foreign newspaper reporters and artists followed the Union and Confederate armies during the Civil War. These correspondents had no official status. They might be tolerated or not by the senior officers of the commands to which they attached themselves. The public had a great hunger for war news.

   Rivalry among newspapers was intense, especially among the New York City papers. In the North, the newspaper industry flourished during the war. Its revenue was inflated by increased advertising and circulation. In the South, however, the newspaper industry struggled as the war dragged on and the blockade of Confederate ports tightened. *Harper's Weekly*, published in the North, was probably the most popular newspaper during the Civil War. The South had no comparable publication. You can access online articles from *Harper's Weekly* magazines published during the Civil War.

3. **Find out who the Copperheads were. Why were they considered dangerous?**

Answer: The Copperheads, or "Peace Democrats," were a faction of northern Democrats who were opposed to the Civil War. In 1861, Republicans began calling these Democrats "Copperheads," a name probably derived from the venomous snake that strikes without warning. The Peace Democrats accepted this label and wore copper liberty-head pennies as badges.

In addition to their strong opposition to the war, the Copperheads considered Lincoln to be a tyrant, bent on destroying American republican values with his arbitrary actions. Some Copperheads tried to persuade Union soldiers to desert, resisted the draft laws, and talked of helping Confederate prisoners of war escape. Of course, Peace Democrats constantly had to defend themselves against charges of disloyalty.

Copperheads were most numerous in the Midwest, in states such as Ohio, Illinois, and Indiana. Midwesterners often had close economic and cultural ties with the South. The influence of the Copperheads varied according to how the war was going for the Union. When the war was going well, Copperheads were dismissed as defeatists. When the war was going badly, more people were willing to consider making peace with the Confederacy. Many northerners believed that the Copperheads were prolonging the war by encouraging the South to continue fighting.

The most famous Copperhead was Ohio Congressman Clement L. Vallandigham, who introduced a bill in 1862 to imprison President Lincoln. Instead, Vallandigham and a number of other Democratic politicians, judges, and newspaper editors were arrested and held in prison for months without a trial on the orders of Lincoln and Secretary of War Edwin Stanton. In 1864, Vallandigham persuaded the Democratic Party to adopt a platform that declared the war a failure. However, the party's presidential candidate, George McClellan, repudiated this platform.

4. **Research the Trent Affair. How did it almost bring Great Britain into the war? Why did Britain decide not to help the Confederacy?**
    Answer: The Trent Affair, also known as the Mason and Slidell Affair, was a diplomatic incident between the United States and Great Britain that occurred during the Civil War. In November 1861, James Mason (Confederate minister to Great Britain) and John Slidell (Confederate minister to France) were dispatched in an attempt to gain support from these nations for the Confederacy. They sailed from Havana, Cuba, on the British mail steamer, the *Trent*.

    However, the *Trent* was stopped in the Bahama Channel by the U.S. warship *San Jacinto*, commanded by Captain Charles Wilkes. Mason and Slidell and their secretaries were forcibly removed from the ship and taken to Boston, where they were interned at Fort Warren. This act was a violation of maritime law as it had been previously upheld by the United States.

    Northern newspapers praised Wilkes's actions, and the U.S. House of Representatives passed a resolution thanking Wilkes. The war had been going badly for the Union, and the Trent Affair was a bright spot in the midst of a dismal year of fighting. However, many people in Great Britain considered the affair to be an insult to British honor, as well as a violation of maritime law. The British government issued an ultimatum to the United States, which demanded an explanation, an apology, and the release of Mason and Slidell. The terms of the ultimatum finally sent were softened by Prince Albert from his deathbed.

    For a time it seemed as if Great Britain might recognize the Confederacy and even declare war against the United States. Britain and the South had close economic links because of their shared involvement in the cotton trade, and many British aristocrats sympathized more with the Confederacy than with the Union. Lincoln and his administration struggled with how to accept the demands of the British government while maintaining American popular support.

    Finally, Secretary of State William Seward crafted a reply to the British, agreeing to free Mason and Slidell but salvaging American pride by asserting that the British had finally adopted the U.S. concept of neutral rights, over which the two countries had fought the War of 1812. In January of 1862, Mason, Slidell, and their two secretaries were released, and war between the United States and Great Britain was averted. Mason and Slidell went on to Europe but did not succeed in convincing any European powers to intervene on behalf of the Confederacy.

Lesson 5: For Further Study Younger Student Adaptations

1. Look for pictures of telegraph lines, transmitters, and receivers and show them to your students. Explain how telegraphy works, as well as how it was used during the Civil War. Introduce them to the Morse code alphabet and have them practice sending messages in code.

2. Show them excerpts from various *Harper's Weekly* newspapers.

3. Share with younger students a photograph of a copperhead snake and read a short description of copperheads. Tell them that a group of people during the Civil War was called Copperheads and have them guess who that group was. Then explain the story of the Copperheads, or Peace Democrats.

4. Explain how the Confederacy was hopeful of gaining allies in their fight with the Union. Tell them the story of James Mason and John Slidell. Ask them to think about how the Civil War might have been different if Great Britain had decided to help the Confederacy.

Lesson 6: For Further Study Questions and Answers

1. **During the Civil War, some people in the Union claimed that Lincoln was making himself a dictator when he suspended writs of habeas corpus. What is a writ of habeas corpus? What does the Constitution say about it? How did Lincoln answer his critics? Do you agree with his explanation?**
   Answer: The writ of habeas corpus protects Americans from illegal arrests and imprisonments. The Latin phrase means to "produce the body." A prisoner who believes that he is unjustly imprisoned may petition a court for a writ of habeas corpus. He is then brought before a judge, who decides whether or not there is "probable cause" for holding the prisoner. If the judge decides that the individual has been imprisoned unlawfully, he can order him released.

   The writ of habeas corpus is an ancient English legal concept that the Founding Fathers assumed to be a fundamental liberty. The only place in the Constitution that the writ of habeas corpus is mentioned occurs in Article I, Section 9, "The privilege of the writ of habeas corpus shall not be suspended, unless when in cases of rebellion or invasion the public safety may require it."

   President Lincoln was the first American president to suspend the writ of habeas corpus, and he did so without consulting Congress. At first Lincoln's suspension applied only to Maryland, a border state sympathetic to the South surrounding Washington, D.C. However, on September 24, 1862, the president issued a proclamation that suspended the writ of habeas corpus everywhere in the United States. Furthermore, Lincoln ordered that those arrested under his proclamation were subject to martial law (trial and punishment by military courts). Lincoln's critics accused him of abusing the power of the presidency, but Lincoln contended that this action was necessary in order to preserve the Union.

2. **Find out about Julia Ward Howe, a noted northern abolitionist and writer, who wrote the "Battle Hymn of the Republic." Read the words to that song.**
   Answer: Julia Ward Howe (1819–1910), the daughter of a wealthy banker, was active in the American Anti-Slavery Society. In 1843, Julia married a fellow abolitionist, a physician named Samuel Gridley Howe. Dr. Howe

founded the Perkins Institute for the Blind. The Howes lived in Boston and eventually had six children. From 1851–1853, they edited the antislavery journal known as the *Commonwealth*. The couple was also active in the Free-Soil Party. Julia's first book of poetry, *Passion Flowers*, was published in 1854.

In November of 1861, Julia Ward Howe visited Washington, D.C., and witnessed a Union battalion marching and singing the song "John Brown's Body." Howe was inspired to write new words for the song, a version that soon became known as the "Battle Hymn of the Republic." The *Atlantic Monthly* published Howe's poem in February of 1862. The "Battle Hymn of the Republic" quickly became one of the most popular songs of the Union army and later a well-loved American patriotic song.

After the war, Julia wrote and lectured on behalf of women's suffrage and pacifism. She became the first woman elected to the American Academy of Arts and published her *Reminiscences 1819–1899*.

3. Watch the scenes in the movie *Gone with the Wind* (**or read the sections in the book**) **that deal with the Union army's Atlanta campaign.**

4. **Research the life of Mary Surratt, owner of a Washington, D.C., boardinghouse, who was arrested and charged with knowledge of the plot to assassinate President Lincoln. What happened to her? Who else was accused of being a part of this conspiracy?**

Answer: Mary Jenkins Surratt (1823–1865) was born in Waterloo, Maryland, and educated at a Catholic female seminary. Married at age seventeen, Mary and her husband, John, eventually settled on 287 acres of farmland in Prince George's County, Maryland. There they built a tavern and a post office and raised three children. In 1862, John Surratt died. Two years later, Mary decided to move to a house that she owned at 541 High Street in Washington. She rented her tavern to a former policeman named John Lloyd, who later testified at her conspiracy trial.

To make money, Mary rented out some of the rooms in her High Street house. One of Surratt's sons was a Confederate secret agent, and his acquaintances included many of the key figures in the Lincoln assassination attempt, including John Wilkes Booth. Booth, an actor who performed throughout the country, was a Confederate sympathizer who hated Lincoln.

By January of 1865, Booth had organized a group of co-conspirators in a plot to kidnap Lincoln. This group apparently included John Surratt, Samuel Arnold, George Atzerodt, David Herold, Michael O'Laughlen, and Lewis Powell. Booth began to use Surratt's boardinghouse as a place to meet with this group. In March, Booth's plans turned toward assassination.

On April 14, Booth learned that the Lincolns were attending a play at Ford's Theatre. Booth agreed to kill Lincoln. Apparently, at least two other assassinations were also planned to occur simultaneously—Atzerodt would kill Vice President Andrew Johnson, and Powell (with Herold accompanying him) would kill Secretary of State Seward. However, Atzerodt did not attempt to kill Johnson, and Powell stabbed Seward but didn't kill him.

After shooting Lincoln, Booth fled with Herold to Surratt's tavern in Maryland, where they picked up supplies. Then they traveled to Dr. Samuel Mudd's home, where the doctor set Booth's broken leg. On April 26, Herold and Booth were found by federal authorities hiding in a barn near Port Royal. Herold gave himself up, while Booth was shot to death. Within days, Booth's co-conspirators, including Mary Surratt, were arrested. They were brought to trial before a military tribunal, and all were found guilty.

Surratt, Powell, Atzerodt, and Herold were hanged on July 7, 1865 (Surratt was the first woman executed by the United States). Mudd, O'Laughlen, and Arnold were given life sentences. Ned Spangler, a stagehand at Ford's Theatre, was convicted of helping Booth escape from the theater. He received a six-year sentence. John Surratt escaped to Canada and then Europe. However, he was eventually captured and tried in a civil court in 1867. Because the jury was deadlocked, Surratt went free. O'Laughlen died in prison in 1867, but President

Andrew Johnson pardoned Mudd, Arnold, and Spangler in 1869. Surratt's and Mudd's convictions have been hotly debated throughout the years.

Lesson 6: For Further Study Younger Student Adaptations

1. Have them read (or read to them) a short biography of Abraham Lincoln.

2. Play for them a recording of the "Battle Hymn of the Republic" and let them read the words. Decide if you would like them to memorize the first verse. Share with them the origin of the song.

3. Decide if you would like your younger students to view an excerpt of *Gone with the Wind*.

4. Explain to your students what an assassination is. The National Park Service has a Ford's Theatre website with interesting information about Lincoln's assassination, as well as photographs that you could show them.

Lesson 7: For Further Study Questions and Answers

1. **Research the life of Thaddeus Stevens. Why did African Americans consider him to be a hero and southerners call him the "vilest of the Yankees"?**
   Answer: Thaddeus Stevens (1792–1868), born in Danville, Vermont, suffered from a club foot and a deformed leg. Although his family was poor, Thaddeus graduated from Dartmouth College and established a successful law practice in Pennsylvania. Stevens was a strong opponent of slavery and became known for defending fugitive slaves without charge. Eventually, he acquired a large amount of property in the area and established an iron business.

   From 1833–1842, Stevens served in the Pennsylvania state legislature. In 1848, he was elected to the U.S. House of Representatives. A member of the Whig Party, he joined the newly formed Republican Party and played a leading role in the fight against the Compromise of 1850 and the Fugitive Slave Act. Known as the "Great Commoner," Stevens passionately opposed the extension of slavery and pushed for African American emancipation and suffrage.

   During the Civil War, Stevens wielded great power in Congress as chairman of the House Ways and Means Committee. He became a leader of the Radical Republicans, who opposed moderate actions against the South and favored a "war of extermination." The Confederacy got even with Stevens by burning one of his forges during the Gettysburg campaign.

   Following the war, Stevens was a leader in the Radical Republican fight against President Johnson's Reconstruction policy. He helped to draft the 1867 Reconstruction Act and the Fourteenth Amendment and argued that southern plantations should be taken from their owners and redistributed among former slaves. A prime instigator of the effort to impeach Johnson, Stevens became so ill during Johnson's trial that he had to be carried into the Senate chambers. He died less than three months after Johnson's acquittal.

2. **The political cartoonist Thomas Nast drew thousands of cartoons during the second half of the nineteenth century. Discover in which newspaper he was regularly published and what enduring American symbols he created. Look for examples of his cartoons from the Reconstruction era. Did he support Andrew Johnson's plan for Reconstruction?**
   Answer: German-born political cartoonist Thomas Nast (1840–1902) gave the United States some of its most enduring symbols: the Republican Party's elephant, the Democratic Party's donkey, Uncle Sam, and the classic version of Santa Claus. Considered to be the father of American political cartooning, the celebrated Nast had his

work published regularly in *Harper's Weekly*. A staunch opponent of slavery, Nast supported President Lincoln during the war and produced patriotic drawings championing the Union's cause and the dignity of African Americans. Lincoln referred to Nast as "the Union's best recruiting sergeant."

Following the war, Nast drew cartoons that attacked President Johnson for undermining Lincoln's policies. In September of 1868, Nast began a campaign against William Tweed, a corrupt New York City political leader, and used his signature Tammany Hall tiger for this successful crusade. A loyal Republican, Nast supported Ulysses Grant in 1868 and 1872 and Rutherford B. Hayes in 1876. However, in 1884, Nast changed sides and supported the Democratic candidate, Grover Cleveland. When Cleveland won, Nast became known as the "presidential maker." In 1892, he returned to the Republicans and supported Benjamin Harrison for president.

During the 1880s, Nast began to attack trade unions and the Catholic church. He also depicted Irish Americans as apes. These cartoons were less popular with his reading audience. However, Nast was sympathetic in his treatment of Native Americans and Chinese Americans. After a disagreement with the owners of *Harper's Weekly*, Nash left that journal in 1886 and started his own, *Nash's Weekly*, which did not succeed. Nash was left with heavy debts and suffered severe financial hardship when other investments of his were not successful. In 1902, President Theodore Roosevelt appointed his old friend to be the U.S. consul to Ecuador. In December of 1902, Thomas Nast died from yellow fever.

To look at some of Nast's work, type "Thomas Nast's political cartoons" into an Internet search engine.

3. **Read more about the black codes enacted by the former Confederate states after the Civil War. Find more specifics concerning restrictions placed upon freed slaves. Why would former slave owners want these codes in place? How were these black codes related to "Jim Crow laws"?**

Answer: Other examples of restrictions that might be found in black codes included not allowing freedmen to rent a house within the town limits, to have their own congregations (of freedmen), to keep livestock, to vote without paying poll taxes, to buy intoxicating liquors, or to be outside after a nightly curfew. Freedmen were required to make annual contracts for their labor in writing, and fugitives from jobs were arrested and carried back to their employers.

White southerners were fearful that freed slaves might commit violent acts against their former masters or refuse to work and bankrupt the planters that depended upon their labor. They wanted to force freedmen to work for them under the conditions that they established. In effect, these black codes created a type of quasi-slavery and led to continuing segregation of the races in the South. In the 1890s, laws maintaining racial segregation became known as Jim Crow laws.

4. **Discover what the phrase "Solid South" means. How did this phenomenon affect American politics for a hundred years after Reconstruction?**

Answer: The "Solid South" refers to the South's consistent electoral support of national Democratic Party candidates for almost a century following Reconstruction (1876–1964). From 1876 until 1948, every Democratic presidential candidate, except Al Smith in 1928, won heavily in the South. The dominance of the Democratic Party in the southern United States originated from the South's bitterness toward the Republican Party because of its role in the Civil War and Reconstruction. During this period, the Democratic Party was willing to fight for racial segregation and Jim Crow laws. Although African American voters today are 90 percent Democratic, they preferred the Republican party into the 1950s.

The Democratic "Solid South" began to erode when President Truman decided to support the civil rights movement. The 1960 election was the first in which a Republican presidential candidate received electoral votes in the South. Presently, the South has a mix of Democratic and Republican governors, senators, and representatives. However, since the 1960s, the region has been a Republican stronghold in presidential elections, which has led to the term "Solid South" acquiring a meaning opposite to its original meaning.

Lesson 7: For Further Study Younger Student Adaptations

1. Discuss with your younger students the difficult job facing the U.S. government after the Civil War ended — deciding how to reintegrate the Confederate states into the Union. Ask them whether or not they think the government should have chosen a plan that was more lenient to the former Confederacy and the reason(s) for their opinion. Explain to them Thaddeus Stevens's ideas about Reconstruction.

2. Show your students Nast's drawings of the Republican Party's elephant, the Democratic Party's donkey, Uncle Sam, and Santa Claus. See if you can find some of Nast's political cartoons that they can understand and have them interpret the cartoons for you. Explain the role of political cartoons.

3. Explain in more detail what the black codes were and why they were adopted by the southern states after the Civil War. Ask your students what they might have done to help the freed slaves if they had been a government leader after the war. See if you can find a short book that describes the lives of African Americans during Reconstruction and read it to them.

4. Make sure they understand that the Democratic and Republican parties have been the two major political parties in the United States since the Civil War. Discuss with them why the South was so heavily Democratic in national politics for one hundred years after the Civil War and why it has been heavily Republican since the 1960s.

Lesson 8: For Further Study Questions and Answers

1. **Research the life of Hiram Revels. Record the information on an African American form.**
   Answer: Hiram Revels (1822?–1901) was born a free man of African American and Indian descent in Fayetteville, North Carolina. He was secretly taught to read by a free black woman. When he was about fifteen, Hiram became apprenticed to his brother as a barber in Lincolnton, North Carolina. After his brother died in 1841, Hiram managed his barber shop for a time.

   However, Revels decided that he wanted to continue his education. He attended a Quaker seminary in Indiana and a black seminary in Ohio. In 1845, Revels was ordained as a minister in the African Methodist Episcopal church. Following his ordination, he traveled extensively, teaching and preaching in the old Northwest Territory states. In the early 1850s, Hiram married and attended Knox College in Illinois for two years. When he left Knox in 1857, Revels became the minister of an AME church in Baltimore and the principal of an African American high school.

   When the Civil War began, Revels helped to organize black Union regiments in Maryland and Missouri. He became affiliated with the Freedmen's Bureau and moved to Mississippi, where he served as a minister and on the Natchez city council. In January of 1870, Revels became the first African American to be elected to the U.S. Senate from Mississippi.

2. **Who was the only president besides Andrew Johnson to be impeached? What were the similarities and differences in these men and their trials?**
   Answer: Bill Clinton was impeached by the U.S. House of Representatives on December 19, 1998, and acquitted by the Senate on February 12, 1999.

Both Johnson and Clinton alienated a majority of Republicans in Congress. Andrew Johnson was the enemy of the Radical Republicans because he refused to accommodate their plans for Reconstruction. Bill Clinton was the enemy of the right-wing Republicans because he sought to block their "Contract with America." He did so by accepting some of its more popular provisions and portraying the rest of its agenda as extremist. In both cases, moderate Republicans played an important role in the final outcome of their trials.

The enemies of both Johnson and Clinton saw them as personally unsuitable to be president. The Radical Republicans considered Johnson unsuitable because he was a stubborn southern Democrat and former slave-holder. Right-wing Republicans considered Clinton unsuitable because of his adulterous lifestyle and liberal values. In both the 1860s and the 1990s, Republicans began wide-ranging inquiries looking for impeachable offenses.

Many historians believe that Johnson's impeachment dealt with a much more substantive constitutional issue than Clinton's — the power of the presidency in relation to the power of Congress. His impeachment arose from differences between the executive and legislative branches concerning how the country would be reunited and what the status of freed slaves would be. However, most historians do not consider Johnson's actions to have been impeachable offenses, just as many do not believe that Clinton's offenses met the constitutional standard of "high crimes and misdemeanors."

3. **Why did a Republican splinter group, known as the Liberal Republicans, oppose Grant's re-election in 1872? With whom did they form an unlikely coalition? Who was the presidential candidate of this coalition and why was he a poor choice?**

Answer: The Liberal Republican Party, formed in 1872, was opposed to the election of President Grant because they wanted to end government corruption and the military occupation of the South. Many of the original founders of the Republican party joined this movement, including Senator Charles Sumner of Massachusetts, the New York newspaper editor Horace Greeley, Senator Carl Schurz from Missouri, Chief Justice Salmon P. Chase, and Charles Francis Adams (son of John Quincy Adams). They formed an unlikely coalition with the Democrats, who agreed with the positions of the Liberal Republicans.

The presidential candidate of the Liberal Republicans in 1872 was Horace Greeley, who was also nominated by the Democrats. This was the only time in American history that a major political party embraced a third-party candidate. However, Greeley was seen as an eccentric who prided himself on taking extreme positions on many social issues. He was ridiculed as a vegetarian, spiritualist, and turncoat, a crazy man who was not an improvement over Grant. The most vicious attacks against Greeley came from Thomas Nast's cartoons in *Harper's Weekly*. When Grant was re-elected in a landslide victory, the Liberal Republican movement vanished quickly. Most of its members returned to the Republican Party, but some switched to the Democratic Party.

4. **Find out why the United States was enjoying economic prosperity in the late 1860s and early 1870s. Discover what led to the Panic of 1873 and the six-year depression that followed.**

Answer: The Civil War had spurred the growth of heavy industry and agriculture in the United States. Business continued to prosper during the shift from wartime to peacetime. However, the nation's economic growth was unregulated, and the nation's railroad system in particular was overbuilt. The country also had too much paper money (greenbacks) in circulation, which pleased debtors but worried bankers and conservative economists. Eventually, the existence of so many greenbacks led to higher prices and inflation.

The Panic of 1873 was set off on September 18 when the Philadelphia banking firm of Jay Cooke and Company declared bankruptcy. This banking company had invested heavily in railroads and planned to provide the financing for a second transcontinental railroad. However, in September the firm realized that it had become overextended and declared bankruptcy, which touched off a series of devastating economic events that ended in a six-year depression.

The New York Stock Exchange closed for ten days. Almost 90 of the nation's 364 railroads went bankrupt, and as many as eighteen thousand American businesses failed between 1873 and 1875. Credit dried up, and factories shut down. By 1876, national unemployment was at 14 percent. During the depression the government pledged to begin redeeming over three hundred thousand dollars in greenbacks for their face value in gold. However, this did not alleviate the depression, which did not lift until the spring of 1879.

Lesson 8: For Further Study Younger Student Adaptations

1. Show your students a photograph of Hiram Revels and share with them details about his life. Explain how rare it was for an African American to know how to read and write and to be elected to a political office during Reconstruction.

2. Many Americans do not really understand what the term *impeachment* means. Explain to your younger students that impeachment is like an indictment in a criminal trial (you will probably need to explain that word, also). If a president is impeached (or an individual indicted), then he must undergo a court trial (in the president's case, the court is the Senate and the chief justice of the Supreme Court presides). At the end of the trial he is either acquitted or convicted. Decide what details you want to share with them concerning the trials of President Johnson and President Clinton.

3. Instead of discussing Liberal Republicans with your younger students, focus on a review of the following terms: *carpetbaggers*, *scalawags*, and *redeemers*. See if you can find photographs and/or political cartoons related to these groups of people. Also find appropriate photographs to show them regarding the activities of the Ku Klux Klan. Help them see how turbulent life in the South was after the war ended.

4. Look for a book that offers a simple explanation of a financial panic, a depression, a recession, and inflation, as well as of the stock market. Find a way to help them become comfortable with these terms. Explain what happened in the 1870s in the United States, and let them know that the country faced other panics and depressions in the years ahead.

UNIT TWO
For Further Study Questions and Answers

Lesson 9: For Further Study Questions and Answers

1. The title "First Lady" was first widely used in 1877 to refer to Lucy Hayes, popular wife of President Rutherford B. Hayes. The press also gave her a nickname. Find out what it was and why they gave it to her. What event for children at the White House was started by this couple? Can you find any other ways that Lucy Hayes was unique?

   Answer: Lucy Hayes was given the name "Lemonade Lucy" by the press because of her refusal to serve alcohol at the White House. Apparently, this nickname came into use only after she had left the White House. However, despite the ban on alcoholic beverages, she and her husband were known for their elegant public receptions and state dinners. They also were the first presidential couple to hold the White House Easter Egg Roll and to use a telephone. In 1880, Lucy accompanied her husband on a train trip to the West Coast, the first transcontinental trip taken by an incumbent president.

   The daughter of a physician, Lucy was the first presidential wife to graduate from college. At the age of eighteen, she received a degree from Wesleyan Female College in Cincinnati, Ohio. Although family inheritances made Lucy a very wealthy woman, she maintained a humble, frugal lifestyle. Her simplicity contrasted with the extravagance of the Grant administration. Lucy was also deeply religious and instituted times of morning worship in the White House.

2. Read more about the Stalwart and Half-Breed factions in the Republican Party. Look into the background of Charles Guiteau, President Garfield's assassin.

   Answer: During the administration of Rutherford B. Hayes, the Republican Party was divided into three factions.

   - The Stalwarts, who saw themselves as "stalwart" in their opposition to Hayes's efforts to reconcile with the South. They opposed civil service reform and backed the protective tariff. Senator Roscoe Conkling was the most prominent Stalwart leader.
   - The Half-Breeds, who backed Hayes's lenient treatment of the South and supported civil service reform. Senator James G. Blaine was the leader of the Stalwarts. He sought the presidential nomination in 1876 and 1880 but failed to secure it either time.
   - The Liberals, or Reform element, who supported civil service reform and a tariff for revenue purposes only.

   As a young man, Charles Julius Guiteau (1841–1882), an Illinois native, joined a controversial religious group, the Oneida Community. However, he never felt accepted by the members of the community and left twice. Eventually, Guiteau filed lawsuits against the founder of the community, John Humphrey Noyes, who considered Guiteau to be insane. Following this chapter in his life, Guiteau used an inheritance to start a law firm in

Chicago that was unsuccessful. He also published a volume of theology called *The Truth*, which was almost entirely plagiarized from the work of Noyes.

In 1880, Guiteau sent the Republican presidential candidate, James Garfield, an unsolicited and barely coherent campaign speech, which he believed was responsible for Garfield's victory. When Garfield took office, Guiteau began insisting that the president make him ambassador to France. However, Garfield and other cabinet members repeatedly ignored his requests. When, on May 14, Secretary of State Blaine finally told Guiteau never to return to the White House, Guiteau borrowed fifteen dollars and bought a British Bulldog revolver with a silver handle. Apparently, Guiteau chose the revolver that he thought would look best as a museum exhibit after the assassination. Ironically, the revolver was lost.

After Guiteau shot Garfield, he was closely followed by the media because of his bizarre behavior. He constantly criticized his defense team and composed his testimony in the form of long epic poems. During his trial, Guiteau solicited advice from spectators in the courtroom by means of passed notes. When he dictated his autobiography to the *New York Herald*, he ended with a personal ad for a nice Christian lady under thirty. Until his execution, Guiteau was making plans to start a lecture tour and run for president.

On the day of his execution in 1882, Guiteau recited a poem he had composed, entitled "I Am Going to the Lordy." His request for an orchestra to play as he sang the poem had been denied. Although his lawyers had wanted to use an insanity defense, Guiteau insisted that he had been legally sane at the time of the shooting.

3. **Research the Greenback-Labor Party and the Populist Party. What were their goals?**
    Answer: The Greenback-Labor Party, or Greenback Party, was an American political party active between 1874 and 1884. Its main support came from farmers, who had been financially hurt by the Panic of 1873 and continued to suffer from declining farm prices and high railroad rates. These farmers tended to blame the depressed economy on eastern financial interests. Urban trade union groups also added their support to the Greenbacks.

    This political party advocated issuing large amounts of paper money, or greenbacks. Its supporters believed this policy would help farmers by raising prices and making debts easier to pay. In 1878, fourteen members of the Greenback-Labor Party were elected to the U.S. Congress. In the 1880 presidential election, the Greenbacks nominated General James Weaver as their candidate on a platform designed to broaden the party's appeal. They called for an eight-hour workday, a graduated income tax, and opposition to railroad land grants. After the 1880 election, the Greenback-Labor Party merged with the Democrats in most states. However, Weaver was against this merger and helped to establish the Populist Party in 1891.

    The Populist Party, or People's Party, was another short-lived American political party in the late nineteenth century. Established in 1891 by members of the Farmers' Alliance and the Knights of Labor, it promoted free and unlimited coinage of silver, the elimination of national banks, a graduated income tax, the direct election of U.S. Senators, an eight-hour workday, and civil service reform. In 1892, James Weaver ran as the Populist candidate for president and carried four states. In the 1894 mid-term elections, the Populists elected six U.S. Senators and seven Representatives.

    In 1896, Populist leaders entered into talks with the proposed Democratic Party candidate, William Jennings Bryan. They gave their support to Bryan because they were led to believe that the Populist leader Tom Watson would be Bryan's running mate. When Bryan announced that he would support a different vice presidential candidate, one who had a record of hostility toward labor unions, a split occurred in the Populist Party. Some Populists campaigned for Bryan, and others refused to do so. When Bryan lost the election, the Populist Party ceased to be a factor in national politics. Although Tom Watson ran as a Populist presidential candidate in 1904 and 1908, he won few popular votes and no electoral votes.

4. Find a copy of William Jennings Bryan's "Cross of Gold" speech and read it. You can listen to an audio excerpt of Bryan giving this speech twenty-five years after he first delivered it. He repeated this speech many times on the Chautauqua lecture circuit.

   Answer: Type the phrase "text of 'Cross of Gold' speech" into an Internet search engine.

Lesson 9: For Further Study Younger Student Adaptations

1. Share with your younger students the information about Lucy Hayes. See if you can find photographs of a White House Easter Egg Roll to show them.

2. Have them read (or read to them) a short biography of James Garfield or chapter(s) in the biography that discuss his assassination.

3. Continue your discussion with them about third parties in American politics. Explain the reason for the formation of the Greenback-Labor and Populist parties. Look for a book in the children's section of the library that gives a simple explanation of political parties and campaigns.

4. Let them listen to the audio excerpt of Bryan's "Cross of Gold" speech or have them read (or read to them) a short biography of William Jennings Bryan.

Lesson 10: For Further Study Questions and Answers

1. **Read about the life of Alfred T. Mahan. Where did he work and what influential books did he write? How did his views affect American policies during the Gilded Age?**

   Answer: Alfred Thayer Mahan (1840–1914) was a U.S. naval officer and historian. Born in West Point, New York, Mahan graduated from the Naval Academy at Annapolis in 1859. As the Civil War broke out, he was beginning a career that would span nearly forty years of naval service. Commissioned as a lieutenant in 1861, Mahan saw action in the war and served as an instructor at the Naval Academy. He progressed in rank until he was promoted to captain in 1885. The following year, Mahan was appointed president of the U.S. Naval War College. There, in 1887, he met a visiting lecturer named Theodore Roosevelt. From Mahan's lectures during this period came two important books — *The Influence of Sea Power upon History, 1660–1783* and *The Influence of Sea Power upon the French Revolution and Empire, 1793–1812.*

   In his books, Mahan argued that naval power, along with a strong industrial economy, was the key to national greatness and success in international affairs. He believed that the nation that controlled the seas would dominate in modern warfare. In the last quarter of the nineteenth century, Mahan's ideas were radical. His books were translated into several languages and closely studied by political leaders in Germany and Great Britain. In the United States, Teddy Roosevelt and others who supported U.S. naval buildup and overseas expansion were greatly influenced by Mahan's writings. As a result, by the turn of the century, the United States had established a well-armed steel naval fleet. Although Mahan retired from active service in 1896, he continued to write. In 1906, Mahan became a Rear Admiral by an act of Congress that promoted all retired captains who served in the Civil War.

2. **Research what role the Rough Riders played in the Spanish-American War. Who led them? How were they portrayed in the American press? Find out how the Buffalo Soldiers were involved in the Spanish-American War. Who gave them their name?**

Answer: "Rough Riders" was the name given by the American press to the 1st U.S. Volunteer Cavalry Regiment during the Spanish-American War. Assistant Secretary of the Navy Theodore Roosevelt asked the Department of War for permission to raise a regiment once the war began. Since Roosevelt had no military experience, he suggested that command of the regiment be given to his close friend, Colonel Leonard Wood, an army doctor and Medal of Honor recipient. Roosevelt was made a lieutenant colonel and second in command of the regiment.

The 1st U.S. Volunteer Cavalry Regiment consisted of over 1,250 men from all over the United States. From over twenty-three thousand applicants, a group was chosen that included cowboys, Native Americans, miners, Texas rangers, Ivy League athletes, New York City policemen, and East Coast polo players. What these men had in common was that they could ride and shoot and thus be ready for war with little training.

The regiment was assembled at San Antonio, Texas, in May of 1898, and shipped from Tampa to Cuba on June 14, 1898. Because of logistical difficulties, almost half of the regiment's men and most of its horses had to be left behind. Upon their arrival on June 22, the Rough Riders, assigned to the Army's 5th Corps, immediately began marching toward Santiago. Two days later, they participated in the Battle of Las Guasimas.

The night of June 30, Colonel Leonard Wood was promoted to the rank of brigadier general and Roosevelt was made a colonel. The following day, Roosevelt led the Rough Riders and elements of the 9th and 10th Regiments up Kettle Hill. After the capture of Kettle Hill, Roosevelt led a second charge up San Juan Hill. After the capture of San Juan Hill, Santiago surrendered, and the Spanish-American War was virtually over. The exploits of the Rough Riders, widely reported in the U.S. press, led to Teddy Roosevelt's becoming a national hero.

As tropical diseases began to kill many of the American soldiers in Cuba, Roosevelt and others began calling for the troops to be brought back to the United States. The Rough Riders were shipped to Long Island and mustered out on September 16, 1898. As many as 37 percent of the regiment's soldiers who fought in Cuba were killed, wounded, or afflicted with a tropical disease.

More than ten thousand African Americans volunteered for military service in the Spanish-American War. Five of these were awarded the Medal of Honor. Among the first American troops mobilized in Cuba were the 9th and 10th Regular Cavalry Regiments. Known as the legendary Buffalo Soldiers, this group of African American soldiers had fought in the Indian Wars in the West for over thirty years. They were given their nickname by the Native Americans—first as a way of comparing their hair to that of the buffalo but later as a sign of respect for their prowess and bravery on the battlefield.

3. **Who was Walter Reed? What problem faced by American soldiers during the Spanish-American War was Reed asked to address?**
    Answer: Walter Reed (1851–1902) was an American army surgeon, bacteriologist, and educator. During the Spanish-American War, yellow fever had been a problem for thousands of American soldiers fighting in Cuba. In May 1900, Reed was appointed president of a board to study infectious diseases in Cuba, particularly yellow fever. The board determined that yellow fever was transmitted by mosquitoes. Its research was done with human volunteers, including some medical personnel who agreed to be deliberately infected with the disease. Walter Reed General Hospital (eventually renamed Walter Reed Army Medical Center), which opened in Washington, D.C., in 1909, was named in Reed's honor.

4. **Why were some Americans referred to as "jingoes" during the Spanish-American War? What does that word mean? How did it originate?**
    Answer: Those who vigorously supported American involvement in Cuba, such as Theodore Roosevelt, were called "jingoes." Apparently, the word was taken from a song that was popular during a war between Turkey and Russia in 1877–1878. The first two lines of the song were: "We don't want to fight, but by Jingo if we do, we've

got the ships, we've got the men, we've got the money too." Since the Spanish-American War, the word *jingo* has been used to refer to a person who supports an aggressive or belligerent foreign policy or to a chauvinistic patriot.

Lesson 10: For Further Study Younger Student Adaptations

1. Share with them who Alfred T. Mahan was and what he believed. Look for a book that offers a simple explanation of the U.S. Navy.

2. Have them read (or read to them) a short biography of Teddy Roosevelt and pay special attention to the chapter(s) that discuss his role in the Spanish-American War.

3. Explain how mosquitoes can cause diseases, such as yellow fever and today's West Nile virus. Share the story of Walter Reed and his discovery of the cause of yellow fever following the Spanish-American War.

4. Discuss with your younger students the meaning of the terms *nationalism*, *chauvinism*, and *jingoism*.

Lesson 11: For Further Study Questions and Answers

1. **Discover who Frederick Jackson Turner was and how his ideas influenced the study of American history at the turn of the century. What was the name of his famous thesis? What pronouncement did the U.S. government make three years before Turner announced his thesis?**
   Answer: Frederick Jackson Turner (1861–1932) was a historian and professor at the University of Wisconsin and then Harvard. In 1893, he read a paper entitled "The Significance of the Frontier in American History" to a group of historians gathered in Chicago, which was then hosting the World's Columbian Exposition. Three years before his presentation, the U.S. Census Bureau had announced the "closing of the frontier," or the disappearance of a frontier line in the continental United States.

   In his lecture Turner presented his "frontier thesis," which maintained that the frontier past was the central story of American history. According to Turner, the American people and their institutions were uniquely shaped by the frontier experience, which had fostered American democracy, individualism, self-reliance, ingenuity, openness to new ideas, and tolerance. Turner's lecture was almost completely ignored at the time, but his ideas eventually became very influential and shaped the writing of American history for a generation. Although most historians today have discarded the frontier thesis, many still debate Turner's ideas and approach.

2. **Find out how the pioneers constructed soddies. What were the advantages and disadvantages of this type of home? Pioneer women were known for their patchwork quilts. How were they made? What were some popular designs? Look for pictures of American patchwork quilts.**
   Answer: Lumber was expensive and not easily available on the prairie, which led many of the early settlers to build sod houses. Sod squares, cut from the soil, were stacked to build the walls and often the roofs of houses. Most of the early sod homes had dirt floors, but a few had rough or planed split logs for flooring. A small amount of lumber was also often used for a door and one or more windows. Settlers tended to live in their soddies for six or seven years. If the exteriors of their homes were covered with stucco or whitewash, their sod houses would last even longer.

Soddies were inexpensive to build. Because of the thickness of their walls, they were warm in the winter and cool in the summer. Sod houses were not a fire danger, but they leaked badly when it rained. Dirt was always falling down from the ceiling. Poor lighting, bugs, and snakes were additional problems.

Quilting is the process of placing a layer of cotton, wool, or stuffing between two pieces of fabric and stitching the layers together. The triple thickness of a quilt provides a very warm bed cover. Patchwork quilting, which is distinctively American, became very popular in the nineteenth century. It involves the arrangement of scraps of cloth in geometric designs and then quilting them together. Some popular designs included the Log Cabin, Schoolhouse, Bear's Paw, Sunburst, and Sawtooth.

3. **Read about American cowboys. What different articles of clothing did they wear and what was the purpose of each? What dangers did these cowboys face on the range? Who were Gustavus Swift and Philip Armour? Look for paintings of cowboys by Frederic Remington.**

   Answer: An American cowboy typically wore or carried:
   - long trousers, made of sturdy canvas, usually black, brown, or tan. Until belt loops were added, suspenders held up the pants.
   - a long-sleeved shirt, made of cotton or wool and buttoned up to the neck.
   - a vest, usually made of wool, to provide storage for a watch, tobacco, and money and to give additional warmth in winter.
   - knee-high boots, made of leather with a narrow toe to fit through the stirrup and high heels to prevent the boot from sliding forward.
   - a hat, with a wide brim and a tall crown (adapted from the Spanish sombrero), used for protection from the rain and sun, to gather food and water, to fan a fire, and to cover the face when sleeping.
   - chaps, made of leather, to protect against rocks, cactus, and thorny bushes.
   - gloves to protect the hands from ropes, reins, and hot irons.
   - a bandana to protect from rain, wind, dust, and sun. Bandanas also served to chase the flies away, to wet and cool the neck, to tie on a hat in the wind, and to bandage wounds.
   - a saddle (which often cost a year's wages).
   - spurs, made of metal or silver, to control the horse.
   - a quirt, made of braided leather, horsehair, or rawhide, to get the horse's attention.
   - a lariat, made of rawhide or later, manila hemp, for roping cows.
   - a canteen for water.
   - a carbine or short rifle.
   - a knife.
   - a bedroll.
   - a saddlebag, which stored food, extra clothing, tools, and other utensils.

The life of a cowboy was dirty, dull, and hard. He faced many dangers, such as unfriendly Native Americans, cattle rustlers, rattlesnakes, heat, hail, blizzards, quicksand, and thirst.

Gustavus Swift (1839–1903), the son of a Massachusetts farmer, first worked as a butcher's apprentice and then as a cattle dealer. Arriving in Chicago when he was thirty-six, Swift founded a meatpacking empire in the Midwest during the last years of the nineteenth century. He was also responsible for developing the first practical refrigerated railroad car, which allowed the Swift company to ship dressed meat all over the country. In addition to this important development, Swift became known as a pioneer in the use of animal byproducts to produce fertilizer, glue, soap, and medical products. When he died in 1903, Swift's company was valued at between twenty-five and thirty-five million dollars.

Philip Armour (1832–1901) was born in upstate New York. When he was nineteen, he left home and traveled west for the California gold rush. By the age of twenty-four, he had made eight thousand dollars, which he used to establish a successful meat market in California. Moving from California to Milwaukee, Armour opened a wholesale grocery business. Together with a brother, he built several meatpacking plants and started a grain business.

In 1867, the Armour brothers formed Armour and Company, a meatpacking enterprise headquartered in Chicago, which soon became the world's largest food-processing business. Armour and Company pioneered an efficient new killing and cutting line and became the first to reduce waste by selling every part of the animal. Armour followed the lead of his rival Swift when he established the Armour Refrigerator Line in 1883. His refrigerator cars carried the message, "We Feed the World."

The Chicago slaughterhouses became tourist attractions and made Armour and Swift world famous. Visitors to the World's Columbian Exposition took day excursions to see the stockyards. In 1898–1899, Armour and Company's reputation was tarnished when it was charged with selling tainted meat. Then in 1906, Upton Sinclair's book *The Jungle*, exposed the squalid and dangerous working conditions that existed for those employed in the Chicago meatpacking industry.

Type the phrase "paintings by Frederic Remington" into an Internet search engine.

4. **Research the lives of one or more of the following people significant in the Wild West of the Gilded Age — Buffalo Bill, Wild Bill Hickok, Calamity Jane, Bat Masterson, and Frank and Jesse James. Find out more about the Native American Ghost Dance movement. Record information about the Lakota and Sitting Bull on a Native American Tribe form.**

Answer: Reading a biography about any of these individuals would be quite interesting.

William F. Cody (1846–1917), "Buffalo Bill," grew up on the prairie and worked as a mounted messenger, prospector, and rider for the Pony Express. During the Civil War, he served as a Union scout and with the 7th Kansas Cavalry. In 1867, he took a job hunting buffalo to feed railroad construction crews and supposedly earned his nickname in a shooting match with a hunter named William Comstock. A year later, Cody returned to work as a scout for the U.S. Army and participated in sixteen battles. As he earned a reputation for bravery in real life, Cody was also becoming a national folk hero because of the exploits of his alter ego, "Buffalo Bill," in Ned Buntline's novels.

In 1872, Buntline asked Cody to assume the role of "Buffalo Bill" on stage in a play. A natural showman, Cody was well received by audiences. He remained an actor for eleven seasons but still regularly led western hunting expeditions between seasons. He was also called back into army service at least two more times. In 1883, Cody organized Buffalo Bill's Wild West, an outdoor extravaganza that dramatized a Pony Express ride, an Indian attack, a buffalo hunt, and a tableau of Custer's Last Stand. This enormously successful show toured the country and Europe for three decades.

James Butler Hickok (1837–1876), better known as "Wild Bill" Hickok, was a legendary gunfighter in the Wild West. In 1855, Hickok left his father's farm in Illinois to become a stagecoach driver on the Oregon and Santa Fe trails. Two years later, he claimed a tract of land in Kansas, where he became a constable. By 1861, he had moved to Nebraska, where again he served as a town constable and single-handedly captured the McCanles gang at Rock Creek Station.

On July 21, 1865, Hickok killed Davis Tutt, Jr., in an incident caused by a dispute over a gambling debt. Some historians consider this shooting to have been the first Wild West gunfight. After the Civil War, Hickok became an army scout and served as a U.S. marshal. By 1873, he had joined Buffalo Bill Cody in a touring stage play that was the forerunner to Cody's Wild West shows. There he befriended Calamity Jane, who later claimed that they shared a romantic relationship. However, Hickok was fired from the show due to drunkenness and was shot to death in 1876 while playing poker in a saloon.

Martha Jane Canary-Burke (1852?–1903), better known as "Calamity Jane," was a frontierswoman known for her association with Bill Hickok. In 1879, she signed on as a scout with George Custer and took part in several campaigns against Native Americans. There are several conflicting stories concerning the origin of her nickname. In 1896, Jane began touring with Wild West shows and continued to do so until her death.

W. B. "Bat" Masterson (1853?–1921), another legendary figure of the American West, worked at a variety of occupations—as a buffalo hunter, army scout, professional gambler, lawman, U.S. marshal, and sports editor and columnist for a New York newspaper. There are several conflicting stories concerning the origin of his nickname.

Jesse James (1847–1882), along with his brother Frank, was a notorious outlaw in the years following the Civil War. The James brothers and their gang committed numerous bank robberies, train robberies, stagecoach robberies, and various other crimes in Missouri, Kansas, Iowa, Minnesota, Arkansas, Alabama, and West Virginia. Jesse was shot dead by a gang member who wanted to claim the large reward offered for his capture.

The Ghost Dance was a Native American messianic movement that expressed a deep longing for a restoration of the past, a time when tribal life was free of disease, hunger, bitter war, and subjugation by the white man. The movement began with the vision of a medicine man named Wovoka (Jack Wilson). His vision embodied the belief that the white man would disappear from the earth after a great flood and that the Indian dead would return to earth and bring with them the old way of life.

The actual ritual dance associated with the Ghost Dance did not originate with Wovoka or die with him. Referred to as the "round dance," it consisted of a circular community dance held around an individual leader. Trances and prophesying often accompanied the dance. Wovoka also insisted that clean and honest living on the part of the tribes was necessary for his vision to become a reality.

Lesson 11: For Further Study Younger Student Adaptations

1. Have your students read (or read to them) a book about frontier life during the Gilded Age.

2. Show your younger students pictures of quilt designs from this period in history. Encourage them to sketch and color designs of their own. If you own a quilt of your own or know someone who quilts, give them an opportunity to examine how a quilt is made.

3. Have them read (or read to them) a book about American cowboys during the years following the Civil War. Hands-on activities related to cowboys are easy to find.

4. Have them read (or read to them) a book about one of the following—Buffalo Bill, Wild Bill Hickok, Calamity Jane, Bat Masterson, Frank and Jesse James, and Sitting Bull. There have been a number of movies and television shows made about these Wild West figures. Some are more accurate than others. Look for one that would be acceptable for you to watch together.

Lesson 12: For Further Study Questions and Answers

1. **Read more about John Rockefeller, Andrew Carnegie, and/or Cornelius Vanderbilt. Find out how they eliminated their competition to become multimillionaires. How did these men treat their workers? For what philanthropic deeds did they become known?**
    Answer: John D. Rockefeller (1839–1937), a native of New York, was the founder of Standard Oil Company, which quickly gained a monopoly in the oil industry. Rockefeller was able to force out his competitors through exclusive deals with the railroads, rate wars, and intimidation. In 1882, he formed the Standard Oil Trust, the first

of the great American corporate trusts. By the 1890s, Standard Oil had become an immense monopoly, able to set its own prices and terms of business.

In 1902, Ida Tarbell began a series of articles in *McClure's Magazine* about how Rockefeller had achieved his monopoly. Eventually, Tarbell's material was published as a book, *History of the Standard Oil Company*. Finally, in 1911, the U.S. Supreme Court broke up the Standard Oil trust into many smaller companies. Although Rockefeller was known for crushing his competitors and ruining hundreds financially, he also gained recognition for giving over 500 million dollars to medical research, universities, and Baptist churches.

Andrew Carnegie (1835–1919) arrived in the United States from Scotland in 1848 at the age of twelve. Settling in Pittsburgh, Carnegie worked in the daytime and went to school at night. In 1879, he erected a blast furnace using the techniques developed by Henry Bessemer in England. Other furnaces were built, and eventually the Carnegie Steel Company was established. Carnegie took on several partners but retained the majority holding in his highly successful enterprise.

Carnegie and his managers controlled every stage of steel manufacturing, a practice known as vertical integration. By 1892, Carnegie Steel Company was valued at twenty-five million dollars, the largest steel company in the world. In an effort to increase profits, the chairman of the company, Henry Frick, lowered the wage rate of the company's employees. When the steelworkers' union went on strike, (the Homestead Strike), Frick hired strikebreakers from outside the area. The union did not succeed in its attempt to force Carnegie Steel to back down.

In 1901, Andrew Carnegie sold his company to Henry Frick and the banker J. P. Morgan, who established the U.S. Steel Corporation. Carnegie spent the next eighteen years giving away 350 million dollars of his fortune. He built nearly three thousand libraries in the United States and around the world, paid for thousands of church organs to be built, established the Carnegie Institute of Technology, and founded the Carnegie Corporation, which still donates to worthy causes today.

Cornelius Vanderbilt (1794–1877), an American entrepreneur who built his wealth in shipping and railroads, was born on Staten Island, New York, to a family of Dutch ancestry. As a young boy, Vanderbilt worked on ferries in New York City. By the age of sixteen, he was operating his own ferry business. In the 1830s and 1840s, Vanderbilt controlled coastal shipping along the Hudson River and along the New England coast. During the California gold rush of 1849, he ran a steamship line from New York to California.

By the early 1860s, Vanderbilt had started withdrawing capital from his steamship business and investing it in railroads. Over time, he acquired the New York and Harlem Railroad, the Hudson River Railroad, and the New York Central Railroad. By the early 1870s, Vanderbilt had extended the lines to Chicago. Ruthless in his business dealings, Vanderbilt had the public image of a mean-spirited man, little concerned about his passengers' safety (many accidents occurred on his trains). Unlike Rockefeller and Carnegie, Cornelius Vanderbilt gave little of his large fortune to charitable works. He bequeathed one million dollars to Vanderbilt University and fifty thousand dollars to the Church of the Strangers in New York City.

2. **Research the Haymarket Square Riot (1886), the Homestead Lockout (1892), and/or the Pullman Strike (1894). Against which companies were the workers in each of these situations striking? Why were they striking? How were they treated by management? What was the end result of each strike?**
   Answer: The Haymarket Square Riot took place in Chicago on May 4, 1886. On May 1, workers at the McCormick Harvesting Machine Company had begun a strike for an eight-hour workday. Two days later, police were called to the McCormick plant to protect strikebreakers (scab workers) from the striking workers. A fight broke out on the picket lines, and the police intervened. Two workers were killed, and several others were wounded. The working community in Chicago was outraged.

   A protest rally was organized, primarily by socialist and anarchist leaders, to be held at Haymarket Square, an important commercial center in Chicago. On May 4, 1,500–2,000 people gathered in the square. The crowd was peaceful until it was ordered to disperse by the police. In the confusion that followed, a dynamite bomb was exploded. Seven policemen were killed by the explosion, and more than fifty people were wounded. The police fired into the crowd and killed four workers.

Eight anarchists were arrested and tried, but no evidence was produced that they made or threw the bomb. They were convicted nonetheless; four of them were hung, one committed suicide, and three were imprisoned and later pardoned. One of the eight anarchists belonged to the Knights of Labor. Although the Knights disavowed a connection to the riot, the incident was used by opponents of organized labor to discredit the Knights of Labor movement.

The Homestead Lockout pitted the Carnegie Steel Company at Homestead, Pennsylvania, against the Amalgamated Association of Iron and Steel Workers, a very successful American craft union. This union was protesting a proposed wage cut. Henry Frick, the company's manager, locked out the striking workers, placed barbed-wire fencing around the plant, and hired three hundred Pinkerton detectives to protect the plant and the strikebreakers. On July 6, 1892, the striking workers attacked the detectives as they arrived on river barges. Seven workers and three Pinkerton detectives were killed, and others were wounded. Frick asked the governor of Pennsylvania to send in the state militia to restore order. The plant reopened, nonunion workers stayed, and the strike was officially called off on November 20. The Homestead strike seriously weakened the steelworkers' union until the 1930s.

The Pullman Strike occurred on May 11, 1894, in Chicago. Workers at the Pullman Palace Car Company went on strike to protest wage cuts and the firing of union representatives. These workers asked for support from the American Railway Union (ARU), led by Eugene V. Debs. On June 26, the ARU called for a boycott of all Pullman railway cars. When thousands of railway workers quickly responded, rail traffic out of Chicago came to a halt. During the weeks of the strike, thirteen striking workers were killed and more than fifty were wounded. The railroad owners asked the federal government to intervene. On July 4, President Cleveland's administration obtained an injunction that forbade interference with trains carrying U.S. mail and sent U.S. cavalry to escort these trains. Debs and three other union officials were arrested and imprisoned for disobeying the injunction.

3. **What was the role of political machines and bosses in large cities during the Gilded Age? Read about "Boss" Tweed who ran the Tammany Hall political machine in the years leading up to the Gilded Age. What role did Thomas Nast play in Boss Tweed's life?**

Answer: A political machine was an unofficial system of political organization that existed in many U.S. cities, especially during the Gilded Age until the end of World War II and in some cases, even today. The key to a political machine was patronage, a system in which those in power offered handouts in return for support. Machines were often run by a boss, who dispensed favors, such as food, shelter, jobs, and Christmas turkeys, primarily to laborers and immigrants in return for their voting as they were told.

William Macy Tweed, commonly known as "Boss Tweed," was the political boss of the Tammany Hall political machine in New York City. Tweed became an alderman in 1851 and built his power through the election and appointment of his friends. During the 1860s, the Tweed Ring controlled almost every Democratic Party nomination for the city and state of New York. By 1870, Tweed had accumulated a fortune of more than twelve million dollars through graft and bribery and had become the third largest landowner in Manhattan. In 1875, political cartoons, drawn by Thomas Nast and published in *Harper's Weekly*, exposed the graft and bribery of the Tweed Ring and led to the election of a number of opposition candidates. Tweed was eventually convicted and imprisoned for stealing millions of dollars from the city.

4. Look for information on the Morrill Land-Grant College Act of 1862 and the Hatch Act of 1887. What impact did they have on American agriculture? When was the Department of Agriculture made a cabinet position?

    Answer: The Morrill Land-Grant College Act of 1862 endowed state agricultural colleges with thirty thousand acres for each U.S. Senator and U.S. Congressman representing the state in the 1860 census. This first act included only states that had remained in the Union. A second Morrill Act in 1890 extended the provisions of the act to include the former Confederate states in the program. One hundred land-grant institutions were established.

    The Hatch Act of 1887 funded experimental agricultural stations.

    The Department of Agriculture was made a cabinet position in 1889.

Lesson 12: For Further Study Younger Student Adaptations

1. Have your students read (or read to them) a biography of John D. Rockefeller, Andrew Carnegie, or Cornelius Vanderbilt.

2. Explain to them what a labor union, a strike, a scab (or strikebreaker), and a lockout are. Share some of the details of the three most famous strikes of the Gilded Age.

3. Share with your younger students one of Thomas Nast's cartoons of Boss Tweed. Discuss with them what a political machine and a boss are.

4. Discuss with them the problems faced by farmers in the Gilded Age and the reasons why the Grange, Farmers' Alliance, and Populist Party were formed. If there are farms near where you live, see if you can visit one and/or talk with a farmer about problems he faces today.

Lesson 13: For Further Study Questions and Answers

1. Define the political terms _referendum_ and _recall_. Why do you think the Progressives favored enacting these measures?

    Answer: A referendum is the submission of a proposed law or public action to a direct popular vote. The referendum power is the creation of state constitutions and is given to the people of a state or a local subdivision of a state.

    A recall is the procedure by which a public official may be removed from office by popular vote.

    Both the referendum and recall were forms of direct democracy, which were favored by the Progressives and adopted by many states in the early twentieth century.

2. Read more about Governor Robert La Follette from Wisconsin. How did his state become a "laboratory for Progressive reform"?

    Answer: Robert La Follette (1855–1925) was one of the leading Progressive politicians in the United States during the late nineteenth and early twentieth centuries. The son of a politically active Republican farmer, La Follette graduated from the University of Wisconsin in 1879 and from its new law school in 1880. In 1884, he was elected to the U.S. House of Representatives. There he attracted the attention of Republican leaders and received an appointment to the Ways and Means Committee. However, the unpopularity of the 1890 tariff that he helped William McKinley draft caused both of them to lose their seats in the 1890 election.

    The following year, La Follette was offered a bribe by a Wisconsin state Republican boss (Senator Philetus Sawyer) in connection with a legal case. He refused the bribe and spent the next six years working to expose the corrupt party machine in the state. Gradually, La Follette built a loyal following within the state Republican Party, although he was opposed by conservatives in both parties. He was supported by angry farmers, small businessmen, professionals, and intellectuals who believed his push for direct popular government would prevent control by a powerful few and improve their economic situation.

In 1900, La Follette was elected governor of Wisconsin. During his six years as governor, he worked to establish more equitable taxation, civil service reform, direct primaries, corporate regulation, and bank reform. La Follette employed political and social scientists and economists from the University of Wisconsin to draft the legislation that he introduced. Wisconsin became the first state to adopt a direct primary for nominations for state offices, and taxes on corporations enabled the state to pay its debts. A civil service law was enacted, funding for education was increased, and a railroad commission was established to regulate rates.

In 1906, La Follette entered the U.S. Senate, where he stirred up controversy almost from the beginning. There "Fighting Bob" La Follette sought to strengthen federal regulation of railroad rates, equalize federal tax assessments, and do whatever else he could to protect the American people from the "selfish interests" of wealthy industrialists and businessmen. He sought and failed to gain the Republican presidential nomination in 1908 and 1912.

When Wilson was elected president in 1912, La Follette approved his social reform legislation but opposed his decision to enter World War I. After war was declared, La Follette opposed the draft and the passage of the Espionage Act. When he continued to criticize the war effort, an attempt was made to expel him from the Senate for treason. In 1924, La Follette ran unsuccessfully for president as the candidate of the Progressive Party. He died the following year.

3. **Who was Gifford Pinchot? Why was he a controversial figure during William Howard Taft's presidency?**
   Answer: Gifford Pinchot (1865–1946), the first chief forester of the redefined U.S. Forest Service (1905–1910), became well known for reforming the management of America's forests and calling for the scientific conservation of the nation's forest reserves. Pinchot believed in efficiency and opposed waste and rose to national prominence under the patronage of President Teddy Roosevelt. During the period in which he headed the Forest Service, Pinchot used massive publicity campaigns in newspapers and magazines to generate discussion concerning the conservation of national resources.

   When Taft succeeded Roosevelt as president, Pinchot became dissatisfied with Taft's refusal to be a strong advocate for conservation programs. Taft believed that public lands should be controlled by the states or private individuals, not by the federal government. Pinchot spoke out against Taft's policies and those of the secretary of the interior, Richard Ballinger. Over time, Pinchot engaged in a series of public attacks against Ballinger in an attempt to force him from office, which led to Pinchot's dismissal by the president in January of 1910. The public was outraged, and a long investigation into Pinchot's firing was in the national headlines for months. The Ballinger-Pinchot controversy hastened the split in the Republican Party that led to the establishment of the Progressive Party, of which Pinchot became a prominent leader.

4. **Find out who Pancho Villa was. Why did President Wilson send General Jack Pershing to look for him?**
   Answer: Pancho Villa (1878–1923) was a Mexican revolutionary leader during the early twentieth century. He is remembered by many as a folk hero and an advocate for the poor and by others as a cold-blooded murderer. By 1896, Villa was leading groups of bandits in stealing cattle and money and committing other crimes against the wealthy. Because Villa stole from the rich and gave to the poor, he became known as a modern-day Robin Hood.

   In 1910, when a revolution broke out, Villa was recruited by revolutionary leaders to put together an army. Villa led the war in the northern part of Mexico, and his success and charisma made him a hero to the people. In 1911, Villa resigned from his command because of differences with another commander. However, political unrest continued in Mexico. Eventually, General Carranza became head of the Mexican government and was recognized by the United States.

At first, Villa was a Carranza supporter. However, in the summer of 1914, the two split and became enemies. For the next several years, a Mexican civil war was fought between the followers of Villa and the followers of General Carranza, who was supported by the United States. In March of 1916, Pancho Villa crossed the border between Mexico and the United States and attacked the town of Columbus, New Mexico. This was the first foreign attack on American soil since the War of 1812. General Jack Pershing was sent with ten thousand troops across the border to hunt for Pancho Villa. Although Pershing and his men searched for Villa for over a year, they never found him. Villa finally retired from his revolutionary activities in 1920. Three years later, he was gunned down by unidentified assassins while driving his car.

Lesson 13: For Further Study Younger Student Adaptations

1. Explain to your younger students what a referendum and a recall are. See if you can find an example of a referendum that was passed or defeated fairly recently in your community. A common example would be a school budget referendum.

2. Show them a photograph of Robert La Follette and share with them why he was called "Fighting Bob" and why Wisconsin became known as a "laboratory for Progressive reform."

3. Discuss with them what conservation of natural resources means. Tell them about the difference in philosophy regarding national conservation of resources between President Teddy Roosevelt and President Taft. Ask them which philosophy they believe. Explain the Ballinger-Pinchot controversy.

4. Share photographs of Pancho Villa and General Jack Pershing. See if they know what a bandit is. Tell them why Pershing was sent to Mexico by President Wilson to search for Pancho Villa.

Lesson 14: For Further Study Questions and Answers

1. **Research the life of Susan B. Anthony. Who was her partner in the suffragist movement? Why was she arrested in 1872? Was she alive when the Nineteenth Amendment was ratified?**
   Answer: Susan Brownell Anthony (1820–1906), the daughter of a Quaker abolitionist, was raised in Massachusetts and New York. A bright, well-educated woman, she taught for fifteen years. Anthony's friendship with Amelia Bloomer led to a meeting in 1851 with Elizabeth Cady Stanton, who became her partner for fifty years in the fight for women's suffrage and property rights. Anthony also helped slaves escape on the Underground Railroad and took a prominent role in the abolitionist and temperance movements before the Civil War.

   In 1869, Stanton and Anthony worked to found the National Woman Suffrage Association (NWSA). In addition to pushing for women's suffrage, this organization called for easier divorce laws and an end to discrimination against women in employment and pay; it also condemned the Fourteenth and Fifteenth amendments as being unjust to women. Anthony, however, opposed abortion, which she considered to be a moral wrong and an imposition of men upon women.

   Elizabeth Cady Stanton was married and a mother, whereas Anthony remained single her entire life. Stanton was apparently more charismatic than Anthony and a more natural speaker. Although Anthony resisted public speaking for a while, she ended up traveling thousands of miles each year in the United States and

Europe to give speeches on women's suffrage. Stanton and Anthony also began publishing a political weekly called *The Revolution* in 1868.

In November of 1872, Anthony voted in Rochester's 8th Ward for Ulysses S. Grant for president of the United States. This violation of the law carried penalties of up to three years in prison and a fine of as much as five hundred dollars. Anthony claimed that the Constitution already permitted women to vote. Two weeks later she was arrested. Out on bail, she spent the next seven months explaining her case in New York, Ohio, Indiana, and Illinois. At her trial, which took place in June of 1873, Anthony was found guilty and fined one hundred dollars. However, she never paid the fine (no attempt was made to force her to do so), and she spent the next thirty-five years continuing her fight for women's rights, even though she was a constant target of ridicule and abuse from the media, political leaders, and private individuals. She died in 1906 before the Nineteenth Amendment was ratified in 1920.

2. **Read about Amelia Bloomer. What was named for her?**
Answer: Amelia Jenks Bloomer (1818–1894), a New York native, was the wife of a Quaker lawyer who encouraged her to write for his newspaper, the *Seneca Falls County Courier*. She wrote articles that favored prohibition and women's rights. In 1849, Amelia began publishing her own biweekly newspaper, which she called *The Lily*. She used the journal to promote women's suffrage, marriage law reform, higher education for women, and temperance.

In 1851, Bloomer began publishing articles in *The Lily* about women's clothing. She advocated abandoning corsets, petticoats, and floor-length dresses for loose bodices, ankle-length pantaloons, and dresses that ended above the knee. The pantaloons, or wide trousers, eventually were called bloomers. Although Anthony, Stanton, and others fighting for women's rights experimented with wearing this type of clothing, most of them did not continue to do so for long. They concluded that the ridicule they frequently received undermined their crusade.

After Bloomer moved to Iowa, she stopped publishing *The Lily*. However, she continued to play an active role in the campaign for equal rights. Bloomer spoke at many public meetings and served as president of the Iowa Woman Suffrage Association in the early 1870s.

3. **For whom was the Little Lord Fauntleroy suit named? What type of hairstyle did little boys often wear with this suit?**
Answer: *Little Lord Fauntleroy*, a children's novel by Frances Hodgson Burnett, was serialized in *St. Nicholas Magazine* in 1885 and published separately in 1886. Both publications were very popular on both sides of the Atlantic. Burnett's descriptions of the Fauntleroy suit and the book's illustrations by Reginald Birch popularized a style of boys' clothing that became very popular among American mothers in the late nineteenth and early twentieth centuries.

The novel's main character is an American boy named Cedric, who discovers at an early age that he is the heir to a British earldom. Cedric leaves New York to live in the ancestral castle with his middle-class mother and his aristocratic British grandfather. Frances Burnett, the author of *Little Lord Fauntleroy*, had been born in England and had lived for a time in France. Her ideas concerning boys' clothing came from European fashions worn by boys from aristocratic families. This style was modeled after the "Van Dyke," eighteenth century court clothing epitomized by Thomas Gainsborough's famous painting *The Blue Boy*.

Burnett adopted this clothing style for her two sons and actually made their clothing herself. The Fauntleroy suit, which many middle-class American boys were forced to wear, consisted of a black velvet pageboy suit with short knee-pants, a fancy blouse, a deep lace collar, black or white stockings, black shoes, and a red or black satin sash. The proper hairstyle, worn by Cedric, was long flowing ringlets.

4. Probably the best-known American cooking authority at the turn of the century was Fannie Farmer. Her *Boston Cooking-School Cook Book* is considered by many to be the best known and most influential of all American cookbooks. From the time of its first printing in 1896, it has been a best seller. It continues in print today. Look through a copy of this cookbook online and pick a recipe to try.

   Answer: Presently, the easiest place to access this cookbook is at the Feeding America: The Historic American Cookbook Project website. Type this name into an Internet search engine.

Lesson 14: For Further Study Younger Student Adaptations

1. Have them read (or read to them) a short biography of Susan B. Anthony.

2. Share with your younger students the story of Amelia Bloomer and her new outfit for women. Show them a picture of her bloomers.

3. Check out a copy of *Little Lord Fauntleroy* with the original Reginald Birch illustrations and show them the drawings of the Fauntleroy suit.

4. Use Fanny Farmer's *Boston Cooking-School Cook Book* to do some cooking with them.

Lesson 15: For Further Study Questions and Answers

1. **Find a copy of the list of Mrs. Astor's "Four Hundred." Does it really contain four hundred names? Is there anything similar to this list today?**

   Answer: You should be able to find a copy of the original list of Mrs. Astor's guests to her ball in February of 1892 (as given by Ward McAllister to *The New York Times*) by typing the phrase "Mrs. Astor's Four Hundred" into an Internet search engine. This list has 309 names, not 400.

   Since 1982, *Forbes*, an American business and financial magazine, has published the Forbes Four Hundred, a list of the 400 wealthiest Americans. However, only 58 of the 400 names remained on the list for the first twenty years, which demonstrates how fluid American capitalism is today.

2. **Research the activities of the Woman's Christian Temperance Union and the Anti-Saloon League. Look for some of their printed materials — flyers, posters, banners, and cartoons.**

   Answer: The Woman's Christian Temperance Union (WCTU) was established in 1874 in Cleveland, Ohio. The purpose of the WCTU was to combat the influence of alcohol on families and society. Under the leadership of Frances Willard and Anna Howard Shaw, the organization established temperance education in schools and promoted women's suffrage, public health, prison reform, and international peace. The WCTU also hoped to persuade all states to prohibit the sale of alcoholic beverages. Of course, the Eighteenth Amendment (Prohibition) was approved in 1919 and became the law for the entire nation when the Volstead Act was passed in 1920.

   The Woman's Christian Temperance Union still exists today. Its members must sign a pledge to abstain from alcohol, which the organization maintains is the nation's number one drug problem. The WCTU also warns against the dangers of tobacco and illegal drugs, which they consider to be harmful to society.

   The Anti-Saloon League was founded as a state society in Oberlin, Ohio, in 1893. Another organization opposed to the sale of alcoholic beverages, the Anti-Saloon League drew most of its support from Protestant churches. By 1895, it had become a national organization that lobbied at all levels of government for prohibition legislation. John D. Rockefeller donated over 350 thousand dollars to the Anti-Saloon League. Even after Prohibition was repealed, the organization continued to exist — first as the Temperance League and then as the National Temperance League. Since 1964, it has been known as the American Council on Alcohol Prohibition.

3. **Read more about the lives of Booker T. Washington and W. E. B. Du Bois. Record the information on African American forms.**

Answer: Booker T. Washington (1856–1915), an African American educator, author, and political leader, was an important figure in U.S. history from 1890 to 1915. Washington's father was an unknown white man, and his mother was a slave in Virginia. At the age of nine, Booker was freed from slavery and moved with his family to West Virginia. He learned to read and write and worked at several manual labor jobs. Then, in 1873, Washington enrolled in Hampton Normal and Agricultural Institute to train as a teacher.

In 1881, Booker T. Washington was named the first leader of the Tuskegee Negro Normal Institute in Alabama. The school taught academic subjects but emphasized practical education, teaching skills such as farming, printing, carpentry, cabinetmaking, and shoemaking. Washington was able to attract good teachers to the school, and his conservative leadership made the school "acceptable" to the surrounding white population.

Washington's 1895 Atlanta Address, which he gave at the opening of the Cotton States and International Exposition, was widely reported by newspapers across the United States. This speech made Washington a nationally prominent figure and led to President McKinley's visiting the Tuskegee Institute. When President Teddy Roosevelt invited Washington to the White House in 1901, many southern whites felt that the president had gone too far.

Although labeled an accommodator by a number of African Americans, Washington cooperated with white philanthropists to raise funds that established dozens of community schools and colleges for African Americans in the South. He also spent much time on the lecture circuit and helped to establish the National Negro Business League, which helped African Americans earn a living and acquire property. Washington's autobiography, *Up From Slavery*, first published in 1901, is still read today.

William Edward Burghardt (W. E. B.) Du Bois (1868–1963) was a distinguished African American educator and the first African American to earn a doctorate from Harvard University. Born in Massachusetts, Du Bois won a scholarship to Fisk University in Nashville. During summers he worked in rural Tennessee and faced Jim Crow laws and racist attitudes firsthand.

After graduation from Fisk, Du Bois studied for two years at the University of Berlin. When he returned to the United States, he entered Harvard to work on his dissertation, *The Suppression of the African Slave Trade*. His paper is still considered to be one of the most comprehensive treatments of this subject.

In 1897, W. E. B. Du Bois began teaching history and economics at Atlanta University. While there he conducted studies of the social conditions of African Americans. In 1903, he published his groundbreaking book, *The Souls of Black Folks*, which included an attack on Booker T. Washington for not doing more to work for black civil rights.

In 1905, Du Bois and other African American leaders founded the Niagara Movement, which renounced Washington's philosophy set forth in his Atlanta Address ten years before. The manifesto of this movement called for aggressive action to secure immediate full suffrage for African Americans, as well as equal economic and educational opportunities and an end to segregation. However, this group never attracted mass support for a variety of reasons and had little impact on those in political power.

Four years later, in 1909, Du Bois joined with others in forming the National Association for the Advancement of Colored People (NAACP). The NAACP started its own magazine called *Crisis* in 1910, and Du Bois wrote articles for the magazine, campaigning against Jim Crow laws and lynchings. Throughout the first half of the twentieth century, W. E. B. Du Bois continued to work as an educator, lecturer, and author. His ideas had a significant influence on those involved in the Civil Rights movement of the 1950s and 1960s.

4. **Find and read one of Dwight L. Moody's sermons and some of Fanny Crosby's gospel songs.**

   Answer: In addition to his revival tours, Dwight L. Moody established Moody Church and the Bible institute that bears his name. You can find some of his sermons by typing the phrase "Dwight L. Moody's sermons" into an Internet search engine. You can find the lyrics (and, on some sites, musical recordings) of Crosby's music by typing in "Fanny Crosby songs."

Lesson 15: For Further Study Younger Student Adaptations

1. Show your younger students Caroline Astor's list. Review what a social class is. Find photographs of Gilded Age mansions to show them, as well as Gilded Age slums and tenements.

2. Share with them samples of flyers, posters, banners, and cartoons published by the Woman's Christian Temperance Union and the Anti-Saloon League. Look at what the Bible has to say about drinking alcohol, and discuss with them your views concerning this subject.

3. Have them read (or read to them) a short biography of Booker T. Washington or W. E. B. Du Bois. Make sure they understand the philosophical differences between these two African American men.

4. Have them read (or read to them) a short biography of Dwight L. Moody or Fanny Crosby.

Lesson 16: For Further Study Questions and Answers

1. **Two of the inventors showcased at the Philadelphia Centennial Exposition were Alexander Graham Bell and Thomas Edison. Read more about their lives and their inventions. Find out what George Eastman invented.**

   Answer: Alexander Graham Bell (1847–1922) was born in Scotland. His mother, who was a talented pianist and portrait painter, was deaf, and his father taught deaf people to speak using a method that he invented and named "Visible Speech." When Alexander was twenty-three, he emigrated with his family to Canada. Two years later, he moved to Boston to open a school for teachers of the deaf. He also became a professor at Boston University. Eventually, he married one of his students, who had become deaf at the age of four due to scarlet fever.

   In 1876, when he was twenty-nine years old, Alexander Graham Bell invented the telephone and secured a patent for his invention. The following year he formed the Bell Telephone Company. Other inventions by Bell included an iron breathing lung, a photo phone, a device for locating icebergs at sea, a method for making phonograph records on a wax disc, and a hydrofoil that set a world speed record of over seventy miles per hour. He was granted eighteen patents in his name alone and twelve patents with collaborators. Along with others, Bell started the National Geographic Society and served as its second president.

   Thomas Alva Edison (1847–1931), the "Wizard of Menlo Park," held patents for 1,093 inventions, including ones for a cylinder phonograph, an incandescent electric lightbulb, a motion picture camera, a motion picture viewer, a mimeograph, and a stock ticker. Although Edison is considered to be one of the most prolific inventors in history, many of the patents credited to him were either improvements of earlier inventions or created by a team of employees working under his direction.

   Born in Ohio, Edison was the last of seven children. He spent much of his childhood in Port Huron, Michigan, and attended school for only three months because he had difficulty paying attention to the teacher. His mom brought him home to teach him and encouraged him to read widely and to experiment. By the age of twelve, Thomas had become partially deaf. During his early adult years he worked as a telegrapher and became friends with Henry Ford.

In 1871, Edison moved to Newark, New Jersey, where he established his first laboratory. In 1874, he produced his first financially successful invention, the quadraplex telegraph system. By 1876, his Newark lab had become too small, and he decided to build a larger laboratory and factory in Menlo Park, New Jersey. Edison's Menlo Park facility has been credited with being the first private industrial research laboratory established for the specific purpose of producing technological inventions. In 1887, Edison moved his lab from Menlo Park to West Orange, New Jersey, where he built what became known as the Edison Laboratory. This facility was eventually surrounded by factories that employed as many as five thousand people.

George Eastman invented the first handheld camera and paper-strip roll film, which made photography possible for the common man. He also registered the trademark Kodak, a combination of some of his favorite letters, and founded the Eastman Kodak Company. Eastman endowed the Eastman School of Music at the University of Rochester and gave away millions of dollars, including substantial gifts to the Hampton Institute and the Tuskegee Institute.

2. **Listen to some of Scott Joplin's ragtime tunes, John Philip Sousa's marches, and George M. Cohan's Broadway hits. Also play some of the popular songs from the period, such as "Daisy Bell" and "My Wild Irish Rose."**

   Answer: Type the following phrases into an Internet search engine: "music of Scott Joplin," "music of John Philip Sousa," and "music of George M. Cohan" — and enjoy! Type in the name of particular songs, such as "Daisy Bell" and "My Wild Irish Rose," to hear them.

3. **Read a novel or a short story written by a realist author from the Gilded Age. Look at some of the paintings of realist painters from the era.**

   Answer: Gilded Age realist authors included Mark Twain, Stephen Crane, Jack London, Henry James, William Dean Howells, and Horatio Alger. You will need to decide which of their works you consider to be appropriate reading.

   Gilded Age realist painters included Winslow Homer, Frederic Remington, Thomas Eakins, John Singer Sargent, and James McNeill Whistler. Mary Cassatt was an Impressionist painter during this time period.

4. **Research the life and work of Louis Sullivan, a famous American architect during the Gilded Age. What type of buildings did he design? How was he an architectural pioneer? For what did Louis Tiffany become known during this period in history? See if there are any homes in your area dating back to this period.**

   Answer: Louis Henry Sullivan (1856–1924) was an American architect who became known as the "father of modern architecture." Born in Boston, Sullivan studied architecture briefly at the Massachusetts Institute of Technology. By the age of seventeen, he was working in Philadelphia with a prominent architect named Frank Furness. When the United States entered a depression in 1873, Furness was forced to let Sullivan go. At this point, Sullivan moved to Chicago and worked for William LeBaron Jenney, who is often credited with designing the first fully steel-frame skyscraper.

   After less than a year in Chicago, Sullivan studied in Paris for several months, where he was influenced by Renaissance art. He returned to Chicago, where he eventually became a partner in the firm of Dankmar Adler and began his most productive years as an architect. Sullivan became the first architect to find the right form for a steel high-rise building — the steel girder. He believed that "form follows function" and designed his buildings so that they pushed up rather than out. Adler and Sullivan became famous for the 1889 Auditorium Building in Chicago, the 1891 Wainwright Building in St. Louis, the 1894 Guaranty Building in Buffalo, and the 1899 Carson Pirie Scott Department Store in Chicago.

In 1890, Sullivan was one of ten architects chosen to build a major structure for the World's Columbian Exposition, to be held in Chicago in 1893. Sullivan's Transportation Building was the only modern-looking design among a number of Beaux-Arts classical copies. His new architecture style became known as the "Chicago School" and was characterized by stripped-down, technology-driven designs. Probably Sullivan's most famous student was Frank Lloyd Wright. During the last twenty years of his life, Sullivan was plagued with financial problems and an emotional decline related to his alcoholism. He had become estranged from both Adler and Wright and died alone and poor in a Chicago hotel room.

Louis Comfort Tiffany (1848–1933) was a celebrated American painter and decorative arts designer who was best known for his work in stained glass. He was also the American artist most associated with the art nouveau movement. His stained-glass windows and lamps, blown glass, glass mosaics, jewelry, ceramics, and enamels were internationally known. Louis was the son of Charles Lewis Tiffany, who founded Tiffany and Company, a prestigious silver and jewelry firm. Instead of joining the family business, Louis established his own New York City firm, which came to be known as Tiffany Studios. In 1919, he established the Louis Comfort Tiffany Foundation, which provides study and travel grants to art students.

Lesson 16: For Further Study Younger Student Adaptations

1. Have them read (or read to them) a short biography of Alexander Graham Bell or Thomas Edison. Talk about what a patent is.

2. Play for them some of Joplin's, Sousa's, and Cohen's music. Discuss what characterizes jazz, marches, and Broadway tunes. Teach them the words to "Daisy Bell."

3. Show them paintings by some of the realist painters of the Gilded Age.

4. Share with your younger students some details about the work of the architect Louis Sullivan. Show them photographs of some of the skyscrapers that Sullivan designed, as well as some examples of the stained-glass work of Louis Comfort Tiffany.

UNIT THREE
For Further Study
Questions and Answers

Lesson 17: For Further Study Questions and Answers

1. **Germany had been planning for a major war for years. The name of its war plan was the Schlieffen Plan. Find out why it had this name and what the plan entailed. Discover what territory Germany had taken from France that the French were determined to recover.**

   Answer: Alfred von Schlieffen, German army chief of staff from 1891–1905, was told to devise a strategy for Germany to use if it faced a two-front war against Great Britain, France, and Russia. Schlieffen's plan called for rapid mobilization of German forces and an overwhelming sweep of the German right wing through Belgium, the Netherlands, Luxembourg, and northern France in a southwesterly direction. The hope was to defeat France quickly before Russia was able to mobilize, a period that was estimated to be about six weeks. The intent was not to conquer cities or industries but to capture most of the French army and force France to surrender. Following the speedy defeat of France, the German army would turn back to the eastern front before Russia could react.

   When Helmuth von Moltke replaced Schlieffen in 1906, he modified the plan by proposing that the Netherlands not be invaded. In August 1914, the Schlieffen plan was executed. German forces invaded Luxembourg and Belgium. Although the Belgian army was just a tenth the size of the German army, their troops (and civilians) offered amazingly strong resistance and delayed the Germans for almost a month. Germany had also not expected the presence and effectiveness of the British Expeditionary Force so early in the war. Because of the delays caused by the Belgians and the British, the French had more time to transfer troops to meet the Germans as they marched into France. The Russians were also able to mobilize more quickly than the Germans anticipated and gained ground in eastern Prussia so rapidly that the Germans were forced to pull men from their main force to reinforce the eastern front. A French counterattack at the Battle of the Marne signaled the failure of the Schlieffen Plan, the institution of trench warfare, and a two-front war.

   The French had suffered a humiliating defeat at the hands of Germany in the Franco-Prussian War (1870–1871) and wanted to recover the territory in Alsace and Lorraine (on its eastern border) captured by Germany in that war.

2. **Read more about trench warfare and the weapons used in World War I, especially poison gas. What challenges were faced by soldiers in the trenches? Look for pictures of German U-boats and find out what a zeppelin was. Who were the "Red Baron" and Eddie Rickenbacker?**

   Answer: During World War I, the soldiers' existence in the trenches was miserable. They were forced to deal with dampness, mud, overflowing latrines, rats (some the size of cats), lice (which caused a very painful disease called trench fever), frogs, nits, pneumonia, influenza, fungus skin diseases, gangrene, the smell of dead bodies, and monotony. A lack of fresh fruits and vegetables made the soldiers prone to illness and disease. Artillery attacks continued for days without stopping, and many men became shell-shocked from the continual noise and fear.

A battalion would serve a period in the front lines, followed by time in the support trenches, and then given a short period of rest. However, even when at rest, a soldier might be given duties that placed him in the line of fire. While some soldiers stood guard, others worked repairing the trenches, bringing food in from behind the battle lines, or keeping the telephone lines in order. Patrols were often sent into no-man's-land (the land between the opposing enemy lines) to set up barbed wire or in the hope of picking up valuable information from the enemy lines.

The development and use of poison gas during World War I came about because both sides were looking for ways to overcome the stalemate of trench warfare. The first time that poison gas (chlorine gas) was used was by the Germans in April of 1915. Within seconds of a soldier's inhaling this chlorine gas, his respiratory organs were destroyed. German use of poison gas was widely condemned by other countries, especially by the United States.

However, the British were quick to respond with a chlorine gas attack of their own in September of 1915. Because the wind shifted and smoke and gas were blown back into the British trenches, the British suffered as many gas casualties as the Germans. All three armies (British, French, and German) would suffer self-inflicted gas reversals in the months to come, which highlighted the need for a more reliable delivery mechanism for the gas. Soon a new more potent gas, phosgene gas, began to be used, followed by mustard gas, which was the most difficult gas against which to provide protection.

The initial protection against poison gas handed out to the troops was very primitive. Cotton pads dipped in bicarbonate of soda were given to soldiers to hold over the face. By 1918, the troops were being supplied with filter respirators that used charcoal or antidote chemicals, which were much more effective but cumbersome to wear. Once the element of surprise had been lost, the number of casualties due to poison gas quickly diminished. However, because of long-term problems, gas victims who survived usually were not able to hold a job once they were discharged from the army.

The machine gun was the weapon that dominated the battlefields during World War I. Machine guns used during the early years of the war overheated quickly. Because they became inoperative without a cooling mechanism, they had to be fired in short bursts. They also jammed frequently, especially in the heat, and their weight made them ill-suited for use by rapidly advancing infantry forces. As the war continued, machine guns were adapted for use in tanks and added to warships, and light machine guns were incorporated into aircraft. The Germans also produced large quantities of oil-cooled machine guns, which were more rapidly firing weapons.

The first combat tank was ready for production by the British in January of 1916. The British had been working for several years on developing this new military weapon. The French, aware of the British experimentation, had proceeded with their own independent designs. However, the French were initially more skeptical about the tank's potential in warfare. The early British tanks used in battle were very unreliable. They often broke down and became stuck in muddy trenches, and the heat and fumes generated inside the tank were overwhelming. Eventually, the United States and the Germans began producing tanks as well. By the end of the war, the British had produced over twenty-six hundred tanks, the French more than thirty-eight hundred, and the Germans only twenty.

A zeppelin is a rigid airship or dirigible, pioneered by Count Ferdinand von Zeppelin in the early twentieth century. Zeppelin's design was based in part on an earlier design by David Schwarz. During World War I, the German military used zeppelins as bombers and for reconnaissance. Zeppelins were almost as fast as traditional aircraft, had a greater bomb-load capacity, carried more guns, and had greater range. However, they were more vulnerable to gunfire. Almost ninety zeppelins were built during the war, and over sixty were lost to accident and enemy action.

Manfred Albrecht Freiherr von Richthofen (1892–1918), a German fighter pilot, was the most successful flying ace of World War I, with as many as eighty kills. Richthofen was also known as "Little Red," "Red Devil," the "Red Knight," and the "Red Baron." By 1918, Richthofen had become such a legend that it was feared his death would be a tremendous blow to German morale. However, when his superiors asked him to retire, Richthofen refused. On April 21, 1918, the Red Baron was shot to death near the Somme River while pursuing a Sopwith Camel piloted by a Canadian. After the war, some American and British authors insisted that Richthofen's reported success had been exaggerated propaganda. However, World War I scholarship in the 1990s confirmed at least seventy-three of the Red Baron's claimed kills.

Eddie Rickenbacker (1890–1973) was a U.S. fighter pilot in World War I. His early jobs included working as a glazer, in a steel mill, and as an auto racer. When the United States declared war on Germany, Rickenbacker quickly enlisted in the army. When he arrived in France in June of 1917, he worked as a staff driver for Colonel William Mitchell. By March of 1918, Rickenbacker had been assigned to the 94th Pursuit Squadron, the first all-American unit to see combat duty in World War I. The next month, he shot down his first plane. By the end of October, Rickenbacker had become America's top-scoring ace by shooting down twenty-six enemy planes.

3. Pick one or more of the battles of the Great War to research. Some of the major battles included Verdun, the Somme, Belleau Wood, St. Mihiel, and the Argonne. If this is an area of interest, compile a World War I Battles Notebook. There are forms in the optional forms section of the *Student Activity Book* to use to do this.

4. Find a copy of Wilson's Fourteen Points and read them. Do you think World War II would have occurred if all these points had been adopted?

Lesson 17: For Further Study Younger Student Adaptations

1. Find a map of Europe in 1914 and use it to explain the Schlieffen plan to your younger students. Share with them the reasons why the Schlieffen plan failed.

2. Look for a children's book that has information and photographs about World War I.

3. Pick a World War I battle about which you and your younger students can become "experts."

4. Explain what Wilson's Fourteen Points were, especially his proposed League of Nations. Share with them how Wilson became very ill on his speaking tour for the League and how his condition was not disclosed to the American public.

Lesson 18: For Further Study Questions and Answers

1. During the 1920s, there were several attempts to bring about international disarmament and world peace. Three of these included the Washington Naval Conference (1921–1922), the Locarno Pact (1925), and the Kellogg-Briand Pact (1928). Discover what each of these sought to accomplish.
    Answer: The Washington Naval Conference (1921–1922), formally known as the International Conference on Naval Limitation, was called by President Harding and held in the nation's capital from November 1921 to February 1922. It was attended by representatives of nine nations that had interests in the Pacific Ocean and East Asia, including Great Britain, France, Italy, Japan, and the United States. Neither the Soviet Union nor the defeated Central Powers were invited, and the conference was conducted outside the auspices of the League of Nations.

The first disarmament conference in history, the Washington Naval Conference resulted in a series of treaties and pacts. Britain, France, Italy, the United States, and Japan pledged to limit new naval construction for ten years and to adhere to limitations on the tonnage of ships. They outlawed the use of poisonous gases as a military weapon and agreed to a series of rules for the use of submarines in future warfare.

The Locarno Pact of 1925 resulted from a conference held in Locarno, Switzerland, in October of 1925. Representatives from Great Britain, France, Italy, Germany, Belgium, Poland, and Czechoslovakia attended the conference. The pact guaranteed the common boundaries of France, Belgium, and Germany as specified in the 1919 Treaty of Versailles. Germany signed treaties with Czechoslovakia and Poland agreeing to change the eastern borders of Germany by arbitration only. The Germans also signed arbitration conventions with France and Belgium, and France signed treaties with Poland and Czechoslovakia pledging mutual assistance in the event of war with Germany. The "spirit of Locarno" led to the admission of Germany to the League of Nations in September of 1926.

The Kellogg-Briand pact, formally known as the Pact of Paris, was signed on August 27, 1928. In June of 1927, Aristide Briand, the French foreign minister, had proposed a treaty to the U.S. government outlawing war between the two countries. Briand hoped to ensure that the United States would ally itself with France if there were another European war. Frank Kellogg, secretary of state, wanted to avoid any U.S. involvement in a European war but knew that he would be attacked by Congress and the press if he opposed the treaty. Kellogg returned to Briand a proposal calling for a multilateral pact against war that would be open to all nations to sign.

After prolonged negotiations, eleven nations signed the Kellogg-Briand Pact in Paris. Ultimately, sixty-two nations would sign the pact, pledging to settle all conflicts that might arise among them by peaceful means and to renounce war as an instrument of national policy. The U.S. Senate approved the treaty 85–1. However, the Senate added a reservation that the treaty must not infringe upon America's right of self-defense and that the United States was not obligated to enforce the treaty by taking action against countries that violated it. Of course, the pact did not live up to its aim of ending war, but it did serve as the legal basis for later developments in international law.

2. **Research the Teapot Dome scandal. To what did "teapot dome" refer? Find out the details of the other scandals that occurred during Harding's administration.**

   Answer: Teapot dome was a reference to an oil field that was located on public land in Wyoming. The oil field had received that name because a rock that resembled a teapot overlooked the field. In 1921, control of naval oil reserves at Teapot Dome, Wyoming, and Elk Hills, California, was transferred from the Department of the Navy to the Department of the Interior by executive order of President Harding. The following year, Secretary of the Interior Albert B. Fall leased the Teapot Dome field to Harry Sinclair of Sinclair Oil and the Elk Hills field to Edward Doheny of Pan American Petroleum without competitive bidding. Eventually, these transactions came under Senate investigation, and Fall was indicted and convicted of accepting large bribes (monetary gifts) from Doheny and Sinclair. He was fined one hundred thousand dollars and sentenced to a year in prison. A Supreme Court decision in 1928 restored these oil fields to the U.S. government.

   Additional scandals during the Harding administration included the following:
   - Charles Forbes, director of the Veterans Bureau, was convicted of taking at least 250 million dollars in bribes and kickbacks. He, too, served time in federal prison. Charles Cramer, an aide to Forbes, committed suicide.
   - Colonel Thomas Miller, head of the Office of Alien Property, was convicted of fraud.
   - Jesse Smith, assistant to the Attorney General, destroyed papers that exposed his role in carrying bribes to and from the Attorney General's office and then committed suicide.

3. **Albert Einstein and Robert Goddard were responsible for important scientific developments during the first twenty-five years of the twentieth century. Read about the lives of these men and their accomplishments.**

    Answer: Albert Einstein (1879–1955) was a theoretical physicist regarded by many as the most important scientist of the twentieth century. He became world-famous for his development of the general and special theories of relativity and for his substantial contributions to quantum and statistical mechanics. Born in Germany, Einstein showed little signs of genius in his early years. He was slow to learn to speak and did not excel during his elementary school years. However, Albert evidently preferred to learn on his own — by the time he was a teenager, he had taught himself advanced mathematics and science.

    The Einstein family moved several times during Albert's childhood and ended up in Italy when Albert was sixteen. At this point, Albert renounced his German citizenship, which freed him from military service; he belonged to no country until he became a Swiss citizen in 1921. In Switzerland Einstein attended the Swiss Federal Institute of Technology, but he hated going to classes regularly and taking exams. Although he graduated with a teaching degree, he was unable to find a teaching job and finally took a position in the Swiss patent office. Einstein worked there for seven years and also obtained his doctorate at the University of Zurich.

    In the years that followed, Einstein held professorships at universities in Zurich, Prague, and Berlin. In 1921, he won the Nobel Prize for Physics for his explanation of the photoelectric effect, and he eventually resumed his German citizenship. When Hitler came to power, Einstein was teaching as a guest professor at Princeton University. The Nazis soon passed a law that forced all Jewish university professors out of their jobs, so Einstein never returned to Germany. He renounced his German citizenship and accepted a position at the newly established Institute for Advanced Studies in Princeton, where he stayed until his death.

    In 1940, Einstein became a U.S. citizen. The year before, he had written a letter to President Roosevelt warning him that the Germans could create an atomic bomb and urging him to complete a bomb before the Germans did. This letter led to the creation of the Manhattan Project, placed under the control of the U.S. Army, which succeeded in building the first atomic bomb.

    Robert H. Goddard (1882–1945), an American physicist and professor, was the father of modern rocket propulsion. Born in Worcester, Massachusetts, Goddard developed a fascination with flight during his childhood. In 1926, he successfully launched the world's first liquid-fueled rocket. During the 1930s, Goddard launched rockets that attained speeds of up to 550 miles per hour. He realized the potential of missiles for space flight and wrote of the possibility of a rocket reaching the moon. Because his work in the field was so revolutionary, Goddard was often ridiculed for his theories, and his work went largely unrecognized in his lifetime.

4. **Find out who the Wobblies (the IWW) are. Look for information about the activities of "Big Bill" Haywood and Eugene V. Debs.**

    Answer: The Industrial Workers of the World (IWW), or the Wobblies, is an international union that has its headquarters in Cincinnati. Its membership peaked in 1923 at some one hundred thousand members. By the mid-1920s, its membership had dramatically declined. Today the IWW has approximately two thousand members worldwide. The origin of the name Wobblies is unclear.

    The IWW was founded in 1905 in Chicago at a convention of two hundred socialists, radical trade unionists, and anarchists from all over the United States who opposed the policies of the American Federation of Labor. They called for the formation of "One Big Union" (the IWW) that would include women, immigrants, and African Americans and called for the eventual overthrow of American capitalism. Some of its early leaders included "Big Bill" Haywood, Daniel De Leon, Eugene V. Debs, "Mother Jones," and Lucy Parsons.

    In 1908, the Wobblies split into two factions. One group, led by De Leon and Debs, advocated political action through the Socialist Party as the best way to attain the IWW's goals. The other group, led by Big Bill Haywood, believed that politics was merely a tool of capitalism and called for direct action in the form of strikes, boycotts, and propaganda. Haywood's views prevailed, and the faction led by De Leon and Debs left the IWW.

During the early years of the IWW, the Wobblies achieved some successes. However, their leaders were often arrested and accused of violent acts. When World War I began, the Wobblies opposed American participation in the war as a capitalist plot to increase profits. Once the United States entered the war in 1917, IWW leaders, including Haywood, were arrested under the Espionage Act. When Haywood was released on bail, he fled to Russia, where he remained until his death.

After the war ended, leaders of the IWW were prosecuted under various laws, and many of them ended up in prison or in exile. Widespread disagreement existed among the Wobblies concerning the future direction of the IWW, and membership in the union dwindled. However, the IWW was successful in demonstrating that large numbers of unskilled workers could be unionized, and it pioneered the use of sit-down strikes and big public demonstrations.

Lesson 18: For Further Study Younger Student Adaptations

1. Share with your younger students the attempts made in the 1920s to bring about international disarmament and world peace. Make sure they understand what disarmament is. Explain that disarmament is still an issue today, and ask what they think would bring about world peace.

2. Have them read (or read to them) a short biography on Warren G. Harding, and concentrate on the chapter(s) that address the scandals that occurred during his administration.

3. Have them read (or read to them) a short biography on Albert Einstein or Robert Goddard.

4. Show your younger students photographs of Big Bill Haywood and Eugene V. Debs. Explain the history of the Wobblies, what they believe, and what happened to them during World War I and in the early 1920s.

Lesson 19: For Further Study Questions and Answers

1. **Look for photographs of American suffragists in action during the early twentieth century. Find out for what activities Carrie Nation became famous.**
   Answer: Carrie Nation (1846–1911) was a famous figure in the American temperance movement. A brief first marriage to an alcoholic contributed to Nation's passion to protect American families from the destructive effects of alcohol. Often accompanied by other hymn-singing women, Nation would march into a bar, sing, pray, and smash the bar fixtures with a hatchet. Between 1900 and 1901, she was arrested as many as thirty times. Nation paid her fines with money from lecture fees and the sale of souvenir hatchets.

   Official records list the spelling of Nation's first name as "Carrie," and she herself used that spelling most of her life. However, her father listed her as "Carry" in the family Bible, and she adopted the name "Carry A. Nation" when she began her temperance activities, apparently because of its value as a slogan. In fact, she had the name registered as a trademark in the state of Kansas.

2. **How did the name flapper originate? The flapper subculture developed many new slang words and expressions. See if you can find what the following mean: "bee's knees," "beeswax," "big cheese," "cat's meow," "dapper," "heebie-jeebies," "hit on all sixes," "now you're on the trolley," "putting on the Ritz," "rag-a-muffin," "the real McCoy," and "wet blanket."**

Answer: The term *flapper* appeared in Great Britain as early as 1912. It was used to describe young girls, whose awkward actions resembled those of young birds trying to leave the nest. Before the 1920s, a flapper was a term for an impetuous teenage girl.

In the 1920s, flappers became a well-defined social group of attractive, independent, and somewhat reckless women in the United States. Writers, such as F. Scott Fitzgerald, popularized the flapper look and lifestyle, and artist John Held, Jr., drew young girls wearing unbuckled galoshes that would make a flapping noise when they walked.

Bee's knees — an extraordinary person, thing, or idea
Beeswax — business
Big cheese — the most important or influential person, the boss
Cat's meow — something stylish, the best or greatest
Dapper — a flapper's dad
Heebie-jeebies — the jitters
Hit on all sixes — perform 100 percent (hitting on all six cylinders)
Now you're on the trolley — now you've got it!
Putting on the Ritz — doing something in high style
Rag-a-muffin — a dirty or disheveled person
The real McCoy — the genuine article
Wet blanket — a solemn person, a killjoy

3. Look for more information on John Dewey and Progressive education. Discuss his ideas with your family and decide what purpose(s) you think schools should serve. Should they teach only "academic" courses? Or should they offer "real-life" courses, such as vocational education and "basic living" classes (how to find a job, ways to improve your self-esteem, keys to a good marriage, etc.)?

4. Jell-O was a popular food in the 1920s. Look for the 1922 cookbook *Jell-O: America's Most Famous Dessert at Home and Everywhere* and try a recipe from it. Find out which of the following foods and drinks would have been available in the Roaring Twenties — Coca Cola, chocolate chip cookies, Kool Aid, Oreos, ice cream cones, devil's food cake, Gatorade, Girl Scout cookies, brownies, and Kraft macaroni and cheese.
    Answer: Coca Cola (1886), devil's food cake (1902), ice cream cones (1904), brownies (1906), Oreos (1912), Girl Scout cookies (1922), and Kool Aid (1927) were available in the 1920s.
    Chocolate chip cookies (1933), Kraft macaroni and cheese (1937), and Gatorade (1967) were not available in the 1920s.

Lesson 19: For Further Study Younger Student Adaptations

1. Show your younger students photographs of suffragists. Make sure they understand what the words *suffrage* and *suffragist* mean. Describe Carrie Nation's temperance activities and share with them a photograph of Nation.

2. Look for one of John Held, Jr.'s drawings of a flapper to show them. Explain the origin of this word, as well as the meaning of the other slang terms from the flapper subculture.

3. Discuss with them how education changed during this period in history. See if they can understand John Dewey's ideas about education. Ask them what they think they should know by the time they finish high school.

4. Have them try a Jell-O recipe from the 1922 Jell-O cookbook. Share with them some of the new food products introduced from 1900–1930. Show them Birds Eye brand vegetables in the freezer section of the grocery store. Introduce them to a White Castle hamburger.

Lesson 20: For Further Study Questions and Answers

1. **Read about George Washington Carver, a famous black southern agricultural leader of this period. What crops did he encourage southern farmers to plant? Why? Record the information about Carver on an African American form. You could also fill out African American forms for any of the following that you are interested in researching — Louis Armstrong, Billie Holiday, Fats Waller, Ella Fitzgerald, and Mahalia Jackson.**
   Answer: George Washington Carver (1864?–1943) was an African American botanist and agricultural chemist. Born into slavery in Missouri, George and his mother were kidnapped by Confederate night raiders and sold in Arkansas. Their owner, Moses Carver, found and reclaimed George after the war, but his mother had disappeared forever. The Carvers raised George and his brother as their own children. On their farm, George became known as the "plant doctor" because of his extensive knowledge of many varieties of wild plants.

   Over a period of years, Carver attended a series of different schools before he earned his high school diploma. He became the first African American student at Simpson College in Indianola, Iowa, and later transferred to Iowa State Agricultural College, where he again was the first African American student. At Iowa State he earned both bachelor's and master's degrees and became the first African American faculty member.

   In 1897, Booker T. Washington recruited Carver to serve as the director of agriculture at the Tuskegee Normal Institute. He remained at Tuskegee for forty-seven years until his death. There Carver developed a crop rotation system that revolutionized agriculture in the South. He taught farmers to alternate soil-depleting cotton and tobacco with soil-enriching crops, such as peanuts, soybeans, peas, and sweet potatoes. In order to make the new crops profitable, Carver worked to develop numerous new uses for them, including more than three hundred uses for the peanut.

2. **Research the life of Billy Sunday and read one or more of his sermons.**
   Answer: William Ashley "Billy" Sunday (1863–1935) was born in Iowa, where he grew up under very difficult conditions. His father died a month after Billy was born, leaving his mother with a newborn and two other sons. Although she later remarried, the family endured great poverty. However, in his teen years Billy was signed to play professional baseball for the Chicago White Stockings. He played on professional teams in Chicago, Pittsburgh, and Philadelphia for eight years and set records for stealing bases.

   In 1887, Sunday was invited to a service at the Pacific Garden mission in Chicago. He began attending services there regularly and eventually accepted Jesus Christ as his Savior. By 1891, Sunday had left his well-paying job in baseball to work in a low-paying ministry position with the Young Men's Christian Association (YMCA). Just five years later he began his evangelistic campaigns.

   You can read some of his sermons by typing the phrase "Billy Sunday's sermons" into an Internet search engine.

3. See if you can find any film clips from the Roaring Twenties to view. Look for photographs of movie stars of the period and recordings of some of the popular songs. Find out why Harry Houdini was famous during this era. See if you can learn one of the dances popular in the 1920s.

   Answer: Harry Houdini (1874–1926) was a popular magician, stunt performer, and escape artist with a great flair for the dramatic. He traveled the United States thrilling audiences. A native of Budapest, Hungary, Houdini's birth name was Erik Weiss. His father was a Jewish rabbi, and the family moved to the United States in 1878. When Weiss became a professional magician in 1891, he began calling himself Harry Houdini and legally changed his name to Harry Houdini in 1913.

   Harry's big break came when he started concentrating on escape acts. By 1899, he had begun performing at the top vaudeville houses in the United States, and a year later he traveled to Europe to perform. When he returned to America in 1905, Harry Houdini had become an international sensation. Time and again his escape from seemingly impossible predicaments thrilled audiences. Houdini also starred in movies and in a one-man show on Broadway, and continued his traveling performances until he died from a ruptured appendix. Perhaps his most famous act was the Chinese Water Torture Cell, in which he was suspended upside-down in a locked cabinet full of water and freed himself in three minutes.

4. Read about one or more of the art movements that developed during the first decades of the twentieth century — fauvism, dadaism, futurism, and cubism. Look for paintings that exemplify these movements. (Parental involvement should take place in choosing which paintings are appropriate to view.)

   Answer: Fauvism was a short-lived movement of artists whose works used simplified lines, exaggerated perspectives, and bold, shocking colors. In French, *fauves* means "wild beasts." An art critic gave the group its name, comparing their unnatural use of color to the painting of wild beasts.

   Dadaism was an art movement born in Europe during World War I. Its artists protested against nationalism, materialism, and anything else that they believed contributed to a senseless war. The reason that the word *dada* was used to name this movement is debated. *Dada* means "hobby horse" in French; others feel that *dada* is just a word that is baby talk. The only rule for this movement was never to follow any rules. Dada art was deliberately absurd and intended to provoke an emotional reaction from the viewer.

   Futurism was a movement of artists who passionately discarded ideas from the past and embraced technological triumphs such as the car, the plane, and the industrial town. Their works demonstrated their love of youth, speed, violence, chaos, and power.

   Cubism was another avant-garde art movement, founded by Georges Braque and Pablo Picasso. Cubist artists broke apart people, landscapes, and objects and reassembled them from several angles, which often resulted in cube-like forms and geometric patterns.

Lesson 20: For Further Study Younger Student Adaptations

1. Have them read (or read to them) a short biography of George Washington Carver.

2. Share with your younger students some excerpts from a Billy Sunday sermon.

3. Have them read (or read to them) a short biography of Harry Houdini. Show them photographs of movie stars of the period and play recordings of some of the popular songs.

4. Show them some examples of avant-garde art from the period. Have them tell you what they like or don't like about the paintings.

Lesson 21: For Further Study Questions and Answers

1. **Learn more about the stock market. Read about the difference between bear and bull markets. Look for newspaper articles from 1929 recounting the stock market crash.**
   Answer: Bear and bull markets are named after the way bears and bulls attack their prey. A bear swipes its paws downward toward its prey, while a bull drives its horns up in the air. A bear market is a prolonged period of time when prices are *falling* substantially in a financial market. A bull market is a prolonged period of time when prices are *rising* substantially. A bear market tends to be accompanied by investor pessimism, whereas a bull market tends to be associated with investor confidence. Many financial analysts believe that markets are characterized by a "herd mentality"—trading occurs in the direction that traders believe the market is going.

   Notable bear markets occurred after the 1929 stock market crash and throughout the late 1960s and early 1970s. Notable bull markets occurred in the 1920s and the 1990s.

2. **Read more about the march of the Bonus Expeditionary Force in Washington, D.C. How long did these protesters stay? How were they treated? Look for photographs documenting this event.**
   Answer: In 1924, the U.S. Congress voted to give bonuses to the nation's World War I veterans—$1.25 for each day served overseas and $1.00 for each day served in the United States. However, the law also stipulated that the payment would not be made until 1945. By 1932, many veterans of the Great War, suffering from the effects of the Great Depression, wanted immediate payment of this bonus. In May of 1932, more than fifteen thousand veterans and many of their families assembled in Washington, D.C., to demonstrate for this cause. They called themselves the Bonus Expeditionary Force; the public often referred to them as the Bonus Army.

   Most of the Bonus Expeditionary Force, led by former sergeant Walter W. Waters, camped in a Hooverville on the Anacostia Flats, a swampy area across the river from the Capitol. They slept in shelters built from materials gathered from a nearby junk pile. Despite the camp's rustic conditions, discipline and order were good. Newcomers were required to register and prove that they were honorably discharged World War I veterans.

   The Patman Bonus Bill, which would have moved forward the date for payment of the bonuses, passed the U.S. House of Representatives on June 15. On June 17, the Bonus Army crowded the Capitol grounds to wait for the outcome of the Senate's vote on the bill. After the crowd received the news that the Senate had defeated the bill, the Bonus Army began a silent "death march" in front of the Capitol that continued until Congress adjourned on July 17.

   On July 28, the Attorney General ordered the evacuation of the Bonus Army from all government property. When Washington police attempted to remove some of the veterans from a federal construction site, they were met with resistance. Shots were fired, and two Bonus Army protesters were killed. Several policemen were injured when protesters assaulted them with blunt weapons following the shooting. The District of Columbia commissioners informed President Hoover that they could no longer maintain the peace, and Hoover ordered federal troops to clear out the Bonus Army.

   Under the command of General Douglas MacArthur, U.S. infantry and cavalry, armed with tear gas and supported by six tanks, routed more than ten thousand people from the Anacostia Flats and burned down their tents and shacks. Hundreds of veterans were injured, and two babies were killed. Over one thousand people (Bonus Army protesters, reporters, ambulance drivers, and private citizens) were exposed to the effects of tear gas.

   The following year, Bonus Army protesters returned to Washington to demonstrate. Franklin Roosevelt was now president. He sent his wife, Eleanor, to meet with the veterans and persuaded many of them to sign up for jobs building a roadway to the Florida Keys. Unfortunately, in 1935, a hurricane claimed the lives of many who took these jobs. When the public saw newsreels of this disaster, Congress could no longer afford to ignore the groundswell of public support for the Bonus Army veterans. In 1936, Congress overrode Roosevelt's veto and gave the World War I veterans their bonus.

3. **Draw a cartoon illustrating FDR's New Deal alphabet soup. Find out which New Deal laws were declared unconstitutional by the Supreme Court.**

    Answer: In _Schechter Poultry Corporation v. the United States_ (1935), the Supreme Court declared the National Industrial Recovery Act (NIRA) unconstitutional. By a unanimous vote, the high court held that the "codes of fair practice" of the NIRA went beyond the regulation of interstate commerce and that Congress had delegated too much legislative power to the president and industrial groups. The Supreme Court declared the Agricultural Adjustment Act (AAA) unconstitutional in _United States v. Butler_ (1936). However, the high court upheld the National Labor Relations Act, a successor to the NIRA, in a 1937 decision.

4. **Research the life of Eleanor Roosevelt, the wife of President Roosevelt. How was she different from the first ladies who had come before her? What did she do after her husband died?**

    Answer: Eleanor Roosevelt (1884–1962), a favorite niece and goddaughter of Theodore Roosevelt, was born to Elliott and Anna Roosevelt in New York City. Following her parents' deaths, Eleanor was raised by her maternal grandmother. Educated by private tutors until she was fifteen, she completed her education at Allenswood, a school for girls in England. At the age of eighteen, Eleanor returned to New York and became involved in social service work. There she joined the Junior League and taught at a settlement house.

    In 1905, Eleanor married a distant cousin, Franklin Delano Roosevelt. Over a period of eleven years (1906–1916), they became the parents of six children. When the United States entered World War I in 1917, Eleanor volunteered through the Red Cross and in navy hospitals. Throughout her husband's political career, Eleanor served as his helpmate. After Franklin was stricken with polio in 1921, she became increasingly active in politics to help her husband maintain his interests and ambitions. She also founded Val-Kill Industries, a nonprofit furniture factory in Hyde Park, New York, and taught at a private girls' school in New York City.

    When the Roosevelts entered the White House in 1933, Eleanor transformed the role of First Lady. She traveled extensively throughout the United States and reported her observations to the president. She also became an advocate of the rights of the poor, disadvantaged, and minorities. She gave lectures and radio broadcasts and entertained thousands at the executive mansion. During World War II, Eleanor traveled to England and the South Pacific to boost the morale of American servicemen and to promote goodwill among the Allies. Eleanor Roosevelt was the first woman to speak to a national convention, hold regular press conferences, and write a syndicated newspaper column ("My Day").

    After her husband's death in 1945, Eleanor moved to a cottage at their Hyde Park estate. She also maintained an apartment in New York City. In 1946, Eleanor began serving the United States as a delegate to the United Nations, a position she held until 1953. President Kennedy reappointed Roosevelt as a UN delegate in 1961, and she served there again until her health deteriorated in 1962. The former first lady also continued to be in great demand as a speaker and radio/TV broadcaster. She wrote many articles and books, including a multivolume autobiography.

Lesson 21: For Further Study Younger Student Adaptations

1. Explain to your younger students the difference between a bull and a bear market. See if you can find cartoons related to the stock market's herd mentality to show them.

2. Share with them photographs of the Bonus Expeditionary Force's march on Washington, D.C. Tell them the story of what happened to the Bonus Army during the summer of 1932.

3. Have them read (or read to them) a short biography of Franklin Roosevelt, paying special attention to the chapter(s) on the New Deal.

4. Have them read (or read to them) a short biography of Eleanor Roosevelt.

Lesson 22: For Further Study Questions and Answers

1. **John Dillinger and Bonnie and Clyde were three famous figures during the depression years. For what were they known? Read about Father Charles Coughlin. Why was he a controversial religious figure during the 1930s?**

    Answer: John Dillinger (1903–1934) was an infamous American bank robber during a period in history sometimes referred to as the public enemy era (1931–1935). During the early 1930s, Dillinger's gangs robbed about a dozen banks and confiscated over three hundred thousand dollars (an enormous amount for that time). The son of an Indiana farmer, Dillinger had a reputation as a rebellious youth and later had difficulty holding a job as an adult. In 1924, he was arrested and convicted of robbing a well-known local grocer in Mooresville, Indiana. While serving time in prison, Dillinger and other prisoners planned robberies to be committed soon after they were released.

    In 1933, Dillinger received his parole, and he and several other ex-convicts began robbing banks in Indiana and Ohio. Within four months, Dillinger was back in jail, but his fellow gang members were able to spring him. His escape created a national sensation. From October through early January of 1934, the Dillinger gang robbed several more banks and killed a police officer during a gunfight. However, Dillinger and most of his gang were soon captured and arrested in Tucson, Arizona. Dillinger was sent back to a prison in Indiana, from which he escaped in March of 1934.

    With a new gang, Dillinger began robbing banks in Minnesota and Wisconsin. Eventually, Dillinger was named Public Enemy Number One by the FBI. The U.S. Department of Justice offered a ten thousand dollar reward for his capture or five thousand dollars for information leading to his capture. On July 22, 1934, Dillinger attended the movie *Manhattan Melodrama* at a theater in Chicago with his girlfriend. A local prostitute named Anna Sage had worked out a deal with the FBI to set up an ambush for Dillinger if they would drop deportation charges against her. When Dillinger and his girlfriend left the theater, Sage tipped off the FBI, and they opened fire on Dillinger and killed him. Many legends have surrounded the life and death of John Dillinger, including rumors that the man killed on July 22 was not Dillinger.

    Bonnie Parker (1910–1934) and Clyde Barrow (1909–1934) were two other notorious robbers who captured the attention of the American press and public during the public enemy era. Both Parker and Barrow were Texas natives who endured poverty-stricken childhoods and ended up in Dallas by the time they were adults. When they met in January of 1930, Bonnie was married to an imprisoned murderer, and Clyde would soon be sent to jail on burglary charges. When Clyde was paroled in 1932, he joined Bonnie and they embarked on a life of crime together.

    Although they are remembered as bank robbers, Bonnie and Clyde actually preferred to rob gas stations or small stores and to steal cars. The FBI became interested in the couple's activities as early as December of 1932. By the time Bonnie and Clyde were killed in 1934, they were believed to have committed at least thirteen murders in addition to numerous robberies and burglaries in Texas, Oklahoma, Louisiana, Missouri, and New Mexico. As their fame grew, government and police detectives were constantly on their trail, and the couple time and time again risked their lives to save each other.

    Many Americans followed the adventures of this romantic couple with great interest. Because Bonnie and Clyde became famous at the height of the depression, they were viewed sympathetically by some as simply poor Americans striking back at the government and business officials who had caused the nation's financial hardships. Finally, in May of 1934, Bonnie and Clyde were ambushed by police officers along a highway near the border of Texas and Louisiana. When the officers opened fire, the couple was killed instantly.

Father Charles Coughlin (1891–1979) was a Canadian-born Roman Catholic priest. Ordained in Toronto in 1916, Coughlin assisted in several parishes in the Detroit area. In 1926, he was assigned to the Shrine of the Little Flower, a new church in Royal Oak, Michigan. That same year he also began his weekly radio broadcasts. Although initially designed for children, these broadcasts soon changed to topics concerned with social reform. Coughlin's broadcasts became so popular that within four years CBS was broadcasting them throughout the nation.

Coughlin, who was highly critical of the government in the Soviet Union, claimed that the antifamily ideas of the communist government were spreading to the United States. However, Coughlin also denounced the greed and corruption of American industrialists and believed that the appeal of communism should be countered by introducing reforms that would make America a more equal society. When Coughlin refused to tone down his criticisms of President Hoover, CBS decided not to renew his contract in 1931. Coughlin responded by organizing his own radio network.

During the 1932 presidential election, Coughlin urged his listeners to vote for Franklin Roosevelt. After the election, he also gave his support to the New Deal. However, by 1935, Coughlin had begun to oppose Roosevelt's policies, accusing him of leaning toward socialism. He announced the formation of the National Union of Social Justice and expressed sympathy for the fascist policies of Hitler and Mussolini to combat communism. His radio broadcasts, which were now reaching thirty million people, became overtly anti-Semitic. In addition to his radio broadcasts, Coughlin also began publishing *Social Justice Weekly*, in which he continued his attacks on Jews, communists, and atheists.

The popularity of Coughlin's broadcasts declined as his radicalism grew. When the United States entered World War II, the National Association of Broadcasters arranged for his broadcasts to be brought to an end. The U.S Post Office also banned his weekly newspaper from the mail, and church authorities ordered Coughlin to bring his political activities to an end. Although Coughlin remained the pastor of the Shrine of the Little Flower until he retired in 1966, he continued to write pamphlets denouncing communism.

2. **View** *Snow White and the Seven Dwarfs*. **Is it different from more recent Disney animated movies? Try some Shirley Temple films or other movies from this period. Why do you think Shirley Temple was so popular during the depression?**
Answer: Shirley Temple starred in movies that promised better times just around the corner. She was a charming little girl who sang and danced and made everything better for the grown-ups around her. At one point, Shirley Temple was more photographed than President Roosevelt and became known for single-handedly saving Fox studios.

3. **See if you can find some audio recordings of radio programs from the depression years, such as** *The Shadow, Fibber McGee,* **and** *The Lone Ranger*. **How is listening to a program on the radio different from viewing a program on TV? Find out who Walter Winchell and Will Rogers were, as well as the significance of Orson Welles's broadcast of** *The War of the Worlds*.
Walter Winchell (1897–1972) was an extremely popular American newspaper and radio commentator who became very influential in shaping public opinion. In his column at the *New York Evening Graphic*, he began exposing the private lives of public figures in a way that permanently changed American journalism and celebrity. Although he concentrated on entertainment gossip, Winchell also frequently expressed political opinions. His inimitable writing style was filled with slang and incomplete sentences.

Winchell was writing a gossip column for the *New York Daily Mirror* when he made his radio debut in 1930. However, his big radio breakthrough came in 1932 when he was selected to host the *Jergens Journal*, a fifteen-minute show that mixed entertainment and political news. Winchell began his broadcasts by pressing on a telegraph key, then speaking in a rapid-fire staccato style of 197 words per minute. Because Winchell was such a colorful and opinionated personality, his show soon became top-rated, and he became a celebrity in his own right.

For most of Winchell's career, his contracts with newspaper and radio employers required them to reimburse him for any damages he might have to pay should he be sued for slander. He often had no credible sources for his accusations and perfected the use of slang to report stories that might have led to legal disputes. Especially in the years following World War II, he attempted to ruin the careers of his enemies and gained a reputation for being arrogant and ruthless. Winchell stayed in radio until 1957, then narrated *The Untouchables* on the ABC television network from 1959–1964.

Will Rogers (1879–1935) was an American humorist and entertainer during the depression years. Born in Indian Territory (later the state of Oklahoma), Rogers had Cherokee ancestry on both his mother's and father's sides. He grew up loving the life of a cowboy and began his show business career as a trick roper. Traveling on the American vaudeville circuits, Rogers began working jokes into his roping act and eventually worked up daily humorous commentaries on the news. From 1916 to 1925, Rogers appeared as a comic act in the Ziegfeld Follies.

From 1925 to 1928, Rogers traveled all over the United States giving witty, entertaining, after-dinner and convention speeches. He became the most widely read newspaper columnist in the United States, and his Sunday night half-hour radio broadcast was the most listened to in the nation. Will Rogers won the admiration of the American people and became a friend to presidents and other important national figures. He also starred in more than twenty feature films and became the number one movie box office draw in 1934. When he died in an airplane crash in Alaska in 1935, Rogers ranked second only to Shirley Temple in popularity.

On October 30, 1938, actor and director Orson Welles and his Mercury Theatre players presented a radio adaptation of H. G. Wells's science fiction novel, *The War of the Worlds*. The live Sunday evening broadcast frightened many listeners into believing that an actual Martian invasion was in progress in Grovers Mill, New Jersey. In adapting the book for radio, Welles made over half of the fifty-minute play a series of "live" news bulletins. Although the broadcast contained several explanations that it was just a performance of a play, anyone who missed the first explanation would not hear the second until forty minutes into the program. People actually loaded guns, hid in cellars, fled their homes, and wrapped their heads in wet towels to protect themselves from the Martians' poison gas.

Later studies indicated that many listeners missed the explanations because the Mercury Theatre ran opposite the very popular Edgar Bergen show. Twelve minutes into the Bergen program an opera number began, and many listeners presumably switched channels and tuned into the Mercury Theatre presentation at the point where Martians were emerging from their spacecraft. Subsequently, news of the reported panic created a public uproar and spawned many urban legends.

4. **Listen to some big band music of the swing era and look at some surrealist and regionalist paintings. Look for information about the Mount Rushmore memorial. Which presidents are included in this monument?**
   Answer: Big band music during the depression years was played by the orchestras of Duke Ellington, Harry James, Glenn Miller, Benny Goodman, and Tommy and Jimmy Dorsey.

   Look for paintings during this period by Edward Hopper, Grant Wood, Man Ray, and Joseph Stella.

   The presidents included on Mount Rushmore are George Washington, Thomas Jefferson, Abraham Lincoln, and Theodore Roosevelt.

Lesson 22: For Further Study Younger Student Adaptations

1. Explain to your younger students what the FBI does and what a "public enemy" is. Share the stories of John Dillinger and Bonnie and Clyde and discuss why people during the depression years might have viewed the actions of these notorious robbers sympathetically.

2. Watch *Snow White and the Seven Dwarfs* with them and ask them how it is different from more recent Disney animated movies. Let them watch an early Shirley Temple movie and ask them why they think she was so popular during the depression years.

3. Have them listen to a 1930s radio program. Have them read (or read to them) a short biography of Will Rogers. Play part of *The War of the Worlds* broadcast for them and make sure they understand why it created a national panic.

4. Play for your students some big band music from the 1930s and show them some surrealist and regionalist paintings from that decade. Let them see a photograph of the Mount Rushmore memorial and tell you the names of the four presidents included in this monument.

Lesson 23: For Further Study Questions and Answers

1. **Learn more about the Japanese attack at Pearl Harbor. On which Hawaiian island was the U.S naval base located? What was the significance of the phrase "Tora, tora, tora"? How long did the attack last? Which battleship was hit at the beginning and sank within minutes with its crew trapped inside? What role did Pearl Harbor play in the rest of the war?**
   Answer: The U. S. naval base was located on the island of Oahu. The Pacific fleet of the U.S. Navy was unaware that the Japanese were in the area and did not expect a sneak attack. At 7:53 on Sunday morning, December 7, 1941, Lieutenant Commander Mitsuo Fuchida in his lead Japanese bomber called out on his radio, "Tora, tora, tora" (code word "tiger" that signaled the Japanese navy that they had achieved maximum strategic surprise at Pearl Harbor). At 7:55, the Japanese let loose their bombs. The attack lasted one hour and forty-five minutes. Then the Japanese planes flew back to their aircraft carriers in the Pacific.

   The USS *Arizona* was hit almost immediately. It exploded and sank within minutes with its crew trapped inside. The *West Virginia* and the *California* were sunk but later raised and repaired. The *Nevada* was heavily damaged. Eighteen ships and hundreds of aircraft and buildings were damaged or destroyed by the thousands of Japanese bombs. Over 2,400 Americans were killed, including 68 civilians, and more than 2,000 were wounded or missing.

   Military forces flooded into Pearl Harbor after the attack. Within a few months, they had rebuilt the harbor and repaired many of the buildings, planes, and ships. However, the *Arizona* remained underwater in the harbor. During the remaining years of World War II, Pearl Harbor served as the center of training and operations for the war in the Pacific.

2. **Several important conferences took place between Allied leaders during the war. Discover who attended the conferences at Cairo and Tehran, when they were held, and what was decided at each.**
   Answer: The Cairo Conference was held November 22–26, 1943, in Cairo, Egypt. In attendance were President Franklin Roosevelt, British Prime Minister Winston Churchill, and General Chiang Kai-shek of the Republic of China. The purpose of the Cairo meeting was to address the Allied position against Japan during the remainder of the war and to make decisions about postwar Asia. The Cairo Declaration pledged continued Allied deploy-

ment of brutal military force against Japan until Japan's unconditional surrender. The declaration also called for Japan to be stripped of all islands in the Pacific that it had seized or occupied since the beginning of World War I (1914) and further, it called for Japan to return all territories stolen from the Republic of China. Korea was promised its independence in "due course."

The Tehran Conference was held November 28–December 1, 1943, in Tehran, Iran. In attendance were President Franklin Roosevelt, British Prime Minister Winston Churchill, and Soviet Premier Joseph Stalin. The purpose of the conference was to strengthen the cooperation of the three world powers in planning the final strategy for the war against the Axis powers. Agreement was reached on the timing and scope of military operations against Germany, including plans for the Allied invasion of France. The three countries also pledged to recognize and maintain the independence of Iran.

3. **Find out for what Lt. Colonel James Doolittle became known during World War II, and which popular wartime movie dramatized Doolittle's story.**

   Answer: James Harold "Jimmy" Doolittle (1896–1993), an American aviation pioneer, served with distinction as a general in the U.S. Army Air Forces during World War II. After serving as a flight instructor during World War I, Doolittle made many pioneering flights during the years between the two world wars. Perhaps his most important aeronautical contribution was the development of instrument flying. In 1929, he became the first pilot to take off, fly, and land using instruments alone.

   In 1940, Doolittle returned to active duty as a major. In January of 1942, he was promoted to lieutenant colonel and became involved in planning the first aerial raid on Japan. Doolittle volunteered and received approval to lead an attack of sixteen B-25 bombers from the aircraft carrier USS *Hornet* on targets in Tokyo, Osaka, Nagoya, and Kobe. This mission on April 18, 1942, stunned the world and lifted American morale. Although several flyers lost their lives in this mission, Doolittle was able to bail out and landed in a rice paddy in China. He was helped by Chinese guerillas until he could return to the United States.

   Doolittle's raid did little damage to the Japanese war industry, but it demonstrated that Japan was not invulnerable. The Japanese, who withdrew several front-line fighter units for homeland defense, were deeply embarrassed by the raid, which was followed by a decisive American victory at the Battle of Midway. President Roosevelt presented Doolittle with the Medal of Honor for planning and leading the operation.

   Following the raid, Doolittle was promoted to major general and in March 1943, became commanding general of the Northwest African Strategic Air Forces. From January 1944 to September 1945, Doolittle commanded the Eighth Air Force in England as a lieutenant general. On May 10, 1946, he returned to inactive reserve status and to Shell Oil as a vice president. In 1944, Spencer Tracy portrayed Doolittle in the movie *Thirty Seconds over Tokyo*.

4. **Pick one or more World War II battles to research. Some of the major battles included Dunkirk, Midway, Guadalcanal, Stalingrad, Normandy, the Bulge, Iwo Jima, and Okinawa. If this is an area of interest, compile a World War II Battles Notebook. There are forms in the optional forms section of the** *Student Activity Book* **to use to do this.**

Lesson 23: For Further Study Younger Student Adaptations

1. Share appropriate details about the Japanese attack at Pearl Harbor. There are various Pearl Harbor websites with photographs and additional information.

2. Explain why the Allied leaders held conferences during the war. Show photographs of the leaders taken at these conferences—see if they can identify Roosevelt, Churchill, and Stalin.

---

3. Show them a photograph of Jimmy Doolittle and tell them about Doolittle's Raid.

4. Pick a World War II battle about which you and your younger students can become "experts."

Lesson 24: For Further Study Questions and Answers

1. Look for an issue of *Look, The Saturday Evening Post, Life,* or another magazine from the World War II period. Pay special attention to the advertisements and clothing fashions, as well as other information about what life was like on the home front.

2. Find out what actions the U.S. government has taken to make restitution to the Japanese Americans sent to relocation centers during the war.
   Answer: In 1968, the U.S. government began giving reparations to Japanese Americans for property they had lost. In 1988, the U.S. Congress passed legislation that issued an official apology and awarded formal payments of twenty thousand dollars each to the surviving internees (about sixty thousand people).

3. Discover who Anne Frank was. Read *The Hiding Place* by Corrie Ten Boom or watch the movie.
   Answer: Anne Frank (1929–1945) was a German-born Jewish girl who wrote a diary while in hiding in Amsterdam with her family and four others during the German occupation of the Netherlands in World War II. In July of 1942, this group of Jews went into hiding in secret rooms in Otto Frank's office building (the Secret Annex). Two years later, they were betrayed and transported to concentration camps. Otto Frank was the only survivor. When he returned to Amsterdam at the end of the war, he found Anne's diary and had it published in English under the name *The Diary of a Young Girl*. Many theatrical productions based on the diary of this Holocaust victim have been presented in the United States.

4. Research the role Hollywood played in World War II. For what was Bob Hope known in the war effort? Look for photographs of movie stars from the era. What did the expression "Kilroy was here" mean?
   Answer: Beginning in World War II (and for the next fifty years), Bob Hope entertained U.S. troops in this country and overseas. After the attack on Pearl Harbor, Hope toured training bases all over the United States with his radio show. In 1943, he started touring bases overseas with his USO (United Service Organizations) variety show to bring entertainment and a touch of home to American troops, wherever stationed. His shows featured comedy monologues songs, dances, celebrity appearances, specialty acts, and skits.

   "Kilroy was here" was a popular American cultural expression, often seen in graffiti drawn by U.S. servicemen in World War II. The expression was often accompanied by the drawing of a face with a long nose and two big round eyes peeking over a wall and sometimes fingers gripping the wall. There are many legends surrounding the origin of the slogan. The Transit Company of America held a nationwide contest in 1946 in an attempt to solve the mystery. James J. Kilroy, an American shipyard inspector, brought his co-workers with him to prove that he was the true Kilroy and received the prize (a trolley car, which he gave to his children to play in).

Lesson 24: For Further Study Younger Student Adaptations

1. Show your younger students magazine advertisements and articles from magazines published during World War II.

2. Discuss with them the Japanese American relocation centers established during the war and the restitution that the U.S. government later made to the internees there.

3. Share with them the story of Anne Frank. Have them read (or read to them) a children's biography of Corrie Ten Boom.

4. Show them a "Kilroy drawing" and explain the significance of the expression "Kilroy was here."

UNIT FOUR
For Further Study
Questions and Answers

Lesson 25: For Further Study Questions and Answers

1. Look for a copy of Winston Churchill's speech (March 5, 1945) in which he warned about the Iron Curtain descending across Europe. Also find President Eisenhower's Farewell Address to the Nation (January 17, 1961) in which he warned about the dangers of the American military-industrial complex. Read one or both of these speeches and decide how effective they were in communicating their messages.
   Answer: To find these speeches, type "Winston Churchill's Iron Curtain Speech" and "Eisenhower's Farewell Address to the Nation" into an Internet search engine.

2. Read more about the Berlin Airlift. What name did the Americans give this operation? How often did Allied planes make drops there? What type(s) of U.S. aircraft were used to make the drops?
   Answer: The U.S. airlift operation in Berlin was given the name "Operation Vittles." The British called their part of the mission "Operation Plane Fare." This massive effort to supply two million West Berliners with food and heating fuel required round-the-clock flights. By the spring of 1949, approximately eight thousand tons of supplies were being flown in daily. C-47s and C-54s were used to make the drops. Because C-54s could carry three times more cargo than C-47s, C-54s gradually took over most of the airlift flights.

3. Find out how many nations belong to NATO today. Is Russia a member? Where are the headquarters for NATO located? What role has NATO played in the war on terrorism?
   Answer: The North Atlantic Treaty Organization is an alliance of twenty-six countries from North America and Europe. Russia is a partner country. NATO headquarters are located in Brussels, Belgium. On September 12, 2001, NATO declared the terrorist attacks against the United States to be an attack against all the NATO member countries. NATO followed this proclamation with practical measures of assistance to the United States in its war on terrorism.

4. Pick one or more of the battles of the Korean War to research. Some of the major battles included Inchon, Chosin Reservoir, Heartbreak Ridge, Unsan, Seoul, and Pork Chop Hill. If this is an area of interest, compile a Korean War Battles Notebook. There are forms in the optional forms section of the _Student Activity Book_ to use to do this.

Lesson 25: For Further Study Younger Student Adaptations

1. Have them read (or read to them) a short children's book giving an overview of the Cold War.

---

2. Show them photographs of the planes used in the Berlin Airlift and share more details about the airlift operation with them.

3. Take your younger students to the NATO website and discuss with them the purpose of NATO today.

4. Pick a Korean War battle about which you and your younger students can become "experts."

Lesson 26: For Further Study Questions and Answers

1. **Look for photographs of cars from the 1950s. How did they differ from today's cars? What was the Edsel?**
   Answer: Cars in the 1950s generally had long lower bodies, tail fins, excessive chrome ornamentation, radiator grilles, and dashboards with push buttons. The more expensive, "flashy" cars had V-8 engines, pointy tail fins, giant red tail lights, hood ornaments, padded dashboards, elegant upholstery, and air conditioning.

   The Edsel, introduced in 1957, was the most famous marketing disaster in U.S. auto history. This car had been carefully researched and designed by Ford to appeal to young executives. However, the Edsel was a flop from the beginning and was responsible for the loss of millions of dollars for the Ford Motor Company. There was no single reason why the Edsel failed. *Consumer Reports* blamed poor workmanship; business analysts pinned the problem on weak support for the Edsel from Ford's executive offices. Marketing experts cited the public's adverse reaction to the car's styling and its failure to meet their expectations of being an entirely new kind of car.

2. **Discover who Wernher von Braun and the Army Redstone Arsenal team were. For what did Chuck Yeager become known in 1947?**
   Answer: Wernher von Braun (1912–1977), a German physicist, was employed by the German Ordnance Department from 1932 to 1937. In 1937, he became the technical director of a German rocket center that developed the V-2 rocket. Near the end of World War II, von Braun led more than one hundred of his rocket team members in surrendering to the Allies. In September of 1945, von Braun came to the United States under contract with the U.S. Army Ordnance Corps.

   By 1950, von Braun had moved to Huntsville, Alabama, where he lived for the next twenty years. From 1950–1956, he led the U.S. Army's rocket development team at Redstone Arsenal. Projects under von Braun's direction included the Redstone rocket, the Jupiter intermediate-range ballistic missile, and the Pershing missile.

   After the 1957 Russian *Sputnik* launch, von Braun and his team were transferred to NASA and became the nucleus of the Marshall Space Flight Center at Redstone Arsenal. The Marshall-developed Saturn V rocket launched the *Apollo 11* crew on their historic moon mission. Von Braun eventually became a naturalized U.S. citizen and retired from NASA in 1972.

   Charles E. "Chuck" Yeager (1923–), a famous American pilot, fought in World War II. When he returned to the United States after the war, he entered test pilot school, where he was chosen from over 125 pilots to fly the X-1. In October of 1947, Yeager was the first person to break the sound barrier in level flight in his X-1.

3. **Read some excerpts from Dr. Benjamin Spock's *Common Sense Book of Baby and Child Care*. See if you agree with his philosophy.**
   Answer: Type "Dr. Benjamin Spock's *Common Sense Book of Baby and Child Care*" into an Internet search engine.

---

4. **Find out the significance of Linda Brown and Elizabeth Eckford. Record the information on African American forms.**

    Answer: Linda Brown (1943–) and her family lived in Topeka, Kansas, during the 1950s. They were one of thirteen Topeka families recruited by the NAACP in the fall of 1950 to attempt to enroll their children in their neighborhood white schools (with the expectation that they would be rejected). As a third grader, Linda Brown walked a mile through a railroad switchyard to reach her African American elementary school, even though a white elementary school was just seven blocks from her home.

    In 1951, the NAACP requested an injunction that would forbid the segregation of Topeka's public schools. This case, which became known as *Brown v. Board of Education of Topeka, Kansas*, went all the way to the Supreme Court. The Browns' name was applied to the case because alphabetically their name appeared first in the list of families involved. In 1979, Linda Brown Smith filed another suit against the Topeka Board of Education, charging that many African American children in Topeka were still attending primarily segregated schools.

    Elizabeth Eckford (1942–) was one of the African American high school students who became known as the Little Rock Nine. On September 4, 1957, she and eight other black students attempted to enter Little Rock Central High School, previously an all-white school. However, they were stopped at the door by Arkansas National Guard troops sent by Governor Orval Faubus.

    That evening, the NAACP reached eight of the Little Rock Nine by phone and advised them that they needed protection and should plan to meet together before entering the school the following day. However, Elizabeth Eckford had no phone and did not receive the warning call. The next day, she attempted to enter Little Rock Central alone through the front entrance and encountered an angry mob that threatened to lynch her as the National Guard looked on. A white *New York Times* reporter and a white woman stepped forward to help Elizabeth get safely on a bus. The other eight were also again denied admittance by the National Guard. Finally, on September 24, President Eisenhower called in the 101st Airborne Division to escort the Little Rock Nine to school.

Lesson 26: For Further Study Younger Student Adaptations

1. Show your younger students photographs of cars from the 1950s. Tell them the story of the Edsel.

2. Have them read (or read to them) a short biography of Wernher von Braun or Chuck Yeager.

3. Read to them a few excerpts from Dr. Benjamin Spock's *Common Sense Book of Baby and Child Care*. Discuss with them differences in parenting philosophies.

4. Share with them the stories of Linda Brown and Elizabeth Eckford, as well as photographs of these girls taken during this time period.

Lesson 27: For Further Study Questions and Answers

1. **Investigate the strategy used by Dr. Martin Luther King, Jr., in leading the civil rights movement in the United States. What leader's ideas influenced his thinking? Fill out an African American form on Martin Luther King, Jr. Read about the lives of Ralph Abernathy and Coretta King and fill out African American forms for them.**

    Answer: Dr. Martin Luther King, Jr. (1929–1968), born in Atlanta to a Baptist minister and his wife, received a B. A. from Morehouse College, a B. D. from Crozer Theological Seminary, and a Ph. D. from Boston University.

In 1954, King became the minister of a Baptist church in Montgomery, Alabama, and the following year, he led the African American bus boycott there. Influenced by the writings of Mohandas Gandhi, he embraced the philosophy of nonviolent resistance or civil disobedience.

When he was twenty-eight, King organized the Southern Christian Leadership Conference (SCLC), a group of churches and organizations that pushed for African American civil rights in a nonviolent fashion. He moved to Atlanta and began traveling across the nation giving speeches, staging sit-ins, walking in marches, and leading rallies. King's leadership of the 1963 Birmingham protests and the March on Washington brought him worldwide attention. In 1964, King became the youngest man to have been awarded the Nobel Peace Prize and announced that he would give the prize money (over fifty-four thousand dollars) to the civil rights movement. Before his death he published three books.

From 1955 until his assassination in 1968, King faced arrest on numerous occasions. His life and the lives of his family were in constant jeopardy. Their house was bombed, and they were the recipients of hate mail and hundreds of phone threats. In 1968, King traveled to Memphis to support striking sanitation workers. On April 4, 1968, he was shot and killed as he stood on the balcony of the Lorraine Motel.

Ralph Abernathy (1926–1990) was a Baptist minister and close friend and advisor of Martin Luther King, Jr. Abernathy and King first worked together when they organized the Montgomery bus boycott in 1955. Two years later, Abernathy was involved with King in founding the Southern Christian Leadership Conference. He moved to Atlanta in 1961 and worked closely with King until King's assassination in 1968. After King's death, Abernathy was chosen president of the SCLC, a position he held until 1977. His autobiography, *And the Walls Came Tumbling Down*, was published in 1989.

Coretta Scott King (1927–2006), the "first lady of the civil rights movement," was the wife of Martin Luther King, Jr. After receiving an undergraduate degree from Antioch College in 1951, Coretta enrolled in a graduate program at the New England Conservatory of Music. While living in Boston, she met her future husband, whom she married in 1953. Coretta strongly supported Martin in his leadership of the civil rights movement and endured with him the anger and hatred directed at him and their family. After her husband's death, Coretta founded the Martin Luther King, Jr. Center for Nonviolent Social Change in Atlanta. She devoted her life to his legacy and worked for decades to have his birthday observed as a federal holiday.

2. **Learn more about Billy Graham and the Billy Graham Evangelistic Association. Whom did Graham choose to succeed him in his ministry?**
Answer: The Reverend Dr. William "Billy" Franklin Graham, Jr. (1918–), an American Protestant evangelist, became well known for advising and praying with ten successive U.S. presidents. Ordained a Baptist minister in 1938, Billy graduated from Wheaton College and married Ruth Bell, whose parents were missionaries in China. From 1945–1948, Graham traveled all over the United States, Canada, and Europe speaking at Youth for Christ rallies and organizing Youth for Christ chapters. Gradually, he began to hold evangelistic rallies on his own. Working with him at these rallies were master of ceremonies Cliff Barrows, soloist George Beverly Shea, and associate evangelist Grady Wilson.

In 1949, Graham led an evangelistic campaign in Los Angeles, which resulted in the dramatic conversion of a well-known disc jockey and an underworld figure. Newspaper magnate William Randolph Hearst sent a telegram to editors of his publications to "puff" Graham, and other newspapers followed Hearst's example. Graham's campaign stretched from three to seven weeks. From Los Angeles, Graham went to Boston for another crusade, which also received national attention. In the decades that followed, he would hold evangelistic campaigns in all major U.S. cities, as well as rallies in Australia, Africa, Asia, South America, and Europe.

To keep his ministry running with integrity and efficiency, Graham incorporated the Billy Graham Evangelistic Association (BGEA) in 1950. The BGEA originally had its headquarters in Minneapolis but later relocated to Charlotte. In addition to planning and coordinating Graham's and his associates' evangelistic meetings, the BGEA published *Decision* magazine, broadcast the *Hour of Decision* radio program and established *World Wide Pictures* (production and distribution of films about BGEA crusades). In 1996, Graham's elder son, William Franklin Graham II, announced that he would be his father's successor when the time came for Billy Graham to leave the ministry.

3. **Listen to some of Elvis Presley's records from the 1950s. Why do you think Elvis is still an important American phenomenon, even after he has been dead for so many years?**
   Answer: Elvis Presley (1935–1977), known as the King of Rock and Roll, redefined popular music in the middle of the twentieth century. "Heartbreak Hotel" was his first across-the-board hit. Other early hits from 1956 and 1957 included "Hound Dog," "All Shook Up," "Love Me Tender," and "Jailhouse Rock." Presley also starred in approximately thirty movies and performed live for capacity crowds until he died at his Graceland mansion in Memphis at the age of forty-two. Elvis Presley holds records for the most Top Ten hits (38), the most Top Forty hits (107), and the most consecutive #1 hits (10).

4. **Discover what Levittown is. See if you can find pictures of it. Look for the words to Peter Seeger's recording of the song, "Little Boxes on the Hillside." What is the meaning of this song?**
   Answer: Levittown, New York, started out as an experiment in low-cost, mass-produced housing after World War II. In 1947, the development firm of Levitt and Sons announced plans to build two thousand rental homes for veterans on some abandoned potato fields known as Island Trees. In order to build these homes quickly and cheaply, Levitt and Sons eliminated basements and garages and built on concrete slabs. All the lumber used was precut and shipped from a lumberyard owned by Levitt and Sons. Nonunion contractors were also employed. All two thousand homes were rented immediately. When hundreds of veterans continued to apply for houses, the Levitts decided to build four thousand additional homes.

   In 1949, Levitt and Sons stopped constructing rental houses and began building a larger home, which they called a "ranch" and sold for just under eight thousand dollars. Each Levitt ranch measured thirty-two feet by twenty-five feet and came in one of five models that differed only in exterior color, window placement, and roof line. Prospective buyers needed a ninety dollar deposit and the ability to make payments of fifty-eight dollars per month. By 1951, Levitt and Sons had constructed 17,447 houses in Levittown and the immediate surrounding area. Their community became a model upon which scores of other suburban communities in the United States were based in the postwar years.

   Levittown was the largest housing development ever constructed by a single builder. Shopping centers, playgrounds, and a community center were built for its residents. Many people in surrounding towns were apprehensive about the building of so many nearly identical, mass-produced homes. The song "Little Boxes" referred to the monotony and sameness of homes like the Levitt ranches. Today, however, nearly all the Levitt houses have been attractively expanded or remodeled, and the average Levitt house can be purchased for around $135,000.

Lesson 27: For Further Study Younger Student Adaptations

1. Have them read (or read to them) a short biography of Martin Luther King, Jr., Coretta King, or Ralph Abernathy.

2. Have them read (or read to them) a short biography of Billy Graham.

3. Listen to a few of Elvis's early recordings with them. Share with them some of the records that Elvis holds and how he changed popular American music.

4. Show your younger students photographs of Levittown. Explain the significance of this suburban community. Play them a recording of "Little Boxes," and ask them what they think it means.

Lesson 28: For Further Study Questions and Answers

1. **Look for footage from the Kennedy/Nixon TV debates, Kennedy's inaugural address, and Kennedy's assassination and funeral. Learn more about his wife Jacqueline's renovation of the White House. What were the findings of the Warren Commission concerning Kennedy's assassination?**
   Answer: After she moved into the White House, Jacqueline Kennedy asked that a fine arts committee be formed to oversee a restoration of the executive mansion. The first lady was committed to making the White House a living museum of history. She inventoried its furniture and artwork, consulted with art experts and interior decorators (such as Henry du Pont, an authority on American historical decoration), interior designers (Stéphane Boudin and Mrs. Henry Parrish), and convinced private collectors to lend or donate period pieces.

   When the renovation project was complete, Mrs. Kennedy conducted an hour-long televised tour of the White House seen by millions of Americans. She also wrote the text for the first historical guidebook to the White House, which was sold to tourists visiting the mansion. These guidebooks raised millions of dollars for the new nonprofit White House Historical Association, established to purchase items for the White House collection.

   The President's Commission on the Assassination of President Kennedy, unofficially known as the Warren Commission, was appointed by President Lyndon Johnson on November 29, 1963. Headed by Chief Justice Earl Warren, the commission conducted a ten-month investigation of the assassination of John F. Kennedy and concluded that Lee Harvey Oswald acted alone in killing Kennedy (refuting the conspiracy theory). The Warren Commission report proved to be extremely controversial, and the commission has been criticized for some of its methods and especially for its failure to comment on the destruction of important evidence by intelligence agencies and law enforcement officials.

2. **Learn more about the Vietnam War. If this is an area of interest, compile a Vietnam War Battles Notebook. There are forms in the optional forms section of the *Student Activity Book* to use to do this. What happened at Kent State University in 1970? Who was William Calley and what happened to him? What were the Pentagon Papers? Who was Daniel Ellsberg?**
   Answer: On May 1, 1970, students at Kent State University in Kent, Ohio, staged a massive antiwar demonstration on the school commons to protest the American invasion of Cambodia announced the day before by President Nixon. That evening a crowd of students, bikers, and out-of-town youth engaged in drunken behavior in the Kent downtown area, which led to looting and vandalism.

   The following day, the mayor of Kent declared a state of emergency and asked the governor to send the National Guard to keep order. When the National Guard arrived the evening of May 2, a large demonstration was underway, and the campus ROTC building was burning. When another rally was held on Sunday evening, May 3, the Guard used tear gas to disperse the crowd.

   A fourth protest demonstration was scheduled for noon on May 4. University officials tried to stop the rally, but approximately two thousand people gathered anyway on the commons. Just before noon, the Guard ordered the crowd to disperse and again used tear gas. Some of the students threw rocks at the guardsmen, and other students picked up tear-gas canisters and began throwing them.

   Before the confrontation was over, the guardsmen had fired more than sixty shots at the unarmed students. Why the shots were fired has been widely debated. The shootings killed four students (two of whom were simply walking to class) and wounded nine. Hundreds of colleges and universities throughout the nation closed, fearing similar outbreaks. What became known as the Kent State Massacre shocked the nation and further galvanized the U.S. antiwar movement.

On September 5, 1969, Lieutenant William Calley was charged with premeditated murder in the deaths of over one hundred unarmed Vietnamese civilians near the village of My Lai. His court martial began in November of 1969. Testimony revealed that Calley had ordered soldiers of Charlie Company, Americal Division, to shoot everyone in the village. According to Calley, he was following the orders of his immediate superior, Captain Ernest Medina. Medina was later acquitted of all charges at a separate trial.

Of the twenty-six officers and soldiers initially charged in connection with the My Lai massacre and cover-up, only Calley was convicted. Many Americans believed that Calley was used as a scapegoat by the U.S. Army for its failure to instill discipline in its troops and officers. A day after Calley was sentenced to life in prison, President Nixon ordered him released and placed under house arrest pending appeal. In 1973, the secretary of the army reduced Calley's sentence to ten years. After more legal maneuvering, Calley was paroled in 1974.

The Pentagon Papers, consisting of forty-seven volumes, was a top-secret government study of U.S. involvement in Southeast Asia from 1945 to 1967 commissioned by Secretary of Defense Robert McNamara. Written by a team of analysts with access to classified documents, the study revealed many blunders and deceptions as well as bureaucratic arrogance on the part of U.S. policymakers. Daniel Ellsberg, a former U.S. military analyst, released the Pentagon Papers to *The New York Times* in 1971. Publication of these documents significantly eroded public support for the Vietnam War. Although Ellsberg was charged with espionage, conspiracy, and theft, all the charges against him were eventually dismissed.

3.   **Why did federal officials investigate Vice President Spiro Agnew? What evidence did they uncover? What role did the Twenty-fifth Amendment play in the events that followed? Find out what the Saturday Night Massacre was. What role did Carl Bernstein and Bob Woodward play in Watergate? What role did Chuck Colson play in Watergate? What has Colson done since serving in the Nixon White House?**

Answer: On October 10, 1973, Spiro Agnew became the second vice president to resign. The first was John C. Calhoun, who resigned to take a seat in the U.S. Senate. Agnew, however, resigned amid accusations of bribery, extortion, and tax violations. The vice president had come under investigation by the U.S. attorney in Baltimore for receiving illegal payments from engineers seeking contracts when he was governor of Maryland. Although Agnew maintained his innocence, he pleaded no contest to a single charge that he had failed to report $29,500 in income received in 1973. Agnew was fined ten thousand dollars and put on three years' probation. His resignation brought about the first use of the Twenty-fifth Amendment when Nixon appointed Gerald Ford as Agnew's successor.

The Saturday Night Massacre (October 20, 1973) was the name given to President Nixon's dismissal of independent special prosecutor Archibald Cox, who was investigating the Watergate scandal. When Cox issued a subpoena to Nixon for copies of conversations taped in the Oval Office, the president ordered Attorney General Elliot Richardson to fire Cox. Richardson refused to do so and resigned in protest. Deputy Attorney General William Ruckelshaus also refused to fire Cox and resigned. Finally, Solicitor General Robert Bork, acting head of the Justice Department, complied with Nixon's order and fired Cox. Congress saw this affair as a gross abuse of presidential power, and several bills of impeachment against the president were introduced in the days that followed.

Bob Woodward (1943–) and Carl Bernstein (1944–), reporters for *The Washington Post* newspaper, investigated the Watergate break-in and broke the story of the scandal in August of 1972. Their work helped the *Post* win a Pulitzer Prize in 1973. The two reporters also co-authored two best-selling books about Nixon and Watergate — *All the President's Men* and *The Final Days*.

Charles "Chuck" Colson (1931–) served as chief counsel to President Richard Nixon from 1969 to 1973. Known as Nixon's "hatchet man," Colson authored a 1971 memo that became known as Nixon's Enemies List. He was also involved in the activities of the Committee to Re-elect the President, a group that agreed to fund the gathering of "intelligence" on the Democratic Party. When the Watergate scandal broke, Colson was given C. S. Lewis's *Mere Christianity* by a friend. He accepted Christ as his Savior and entered a plea of no contest to obstruction of justice in the Daniel Ellsberg case. Given a one- to three-year sentence, Colson served seven months at Maxwell Correctional Facility in Alabama. After being released, he founded Prison Fellowship Ministries, an outreach to prisoners, ex-prisoners, their families, and crime victims. Colson has written a number of books discussing contemporary issues from a politically conservative, evangelical Christian worldview.

4. **Research the terms of the new treaties negotiated between the United States and Panama in 1977. Why were some Americans opposed to these treaties?**
   Answer: In 1977, the United States negotiated two new treaties with Panama, which allowed the two countries to operate the Panama Canal jointly until the year 2000. At that point, Panama would be authorized to take over sole control of canal operations and given primary responsibility for defense of the canal. The canal's neutrality was guaranteed, and the United States was given the permanent right to defend the canal from any threats to its continued neutral service to ships of all nations.

   Opponents of these Torrijos-Carter Treaties (named for U.S President Carter and Panama leader Omar Torrijos) believed that surrender of the canal to an unstable government was unwise. However, supporters of the treaties maintained that the Panama Canal's narrow width and the growth in importance of air power made the canal relatively unimportant to the United States militarily or economically.

Lesson 28: For Further Study Younger Student Adaptations

1. Share clips from the Kennedy/Nixon debate, Kennedy's inaugural address, Kennedy's funeral, and/or Jacqueline's White House tour with your younger students.

2. Discuss with them the widespread opposition to the Vietnam War in the United States. Explain what happened at Kent State, what charges William Calley faced, and why the Pentagon Papers were significant.

3. Have them read (or read to them) a book explaining the Watergate scandal or a short biography of Charles Colson.

4. Explain how the United States relationship to the Panama Canal changed on January 1, 2000.

Lesson 29: For Further Study Questions and Answers

1. **Discover what happened at Three Mile Island in 1979. When was the first Earth Day? What books did Rachel Carson and Ralph Nader write that made them famous?**
   Answer: Three Mile Island is located in the Susquehanna River southeast of Harrisburg, Pennsylvania. On March 28, 1979, a nuclear power plant on Three Mile Island suffered a partial core meltdown due to technical malfunctions and human error. Although the meltdown resulted in very little radiation leakage, the accident created panic among nearby residents, and the subsequent cleanup process cost millions of dollars. After the Three Mile Island accident, public support for nuclear power across the country fell from 70 to 50 percent, and no new nuclear plant has been built in the United States since the accident.

The first Earth Day, held on April 22, 1970, involved as many as twenty million Americans (primarily students in universities, colleges, and primary and secondary schools) demonstrating in support of an environmental agenda. Senator Gaylord Nelson, an environmental activist in the Senate, took a leading role in organizing the day. The first nationwide event also included speeches opposing the Vietnam War. Soon after the first Earth Day, Congress passed the Clean Air Act, as well as laws that protected drinking water and wild lands. The Environmental Protection Agency (EPA) was also created.

Rachel Carson (1907–1964), a noted marine biologist and one of America's first ecologists, was the author of a landmark book, *Silent Spring*, published in 1962. This carefully researched book focused worldwide attention on the environment and spurred a reversal in the nation's pesticide policy.

Ralph Nader (1934–), an American attorney and political activist, became famous for pointing out safety problems with automobiles. In 1965, he released *Unsafe at Any Speed* — a book that illustrated the fundamentally unsafe engineering of many American cars.

2. **Find pictures of cars from the 1960s and 1970s. How did they differ from the cars of today? Look for pictures of U.S. Mercury, Gemini, and Apollo spacecraft. Read about the moonwalks taken by American astronauts.**

Answer: "Pony cars" and "muscle cars" were hot-selling automobiles in the United States during the 1960s. A pony car was a class of compact, sporty automobiles, inspired by the 1964 Ford Mustang. A muscle car was a mid-size car with a large powerful engine (usually a V-8 engine) intended for maximum acceleration. The Pontiac GTO of 1964 is usually credited with starting the muscle car trend, which lasted until 1971.

The U.S. automobile industry was dramatically changed by the 1973 oil crisis, the passage of laws controlling automobile emissions, and increasing competition from Japanese and European imports. During the 1970s, small imported cars from Toyota, Nissan, and BMW outsold big-engine American cars.

Type "Mercury space program," "Gemini space program," and "Apollo space program" into an Internet search engine to find information and pictures.

3. **Read about the life of Bill Gates. What has he done in the years since he made his millions?**

Answer: William Henry "Bill" Gates (1955–), co-founder and chief software architect of Microsoft Corporation, became the world's first centibillionaire in 1999 when his wealth briefly surpassed the 100-billion-dollar mark. Gates began programming computers at the age of thirteen and left Harvard University his junior year to concentrate on developing Microsoft, a corporation that he formed with his childhood friend Paul Allen. In 2000, he and his wife founded the Bill and Melinda Gates Foundation to support philanthropic endeavors in the areas of education and global health.

4. **Research *Engel v. Vitale* (1962), *Wallace v. Jaffree* (1985), *Lee v. Weisman* (1992), and *Santa Fe ISD v. Doe.* (2000). What was the significance of the rulings by the Supreme Court in each of these cases?**

Answer: *Engel v. Vitale* (1962) was a landmark Supreme Court decision which established that it is unconstitutional for state officials to compose an official school prayer and require that it be recited in public schools (even if the prayer is nondenominational and students can be excused from participation). This decision became the basis for several subsequent decisions limiting government-directed prayer in school. In *Wallace v. Jaffree* (1985), the Supreme Court ruled that an Alabama law authorizing a one-minute period of silence in all public schools for voluntary prayer or meditation was unconstitutional. In *Lee v. Weisman* (1992), the Court prohibited clergy-led prayer as part of an official public school graduation ceremony. *Lee v. Weisman*, in turn, was a basis for *Santa Fe ISD v. Doe* (2000), in which the Court ruled that a policy allowing student-led, student-initiated prayer at football games was unconstitutional.

Lesson 29: For Further Study Younger Student Adaptations

1. Share with your younger students what happened at Three Mile Island and why Earth Day was established, as well as the causes promoted by Rachel Carson and Ralph Nader.

2. Show your younger students photographs of cars from the 1960s and 1970s, as well as pictures from the Mercury, Gemini, and Apollo space programs.

3. Have them read (or read to them) a short biography of Bill Gates.

4. Explain these four Supreme Court rulings on prayer in public schools.

Lesson 30: For Further Study Questions and Answers

1. **Read about the lives of Thurgood Marshall and Medgar Evers. For what are they remembered? Fill out African American forms on Marshall and Evers.**
   Answer: Thurgood Marshall (1909–1993) was the first African American to serve on the U.S. Supreme Court. A graduate of Howard University Law School, he became a counsel for the NAACP in 1938. Over a period of more than twenty years, Marshall won twenty-nine of the thirty-two cases that he undertook for the NAACP, opening many doors for African Americans. The most famous of these cases was _Brown v. Board of Education of Topeka, Kansas_.

   In 1961, President Kennedy appointed Marshall to the U.S. Court of Appeals for the Second Circuit. Four years later, President Johnson named him U.S. Solicitor General, and in 1967, Johnson appointed Thurgood Marshall to the Supreme Court. Marshall, who served on the high court for twenty-four years, was a steadfast liberal during his tenure and was known for his strong support for constitutional protection of individual rights.

   Medgar Evers (1925–1963) was an African American civil rights leader from Mississippi. A World War II veteran and college graduate, Evers applied to the all-white University of Mississippi law school in 1954. When Evers's application was rejected, he became the focus of an NAACP campaign to desegregate the school. In December 1954, Evers became the first NAACP field officer in Mississippi and moved to Jackson. There he was involved in a boycott against white merchants and fought for the enforcement of _Brown v. Board of Education of Topeka, Kansas_.

   Evers became the target of an increasing number of violent threats. On June 13, 1963, he pulled into his driveway after a late meeting. When Evers emerged from his car, he was shot in the back. Byron de La Beckwith, a member of the White Citizens' Council, was arrested for Evers's murder. Despite convincing evidence against Beckwith, two trials with all-white juries ended in deadlocks. More than three decades later, Beckwith was retried by a multiracial jury and found guilty.

2. **Find out more details concerning the 1960 sit-in at the Woolworth's in Greensboro, North Carolina, and the 1963 Birmingham demonstrations.**
   Answer: On February 1, 1960, four college freshmen from North Carolina Agricultural and Technical College bought some items at the local Woolworth's store in Greensboro, North Carolina. They then proceeded past the end of the store's lunch counter assigned to "coloreds" (a stand-up/take-out only section) and sat down on counter stools in the "whites only" section. Although they requested service, they knew they would be refused. In fact, they expected to be arrested or beaten. The four remained seated until the store closed.

In the days that followed, the Greensboro Four were joined by other students at the Woolworth's counter and at the nearby Kress 5 & 10 counter. Over the next six months, hundreds of students joined the sit-in. By the end of the summer, the counter was open to all races. By the end of 1961, student-led sit-ins had desegregated hundreds of stores and lunch counters throughout the South.

Martin Luther King, Jr., and the SCLC were invited to initiate a civil rights campaign in Birmingham, Alabama, in 1963. Birmingham, a stronghold of the Ku Klux Klan, had been nicknamed "Bombingham" because it had been the site of eighteen unsolved bombings in African American neighborhoods over a six-year period. In April of 1963, the SCLC began staging sit-ins in Birmingham. A number of protesters were arrested on Palm Sunday, and King was arrested on Good Friday. Placed in solitary confinement, King wrote his famous "Letter from Birmingham Jail."

After King was released from jail on April 20, SCLC organizers began planning a demonstration using African American children. On May 2, children ranging in age from six to eighteen gathered in a park across from the Sixteenth Street Baptist church. As groups of children left the area and headed downtown, they were arrested. Eventually, over 950 children were packed into the city jails. The next day, over 1,000 more children met in the park to demonstrate. Police Commissioner Eugene "Bull" Connor ordered his officers to use police dogs and fire hoses to break up the crowd of children and other protesters.

Photographs of the confrontation between the police and children shocked the entire country. The demonstrations continued, and Birmingham's jails overflowed. Finally, the Birmingham business community agreed to hire more African American sales and office workers and to integrate city lunch counters.

3. **For what did the X in Malcolm X stand? What happened to Malcolm X? Fill out an African American form on Malcolm X.**

Answer: Malcolm X (1925–1965), born Malcolm Little in Omaha, Nebraska, was the son of an African American Baptist preacher. In 1929, Malcolm moved with his family to Lansing, Michigan. Two years later, his father was found dead by a streetcar railway track. Malcolm believed that his father had been murdered by white supremacists. His mother, who never recovered from her husband's death, was committed to a mental institution.

Leaving school after the eighth grade, Malcolm moved east and lived in Boston and Harlem. He soon began selling and using drugs. Convicted of burglary in 1946, he was sentenced to a ten-year prison term. While in prison, Malcolm was converted to the Black Muslim faith, a sect headed by Elijah Muhammad. Muhammad taught that white society actively worked to keep African Americans from achieving political, economic, and social success. The Black Muslims sought to establish a state of their own, the Nation of Islam, separate from white society.

After his parole in 1952, Malcolm became a leading figure in the Nation of Islam. He changed his last name to X, a custom among Muhammad's followers, who believed that their last names had originated with white slaveholders. Malcolm chose *X* to signify his lost tribal name. Embarking on several speaking tours, he soon became well known for his inflammatory comments concerning the evils of white society and the need for black vengeance. Malcolm helped to establish several mosques and founded and edited *Muhammad Speaks*.

In March of 1964, Malcolm created his own religious organization, the Organization of Afro-American Unity. That same year he made a pilgrimage to Mecca and rejected his former extremist separatist views. He began urging African Americans to work with sympathetic whites to bring an end to racism. As a result of his changed views, Malcolm became the victim of death threats. His home was firebombed on February 14, 1965, and a week later, Malcolm was shot and killed at the Audubon Ballroom in Harlem. Three Black Muslims were later convicted of his murder. *The Autobiography of Malcolm X*, based on interviews that he had given to Alex Haley, was published in 1965.

4. **Discover the significance of Patricia Hearst and the Symbionese Liberation Army (SLA).**

    Answer: Patricia "Patty" Hearst (1954–), the granddaughter of publishing magnate William Randolph Hearst, became famous in February of 1974, when she was kidnapped from her Berkeley apartment by a group known as the Symbionese Liberation Army (SLA). The SLA, an urban terrorist group, demanded a ransom of four million dollars in food for the poor, which Hearst's parents paid. However, the nineteen-year-old heiress was not released.

    On April 15, 1974, Patty was photographed wielding an assault rifle while robbing a San Francisco bank. Later communications from Patty indicated that she had changed her name to Tania and had become committed to the goals of the SLA. A warrant was issued for Hearst's arrest, and she was arrested with other SLA members in September of 1975.

    In her trial, Hearst claimed that her actions were the result of being brainwashed by the SLA. Others believed that she suffered from "Stockholm syndrome," in which a captive becomes sympathetic to his or her captors. However, Hearst was convicted of bank robbery and sentenced to seven years in prison. Her sentence was eventually commuted by President Carter in 1979, and she was granted a full pardon by President Clinton on his last day in office in 2001.

Lesson 30: For Further Study Younger Student Adaptations

1. Have them read (or read to them) a short biography of Thurgood Marshall or Medgar Evers.

2. Share with them photographs and details concerning the 1960 Woolworth's sit-in and the 1963 Birmingham demonstrations.

3. Explain to your younger students who Malcolm X was and what he believed.

4. Show them photographs of Patricia Hearst (Tania) and tell them what the Symbionese Liberation Army was. Explain what brainwashing and the Stockholm syndrome are.

Lesson 31: For Further Study Questions and Answers

1. **Read about the Iran-Contra affair. What role did Oliver North play?**

    Answer: The Iran-Contra affair was a secret arrangement by several members of President Reagan's administration to provide funds to the Contra rebels in Nicaragua from profits gained from selling arms to Iran. The sale of American weapons to Iran was in violation of an American embargo on arms sales to nations supporting terrorism. This sale was arranged in the hope that it would lead to the release of six U.S. hostages held in Lebanon by Islamic militants friendly to Iran. Profits from selling these illegal arms were used to help right-wing Nicaraguan rebels known as the Contras, which was a violation of the Boland Amendment (prohibiting the federal government from providing military support for the purpose of overthrowing the government of Nicaragua).

    Oliver North, a member of the National Security Council, oversaw the arms sales to Iran and arranged to divert money to the Contras. In 1986, these activities became known to the American public, and in 1987, televised hearings concerning the Iran-Contra affair were held in Congress. President Reagan insisted that he knew nothing about the operation. A special review board, known as the Tower Commission, was appointed to look into the matter.

    The Tower Commission Report did not determine that the president had knowledge of the operation, but it did criticize him for not properly supervising his subordinates at the National Security Council. North and others were convicted of wrongdoing, but their convictions were overturned on a technicality by an appeals court. President Reagan survived the scandal, and his approval ratings returned to their previously high levels.

2. **Find out what NAFTA is and why it is significant.**

   Answer: The North American Free Trade Agreement (NAFTA) was signed in December of 1992 by U.S. President George H. W. Bush, Canadian Prime Minister Brian Mulroney, and Mexican President Carlos Salinas. It was approved by the U.S. Congress by the end of 1993 and then signed into law by President Bill Clinton. This agreement removed most barriers to trade and investments among the three countries. The United States and Canada had had a free trade agreement since 1989. NAFTA eliminated about half of the tariffs on trade between the United States and Mexico immediately and phased out most of the remaining tariffs and restrictions over a fifteen-year period. Under NAFTA, the three North American nations became a single, enormous, integrated market.

3. **Research the ratification of the Twenty-seventh Amendment. What was unique about this amendment?**

   Answer: The Twenty-seventh Amendment was first presented by James Madison on September 25, 1789, as one of the articles in the original Bill of Rights. However, it did not pass the required number of state legislatures for ratification and sat unratified with no expiration date for more than eighty years. The state of Ohio then ratified the Twenty-seventh Amendment as a protest to a congressional pay hike. Over one hundred more years passed until another state, Wyoming, ratified the amendment in 1978.

   In the early 1980s, Gregory Watson, an aide to a Texas legislator, began a campaign to push for ratification of the Twenty-seventh Amendment. Between 1983 and 1992, the required number of states ratified the amendment, and on May 7, 1992, it became the Twenty-seventh Amendment to the U.S. Constitution. This amendment has been nicknamed the "Congressional Compensation Amendment of 1789" and the "Congressional Pay Amendment."

4. **What happened in Waco, Texas, in April of 1993 and in Oklahoma City in April of 1995? Discover how these two events were connected. Research the activities of Theodore Kaczynski. Determine what the right-wing militia movement of this era believed and what actions they took.**

   Answer: The Branch Davidians, a religious paramilitary organization, had established their headquarters at a ranch about ten miles outside Waco and named it Mount Carmel Center. In 1993, this sect of more than one hundred followers was headed by a charismatic leader who called himself David Koresh (1959–1993). Federal agents from the FBI and the Bureau of Alcohol, Tobacco, and Firearms (ATF) were investigating their frequent shipments of large quantities of firearms, as well as allegations of child abuse and polygamy made against the group.

   At the end of February of 1993, more than seventy agents from the ATF attempted to serve a search warrant on Koresh and his followers at the Mount Carmel Center. As they charged the house, they were met with gunfire. Six members of the Branch Davidians and four ATF agents were killed. Koresh, who was seriously injured, and his followers refused to leave the compound. The FBI took command of the operation for the federal government, and negotiations continued between the Branch Davidians and the FBI for the next fifty-one days.

   Finally, Attorney General Janet Reno approved an FBI recommendation to remove the Branch Davidians from their compound by force. During the assault on April 19, the church building caught fire, and seventy-six Branch Davidians (including Koresh) died. The Danforth Report, commissioned by the federal government, determined that the fire was deliberately set by the Branch Davidians inside the building. Others groups presented evidence that the fire was caused by the FBI's firing of an incendiary device into the building after filling it with flammable gas. Autopsy reports indicated that at least twenty of the Branch Davidians actually died from gunshot wounds. The Danforth Report maintained that the adults shot themselves after shooting the children, while others pointed to evidence that FBI sharpshooters shot the Branch Davidians as they were attempting to escape the fire.

On April 19, 1995, a truck bomb blew a nine-story hole in the Alfred P. Murrah Federal Building in Oklahoma City. This building housed the offices of the FBI; the Bureau of Alcohol, Tobacco, and Firearms; Social Security; and other federal agencies. The final death toll was 168, including 19 children who were being cared for in a day-care facility in the Murrah building. Over 800 were injured, and many buildings in the surrounding area were damaged. The terrorist responsible for this deadliest domestic terrorist attack in U.S. history was a 27-year-old Gulf War veteran named Timothy McVeigh, along with his accomplice Terry Nichols. The attack was staged on the second anniversary of the Waco siege.

McVeigh, who saw himself as a crusader and a defender of the U.S. Constitution, was reported to have had connections to right-wing militia groups. These suspected links led to the focusing of widespread national media attention upon the American militia movement. These antigovernment groups claimed immunity from U.S. laws and regulations and believed that the Constitution sanctioned any means (including violence) to overthrow a tyrannical government. They collected weapons and ammunition, had links to white supremacists, and believed in elaborate conspiracy theories. In the weeks following the Oklahoma City bombing, federal government buildings in all major cities were surrounded with barriers as protection against other paramilitary attacks. McVeigh was sentenced to death and executed by lethal injection in 2001, and Nichols was sentenced to life in prison.

From 1978 to 1995, a terrorist named Theodore "Ted" Kaczynski (1942–) mailed homemade bombs to Americans working in high-tech fields. He eventually killed three people and injured twenty-nine with his bombs and became the target of the most expensive manhunt in FBI history. In 1995, Kaczynski, who became known as the Unabomber, contacted officials to let them know that the killings would stop if his thirty-five-thousand-word attack against modern society was published in a major national newspaper. He justified his crimes as a fight against the evils of technological progress.

When *The New York Times* and *The Washington Post* printed the article, Kaczynski's brother recognized Ted's writings and contacted the FBI. When a team of forensic linguists compared writing samples provided by Ted's brother and mother with the Unabomber's writings, they determined that they had been written by the same person. Kaczynski was arrested in April of 1996 and was sentenced to a life sentence without possibility of parole.

Lesson 31: For Further Study Younger Student Adaptations

1. Have them read (or read to them) a short biography of Reagan and concentrate on the chapter that addresses the Iran-Contra affair.

2. Review with your younger students the meaning of a tariff. Explain to them what NAFTA is and why it is significant.

3. Explain the unique history behind the Twenty-seventh Amendment.

4. Share with them the stories of the Waco siege, the Oklahoma City bombing, and the Unabomber. Describe the right-wing militia movement of this period in U.S. history.

Lesson 32: For Further Study Questions and Answers

1. Discover the significance of Rodney King and the 1995 Million Man March. Read about the lives of Jesse Jackson and Ben Carson and fill out African American forms for them.

    Answer: In March of 1991, an African American motorist named Rodney King and two passengers led police on a high-speed chase near Los Angeles. When the car was finally stopped, King resisted arrest. The four white policemen beat King repeatedly, mostly with their nightsticks, and a witness videotaped the incident. This tape was played over and over again on national television. King suffered eleven skull fractures, broken teeth and bones, and permanent brain damage. When the white policemen were acquitted of assault charges in April of 1992, a major riot broke out in Los Angeles. By the second day of these riots, fire had consumed twenty-five blocks of the city, and looting, arson, and assaults had taken a huge toll. Forty people were killed, over two thousand were injured, and more than eight thousand were arrested. Rodney King himself pleaded for peace. Violent incidents also occurred in other U.S. cities.

    The Million Man March, an African American march of protest and unity, took place in Washington, D.C., on October 16, 1995. Organized by Nation of Islam leader Louis Farrakhan, the male-only event sought to renew African American commitment to marriage, family, voting, political activism, and volunteerism. The hope of the march's organizers was to defy negative stereotypes of black males in the United States. However, some called the event sexist, and others criticized the participation of racist and anti-Semitic leaders. The actual number of participants in the Million Man March is disputed.

    Jesse L. Jackson, Jr. (1941–), a prominent African American civil rights activist, politician, and Baptist minister, was a candidate for the Democratic presidential nomination in 1984 and 1988. A close associate of Martin Luther King, Jr., Jackson served as head of the SCLC's economic program, Operation Breadbasket. He was present in Memphis when King was assassinated.

    After King's death, Jackson increasingly clashed with Ralph Abernathy, King's successor as head of the SCLC. In 1971, Abernathy suspended Jackson for administrative "improprieties," and Jackson resigned from the SCLC and founded Operation PUSH (People United to Serve Humanity), an organization that pushed for jobs and economic opportunities for African Americans and other minorities. In 1985, Jackson formed another nonprofit organization, the National Rainbow Coalition, which merged with Operation PUSH in 1996. The RainbowPUSH Coalition (RPC) is a political organization that states that its mission is to fight for equal protection under the law, equal opportunity, and equal access for people of all races, religions, and cultures.

    Benjamin S. "Ben" Carson (1951–), a noted African American neurosurgeon, became the director of pediatric neurosurgery at Johns Hopkins Hospital when he was only thirty-two years old. In 1987, he won national attention when he separated conjoined twins who shared part of the same brain. In addition to being a surgeon, Carson has authored several books that incorporate his belief in hard work and faith in God. He has also been a spokesman for creationism over evolution in both the scientific and religious communities.

2. Find out the meaning of the following financial terms — junk bonds, corporate raids, and insider trading. Learn what the Y2K bug was.

    Answer: A junk bond is the popular name for a high-risk investment offered by corporations. Money for many takeovers is raised by the sale of junk bonds.

    A corporate raid is a hostile takeover in which the assets of the purchased company are immediately sold off and the target company disappears. In the 1970s and 1980s, a handful of U.S. corporate raiders built up large lines of credit and purchased large companies for little or no cash, often through issuing junk bonds.

    Insider trading is making an investment decision based on information not available to the general public. The information may allow the individual to profit or to avoid loss. This practice is illegal; penalties for insider trading generally consist of jail time and a fine. Examples of individuals convicted of insider trading include Michael Milken, Ivan Boesky, and Martha Stewart.

The Y2K bug, or the millennium bug, was the speculation that computer programs would stop working or produce errors on January 1, 2000, because they stored years with only two digits. Thus, the year 2000 would be represented by 00 and interpreted by software as the year 1900. The fear that critical industries (financial, electrical) would stop working was fueled by media speculation, as well as by government and corporation reports. Billions of dollars were spent to make companies Y2K-compliant. When January 1, 2000, arrived, only minor problems were reported, and many of the problems did not occur precisely at midnight.

3. **Read about Christa McAuliffe, who died in the *Challenger* space shuttle explosion. Why was McAuliffe chosen to fly on this mission? What did she hope to accomplish on the flight? Why did the shuttle explode?**

   Answer: Christa McAuliffe (1948–1986), a teacher from Concord, New Hampshire, was selected from more than eleven thousand applicants to be the first teacher in space. In the fall of 1985, McAuliffe and her backup teacher took a yearlong leave of absence from teaching to train with NASA for an early 1986 space shuttle mission. McAuliffe believed that students learned best with hands-on experiences, and she referred to her trip on the space shuttle *Challenger* as the "ultimate field trip." She had excellent rapport with the media and succeeded in generating widespread popular attention for NASA's Teacher in Space program.

   Just seventy-three seconds after liftoff, the *Challenger* exploded because of an O-ring seal failure in the booster system. All astronauts on board, including McAuliffe, were killed. While in space, Christa would have taught two lessons. In her first lesson, she had planned to introduce each flight member; explain each person's role; show the cockpit; and describe how crew members ate, slept, and exercised. In her second lesson, she had planned to offer an explanation of how the shuttle flew, the reasons for space exploration, and the technological advances created by the space program. Throughout the mission, McAuliffe would also have kept a journal, inspired by the journals of the pioneer women who left home for the frontier. Christa believed that space was the "new frontier," and her motto was: "I touch the future. I teach."

4. **Learn who founded the Parents Music Resource Center and why it was founded. Determine who started CNN and why its launching was significant.**

   The Parents Music Resource Center (PMRC) was founded in 1985 by the wives of several U.S. congressmen, including Tipper Gore, Susan Baker, and Nancy Thurmond. The mission of the committee was to educate parents about trends in rock music that they considered alarming — glorification of drug use, rape, murder, suicide, and other violent acts. They pressured the Recording Industry Association of America (RIAA) to require that labels be put on all records containing explicit content. Opponents claimed that record labeling violated First Amendment rights.

   Under pressure from the PMRC, in the fall of 1985, hearings were held by the U.S. Senate Committee on Commerce, Science, and Transportation to investigate the pornographic content of rock music. Before the hearings were over, the RIAA agreed to put labels on records containing what the PMRC saw as explicit content. The label became known as the "tipper sticker." Some stores, such as Wal-Mart, refused to sell albums containing the sticker, while others would not sell such albums to minors.

   The Cable News Network (CNN) was founded by Ted Turner on June 1, 1980. CNN introduced the concept of twenty-four-hour television news coverage. Its global reputation was enhanced by its coverage of the Gulf War in 1991.

Lesson 32: For Further Study Younger Student Adaptations

1. Have your younger students read (or read to them) a short biography of Jesse Jackson or Ben Carson.

2. Explain the Y2K bug.

3. Share with them the story of Christa McAuliffe and NASA's Teacher in Space program, as well as the details of the *Challenger* explosion.

4. Discuss with your students the significance of the Parents Music Resource Center.

Section Five

ANSWER KEY TO THE
FORMS, MAPS, AND
FOR REVIEW QUESTIONS

Lessons 1 — 32
in the Student Activity Book

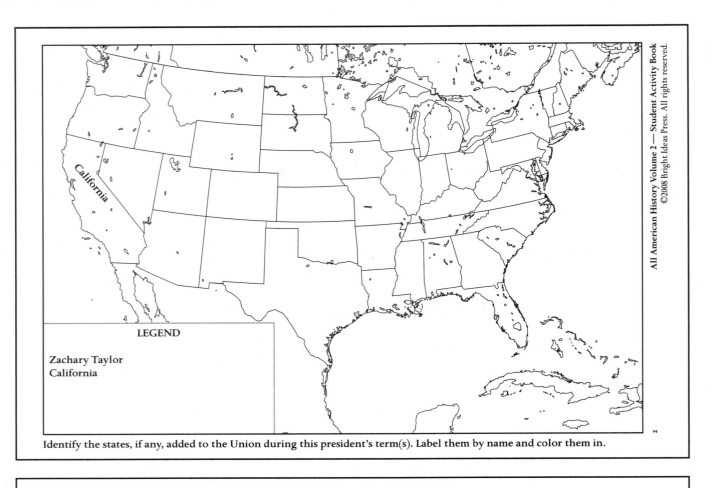

California

LEGEND

Zachary Taylor
California

Identify the states, if any, added to the Union during this president's term(s). Label them by name and color them in.

2

Name _____ Date _____

LESSON 1: ZACHARY TAYLOR

Picture of the president

Year born ___1784___

Year died ___1850___

In which state was he born? ___Virginia___

What jobs did he hold before becoming president? ___40 years of service in the U.S. military – popular general and war hero ("Old Rough and Ready")___

With what political party was this president affiliated? ___Whig___

Vice President: ___Millard Fillmore___

What were the years of his presidency? ___1849 – 1850___

List some significant developments during his administration ___Debate over whether the territories taken from Mexico (after the Mexican War) should be open to slaves___

___Congressional work on what would become known as the Compromise of 1850___

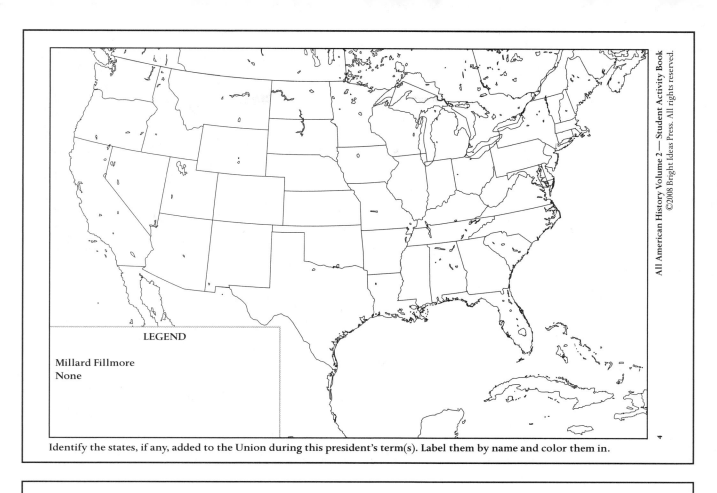

Identify the states, if any, added to the Union during this president's term(s). **Label them by name and color them in.**

Name _____ Date _____

LESSON 1: MILLARD FILLMORE

Picture of the president

Year born _____ 1800_____

Year died _____ 1874_____

In which state was he born? _____ New York_____

What jobs did he hold before becoming president? _____ Lawyer, N.Y. state senator,_____

U.S. Representative, Vice President

With what political party was this president affiliated? _____ **Whig**_____

Vice President: _____ None_____

What were the years of his presidency? _____ **1850 – 1853**_____

List some significant developments during his administration _____ **Ratification of the**

Compromise of 1850

Commodore Matthew Perry's trade mission to Japan (led to the Treaty of

Kanagawa a year after Fillmore left office)

First federal aid for the building of railroads

Lesson 1: Prelude to the Civil War
©2008 Bright Ideas Press. All rights reserved.

Answer Key to the Forms, Maps, and For Review Questions in the Student Activity Book

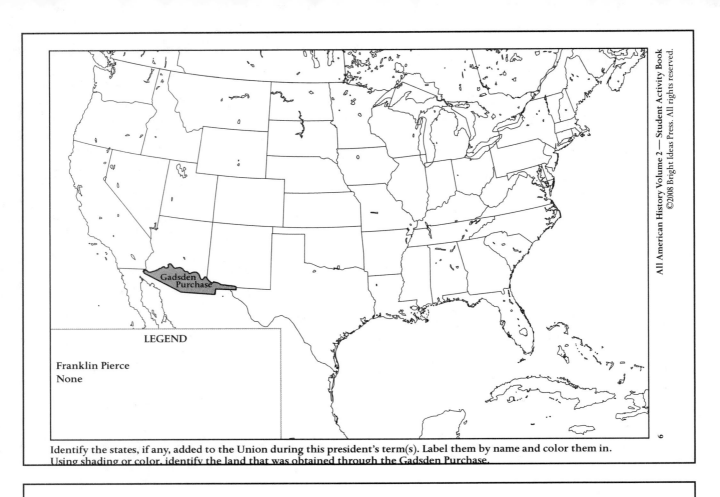

Identify the states, if any, added to the Union during this president's term(s). Label them by name and color them in.
Using shading or color, identify the land that was obtained through the Gadsden Purchase.

6

Name _____   Date _____

LESSON 1: FRANKLIN PIERCE

Picture of the president

Year born ___1804___

Year died ___1869___

In which state was he born?   New Hampshire

What jobs did he hold before becoming president?   Lawyer, U.S. military,
U.S. Representative, U.S. Senator

With what political party was this president affiliated?   Democratic

Vice President: William R. King, None

What were the years of his presidency?   1853 – 1857

List some significant developments during his administration

Kansas-Nebraska Act of 1854

"Bleeding Kansas" controversy

Founding of the Republican Party

Gadsden Purchase

Treaty of Kanagawa (with Japan)

Treaty with Britain for fishing rights off Newfoundland

Lesson 1: Prelude to the Civil War
©2008 Bright Ideas Press. All rights reserved.

5

All American History, Vol. II: Teacher's Guide — Section Five

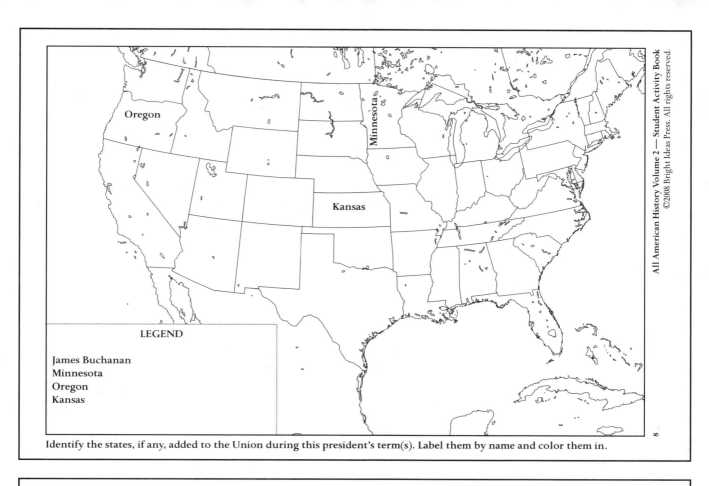

Identify the states, if any, added to the Union during this president's term(s). Label them by name and color them in.

8

Name _____ Date _____

LESSON 1: JAMES BUCHANAN

Picture of the president

Year born ____ 1791 ____

Year died ____ 1868 ____

In which state was he born? ____ Pennsylvania ____

What jobs did he hold before becoming president? ____ Pennsylvania state legislator, ____

____ U.S. Representative, U.S. minister to Russia, U.S. Senator, Secretary of State, ____

____ U.S. minister to Britain ____

With what political party was this president affiliated? ____ Democratic ____

Vice President: ____ John C. Breckinridge ____

What were the years of his presidency? ____ 1857 – 1861 ____

List some significant developments during his administration ____ Scott v. Sandford ____

____ Panic of 1857 ____

____ Southern threats of secession ____

Answer Key to the Forms, Maps, and For Review Questions in the Student Activity Book
145

LESSON 1: FOR REVIEW

Write T for True and F for False in the space provided.

__T__ 1. For more than forty years before the Civil War began, American political parties were forced to cope with the different outlooks and needs of the slave-based southern economy and industrial-based northern economy.

__F__ 2. The Constitution of the United States made slavery illegal in the United States, but the South only half-heartedly enforced this prohibition of slavery.

__F__ 3. Charleston, South Carolina, served as the center of the American slave market.

__T__ 4. The 1820 Compromise allowed Missouri to enter the Union as a slave state if Maine came in as a free state.

__T__ 5. The Underground Railroad made it possible for thousands of American slaves to escape to freedom before the Civil War.

__F__ 6. Perhaps the best known of all the conductors on the Underground Railroad was Harriet Beecher Stowe.

__F__ 7. From 1849 until 1861, the American presidency was occupied by strong leaders, who worked successfully to stem the rising tide of American sectionalism.

__T__ 8. President Zachary Taylor stood firmly against the threats of secession from southern leaders, declaring that he would personally lead the army sent to put down their rebellion.

__F__ 9. If President Taylor had not died unexpectedly, he would certainly have signed into law the bills comprising the 1850 Compromise.

__F__ 10. Millard Fillmore, elected president by an overwhelming majority, refused to sign the Compromise of 1850.

__F__ 11. The 1850 Compromise allowed the slave trade in the District of Columbia to continue but made it harder for slave owners to capture fugitive slaves.

__F__ 12. Under the terms of the 1850 Compromise, California entered the Union as a slave state, and the Utah and New Mexico territories would enter as free states.

__T__ 13. The more militant northern Whigs became angry with Fillmore for supporting the Fugitive Slave Act and worked to prevent him from receiving the 1852 presidential nomination.

__T__ 14. President Fillmore believed that the federal government should encourage and help business at home and abroad and sent Commodore Matthew Perry on a trade mission to Japan.

__T__ 15. The greatest controversy during the administration of Franklin Pierce was the Kansas-Nebraska Act of 1854, which in essence repealed the Missouri Compromise of 1820.

__F__ 16. President Pierce succeeded in restoring order to "Bleeding Kansas."

__F__ 17. Secretary of War Jefferson Davis was unable to persuade Pierce to agree to the Gadsden Purchase, and Pierce also refused to work for the purchase of Cuba, Alaska, and Hawaii.

__T__ 18. Unfortunately, two days into the presidency of James Buchanan, the Supreme Court issued its highly controversial decision in *Scott v. Sandford*.

__T__ 19. There were four presidential candidates in the 1860 election.

__F__ 20. After Lincoln's election as president in 1860, President Buchanan maintained that the southern states had a legal right to secede.

LESSON 1: FOR FURTHER STUDY

For even more interesting information about this period of history, please refer to the For Further Study answers for this lesson in the Teacher's Guide.

1. Research the life of Levi Coffin, a Quaker known as the "president" of the Underground Railroad. How many slaves did he help to escape? See if you can find an excerpt from his book, *Reminiscences of Levi Coffin*, and read it. Where is the National Historic Landmark Levi Coffin House located?

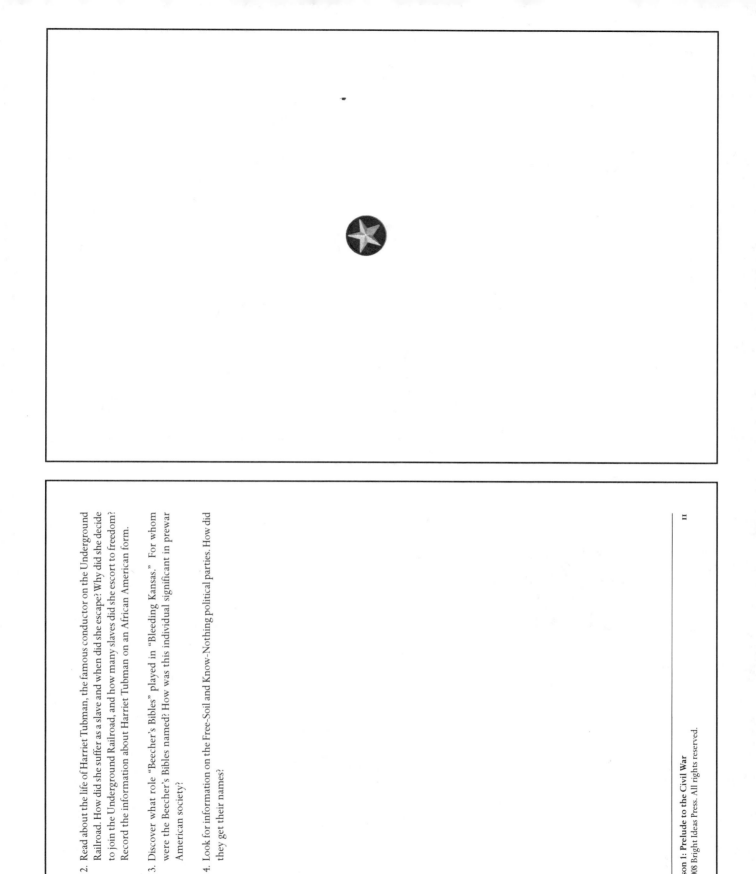

2. Read about the life of Harriet Tubman, the famous conductor on the Underground Railroad. How did she suffer as a slave and when did she escape? Why did she decide to join the Underground Railroad, and how many slaves did she escort to freedom? Record the information about Harriet Tubman on an African American form.

3. Discover what role "Beecher's Bibles" played in "Bleeding Kansas." For whom were the Beecher's Bibles named? How was this individual significant in prewar American society?

4. Look for information on the Free-Soil and Know-Nothing political parties. How did they get their names?

Lesson 1: Prelude to the Civil War
©2008 Bright Ideas Press. All rights reserved.

11

Answer Key to the Forms, Maps, and For Review Questions in the Student Activity Book

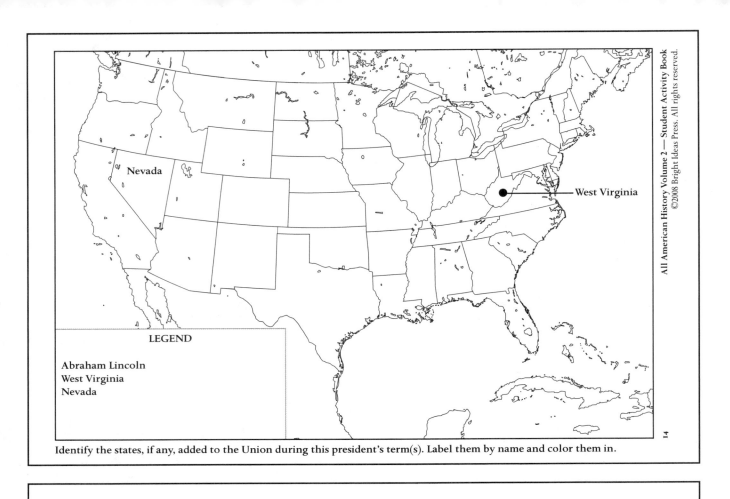

Identify the states, if any, added to the Union during this president's term(s). Label them by name and color them in.

14

Name _____ Date _____

LESSON 2: ABRAHAM LINCOLN

Picture of the president

Year born ___1809___

Year died ___1865___

In which state was he born? ___Kentucky___

What jobs did he hold before becoming president? ___Lawyer, Illinois state legislator,___

___U.S. Representative___

With what political party was this president affiliated? ___Republican___

Vice President: ___Hannibal Hamlin, Andrew Johnson___

What were the years of his presidency? ___1861 - 1865___

List some significant developments during his administration ___Civil War___

___Emancipation Proclamation___

13

148

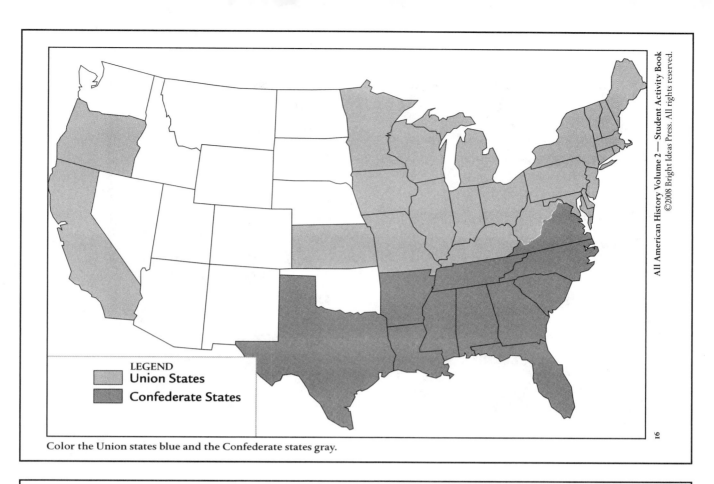

Color the Union states blue and the Confederate states gray.

LESSON 2: UNION AND CONFEDERATE STATES

Fill in the blanks with the appropriate Union and Confederate states.

Union States	Confederate States
Maine	Virginia
New Hampshire	North Carolina
Vermont	South Carolina
Massachusetts	Georgia
Rhode Island	Florida
Connecticut	Tennessee
New York	Alabama
New Jersey	Mississippi
Delaware	Arkansas
Maryland	Louisiana
Pennsylvania	Texas
Ohio	
Michigan	
Indiana	
Kentucky	
Illinois	
Wisconsin	
Minnesota	
Iowa	
Missouri	
Kansas	
Oregon	
California	
West Virginia	
Nevada	

Answer Key to the Forms, Maps, and For Review Questions in the Student Activity Book

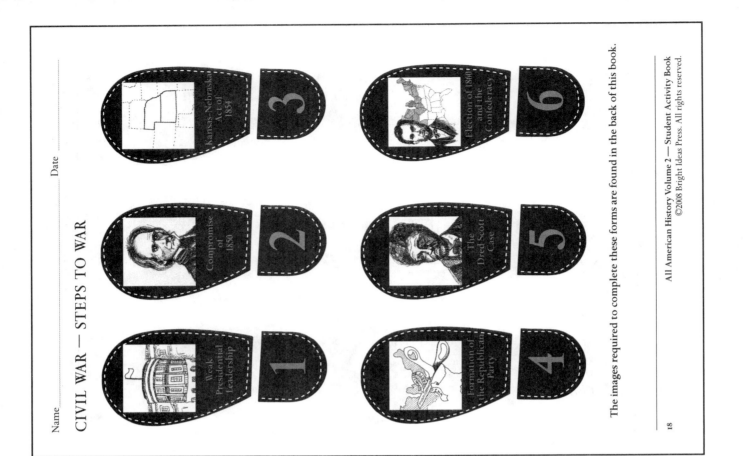

Name _____ Date _____

CIVIL WAR — STEPS TO WAR

3 — Kansas-Nebraska Act of 1854

6 — Election of 1860 and the Confederacy

2 — Compromise of 1850

5 — The Dred Scott Case

1 — Weak Presidential Leadership

4 — Formation of the Republican Party

The images required to complete these forms are found in the back of this book.

All American History Volume 2 — Student Activity Book
©2008 Bright Ideas Press. All rights reserved.

18

Name _____ Date _____

CIVIL WAR HALL OF FAME AND STEPS TO WAR

LESSONS 1–3

Harriet Tubman

Dred Scott

William Lloyd Garrison

Harriet Beecher Stowe

Frederick Douglass

Sojourner Truth

John Brown

Abraham Lincoln

Jefferson Davis

Brigadier General Pierre Beauregard

General Robert E. Lee

General Ulysses S. Grant

The images required to complete these forms are found in the back of this book. Cut and paste them in the appropriate squares. (The corresponding lesson number is in each square.)

Lesson 2: The Civil War Begins
©2008 Bright Ideas Press. All rights reserved.

17

LESSON 2: FOR REVIEW

Write the corresponding letter of the correct answer in the space provided.

A. Major Robert Anderson
B. Brigadier General Pierre Beauregard
C. John Brown
D. Jefferson Davis
E. Frederick Douglass
F. William Lloyd Garrison
G. Colonel Robert E. Lee
H. Abraham Lincoln
I. Harriet Beecher Stowe

C 1. Fanatical abolitionist, who attempted to start a slave rebellion in Harpers Ferry, Virginia

H 2. Sixteenth president of the United States

E 3. Freed slave who worked in the abolitionist movement

I 4. Author of *Uncle Tom's Cabin*

B 5. Commander of the Confederate troops who fired the first shots of the Civil War at Fort Sumter

G 6. Leader of the battalion of U.S. Marines sent to capture John Brown

D 7. President of the Confederate States of America

A 8. U.S. Army officer in charge of the Union troops at Fort Sumter

F 9. Editor of the abolitionist newspaper, *The Liberator*

Write the missing word or words in the spaces provided.

1. The first state to secede from the Union was __South Carolina__ . By early February, __6__ more states had seceded.

2. The Confederate constitution was adopted in the city of __Montgomery, Alabama.__

---

3. The Civil War can be measured in how many Aprils? __5__ months.

4. Both the Union and Confederacy hoped to end the war in __3__ months.

5. By the summer of 1861, Lincoln had called for a __naval blockade__ of all the ports of seceding states.

6. The total number of states in the Confederacy was __11__ .

7. The number of states that remained in the Union was __23__ .

8. By the end of May, the Confederate capital had been moved to __Richmond, Virginia.__

9. The new state that entered the Union in 1863 was __West Virginia__ .

10. During the war, the Union flag had __0__ stars removed.

11. Many believed that the Confederacy had a possibility of winning the war if it captured the city of __Washington, D.C.__ or inflicted a major defeat on the Union quickly.

Write U for Union and C for Confederacy in the space provided.

U 1. Nation with more financial resources

C 2. Nation with more military colleges

U 3. Nation with greater industrial strength

U _____ 4. Nation with larger population

C _____ 5. Nation with psychological advantage of defending its homeland

U _____ 6. Nation with larger army and navy

U _____ 7. Nation with greater railroad mileage

LESSON 2: FOR FURTHER STUDY
For even more interesting information about this period of history, please refer to the For Further Study answers for this lesson in the Teacher's Guide.

1. Look for information on the life of Angelina Grimke, a southerner who moved to the North to join the abolitionist movement. See if you can find excerpts from her pamphlet, *An Appeal to the Christian Women of the South*. Do you agree with what she wrote?

2. Research the lives of Frederick Douglass and/or Sojourner Truth. Record the information on an African American form.

3. Find out more about the abolitionist activities of John Brown. What role did he play in "Bleeding Kansas"?

4. Mary Chesnut, whose husband served in the Confederate army, lived in Richmond for much of the Civil War. She knew President and Mrs. Davis and many other important Confederate government officials personally. Mrs. Chesnut kept a diary throughout the war. See if you can find excerpts from her diary to read.

21

All American History, Vol. II: Teacher's Guide — Section Five

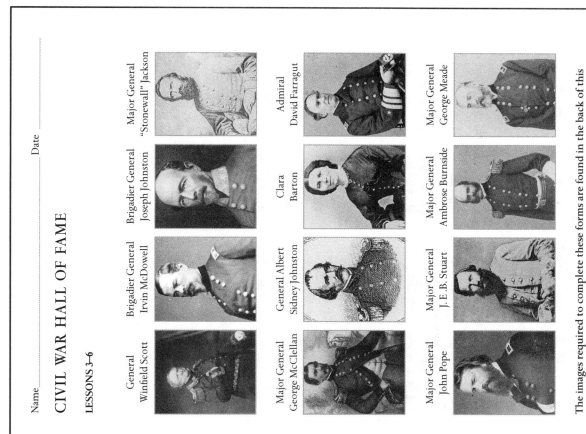

Name _____ Date _____

CIVIL WAR HALL OF FAME

LESSONS 3–6

Major General
William Rosecrans

General
Braxton Bragg

General William
Tecumseh Sherman

Brigadier General
John Hood

All American History Volume 2 — Student Activity Book
©2008 Bright Ideas Press. All rights reserved.

Name _____ Date _____

CIVIL WAR HALL OF FAME

LESSONS 3–6

General
Winfield Scott

Brigadier General
Irvin McDowell

Brigadier General
Joseph Johnston

Major General
"Stonewall" Jackson

Major General
George McClellan

General Albert
Sidney Johnston

Clara
Barton

Admiral
David Farragut

Major General
John Pope

Major General
J. E .B. Stuart

Major General
Ambrose Burnside

Major General
George Meade

The images required to complete these forms are found in the back of this book. Cut and paste them in the appropriate squares. (The corresponding lesson number is in each square.)

Lesson 3: First Year of the Civil War
©2008 Bright Ideas Press. All rights reserved.

Answer Key to the Forms, Maps, and For Review Questions in the Student Activity Book

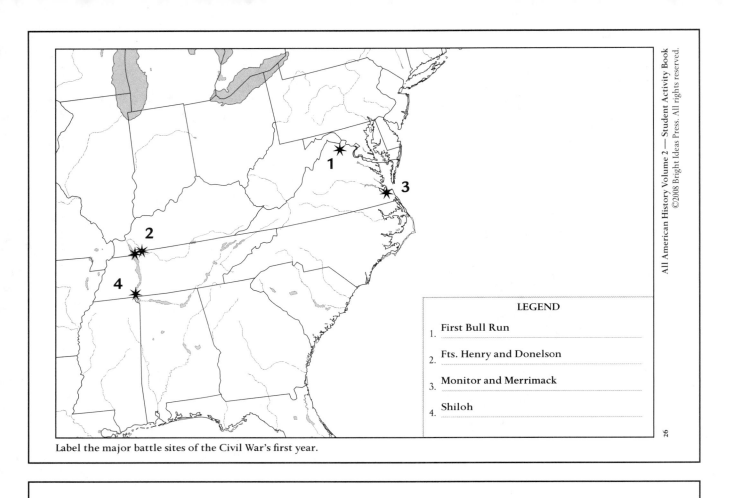

Label the major battle sites of the Civil War's first year.

LEGEND

1. First Bull Run _____

2. Fts. Henry and Donelson _____

3. Monitor and Merrimack _____

4. Shiloh _____

26

Name _____   Date _____

LESSON 3: FIRST YEAR OF THE CIVIL WAR

MAJOR BATTLES OF THE CIVIL WAR'S FIRST YEAR

Color the square blue if the battle was a Union victory. Color the square gray if the battle was a Confederate victory, or write a *D* in the square if the battle was a draw. Record the date of the battle in the parentheses. Write the name of the state, territory, or body of water in which the battle took place, and write the name(s) of the important Union and Confederate leaders involved.

[C] First Battle of Bull Run, or First Battle of Manassas (July 21, 1861)

Location: _____ Manassas, Virginia

Union leaders: Irvin McDowell

Confederate leaders: _____

Pierre Beauregard, Joseph Johnston,

Stonewall Jackson, Bernard Bee

[U] Battle of Fort Henry
(Feb. 6, 1862)

Location: _____ Tennessee River

(Tennessee & Kentucky)

Union leaders: _____ U. S. Grant

[U] Battle of Fort Donelson
(Feb. 16, 1862)

Location: _____ Cumberland River

(Tennessee)

Union leaders: _____ U. S. Grant

Confederate leaders: _____ Simon Bolivar

Buckner

[D] Monitor vs. Merrimack
(March 8 - 9, 1862)

Location: _____ Hampton Roads,

Virginia

[U] Battle of Pittsburg Landing, or Battle of Shiloh (April 6 - 7, 1862)

Location: _____ Pittsburg Landing,

Tennessee

Union leaders: _____ U. S. Grant

Confederate leaders: _____ Albert Sidney

Johnston, Pierre Beauregard

LESSON 3: FOR REVIEW

Write the letter of the correct answer in the space provided.

B _____ 1. The Civil War was fought on
  A. one front
  B. two fronts
  C. three fronts
  D. four fronts

C _____ 2. Which of the following is a true statement about the Civil War?
  A. all the battles were fought east of the Mississippi
  B. most historians have concentrated on the battles fought west of the Mississippi
  C. battles were fought as far away as New Mexico
  D. fewer than thirty battles were fought during the four years of the war

D _____ 3. Most battles in the Civil War were
  A. given only one name
  B. named for states
  C. fought using guerilla tactics
  D. given different names by the Confederacy and the Union

C _____ 4. Confederate armies were
  A. named for rivers
  B. concentrated primarily in Florida and Georgia
  C. hopeful of gaining European allies
  D. constantly moving, not willing merely to hold their own until the Union became weary of the war

---

C _____ 5. Robert E. Lee
  A. found it easy to turn down the offer of field command of the Union army
  B. assumed command of all the Confederate armies at the very beginning of the war
  C. displayed boldness and an ability to anticipate his opponent's next moves
  D. worked out a long-range battle strategy for Confederate forces

B _____ 6. Union armies were
  A. named for mountains
  B. at first led by generals who did not meet Lincoln's expectations
  C. successful in executing the Anaconda Plan from the very beginning
  D. always commanded by Ulysses S. Grant

A _____ 7. Which of the following was NOT true of the Anaconda Plan?
  A. it was developed by Major General George McClellan
  B. it called for a naval blockade of the South
  C. it advocated sealing off the South's inland borders
  D. it called for advancing south by means of the four great southern rivers

A _____ 8. The First Battle of Bull Run
  A. was fought to gain control of a railroad junction at Manassas, Virginia
  B. ended in Union victory
  C. convinced the Lincoln administration that the war could be won quickly
  D. led to a change in command for the Confederate forces

B _____ 9. Fort Henry and Fort Donelson were
  A. located in Virginia
  B. captured by Union troops led by Ulysses S. Grant
  C. not significant to the Union
  D. able to hold off the attacking Union troops

Answer Key to the Forms, Maps, and For Review Questions in the Student Activity Book

LESSON 3: FOR FURTHER STUDY

For even more interesting information about this period of history, please refer to the For Further Study answers for this lesson in the Teacher's Guide.

1. There were many names given to the conflict that we know today as the Civil War. What name for the war did most southerners prefer? See how many of these names you can find and decide which side would have preferred each name.

2. Research the history of the Confederate flag. Explain its symbolism. How is this flag controversial today?

3. One of the first accounts of the infamous "rebel yell" came from the First Battle of Bull Run. What was the purpose of this yell? How did it sound and from where did it originate?

4. Many new words came from the Civil War. Three of these were *sideburns, chignon,* and *greenbacks.* Look for the origin and definition of these words.

C___ 10. The *Merrimack*

    A. sank the *Monitor*

    B. was responsible for making ironclad ships obsolete

    C. prevented McClellan from using the James River in his campaign to capture Richmond

    D. was captured by the *Monitor*

D___ 11. General Albert Sidney Johnston

    A. secured a Confederate victory at Shiloh

    B. succeeded in recovering much of Tennessee for the Confederacy

    C. chose Chattanooga as the staging area for a Confederate offensive

    D. died at Shiloh

Write the corresponding letter of the correct answer in the space provided.

A. Pierre G. T. Beauregard   E. Irvin McDowell
B. Ulysses S. Grant   F. Thomas Jackson
C. Robert E. Lee   G. Albert Sidney Johnston
D. George McClellan   H. Joseph E. Johnston
    I. Winfield Scott

F___ 1. Received the nickname "Stonewall" at the First Battle of Bull Run

I___ 2. Developed the Anaconda Plan

C___ 3. Refused the offer of field command of the Union army

D___ 4. Replaced Irvin McDowell after the Union loss at Bull Run

H___ 5. Brought Confederate reinforcements to the First Battle of Bull Run

B___ 6. Led Union forces that captured Fort Henry and Fort Donelson

A___ 7. Commanded Confederate troops at the battles of Bull Run and Shiloh

G___ 8. Died at the Battle of Shiloh

E___ 9. Led Union forces that lost the Battle of Bull Run

Lesson 3: First Year of the Civil War

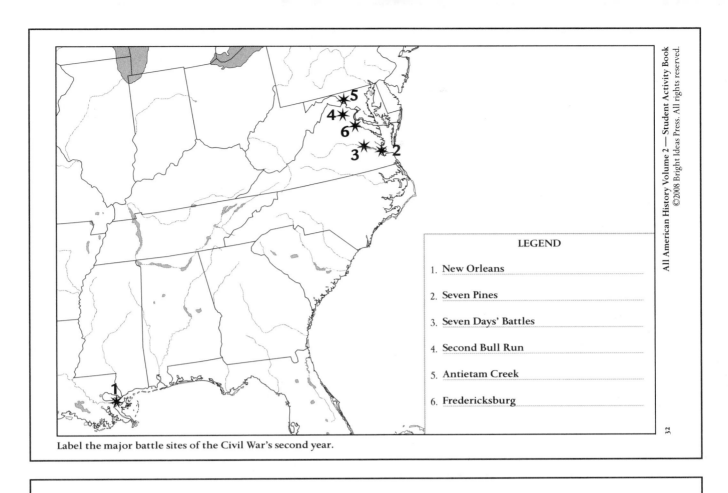

Label the major battle sites of the Civil War's second year.

LEGEND

1. New Orleans

2. Seven Pines

3. Seven Days' Battles

4. Second Bull Run

5. Antietam Creek

6. Fredericksburg

Name _____ Date _____

LESSON 4: SECOND YEAR OF THE CIVIL WAR

MAJOR BATTLES OF THE CIVIL WAR'S SECOND YEAR

Color the square blue if the battle was a Union victory. Color the square gray if the battle was a Confederate victory, or write a *D* in the square if the battle was a draw. Record the date of the battle in the parentheses. Write the name of the state, territory, or body of water in which the battle took place, and write the name(s) of the important Union and Confederate leaders involved.

U Battle of New Orleans
(April 24 - 25, 1862)

Location: New Orleans, Louisiana

Union leaders: Admiral David Farragut

D Battle of Seven Pines, or Battle of Fair Oaks (May 31 - June 1, 1862)

Location: Seven Pines, Virginia

Union leaders: George McClellan

Confederate leaders: Joseph Johnston

C Seven Days' Battles
(June 25 - July 1, 1862)

Location: near Richmond, Virginia

Union leaders: George McClellan

Confederate leaders: Robert E. Lee,

Stonewall Jackson

C Second Battle of Bull Run, or Second Battle of Manassas
(Aug. 29 - 30, 1862)

Location: Manassas, Virginia

Union leaders: John Pope

Confederate leaders: Robert E. Lee,

J. E. B. Stuart, Stonewall Jackson

D Battle of Antietam Creek, or Battle of Sharpsburg (Sept. 17, 1862)

Location: Sharpsburg, Maryland

Union leaders: George McClellan

Confederate leaders: Robert E. Lee

C Battle of Fredericksburg
(Dec. 11 - 15, 1862)

Location: Fredericksburg, Virginia

Union leaders: Ambrose Burnside

Confederate leaders: Robert E. Lee

LESSON 4: FOR REVIEW
Write the letter of the correct answer in the space provided.

A _____ 1. Which was NOT true of the majority of American soldiers in the Civil War?
- A. they came from a big city
- B. they were between 18 and 30 years old
- C. they had little formal education
- D. they had only superficial military training

B _____ 2. The Union and Confederate governments
- A. never needed to draft soldiers
- B. met their enlistment quotas easily early in the war
- C. refused to allow men drafted to pay substitutes to serve for them
- D. met their enlistment quotas throughout the entire war

D _____ 3. Both the Union and Confederate armies
- A. were careful to require standard forms of identification to prevent young boys from joining
- B. welcomed women as soldiers
- C. recruited as many African American soldiers as possible
- D. had men from Europe and Native Americans fighting for them

D _____ 4. Which of the following was NOT true concerning African Americans in the Union army?
- A. they were not allowed to enlist until 1863
- B. they were paid less than white soldiers
- C. they were given poor equipment and inferior uniforms
- D. they were delegated to labor details and never allowed to see action

A _____ 5. During the war, African Americans
- A. who were southern slaves worked as drivers and farm laborers
- B. who fought in the Union army were regarded as freed men by the Confederates
- C. who were captured by the Confederates were usually treated with kindness
- D. who sought protection from Union forces never had to fear being returned to their masters

B _____ 6. The Civil War nurse, whose kindness and bravery were legendary and who later founded the American Red Cross, was
- A. Dorothea Dix
- B. Clara Barton
- C. Louisa May Alcott
- D. Mary Chesnut

C _____ 7. The Union general who led the Peninsula Campaign was
- A. Ulysses S. Grant
- B. Irvin McDowell
- C. George McClellan
- D. John Pope

C _____ 8. The Confederate soldiers known as the "foot cavalry" were led by
- A. Pierre Beauregard
- B. Joseph Johnston
- C. Stonewall Jackson
- D. Robert E. Lee

A _____ 9. The Union commander of the Army of the Mississippi, who was called east to take charge of the newly formed Army of Virginia, was
- A. John Pope
- B. George McClellan
- C. Ambrose Burnside
- D. Joseph Hooker

Write the corresponding letter of the correct answer in the space provided.

A. Antietam Creek   D. Second Bull Run
B. Fredericksburg   E. Seven Days'
C. New Orleans   F. Seven Pines

C ___ 1. Occupation of the largest seaport in the South due to the naval success of the squadron led by David Farragut

B ___ 2. Terrible defeat of the Union army in the one battle in which it was commanded by General Burnside

A ___ 3. Bloodiest single day of fighting in the Civil War

E ___ 4. Series of battles between McClellan and Lee that failed to lead to the Union capture of Richmond

D ___ 5. Confederate victory commanded by Lee and Jackson against McClellan and Pope that led to the South's regaining almost all of Virginia

F ___ 6. Battle that ended in a tactical draw and led to the replacement of the badly wounded Johnston by Lee

LESSON 4: FOR FURTHER STUDY

For even more interesting information about this period of history, please refer to the For Further Study answers for this lesson in the Teacher's Guide.

1. Read about Belle Boyd (Confederate spy) and Emma Edmonds (Union spy). What spying techniques did they use?

2. Research the life of Dorothea Dix. What position did she hold during the Civil War? Why was she known as "Dragon Dix"? With what had she been involved before the war?

3. Read about the life of Mathew Brady, a photographer of the Civil War. Look for photographs that he took. He and other photographers followed the armed forces in wagons that served as traveling darkrooms.

4. Find out what famous military song came from the Seven Days' Battles. See if you can find the conflicting stories concerning the origin of this song. Read the words and listen to the music of the song.

B ___ 10. After the Second Battle of Bull Run, Lee
A. moved north to attack Washington, D.C.
B. decided to invade Maryland
C. realized that the Confederacy would never receive European support
D. won an amazing victory against Union forces led by George McClellan

C ___ 11. The Battle of Antietam
A. caused Lincoln to delay issuing the preliminary Emancipation Proclamation
B. led to French recognition of the Confederacy
C. doomed Lee's campaign of northern invasion
D. ended in a strategic victory for the Confederacy

D ___ 12. Following the Battle of Antietam, Lincoln replaced George McClellan with
A. Joseph Hooker
B. John Pope
C. Ulysses S. Grant
D. Ambrose Burnside

A ___ 13. At the Battle of Fredericksburg,
A. Union forces crossed the Rappahannock River on pontoon bridges
B. the Union won an overwhelming victory
C. the civilian population suffered heavy loss of life
D. Burnside's performance pleased Lincoln

A ___ 14. The Emancipation Proclamation
A. was issued in its final form on January 1, 1863
B. prohibited slavery throughout the United States
C. was welcomed by Confederate leaders
D. prohibited slavery only in border states and in the Confederate states controlled by the Union

Answer Key to the Forms, Maps, and For Review Questions in the Student Activity Book

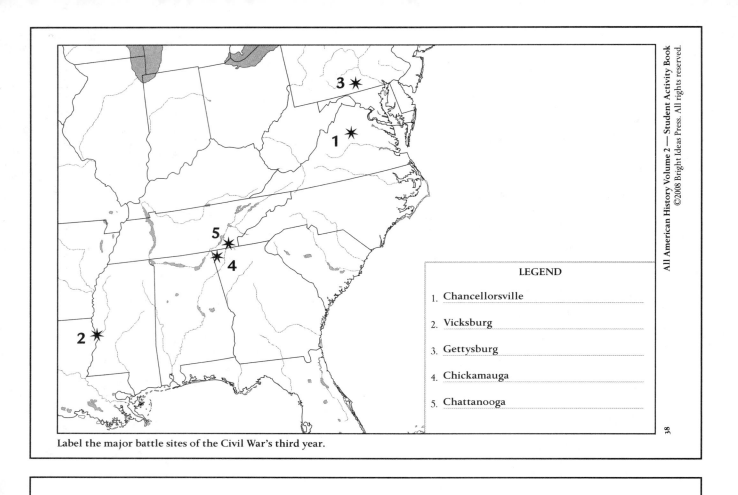

Label the major battle sites of the Civil War's third year.

All American History Volume 2 — Student Activity Book
©2008 Bright Ideas Press. All rights reserved.

LEGEND

1. Chancellorsville ....
2. Vicksburg ....
3. Gettysburg ....
4. Chickamauga ....
5. Chattanooga ....

Name .... Date ....

LESSON 5: THIRD YEAR OF THE CIVIL WAR

MAJOR BATTLES OF THE CIVIL WAR'S THIRD YEAR

Color the square blue if the battle was a Union victory. Color the square gray if the battle was a Confederate victory, or write a *D* in the square if the battle was a draw. Record the date of the battle in the parentheses. Write the name of the state, territory, or body of water in which the battle took place, and write the name(s) of the important Union and Confederate leaders involved.

[C] **Battle of Chancellorsville**
(May 2 - 5, 1863)

Location: Chancellorsville, Virginia

Union leaders: Joseph Hooker

Confederate leaders: Robert E. Lee,

Stonewall Jackson, J. E. B. Stuart

[U] **Siege of Vicksburg**
(May 18 - July 4, 1863)

Location: Vicksburg, Mississippi

Union leaders: U. S. Grant

[U] **Battle of Gettysburg**
(July 1 - 3, 1863)

Location: Gettysburg, Pennsylvania

Union leaders: George Meade

Confederate leaders: Robert E. Lee,

George E. Pickett

[C] **Battle of Chickamauga**
(Sept. 19 - 20, 1863)

Location: Chickamauga Creek, GA

(12 miles south of Chattanooga)

Union leaders: William Rosecrans

Confederate leaders: Braxton Bragg

[U] **Battle of Chattanooga**
(Nov. 23 - 25, 1863)

Location: Chattanooga, Tennessee

Union leaders: U. S. Grant

Confederate leaders: Braxton Bragg

Lesson 5: Third Year of the Civil War
©2008 Bright Ideas Press. All rights reserved.

All American History, Vol. II: Teacher's Guide — Section Five

LESSON 5: FOR REVIEW
Write T for True and F for False in the space provided.

T 1. During the Civil War, soldiers on both sides wore a wide variety of uniforms.

T 2. The principal weapon of all Civil War infantrymen was the rifle-musket.

F 3. Neither Union nor Confederate troops faced a shortage of weapons during the war.

F 4. Only the Confederacy experimented with land mines and machine guns.

T 5. Many historians considered Lee's victory at Chancellorsville to be his greatest.

F 6. While making a night reconnaissance, Stonewall Jackson was wounded by friendly fire; but fortunately his wounds were not fatal.

T 7. Vicksburg was the key Confederate city that guarded the Mississippi River between New Orleans and Memphis.

F 8. Vicksburg fell to Union forces after two days of fierce fighting.

F 9. Grant's reputation was tarnished by his role in the Siege of Vicksburg.

F 10. Lee was not interested in invading the North and was tricked into doing so by General Meade.

F 11. With the Battle of Gettysburg, the tide of war turned in favor of the Confederacy.

T 12. Pickett's Charge showed the hopelessness of a frontal assault against a strong enemy over open ground.

T 13. Although Lincoln did not think his speech at the dedication of the Gettysburg battlefield was well received, his Gettysburg Address became one of the most famous speeches in American history.

T 14. At the Battle of Chattanooga, the Union forces avenged their defeat at Chickamauga.

T 15. By the beginning of 1864, all signs pointed to a Union victory.

Write the corresponding letter of the correct answer in the space provided.

A. Chancellorsville   C. Chickamauga
B. Chattanooga   D. Gettysburg
               E. Vicksburg

E 1. Union victory that led to Union control of the Mississippi River

D 2. Union victory in Pennsylvania that marked a turning point in the war

A 3. An amazing Confederate victory in which Stonewall Jackson suffered a fatal injury

C 4. Perhaps the greatest Confederate victory in the western theater

B 5. Union victory that split the eastern Confederacy in half

LESSON 5: FOR FURTHER STUDY
For even more interesting information about this period of history, please refer to the For Further Study answers for this lesson in the Teacher's Guide.

1. Research the role that telegraphs played during the war.

2. What was the most popular newspaper during the Civil War? Look for examples of newspaper reporting during the war.

3. Find out who the Copperheads were. Why were they considered dangerous?

4. Research the Trent Affair. How did it almost bring Great Britain into the war? Why did Britain decide not to help the Confederacy?

Answer Key to the Forms, Maps, and For Review Questions in the Student Activity Book

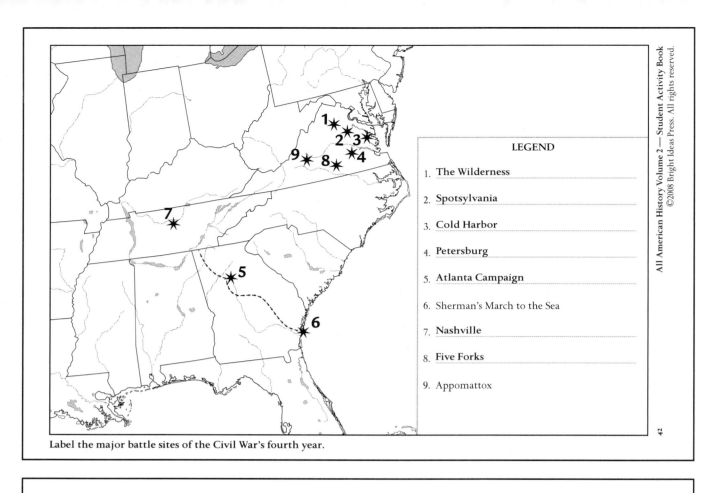

Label the major battle sites of the Civil War's fourth year.

42

Name _____   Date _____

LESSON 6: FOURTH YEAR OF THE CIVIL WAR

MAJOR BATTLES OF THE CIVIL WAR'S FOURTH YEAR

Color the square blue if the battle was a Union victory. Color the square gray if the battle was a Confederate victory, or write a *D* in the square if the battle was a draw. Record the date of the battle in the parentheses. Write the name of the state, territory, or body of water in which the battle took place, and write the name(s) of the important Union and Confederate leaders involved.

☐ D ☐ **Battle of the Wilderness**
(May 5 – 7, 1864)

Location: ___ the Wilderness, Virginia

Union leaders: ___ U. S. Grant

Confederate leaders: ___ Robert E. Lee

☐ D ☐ **Battle of Spotsylvania**
Court House (May 8 – 19, 1864)

Location: Spotsylvania Court House, VA

Union leaders: ___ U. S. Grant

Confederate leaders: ___ Robert E. Lee,
___ J. E. B. Stuart

☐ C ☐ **Battle of Cold Harbor**
(May 31 – June 12, 1864)

Location: ___ Cold Harbor, Virginia

Union leaders: ___ U. S. Grant

Confederate leaders: ___ Robert E. Lee

☐ U ☐ **Siege of Petersburg**
(June 16, 1864 - April 2, 1865)
Location: ___ Petersburg, Virginia

Union leaders: ___ U. S. Grant

Confederate leaders: ___ Robert E. Lee

☐ U ☐ **Atlanta Campaign** (May 1 - Sept. 2, 1864)

Location: ___ Atlanta

Union leaders: ___ William Sherman

Confederate leaders: ___ Joseph Johnston
___ John Hood

☐ U ☐ **Battle of Nashville** (Dec. 15 - 16, 1864)

Location: ___ Nashville, Tennessee

Confederate leaders: ___ John Hood

☐ U ☐ **Battle of Five Forks and the**
Fall of Richmond (April 1 - 3, 1865)

Location: ___ Five Forks/Richmond, VA

Union leaders: ___ U. S. Grant,
___ Philip Sheridan

Confederate leaders: ___ Robert E. Lee

LESSON 6: FOR REVIEW
Write the missing word or words in the spaces provided.

1. When not engaged in battle, soldiers during the Civil War spent much of their time in the monotonous exercise of **drilling** .

2. In the early months of 1863, a religious revival swept over the **Confederate** army, with thousands professing faith in Christ.

3. Filthy water and generally unsanitary conditions led to the prevalence of **disease** among soldiers on both sides in the war.

4. Many soldiers contracted **scurvy** due to the insufficiency of fresh fruit and vegetables in their diet.

5. Because of such heavy casualties, soldiers in the Civil War developed the first **"dog tags"** to help identify those who died in battle.

6. In early March of 1863, President Lincoln appointed **Ulysses S. Grant** to command all the armies of the United States.

7. The first direct confrontation between Lee and Grant occurred at the Battle of **the Wilderness** .

---

8. **J. E. B. Stuart** , commander of Lee's cavalry corps, was mortally wounded at the Battle of Spotsylvania Court House.

9. The longest pontoon bridges used in warfare until World War II were built by Grant and his forces as they advanced toward **Petersburg** .

10. The Union commander in the West responsible for the burning of Atlanta and the destructive March to the Sea was **William Tecumseh Sherman** .

11. The man elected president of the United States in 1864 was **Abraham Lincoln** .

12. The Civil War ended on **April 9, 1865** .

Write the corresponding letter of the correct answer in the space provided.

A. Appomattox Court House   E. Five Forks
B. Atlanta   F. Petersburg
C. Cold Harbor   G. Spotsylvania Court House
D. Nashville   H. the Wilderness

G 1. Five-day battle in which no side could claim victory

F 2. City that underwent a nine-month Union siege

B 3. Union victory that helped Lincoln in his bid for re-election

A 4. Site of Lee's surrender to Grant

H 5. Forest battle where many soldiers burned to death as a result of an under-brush fire

C 6. The only attack that Grant indicated that he wished he had never ordered

---

E _____ 7. Last battle for the Army of Northern Virginia

D _____ 8. Crushing defeat of Confederate forces under Hood following the fall of Atlanta

LESSON 6: FOR FURTHER STUDY

For even more interesting information about this period of history, please refer to the For Further Study answers for this lesson in the Teacher's Guide.

1. During the Civil War, some people in the Union claimed that Lincoln was making himself a dictator when he suspended writs of habeas corpus. What is a writ of habeas corpus? What does the Constitution say about it? How did Lincoln answer his critics? Do you agree with his explanation?

2. Find out about Julia Ward Howe, a noted northern abolitionist and writer, who wrote the "Battle Hymn of the Republic." Read the words to that song.

3. Watch the scenes in the movie *Gone with the Wind* (or read the sections in the book) that deal with the Union army's Atlanta campaign.

4. Research the life of Mary Surratt, owner of a Washington, D.C., boardinghouse, who was arrested and charged with knowledge of the plot to assassinate President Lincoln. What happened to her? Who else was accused of being a part of this conspiracy?

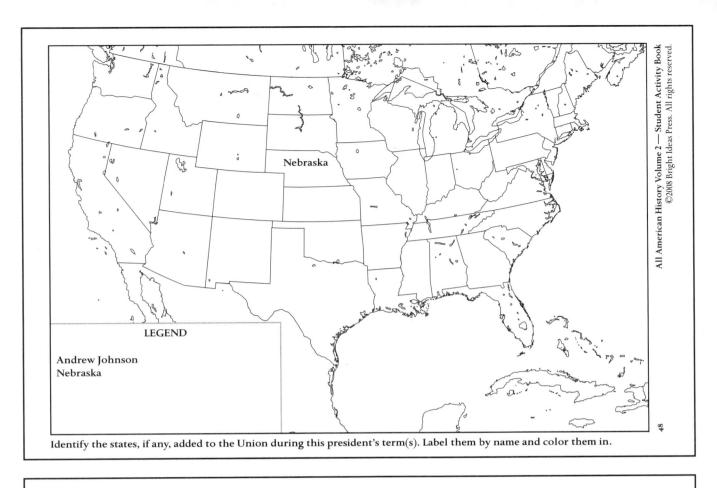

Nebraska

LEGEND

Andrew Johnson
Nebraska

48

Identify the states, if any, added to the Union during this president's term(s). Label them by name and color them in.

Name _____ Date _____

LESSONS 7 AND 8: ANDREW JOHNSON

Picture of the president

Year born ___1808___

Year died ___1875___

In which state was he born? ___North Carolina___

What jobs did he hold before becoming president? ___Tailor, U.S. Representative,___
___Governor of Tennessee, U.S. Senator, military Governor of Tennessee,___
___Vice President___

With what political party was this president affiliated? ___Democratic___
___(although elected vice president on the Republican ticket)___

Vice President: ___None___

What were the years of his presidency? ___1865 – 1869___

List some significant developments during his administration ___13th Amendment___
___14th Amendment___
___Controversy over plans for Reconstruction___
___1867 Reconstruction Act___
___Presidential impeachment___

Answer Key to the Forms, Maps, and For Review Questions in the Student Activity Book

LESSON 7: FOR REVIEW

Write the letter of the correct answer in the space provided.

D 1. The Reconstruction period in American history
    A. lasted over fifty years
    B. did not begin until several years after the Civil War ended
    C. was a simple and easily understood era
    D. was a time when the U.S. government worked to reintegrate the former Confederate states into the Union

B 2. Which of the following was NOT true about the Reconstruction era?
    A. much debate took place concerning what civil rights should be given to freed slaves
    B. President Johnson and Congress negotiated a workable compromise concerning a program for Reconstruction
    C. both Lincoln and Johnson favored a plan for Reconstruction that was lenient toward the ex-Confederate states
    D. the Radical Republicans believed that Reconstruction should be a legislative responsibility

C 3. Lincoln's Ten Percent Plan
    A. required all Confederate citizens to be pardoned by the president
    B. took all property away from Confederate citizens
    C. required new state constitutions to recognize emancipation of slaves as final
    D. did not allow former Confederate states to resume their place in the Union on equal footing with the other states

C 4. Two important Radical Republican leaders in Congress were Charles Sumner and
    A. Wade Hampton
    B. Henry Clay
    C. Thaddeus Stevens
    D. Rutherford B. Hayes

B 5. Radical Republicans
    A. supported Lincoln's Ten Percent Plan
    B. insisted that the prewar white power structure in the South must be dismantled
    C. saw Confederates as rebellious brothers to be forgiven
    D. came alongside President Johnson with their support of his policies after Lincoln's assassination

B 6. The Wade-Davis Act
    A. set forth Lincoln's plan for Reconstruction
    B. allowed only those former Confederates who took an "ironclad" oath of loyalty to vote for delegates or serve as delegates at state constitutional conventions
    C. placed no requirements upon new state constitutions
    D. was signed into law by President Lincoln before he died

A 7. The Freedmen's Bureau
    A. issued food, clothing, and other supplies to freedmen
    B. was only in operation for two years after the war
    C. did not attempt to establish schools or hospitals in the South
    D. solved most of the serious economic problems of freed slaves

C 8. Andrew Johnson
    A. was an old-fashioned southern Republican
    B. championed the interests of the southern plantation aristocracy
    C. battled the Radical Republicans for three years until no compromise was possible
    D. had served in the Confederate government before becoming Lincoln's vice president

C 9. When Johnson became president, he
    A. made overtures of friendship to the Radical Republicans in Congress
    B. refused to recognize the four states organized under Lincoln's Ten Percent Plan
    C. set forth his own program of Reconstruction
    D. decided not to make any plans while Congress was not in session

A_____ 10. Black codes passed in the fall of 1865
  A. restricted the legal and civil rights of former slaves
  B. had no reference to employment and economic opportunities of freedmen
  C. affirmed the right of freedmen to vote and serve on juries
  D. were supported by most African Americans and white Republicans

C_____ 11. The Thirteenth Amendment
  A. was ratified during the Civil War
  B. gave newly freed slaves the right to vote
  C. made the three-fifths clause of the U.S. Constitution inoperative
  D. led to a decrease in southern representation in the U. S. House of Representatives

C_____ 12. The Fourteenth Amendment
  A. was opposed by the Radical Republicans
  B. was supported by President Johnson
  C. guaranteed citizenship to all persons born or naturalized in the United States
  D. gave former slaves the right to vote

D_____ 13. When Congress returned from its recess in December of 1865,
  A. most of the former Confederate states had not yet restored their governments
  B. few prominent former Confederate officials had been elected to state or federal positions
  C. it endorsed Johnson's plan for Reconstruction
  D. it refused to seat any senators or representatives from the former Confederate states

A_____ 14. In 1866, Congress
  A. passed the Civil Rights Act over Johnson's veto
  B. was hopeful that Johnson's Reconstruction plan would succeed
  C. defeated the Fourteenth Amendment
  D. passed the Fifteenth Amendment

C_____ 15. Which of the following was NOT true concerning the election of 1866?
  A. President Johnson was not well received on his speaking tour
  B. the Republicans won a three-fourths majority in Congress
  C. the Radicals strongly supported President Johnson
  D. newspapers printed cartoons depicting the president as "King Andy"

LESSON 7: FOR FURTHER STUDY

For even more interesting information about this period of history, please refer to the For Further Study answers for this lesson in the Teacher's Guide.

1. Research the life of Thaddeus Stevens. Why did African Americans consider him to be a hero and southerners call him the "vilest of the Yankees"?

2. The political cartoonist Thomas Nast drew thousands of cartoons during the second half of the nineteenth century. Discover in which newspaper he was regularly published and what enduring American symbols he created. Look for examples of his cartoons from the Reconstruction era. Did he support Andrew Johnson's plan for Reconstruction?

3. Read more about the black codes enacted by the former Confederate states after the Civil War. Find more specifics concerning restrictions placed upon freed slaves. Why would former slave owners want these codes in place? How were these black codes related to "Jim Crow laws"?

4. Discover what the phrase "Solid South" means. How did this phenomenon affect American politics for a hundred years after Reconstruction?

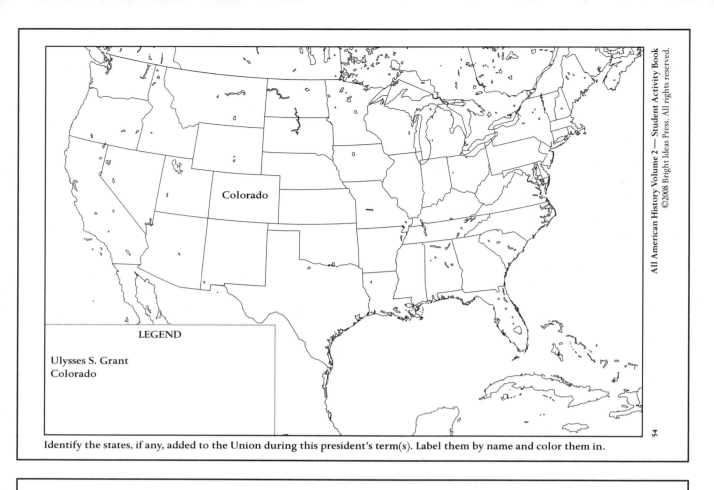

Colorado

LEGEND

Ulysses S. Grant
Colorado

54

Identify the states, if any, added to the Union during this president's term(s). Label them by name and color them in.

Name _____ Date _____

LESSON 8: ULYSSES S. GRANT

Picture of the president

Year born _____ 1822

Year died _____ 1885

In which state was he born? _____ Ohio

What jobs did he hold before becoming president? _____ Union general and
eventual commander of all Union forces, Secretary of War

With what political party was this president affiliated? _____ Republican

Vice President: _____ Schuyler Colfax, Henry Wilson

What were the years of his presidency? _____ 1869 – 1877

List some significant developments during his administration Gould/Fisk attempt
to corner the gold market

"Black Friday"

Crédit Mobilier scandal

Whiskey Ring scandal

15th Amendment

Ku Klux Klan Act of 1871

Civil Rights Act of 1875

Lesson 8: Congressional Reconstruction

53

LESSON 8: FOR REVIEW
Write T for True and F for False in the space provided.

F ___ 1. During Reconstruction a new agricultural system, known as sharecropping, became popular in the North.

F ___ 2. Carpetbaggers and scalawags were strongly supported by most white southerners.

F ___ 3. Newly freed slaves in the South were not easily manipulated and were known for voting independently.

T ___ 4. The Ku Klux Klan was organized by ex-Confederates to maintain white supremacy in the South and to keep freed slaves from exercising their rights.

T ___ 5. The Panic of 1873 caused many Republicans to focus more on economic issues and less on southern Reconstruction.

F ___ 6. Liberal Republicans, known as Redeemers, began to stamp out racial inequalities in the South during the 1870s.

T ___ 7. The Radical Republicans believed that the outcome of the 1866 Congressional election was a mandate for their policies.

T ___ 8. Under the terms of the Reconstruction Act of 1867, the former Confederacy (except for Tennessee) was divided into five military districts, each under the command of a major general.

F ___ 9. The Reconstruction Act of 1867 did not disenfranchise most former Confederate military officers and officeholders.

T ___ 10. Under the Radical Reconstruction plan, a state's Congressional representatives would not be seated until its state legislature ratified the Fourteenth Amendment.

T ___ 11. By 1879, all the former Confederate states had been readmitted to the Union under the Congressional plan of Reconstruction.

T ___ 12. In 1868, the U.S. House of Representatives succeeded in impeaching President Johnson on the basis of the Tenure of Office Act.

Lesson 8: Congressional Reconstruction
©2008 Bright Ideas Press. All rights reserved.

55

F ___ 13. The Senate convicted Johnson in May of 1868 and removed him from office.

F ___ 14. President Grant was an inexperienced political leader but managed to avoid controversy and scandal during his two terms in office.

F ___ 15. The Fifteenth Amendment prohibited slavery throughout the United States.

F ___ 16. No action was taken by Congress to enforce the Fifteenth Amendment or to protect African Americans from acts of violence by the Ku Klux Klan and other organizations.

T ___ 17. The Civil Rights Act of 1875 was the last effort by Congress to protect the civil rights of African Americans for more than a century.

F ___ 18. The Supreme Court upheld the constitutionality of the 1875 Civil Rights Act.

T ___ 19. The compromise settling the 1876 disputed presidential election called for the removal of the remaining federal troops in the South.

F ___ 20. By the end of 1877, Republicans held power in all the southern state governments.

LESSON 8: FOR FURTHER STUDY
For even more interesting information about this period of history, please refer to the For Further Study answers for this lesson in the Teacher's Guide.

1. Research the life of Hiram Revels. Record the information on an African American form.

2. Who was the only president besides Andrew Johnson to be impeached? What were the similarities and differences in these men and their trials?

3. Why did a Republican splinter group, known as the Liberal Republicans, oppose Grant's re-election in 1872? With whom did they form an unlikely coalition? Who was the presidential candidate of this coalition and why was he a poor choice?

4. Find out why the United States was enjoying economic prosperity in the late 1860s and early 1870s. Discover what led to the Panic of 1873 and the six-year depression that followed.

56

All American History Volume 2 — Student Activity Book
©2008 Bright Ideas Press. All rights reserved.

Answer Key to the Forms, Maps, and For Review Questions in the Student Activity Book
©2008 Bright Ideas Press. All rights reserved.

169

UNIT I: FINAL REVIEW

Write the corresponding letter of the correct answer in the space provided.

A. Clara Barton
B. Pierre G. T. Beauregard
C. John Wilkes Booth
D. John Brown
E. William Buchanan
F. Henry Clay
G. Jefferson Davis
H. Stephen Douglas
I. Frederick Douglass
J. Millard Fillmore
K. William Lloyd Garrison
L. Ulysses S. Grant
M. Thomas Jackson
N. Andrew Johnson
O. Robert E. Lee
P. Abraham Lincoln
Q. George McClellan
R. George Pickett
S. Franklin Pierce
T. Winfield Scott
U. William Tecumseh Sherman
V. Thaddeus Stevens
W. Harriet Beecher Stowe
X. J. E. B. Stuart
Y. Zachary Taylor
Z. Harriet Tubman

X 1. Commander of Lee's cavalry corps

J 2. President who signed the Compromise of 1850

T 3. Developer of the Anaconda Plan

M 4. Leader of the "foot cavalry," who received the name "Stonewall" at the First Battle of Bull Run

L 5. Union general who won significant victories in the western theater and then was appointed supreme commander of all Union forces

Y 6. Whig president who had served in the Mexican War and had received the nickname "Old Rough and Ready"

H 7. Lincoln's opponent in his 1858 race for the Senate and driving force behind the Kansas-Nebraska Act

R 8. Confederate general who led the charge up Cemetery Ridge at Gettysburg

D 9. Fanatical abolitionist who attempted to start a slave rebellion in Harpers Ferry, Virginia

P 10. Sixteenth president of the United States

A. Clara Barton
B. Pierre G. T. Beauregard
C. John Wilkes Booth
D. John Brown
E. William Buchanan
F. Henry Clay
G. Jefferson Davis
H. Stephen Douglas
I. Frederick Douglass
J. Millard Fillmore
K. William Lloyd Garrison
L. Ulysses S. Grant
M. Thomas Jackson
N. Andrew Johnson
O. Robert E. Lee
P. Abraham Lincoln
Q. George McClellan
R. George Pickett
S. Franklin Pierce
T. Winfield Scott
U. William Tecumseh Sherman
V. Thaddeus Stevens
W. Harriet Beecher Stowe
X. J. E. B. Stuart
Y. Zachary Taylor
Z. Harriet Tubman

O 11. Commander of the Army of Northern Virginia and eventually supreme commander of all Confederate forces

B 12. Confederate general present at Fort Sumter and Petersburg

S 13. President who had to deal with the controversy surrounding the Kansas-Nebraska Act

C 14. Lincoln's assassin

V 15. Radical Republican who was the chief author of the Fourteenth Amendment

U 16. Union commander in the West responsible for the burning of Atlanta and the destructive March to the Sea

I 17. Freed slave who worked in the abolitionist movement

F 18. "Great Compromiser" who helped to negotiate the Missouri Compromise of 1820 and the Compromise of 1850

W 19. Author of *Uncle Tom's Cabin*

E 20. Only bachelor president, whose term in office was the last before the Civil War began

A 21. Civil War nurse, whose kindness and bravery were legendary and who later founded the American Red Cross

K 22. Editor of the abolitionist newspaper, *The Liberator*

Q 23. Former Union general who ran for president in 1864

N 24. President who lost his fight with the Radical Republicans to control Reconstruction

Z 25. Underground Railroad conductor known as "Moses"

G 26. President of the Confederate States of America

Write the corresponding letter of the correct answer in the space provided.

A. Antietam Creek	L. Fort Sumter
B. Appomattox Court House	M. Nashville
C. Atlanta	N. New Orleans
D. Chancellorsville	O. Second Bull Run
E. Chattanooga	P. Seven Days'
F. Chickamauga	Q. Seven Pines
G. Cold Harbor	R. Shiloh
H. First Bull Run	S. Spotsylvania Court House
I. Forts Henry and Donelson	T. Petersburg
J. Fredericksburg	U. Vicksburg
K. Gettysburg	V. Wilderness

F 1. Greatest Confederate victory in the western theater of the war

K 2. Union victory in Pennsylvania that marked a turning point in the war

A 3. Bloodiest single day of fighting in the Civil War

N 4. Union occupation of the largest seaport in the South

L 5. Site of the opening shots of the Civil War

R 6. Confederate surprise attack upon Union troops near an abandoned Methodist church near Pittsburg Landing, Tennessee

H 7. First battle of the Civil War

A. Antietam Creek	L. Fort Sumter
B. Appomattox Court House	M. Nashville
C. Atlanta	N. New Orleans
D. Chancellorsville	O. Second Bull Run
E. Chattanooga	P. Seven Days'
F. Chickamauga	Q. Seven Pines
G. Cold Harbor	R. Shiloh
H. First Bull Run	S. Spotsylvania Court House
I. Forts Henry and Donelson	T. Petersburg
J. Fredericksburg	U. Vicksburg
K. Gettysburg	V. Wilderness

U 8. Union victory that led to Union control of the Mississippi River

P 9. Series of battles between McClellan and Lee in Virginia that failed to lead to Union capture of Richmond early in the war

J 10. Terrible defeat of the Union army in the one battle in which it was commanded by General Burnside

E 11. Union victory that split the eastern Confederacy in half and paved the way for Union invasion of Georgia

T 12. City that underwent a nine-month siege in the last year of the war

I 13. Union capture that led to control of the Tennessee and Cumberland Rivers

D 14. Amazing Confederate victory in which Stonewall Jackson was fatally wounded

G 15. The only attack that Grant indicated that he wished that he had never ordered

M 16. Crushing defeat of Confederate forces in Tennessee following the fall of Atlanta

S 17. Five-day battle in which neither side could claim victory and J. E. B. Stuart was mortally wounded

C 18. Union victory that helped Lincoln in his bid for re-election in 1864

Answer Key to the Forms, Maps, and For Review Questions in the Student Activity Book

UNIT TWO

THE GILDED AGE

Lessons 9 – 16

Q ___ 19. Battle in Virginia that ended in a tactical draw and led to Lee's replacement of the badly wounded Johnston

B ___ 20. Site of Lee's surrender to Grant

V ___ 21. Forest battle where many soldiers burned to death as a result of an underbrush fire

O ___ 22. Confederate victory against Union troops led by McClellan and Pope that led to the South's regaining almost all of Virginia

61

Unit 1: **Final Review**
©2008 Bright Ideas Press. All rights reserved.

All American History, Vol. II: Teacher's Guide — Section Five

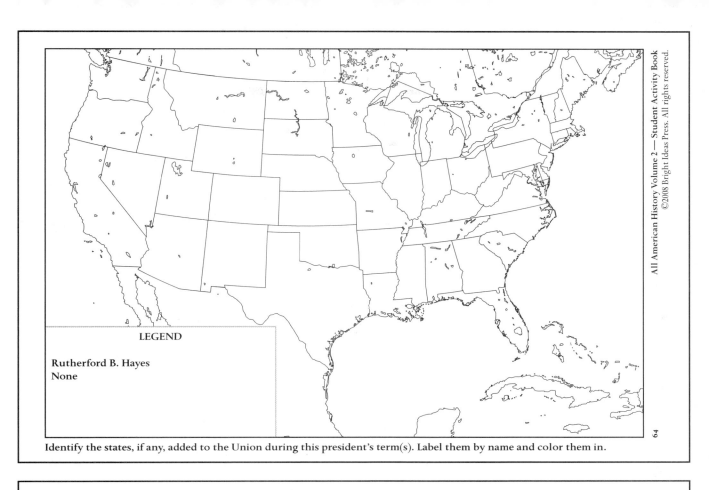

Identify the states, if any, added to the Union during this president's term(s). Label them by name and color them in.

64

Name _____   Date _____

LESSON 9: RUTHERFORD B. HAYES

Picture of the president

Year born ___ 1822

Year died ___ 1893

In which state was he born? ___ Ohio

What jobs did he hold before becoming president? ___ Lawyer, Major General

in Union army, U.S. Representative, Governor of Ohio

With what political party was this president affiliated? ___ Republican

Vice President: ___ William A. Wheeler

What were the years of his presidency? ___ 1877 - 1881

List some significant developments during his administration ___ Removal of

remaining federal troops in the South

Resumption of payment of gold for government bonds issued to

finance the Civil War

Weakening of the spoils system

63

Answer Key to the Forms, Maps, and For Review Questions in the Student Activity Book

173

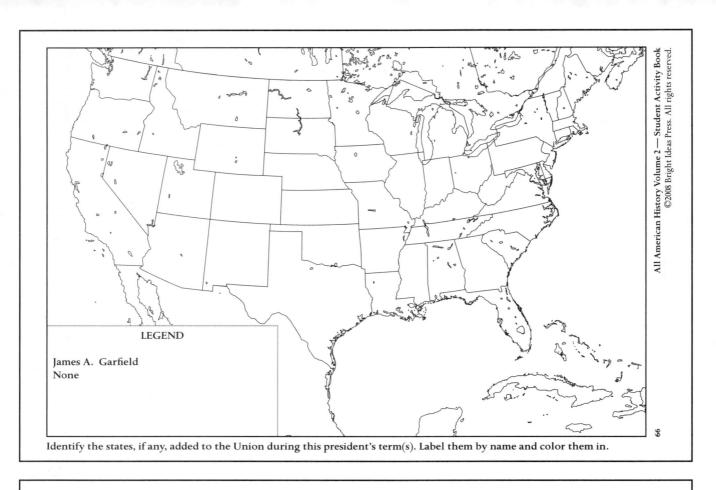

66

Identify the states, if any, added to the Union during this president's term(s). Label them by name and color them in.

Name _____ Date _____

LESSON 9: JAMES A. GARFIELD

Picture of the president

Year born __1831__

Year died __1881__

In which state was he born? __Ohio__

What jobs did he hold before becoming president? __Major General in Union army,__

__U.S. Representative, U.S. Senator__

With what political party was this president affiliated? __Republican__

Vice President: __Chester A. Arthur__

What were the years of his presidency? __1881__

List some significant developments during his administration __Strengthening of__

__federal authority over the N.Y. Customs House__

__Garfield's assassination__

All American History, Vol. II: Teacher's Guide — Section Five

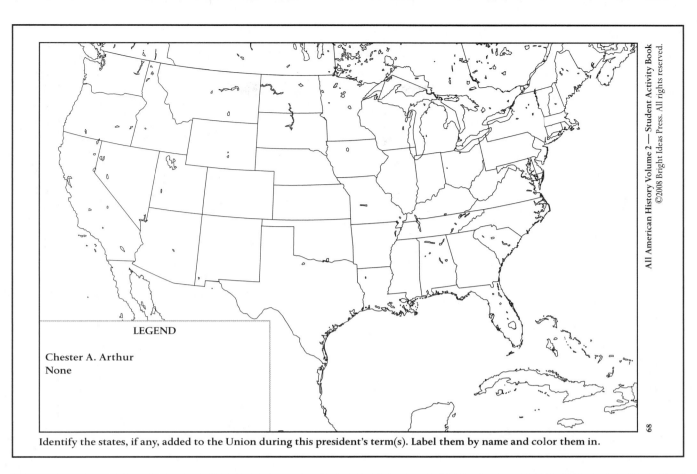

Identify the states, if any, added to the Union during this president's term(s). Label them by name and color them in.

All American History Volume 2 — Student Activity Book
©2008 Bright Ideas Press. All rights reserved.

LEGEND

Chester A. Arthur
None

Name _____ Date _____

LESSON 9: CHESTER A. ARTHUR

Picture of the president

Year born _____ 1830 _____

Year died _____ 1886 _____

In which state was he born? _____ Vermont _____

What jobs did he hold before becoming president? _____ Lawyer, _____

_____ administrator for the Union army _____

With what political party was this president affiliated? _____ Republican _____

Vice President: _____ None _____

What were the years of his presidency? _____ 1881 – 1885 _____

List some significant developments during his administration _____ Pendleton Act _____

_____ (civil service reform) _____

_____ Mongrel Tariff _____

Lesson 9: Presidents of the Gilded Age
©2008 Bright Ideas Press. All rights reserved.

Answer Key to the Forms, Maps, and For Review Questions in the Student Activity Book   175
©2008 Bright Ideas Press. All rights reserved.

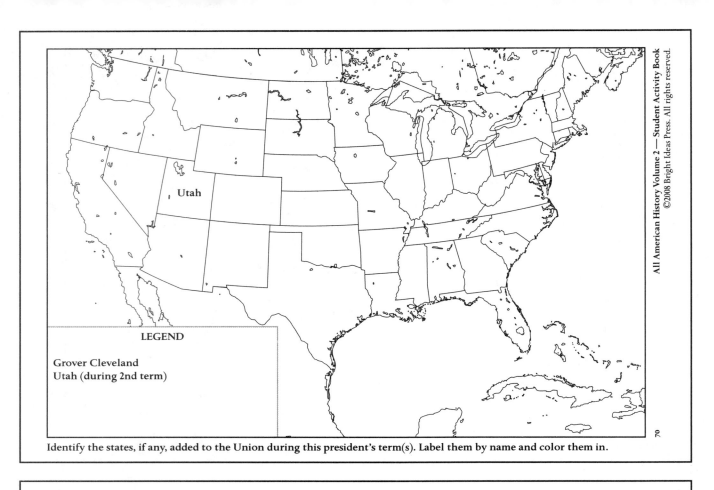

LEGEND

Grover Cleveland
Utah (during 2nd term)

Utah

Identify the states, if any, added to the Union during this president's term(s). Label them by name and color them in.

Name _____ Date _____

LESSON 9: GROVER CLEVELAND—BOTH TERMS

Picture of the president

Year born ___1837___

Year died ___1908___

In which state was he born? ___New Jersey___

What jobs did he hold before becoming president? ___Lawyer,___
___Mayor of Buffalo, Governor of New York___

With what political party was this president affiliated? ___Democratic___

Vice President: ___Thomas A. Hendricks, Adlai E. Stevenson___

What were the years of the two (nonconsecutive) terms of his presidency?
___1885 – 1889, 1893 – 1897___

List some significant developments during each of his administrations

TERM 1	TERM 2
Interstate Commerce Act	Panic of 1893
Forcing the railroads to return	Four-year depression
81 million acres that they held by	Repeal of Sherman Silver Purchase Act
government grant	Pullman Strike
	British threat of intervention in
	Venezuela (violation of Monroe
	Doctrine)

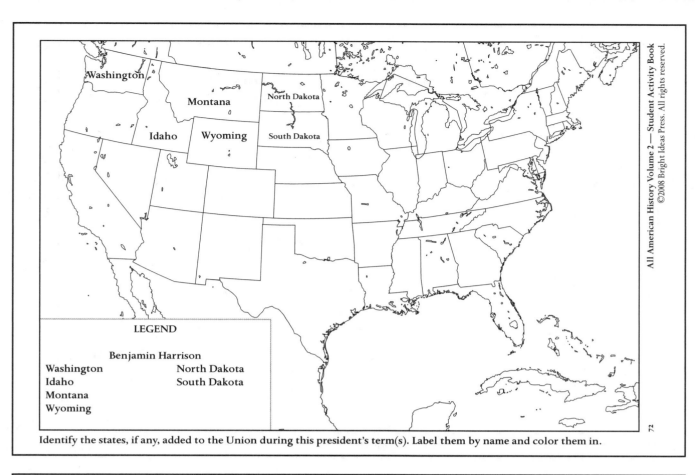

LEGEND

Benjamin Harrison

Washington   North Dakota
Idaho   South Dakota
Montana
Wyoming

Identify the states, if any, added to the Union during this president's term(s). Label them by name and color them in.

Name _____   Date _____

LESSON 9: BENJAMIN HARRISON

Picture of the president

Year born _____ 1833 _____

Year died _____ 1901 _____

In which state was he born? _____ Ohio _____

What jobs did he hold before becoming president? _____ Lawyer, _____
_____ Civil War hero, U.S. Senator _____

With what political party was this president affiliated? _____ Republican _____

Vice President: _____ Levi P. Morton _____

What were the years of his presidency? _____ 1889 - 1893 _____

List some significant developments during his administration _____ Expansion of the _____
_____ U.S. Navy and the merchant marine _____
_____ Sherman Antitrust Act _____
_____ McKinley Tariff _____
_____ Sherman Silver Purchase Act _____

Answer Key to the Forms, Maps, and For Review Questions in the Student Activity Book
©2008 Bright Ideas Press. All rights reserved.   177

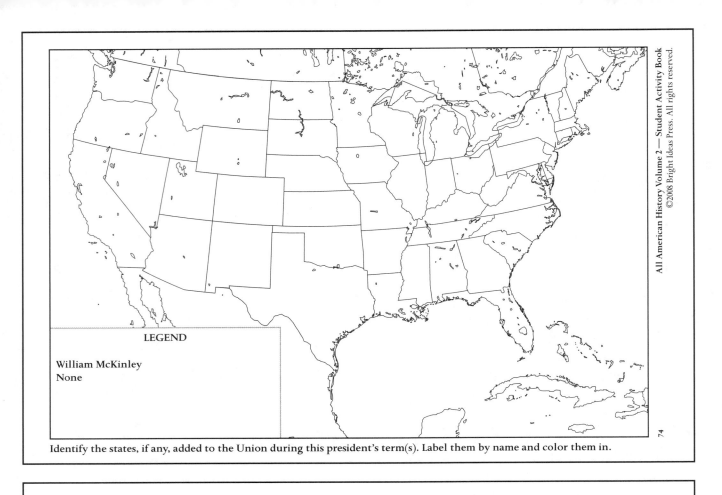

LEGEND

William McKinley
None

74

Identify the states, if any, added to the Union during this president's term(s). Label them by name and color them in.

Name _____ Date _____

LESSON 9: WILLIAM McKINLEY

Picture of the president

Year born _____ 1843

Year died _____ 1901

In which state was he born? _____ Ohio

What jobs did he hold before becoming president? _____ Lawyer,
Civil War veteran, U.S. Representative, Governor of Ohio

With what political party was this president affiliated? _____ Republican

Vice President: _____ Garret A. Hobart, Theodore Roosevelt

What were the years of his presidency? _____ 1897 – 1901

List some significant developments during his administration _____ Dingley Tariff

Spanish-American War

"Open Door" Policy in China; U.S. assistance in putting down the

Boxer Rebellion in China

McKinley's assassination at the Pan-American Exposition

Lesson 9: Presidents of the Gilded Age
©2008 Bright Ideas Press. All rights reserved.

73

All American History, Vol. II: Teacher's Guide — Section Five

LESSON 9: FOR REVIEW

Write T for True and F for False in the space provided.

F   1. The disputed presidential election of 1876 was dominated by the themes of Democratic corruption and economic prosperity.

F   2. The electoral commission appointed by Congress gave the disputed electoral votes to the Democratic candidate, Samuel Tilden.

F   3. The Compromise of 1877 was necessary to gain Republican support for the result of the 1876 presidential election.

F   4. Most of the presidents during the Gilded Age won election by large majorities and had a reputation for strong, effective leadership.

T   5. Hayes hoped that that he would be able to build a new Republican Party that southern businessmen and other conservatives would be willing to support.

F   6. During his term in office, Hayes worked hard to strengthen the spoils system.

F   7. Both Garfield and Arthur were Half-Breeds, united in their contempt for the Stalwart faction of the Republican Party.

F   8. President Arthur was a Half-Breed Republican who provided his friends with special favors.

T   9. The tariff passed during Arthur's term in office became known as the Mongrel Tariff.

T   10. Grover Cleveland was the first Democrat to be elected president after the Civil War.

F   11. Cleveland was criticized for giving special favors to different economic groups and for refusing to use his veto powers.

T   12. The Interstate Commerce Act was the first law attempting to place railroads under federal regulation.

T   13. Benjamin Harrison became president in 1889, even though he received one hundred thousand fewer popular votes than Cleveland.

F   14. The Sherman Antitrust Act, which expanded the power of Congress to regulate business, was easily enforced.

F   15. The Sherman Silver Purchase Act made the purchase of silver by the U.S. Treasury illegal.

T   16. Cleveland's handling of the depression was unpopular, but the public supported his dealings with striking railroad workers in the Pullman Strike.

F   17. William Jennings Bryan campaigned from his front porch, whereas William McKinley traveled across the nation on a whistle-stop campaign.

T   18. The most significant event of McKinley's administration was the Spanish-American War.

Write the corresponding letter of the correct answer in the space provided.

A. Rutherford B. Hayes   D. Grover Cleveland
B. James A. Garfield   E. Benjamin Harrison
C. Chester A. Arthur   F. William McKinley

D   1. Became the only U.S. president to serve two nonconsecutive terms

A   2. Ordered the last federal troops out of the South

B   3. Assassinated by an embittered government office-seeker

D   4. Signed into law the Interstate Commerce Act

D   5. Assumed the presidency just as the country plunged into a four-year depression

F   6. Assassinated by a mentally unstable anarchist at the Pan-American Exposition

C   7. Supported the Pendleton Act that provided civil service reform

E   8. Signed into law the Sherman Antitrust Act and supported the McKinley Tariff

Answer Key to the Forms, Maps, and For Review Questions in the Student Activity Book

F _____ 9. Took the initiative in establishing an open door policy in China

F _____ 10. Hoped to keep the United States out of war with Spain in 1898

LESSON 9: FOR FURTHER STUDY
For even more interesting information about this period of history, please refer to the For Further Study answers for this lesson in the Teacher's Guide.

1. The title "First Lady" was first widely used in 1877 to refer to Lucy Hayes, popular wife of President Rutherford B. Hayes. The press also gave her a nickname. Find out what it was and why they gave it to her. What event for children at the White House was started by this couple? Can you find any other ways that Lucy Hayes was unique?

2. Read more about the Stalwart and Half-Breed factions in the Republican Party. Look into the background of Charles Guiteau, President Garfield's assassin.

3. Research the Greenback-Labor Party and the Populist Party. What were their goals?

4. Find a copy of William Jennings Bryan's "Cross of Gold" speech and read it. You can listen to an audio excerpt of Bryan giving this speech twenty-five years after he first delivered it. He repeated this speech many times on the Chautauqua lecture circuit.

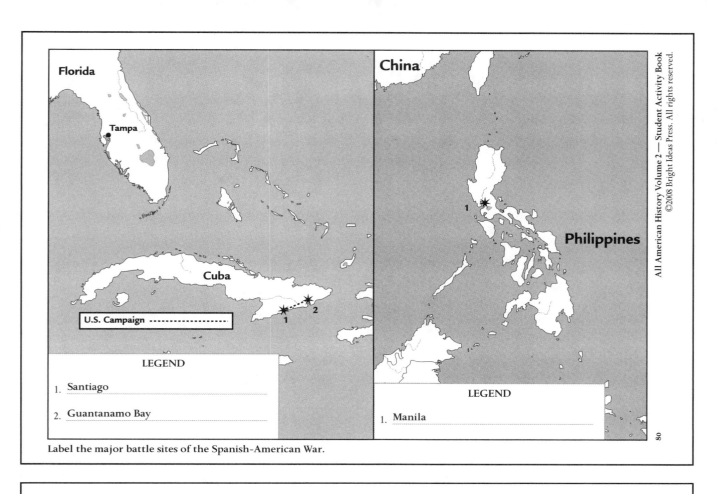

Florida

Tampa

Cuba

U.S. Campaign - - - - - - - -

LEGEND

1. Santiago

2. Guantanamo Bay

China

Philippines

LEGEND

1. Manila

Label the major battle sites of the Spanish-American War.

80

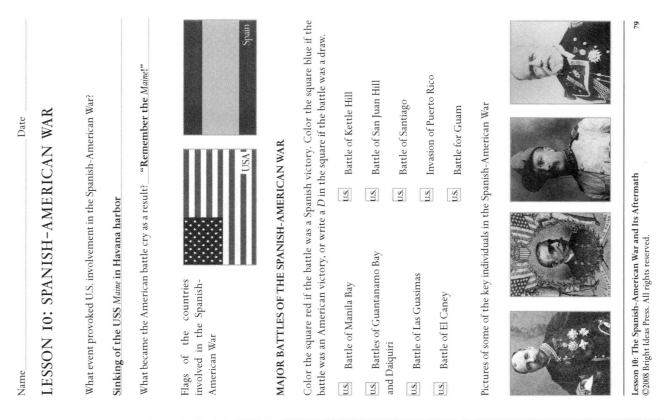

Name _____ Date _____

LESSON 10: SPANISH–AMERICAN WAR

What event provoked U.S. involvement in the Spanish-American War?

Sinking of the USS *Maine* in Havana harbor

What became the American battle cry as a result? **"Remember the *Maine!*"**

Flags of the countries involved in the Spanish-American War

USA

Spain

MAJOR BATTLES OF THE SPANISH-AMERICAN WAR

Color the square red if the battle was a Spanish victory. Color the square blue if the battle was an American victory, or write a *D* in the square if the battle was a draw.

U.S.	Battle of Manila Bay	U.S.	Battle of Kettle Hill
U.S.	Battles of Guantanamo Bay and Daiquiri	U.S.	Battle of San Juan Hill
U.S.	Battle of Las Guasimas	U.S.	Battle of Santiago
U.S.	Battle of El Caney	U.S.	Invasion of Puerto Rico
		U.S.	Battle for Guam

Pictures of some of the key individuals in the Spanish-American War

79

Answer Key to the Forms, Maps, and For Review Questions in the Student Activity Book

182

LESSON 10: FOR REVIEW
Write the letter of the correct answer in the space provided.

B _____ 1. By the time that the Spanish-American War began,
A. Cuba had been granted its independence by Spain
B. all that remained of Spain's New World empire was Puerto Rico and Cuba
C. the Spanish had restored many of the Cubans' political and religious liberties
D. American businessmen had few investments in Cuba

C _____ 2. In February of 1898, the USS *Maine*
A. was sent to Manila to become a part of Admiral Dewey's fleet
B. returned to the United States from duty in Cuba
C. was mysteriously sunk in Havana harbor
D. lost many of its crew members to a mysterious disease

D _____ 3. By the spring of 1898,
A. most of the American public had lost interest in the plight of the Cuban revolutionaries
B. the American press was calling for an end to America's war with Spain
C. most American government officials were dead set against the United States going to war
D. the American press, bankers, and manufacturers were clamoring for the United States to become involved in Cuba against imperialist Spain

A _____ 4. During the months leading up to the Spanish-American War,
A. Hearst's newspaper published a stolen letter written by the Spanish minister criticizing McKinley
B. most newspapers supported McKinley's desire to maintain an American position of neutrality
C. Theodore Roosevelt denounced Social Darwinism and called upon McKinley to avoid war at all costs
D. the Spanish board of inquiry admitted that the explosion on the *Maine* had been caused by a mine

Lesson 10: The Spanish-American War and Its Aftermath
©2008 Bright Ideas Press. All rights reserved.

A _____ 5. When the Spanish-American War began,
A. the U.S. Navy had been recently rebuilt as a modern steel navy
B. the U.S. Army was well trained and equipped for conflict
C. the United States did not have any naval stations at home or abroad
D. most U.S. troops were stationed in Florida

B _____ 6. Which of the following was NOT true of the U.S. military during the Spanish-American War?
A. U.S. troops going to Cuba shipped out of Tampa, Florida
B. few mistakes were made by the supply staff organizing the soldiers and their equipment
C. American military leaders had very little information on the enemy that their troops would be facing in Cuba
D. Spanish soldiers in Cuba were equipped with more advanced weapons than were the U.S. soldiers

B _____ 7. U.S. soldiers in Cuba
A. did not arrive on the island until September
B. suffered from the heat in their wool uniforms
C. were defeated at San Juan Hill
D. were not bothered by diseases like malaria

B _____ 8. The first major action of the Spanish-American War took place in
A. Santiago, Cuba
B. Manila Bay, the Philippines
C. Honolulu, Hawaii
D. San Juan, Puerto Rico

A _____ 9. American Commodore George Dewey
A. destroyed the Spanish fleet in Manila Bay
B. led the charge up San Juan Hill
C. defeated the Spanish at El Caney
D. was killed at the Battle of Kettle Hill

All American History Volume 2 — Student Activity Book
©2008 Bright Ideas Press. All rights reserved.

A _____ 15. At the turn of the century,

A. the Anti-Imperialist League had just been founded in the United States

B. Social Darwinists discouraged American expansionism

C. few Americans believed that the "manifest destiny" of the United States was to become a world power

D. the United States had refused to take over the Philippines, because doing so would be a violation of the Monroe Doctrine

LESSON 10: FOR FURTHER STUDY

For even more interesting information about this period of history, please refer to the For Further Study answers for this lesson in the Teacher's Guide.

1. Read about the life of Alfred T. Mahan. Where did he work and what influential books did he write? How did his views affect American policies during the Gilded Age?

2. Research what role the Rough Riders played in the Spanish-American War. Who led them? How were they portrayed in the American press? Find out how the Buffalo Soldiers were involved in the Spanish-American War. Who gave them their name?

3. Who was Walter Reed? What problem faced by American soldiers during the Spanish-American War was Reed asked to address?

4. Why were some Americans referred to as "jingoes" during the Spanish-American War? What does that word mean? How did it originate?

D _____ 10. Which of the following was an American victory in the Spanish-American War?

A. Guasimas

B. El Caney

C. Kettle Hill and San Juan Hill

D. all of the above

D _____ 11. During the Spanish-American War, Puerto Ricans

A. forced all Americans off their island

B. suffered devastating losses from a hurricane

C. never experienced an attack by American forces

D. offered little resistance to invading American troops

C _____ 12. After the fighting in Cuba ended,

A. Spain refused to sign an armistice with the United States

B. peace negotiations took place in London

C. the major issue in the peace negotiations concerned the Philippines

D. Puerto Rico and Guam both were granted independence

C _____ 13. In the years immediately following the end of the Spanish-American War, the Philippines

A. became an independent nation

B. quickly submitted to American rule

C. saw much bloodshed because of guerilla resistance to American control

D. remained under Spanish rule

A _____ 14. The Spanish-American War

A. lasted for approximately four months

B. was a very unpopular war in the United States

C. caused greater disunity between northerners and southerners

D. ended forever the possibility of the United States becoming an imperialist power

Lesson 10: The Spanish-American War and Its Aftermath

Answer Key to the Forms, Maps, and For Review Questions in the Student Activity Book

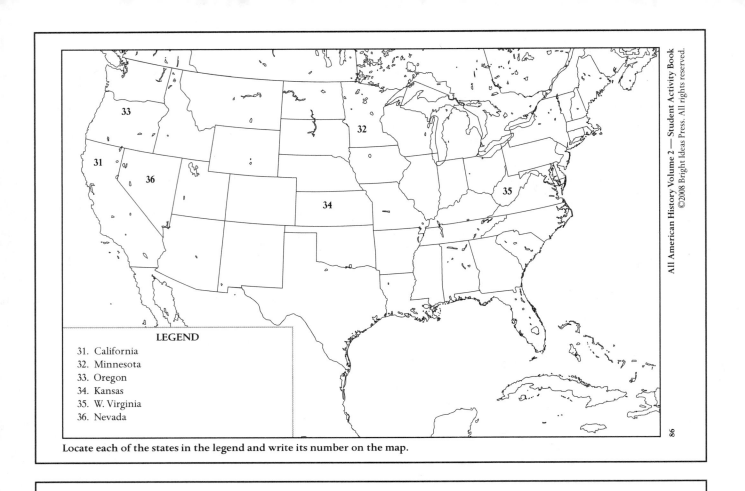

LEGEND

31. California
32. Minnesota
33. Oregon
34. Kansas
35. W. Virginia
36. Nevada

Locate each of the states in the legend and write its number on the map.

Name _____   Date _____

LESSON 11: STATES AND CAPITALS
(LESSONS 1–10)

Fill in the blanks with the names of the state capitals.

# State	Capital City
31. California:	Sacramento
32. Minnesota:	St. Paul
33. Oregon:	Salem
34. Kansas:	Topeka
35. West Virginia:	Charleston
36. Nevada:	Carson City
37. Nebraska:	Lincoln
38. Colorado:	Denver
39. North Dakota:	Bismarck
40. South Dakota:	Pierre
41. Montana:	Helena
42. Washington:	Olympia
43. Idaho:	Boise
44. Wyoming:	Cheyenne
45. Utah:	Salt Lake City

States 1–30 and their capitals were taught in *All American History, Volume I*. You will have the opportunity to learn (or review) these states and their capitals in Lessons 15, 20, 26, and 29. States 46, 47, and 48 are taught in Lesson 15. States 49 and 50 are taught in Lesson 26.

All American History, Vol. II: Teacher's Guide — Section Five

LESSON 11: FOR REVIEW

Write the missing word or words in the spaces provided.

1. The Great Plains became known as the __Great American Desert__ because early settlers believed that its sod was too hard to plow and its climate too harsh for cultivating crops.

2. On May 10, 1869, at Promontory Point, Utah, the Central Pacific and Union Pacific railroads joined to form the first __transcontinental__ railroad in the United States.

3. The __Homestead__ Act of 1862 promised American settlers 160 acres of public land in the West if they would live on it for five years, cultivate it, and pay a small fee.

4. In 1869, silver was discovered at __the Comstock Lode__, in what is now the state of Nevada.

5. With the expansion of the railroads and the invention of __barbed wire__ by Joseph Glidden, the long American cattle drives began to come to an end.

6. The most important animal to the Native American tribes of the Great Plains was the __buffalo__.

7. The U.S. 7th Cavalry, under the leadership of __Lt. Col. George Armstrong Custer__, was massacred by native warriors under Sitting Bull near the Little Big Horn River in Montana.

8. Sitting Bull eventually was allowed to join his tribe at the Standing Rock Reservation and to leave periodically to travel with __Buffalo Bill's Wild West Show__.

9. The Sioux chief Big Foot and over three hundred of his warriors were massacred by three hundred U.S. troops on the banks of __Wounded Knee Creek__ in South Dakota.

10. The __Dawes__ Act of 1887 broke up tribal lands into 160-acre plots, which were distributed among individual Indians who could acquire U.S. citizenship with the land grant.

Write T for True and F for False in the space provided.

__T__ 1. At the end of the Civil War, as much as one-third of the United States was still considered frontier.

__F__ 2. Even to this day, the Great Plains area of the United States is not a very productive agricultural region.

__T__ 3. During the Gilded Age, the Great Plains looked appealing to newly freed slaves and newly arrived European immigrants.

__F__ 4. The federal government was not involved in any way in the building of the first U.S. transcontinental railroad.

Answer Key to the Forms, Maps, and For Review Questions in the Student Activity Book
©2008 Bright Ideas Press. All rights reserved.

range? Who were Gustavus Swift and Philip Armour? Look for paintings of cowboys by Frederic Remington.

4. Research the lives of one or more of the following people significant in the Wild West of the Gilded Age — Buffalo Bill, Wild Bill Hickok, Calamity Jane, Bat Masterson, and Frank and Jesse James. Find out more about the Native American Ghost Dance movement. Record information about the Lakota and Sitting Bull on a Native American Tribe form.

T _____ 5. American pioneers usually migrated westward in trains of Conestoga wagons and often settled with other families who hailed from the same area back East.

F _____ 6. There was a competitive and unfriendly spirit among most of the American pioneers of the Gilded Age.

T _____ 7. Grasshopper plows enabled Great Plains farmers to cut the tough prairie ground to plant their crops.

T _____ 8. Mining fever began with the California gold rush in 1849, reached its peak in the Civil War, and ended with the Alaska gold rush in 1898.

T _____ 9. Mining boomtowns were boisterous places that made legends of men like Bat Masterson and "Wild Bill" Hickok.

F _____ 10. There was only one principal cow trail after the end of the Civil War — the Chisholm Trail.

T _____ 11. By the 1890s, almost all the Great Plains Indians had been forced onto reservations.

F _____ 12. The Native American Ghost Dance movement called for tribes to submit to the dictates of the U.S. federal government.

LESSON II: FOR FURTHER STUDY

For even more interesting information about this period of history, please refer to the For Further Study answers for this lesson in the Teacher's Guide.

1. Discover who Frederick Jackson Turner was and how his ideas influenced the study of American history at the turn of the century. What was the name of his famous thesis? What pronouncement did the U.S. government make three years before Turner announced his thesis?

2. Find out how the pioneers constructed soddies. What were the advantages and disadvantages of this type of home? Pioneer women were known for their patchwork quilts. How were they made? What were some popular designs? Look for pictures of American patchwork quilts.

3. Read about American cowboys. What different articles of clothing did they wear and what was the purpose of each? What dangers did these cowboys face on the

LESSON 12: SECOND INDUSTRIAL REVOLUTION

INDUSTRIALIZATION AND URBANIZATION

List three American industries that grew at an amazing pace during the Gilded Age. Beside each industry, write the name of an important individual associated with that industry.

Oil – John D. Rockefeller

Steel – Andrew Carnegie

Railroad – Cornelius Vanderbilt

List three industries that prospered in the South during the Gilded Age. Beside each industry, write the area in the South associated with that industry.

Lumber and turpentine – coastal plains

Textiles – Piedmont

Cigarettes – Durham and Winston-Salem, NC

What were problems associated with increasing U.S. urbanization? _____ noise, air pollution, slums, sanitation and garbage problems, and health issues

Identify the two large labor unions established in the United States during this period. American Federation of Labor (AFL), Knights of Labor

Why were immigrants not welcomed by some Americans? They feared the job competition that immigrants represented and resented the use of taxpayer money to provide immigrant children with the extra help that they needed at school.

AGRICULTURE

What problems did American farmers face in the Gilded Age? _____ Many small farmers were forced into foreclosure on their farms due to the decline in crop prices caused by overproduction and foreign competition. Many southern farmers became ensnared in the crop lien system. Railroads, bankers, and middlemen reduced the profits of all farmers.

List three organizations that American farmers helped to establish during the second half of the nineteenth century. National Grange, Farmers' Alliance, Populist Party

TRANSPORTATION

What problems did U.S. railroads create during the Gilded Age? _____ Railroad workers went on strike because they labored long hours for low pay, and farmers resented the high fees that railroads charged to haul their produce.

List two types of water transportation that continued to be important in this period. steamboats, barges

COMMUNICATION

Which method of communication was most popular in the United States during the period between 1860 and 1920? _____ magazines and newspapers

How did the term "yellow journalism" derive its name? _____ from a daily cartoon character known as the "Yellow Kid"

Answer Key to the Forms, Maps, and For Review Questions in the Student Activity Book

LESSON 12: FOR REVIEW

Write the letter of the correct answer in the space provided.

A _____ 1. During the Gilded Age,
A. railroad and steel industries grew at a phenomenal rate
B. oil and electric industries failed to grow
C. the United States was not among the top industrial world powers
D. the South became more industrialized than the North

D _____ 2. Which of the following was NOT an important southern industry during the Gilded Age?
A. lumber
B. textiles
C. cigarettes
D. steel

B _____ 3. In the last quarter of the nineteenth century,
A. most immigrants settled on farms in the South
B. the United States became increasingly urbanized
C. most factories were not located in major cities
D. American industries had tremendous difficulty finding workers

C _____ 4. American cities during the Gilded Age
A. were not interested in building mass transit systems
B. were not usually bothered by air and noise pollution
C. had significant sanitation and garbage problems
D. offered few cultural activities for the people living there

A _____ 5. With rapid growth in industrialization, America during the last quarter of the nineteenth century
A. witnessed the amassing of great fortunes by a small group of industrialists
B. rejected capitalism
C. saw few businessmen involved in ruthless practices to wipe out competitors
D. developed an upper class whose wealth was based upon titles and landed estates

D _____ 6. Which of the following was NOT an American "captain of industry" during the Gilded Age?
A. Cornelius Vanderbilt
B. John D. Rockefeller
C. Andrew Carnegie
D. Samuel Gompers

C _____ 7. The Noble Order of the Knights of Labor
A. was founded by Oliver Kelley
B. did not want to unite unskilled and skilled workers in one union
C. reached the height of its influence under Terence Powderly
D. continued to grow rapidly well into the twentieth century

A _____ 8. The American Federation of Labor
A. was composed of trade or craft unions representing skilled labor
B. declined in membership after 1890
C. had long-term political goals
D. opened its membership to all workers, regardless of race, gender, nationality, or skills

B _____ 9. During the 1880s,
A. there were few labor strikes
B. the federal government did not recognize the right of workers to organize
C. state governments refused to send out militia to deal with labor unrest
D. violent labor strikes occurred every few years

A _____ 15. During the Gilded Age, U.S. railroads
   A. caused a decline in the importance of water transportation in the country
   B. paid their workers excellent wages
   C. were able to avoid being subject to federal regulation
   D. never worried about their workers going on strike

D _____ 16. Which of the following is NOT true of communication in the United States during the Gilded Age?
   A. magazines and newspapers benefited from technological advances
   B. over 650,000 telephones were in use
   C. yellow journalism had not yet become a problem
   D. the telegraph had not yet been developed

LESSON 12: FOR FURTHER STUDY

For even more interesting information about this period of history, please refer to the For Further Study answers for this lesson in the Teacher's Guide.

1. Read more about John Rockefeller, Andrew Carnegie, and/or Cornelius Vanderbilt. Find out how they eliminated their competition to become multimillionaires. How did these men treat their workers? For what philanthropic deeds did they become known?

2. Research the Haymarket Square Riot (1886), the Homestead Lockout (1892), and/or the Pullman Strike (1894). Against which companies were the workers in each of these situations striking? Why were they striking? How were they treated by management? What was the end result of each strike?

3. What was the role of political machines and bosses in large cities during the Gilded Age? Read about "Boss" Tweed who ran the Tammany Hall political machine in the years leading up to the Gilded Age. What role did Thomas Nast play in Boss Tweed's life?

4. Look for information on the Morrill Land-Grant College Act of 1862 and the Hatch Act of 1887. What impact did they have on American agriculture? When was the Department of Agriculture made a cabinet position?

B _____ 10. From 1880 until the turn of the century,
   A. the number of immigrants arriving in the United States declined
   B. more and more immigrants began coming from southern and eastern Europe
   C. most immigrants arrived in the United States at Miami
   D. Chinese immigrants were highly valued and welcomed by Americans

C _____ 11. Which of the following was NOT true of immigration during the Gilded Age?
   A. immigrants often crowded into American urban enclaves
   B. American public schools sought to teach immigrant children English
   C. almost all immigrants made America their permanent home
   D. many established Americans feared the job competition that immigrants represented

D _____ 12. American farmers during the Gilded Age
   A. experienced a time of great prosperity
   B. were able to prevent American agriculture from becoming mechanized and specialized
   C. remained the self-sufficient Jeffersonian ideal that formed the backbone of the nation
   D. struggled desperately due to falling cotton and wheat prices

C _____ 13. The Grange
   A. grew most rapidly in New Hampshire and Maine
   B. served only as a social organization for farmers
   C. helped to establish the federal government's right and responsibility to regulate railroads
   D. disapproved of cooperative stores and mills

B _____ 14. William Jennings Bryan
   A. vehemently opposed the free coinage of silver
   B. was sympathetic to the plight of American farmers
   C. was elected president of the United States in 1896
   D. believed that the gold standard was the only hope for American farmers economically

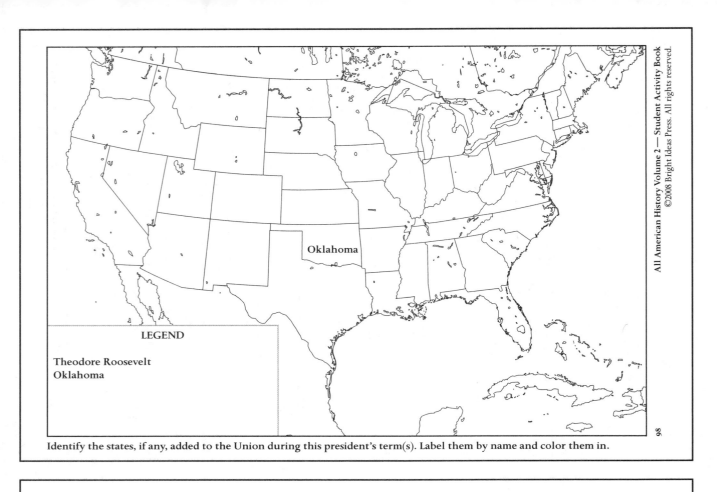

Identify the states, if any, added to the Union during this president's term(s). Label them by name and color them in.

Name _____ Date _____

LESSON 13: THEODORE ROOSEVELT

Picture of the president

Year born _____ 1858

Year died _____ 1919

In which state was he born? _____ New York

What jobs did he hold before becoming president? _____ Governor of New York,
Assistant Secretary of the Navy, Rough Rider, Vice President

With what political party was this president affiliated? _____ Republican

Vice President: _____ None, Charles Warren Fairbanks

What were the years of his presidency? _____ 1901 – 1909

List some significant developments during his administration _____ Trustbusting;

Northern Securities Company lawsuit

Hepburn Act (strengthening of Interstate Commerce Commission)

United Mine Workers strike

Establishment of Dept. of Commerce and Labor

Reclamation Act, Pure Food & Drug Act, Meat Inspection Act

Establishment of the U.S. Forest Service

"Big Stick" foreign policy: Roosevelt Corollary to the Monroe Doctrine

Panama Canal Treaty

Great White Fleet Tour; Gentleman's Agreement with Japan

Lesson 13: The Progressive Movement
©2008 Bright Ideas Press. All rights reserved.

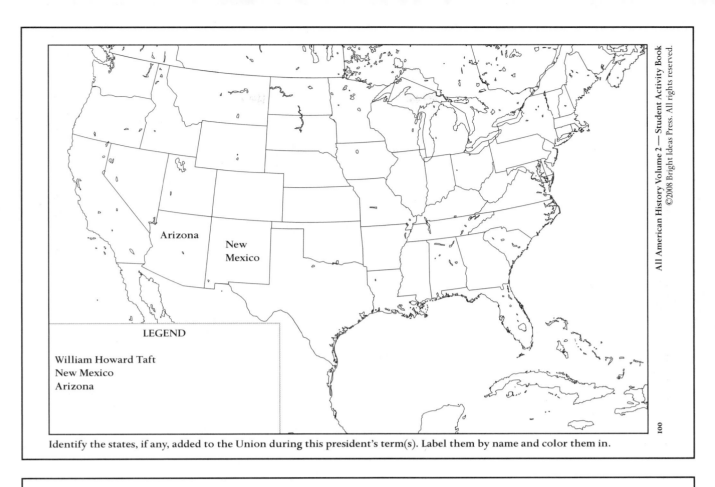

Arizona

New
Mexico

LEGEND

William Howard Taft
New Mexico
Arizona

100

Identify the states, if any, added to the Union during this president's term(s). Label them by name and color them in.

Name _____ Date _____

LESSON 13: WILLIAM HOWARD TAFT

Picture of the president

Year born _____ 1857

Year died _____ 1930

In which state was he born? _____ Ohio

What jobs did he hold before becoming president? _____ Lawyer, judge,
Governor of the Philippines, Secretary of War

With what political party was this president affiliated? _____ Republican

Vice President: _____ James S. Sherman

What were the years of his presidency? _____ 1909 - 1913

List some significant developments during his administration _____ Trustbusting
(nearly twice the number of antitrust suits as in Teddy Roosevelt's administration)

16th Amendment

Establishment of a separate Dept. of Labor

Payne-Aldrich Act (continuation of high tariff rates)

"Dollar diplomacy" foreign policy

Answer Key to the Forms, Maps, and For Review Questions in the Student Activity Book

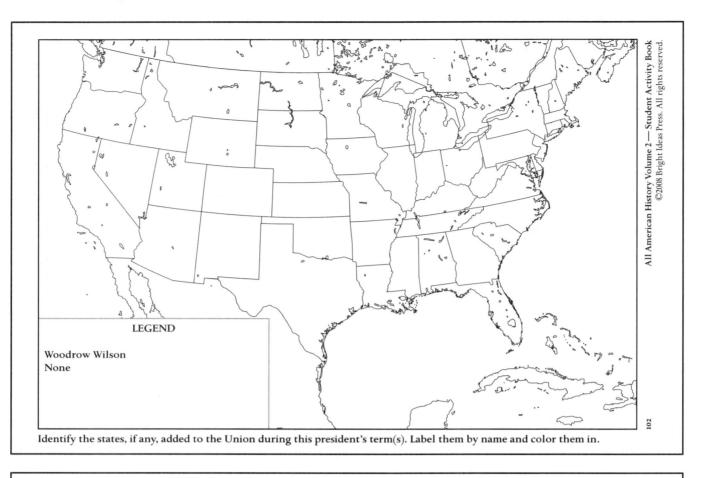

102

Identify the states, if any, added to the Union during this president's term(s). Label them by name and color them in.

Name _____ Date _____

LESSON 13: WOODROW WILSON

Picture of the president

Year born _____ 1856 _____

Year died _____ 1924 _____

In which state was he born? _____ Virginia _____

What jobs did he hold before becoming president? _____ Lawyer, president of Princeton University, Governor of New Jersey _____

With what political party was this president affiliated? _____ Democratic _____

Vice President: _____ Thomas R. Marshall, Thomas R. Marshall _____

What were the years of his presidency? _____ 1913 – 1921 _____

List some significant developments during his administration _____ 17th, 18th, and 19th ("Progressive") amendments

Underwood Tariff (first tariff reduction in almost 20 years)

Establishment of the Federal Trade Commission

Federal Reserve Act (reform of federal banking system)

Clayton Antitrust Act (legalization of strikes/boycotts/picketing and outlawing of price discrimination and of the formation of holding companies)

World War I

101

Lesson 13: The Progressive Movement
©2008 Bright Ideas Press. All rights reserved.

T ___ 13. Taft's administration actually busted more trusts than Teddy Roosevelt's.

T ___ 14. Taft alienated Progressives by refusing to veto the Payne-Aldrich Act.

T ___ 15. When Roosevelt decided to run for president on the Bull Moose ticket in 1912, he assured Taft's defeat by Wilson.

T ___ 16. Woodrow Wilson ran for president on a program that he called the "New Freedom."

F ___ 17. The Nineteenth Amendment to the U.S. Constitution called for the direct election of U.S. senators by the voters.

T ___ 18. The Eighteenth Amendment focused upon the controversial issue of the pro- hibition of the manufacture, sale, and transportation of alcoholic beverages.

Write the corresponding letter of the correct answer in the space provided.

A. Teddy Roosevelt   C. Woodrow Wilson
B. William Howard Taft

B ___ 1. Only president also to serve as chief justice of the Supreme Court

C ___ 2. President during World War I

A ___ 3. The first trustbusting president

A ___ 4. Advocate of carrying a "big stick" in foreign policy

C ___ 5. President when the Seventeenth, Eighteenth, and Nineteenth Amendments were added to the U.S. Constitution

B ___ 6. President who took the first steps toward establishing a federal budget

A ___ 7. Winner of the Nobel Peace Prize

A ___ 8. Youngest president of the United States

B ___ 9. Advocate of "dollar diplomacy"

All American History Volume 2 — Student Activity Book
©2008 Bright Ideas Press. All rights reserved.

LESSON 13: FOR REVIEW
Write T for True and F for False in the space provided.

T ___ 1. The Progressive movement called for wider political participation and rejec- tion of laissez-faire economics.

T ___ 2. Progressives believed in government regulation of trusts and government ownership of businesses.

T ___ 3. Teddy Roosevelt was a dynamic and energetic president, who sought to use the presidency as a "bully pulpit."

F ___ 4. Roosevelt was careful not to take any actions as president that were not clearly specified either in the U.S. Constitution or in a federal law.

F ___ 5. Large business monopolies were not a big problem in the United States during the early years of the twentieth century.

T ___ 6. President Roosevelt believed that the federal government should arbitrate between conflicting economic forces in the United States, especially between labor and management.

F ___ 7. The new cabinet position created during Roosevelt's presidency was the Department of Energy.

F ___ 8. Conservation of America's natural resources was not very important to Teddy Roosevelt.

F ___ 9. The Roosevelt Corollary to the Monroe Doctrine emphasized that the United States should stay out of the affairs of other nations in the Western Hemisphere.

T ___ 10. Roosevelt signed a treaty with Panama, granting the United States use and control of a strip of land on which to build a canal.

F ___ 11. During his time in office, Teddy Roosevelt refused to allow the Great White Fleet to leave the United States.

F ___ 12. William Howard Taft was a charismatic politician who took on the office of the presidency with great enthusiasm.

Lesson 13: The Progressive Movement
©2008 Bright Ideas Press. All rights reserved.

Answer Key to the Forms, Maps, and For Review Questions in the Student Activity Book

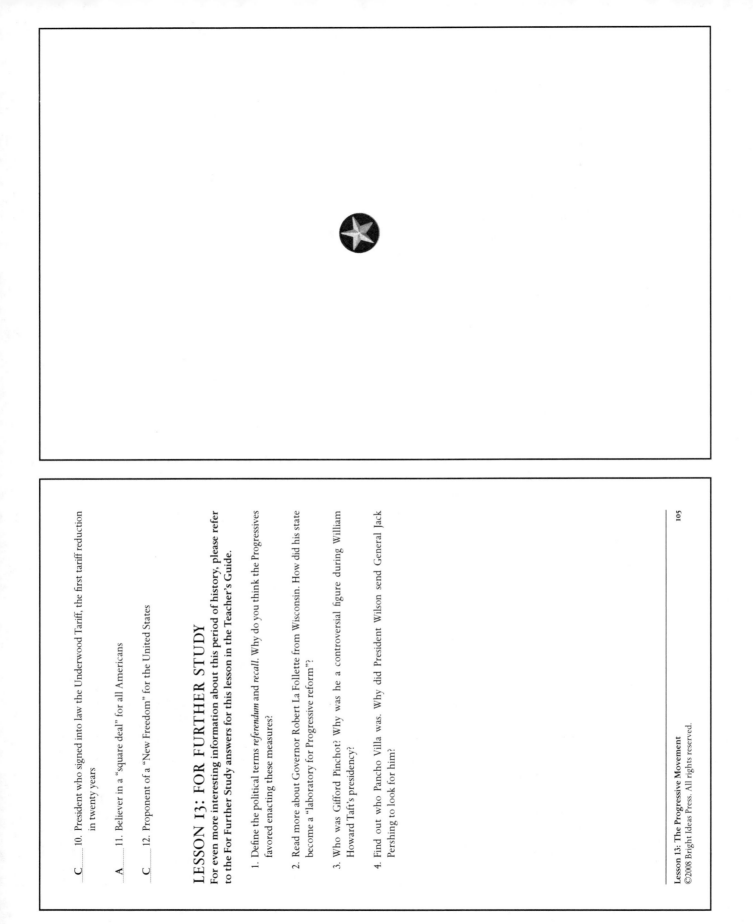

C ___ 10. President who signed into law the Underwood Tariff, the first tariff reduction in twenty years

A ___ 11. Believer in a "square deal" for all Americans

C ___ 12. Proponent of a "New Freedom" for the United States

LESSON 13: FOR FURTHER STUDY

For even more interesting information about this period of history, please refer to the For Further Study answers for this lesson in the Teacher's Guide.

1. Define the political terms *referendum* and *recall*. Why do you think the Progressives favored enacting these measures?

2. Read more about Governor Robert La Follette from Wisconsin. How did his state become a "laboratory for Progressive reform"?

3. Who was Gifford Pinchot? Why was he a controversial figure during William Howard Taft's presidency?

4. Find out who Pancho Villa was. Why did President Wilson send General Jack Pershing to look for him?

Lesson 13: The Progressive Movement
©2008 Bright Ideas Press. All rights reserved.

All American History, Vol. II: Teacher's Guide — Section Five

©2008 Bright Ideas Press. All rights reserved.

Name _____ Date _____

LESSON 14: REVIEW OF PRESIDENTS

Fill in the blanks with the names of the first twenty-five presidents in order.
The acrostic is provided as a tool to help you remember.

#	Acrostic	President's Name
	First Set	
1.	Why:	George Washington
2.	Are:	John Adams
3.	Jeff:	Thomas Jefferson
4.	Madison:	James Madison
5.	Monty:	James Monroe
6.	and:	John Quincy Adams
7.	Jack:	Andrew Jackson
8.	Buying:	Martin van Buren
9.	Horses?:	William Henry Harrison
	Second Set	
10.	Take:	John Tyler
11.	Poor:	James Polk
12.	Taylor's:	Zachary Taylor
13.	Filly:	Millard Fillmore
14.	Past:	Franklin Pierce
15.	Both:	James Buchanan
16.	Lincoln's:	Abraham Lincoln
17.	Jogging:	Andrew Johnson
18.	Goats:	Ulysses S. Grant
	Third Set	
19.	Happy:	Rutherford B. Hayes
20.	Goats:	James A. Garfield
21.	Always:	Chester A. Arthur
22.	Catch:	Grover Cleveland
23.	Horses:	Benjamin Harrison
24.	Creating:	Grover Cleveland
25.	Mischief:	William McKinley

Lesson 14: Gilded Age Family Life

107

Answer Key to the Forms, Maps, and For Review Questions in the Student Activity Book   195

LESSON 14: FOR REVIEW
Write the missing word or words in the spaces provided.

1. Female suffragists in the late nineteenth century worked to secure the adoption of a constitutional amendment that would give American women the right to ____vote____.

2. The American female suffragist who founded the magazine *Revolution* and insisted that American women were subjected to "taxation without representation" was ____Susan B. Anthony____.

3. The ____Chautauqua____ movement, started in 1874, gave Americans in various communities the opportunity to gather for three to seven days to enjoy a series of lectures on a variety of subjects.

4. The first major mail-order company in the United States was ____Montgomery Ward____, founded in 1872.

5. The American mail-order company that published a catalog called *The Farmer's Friend* was ____Sears, Roebuck and Company____.

6. Lord and Taylor was an example of a new American phenomenon during the Gilded Age, the ____department store____.

7. By the 1890s, most American women liked the ____Gibson Girl____ look, inspired by the sketches of the American artist Charles Gibson.

8. During the 1880s and 1890s, ____Little Lord Fauntleroy____ suits were popular for boys two to nine years old.

Write T for True and F for False in the space provided.

F   1. The average life span of an American in 1900 was not much longer than that of an American in 1800.

F   2. Americans during the Gilded Age were marrying earlier than in previous periods and having many more children.

T   3. Before proposing marriage to a young lady, a young man at the turn of the century usually engaged in a period of courtship with her and needed to ask her father for permission to marry her.

F   4. The majority of American women during the Gilded Age worked outside their homes.

T   5. The invention of the typewriter and telephone affected the role of American women in the work world.

T   6. During the second half of the nineteenth century, many states passed compulsory education laws.

F   7. By 1900, there were few one-room schoolhouses left in the United States, and McGuffey Readers were no longer used.

F   8. During the Gilded Age, it was rare for a woman to make her family's clothes at home.

F   9. Men's clothing at the turn of the century was very informal and innovative.

T   10. A man in the late 1800s was considered to be clean shaven if he shaved two times a week.

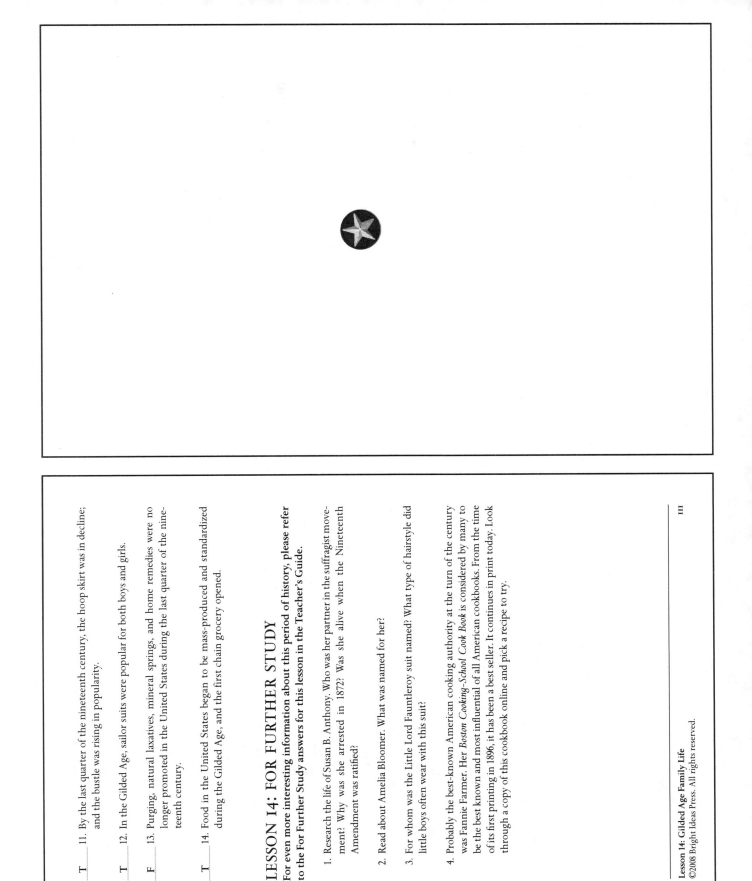

T 11. By the last quarter of the nineteenth century, the hoop skirt was in decline; and the bustle was rising in popularity.

T 12. In the Gilded Age, sailor suits were popular for both boys and girls.

F 13. Purging, natural laxatives, mineral springs, and home remedies were no longer promoted in the United States during the last quarter of the nineteenth century.

T 14. Food in the United States began to be mass-produced and standardized during the Gilded Age, and the first chain grocery opened.

LESSON 14: FOR FURTHER STUDY
For even more interesting information about this period of history, please refer to the For Further Study answers for this lesson in the Teacher's Guide.

1. Research the life of Susan B. Anthony. Who was her partner in the suffragist movement? Why was she arrested in 1872? Was she alive when the Nineteenth Amendment was ratified?

2. Read about Amelia Bloomer. What was named for her?

3. For whom was the Little Lord Fauntleroy suit named? What type of hairstyle did little boys often wear with this suit?

4. Probably the best-known American cooking authority at the turn of the century was Fannie Farmer. Her *Boston Cooking-School Cook Book* is considered by many to be the best known and most influential of all American cookbooks. From the time of its first printing in 1896, it has been a best seller. It continues in print today. Look through a copy of this cookbook online and pick a recipe to try.

III

Lesson 14: Gilded Age Family Life

Answer Key to the Forms, Maps, and For Review Questions in the Student Activity Book

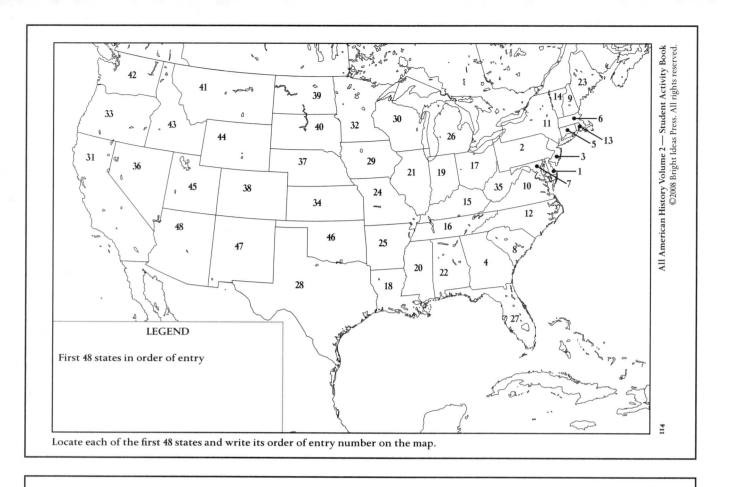

Locate each of the first 48 states and write its order of entry number on the map.

114

Name _____ Date _____

LESSON 15: REVIEW OF STATES AND CAPITALS

Fill in the blanks with the names of the state capitals.

#	State	Capital City	#	State	Capital City
1.	Delaware:	Dover	30.	Wisconsin:	Madison
2.	Pennsylvania:	Harrisburg	31.	California:	Sacramento
3.	New Jersey:	Trenton	32.	Minnesota:	St. Paul
4.	Georgia:	Atlanta	33.	Oregon:	Salem
5.	Connecticut:	Hartford	34.	Kansas:	Topeka
6.	Massachusetts:	Boston	35.	West Virginia:	Charleston
7.	Maryland:	Annapolis	36.	Nevada:	Carson City
8.	South Carolina:	Columbia	37.	Nebraska:	Lincoln
9.	New Hampshire:	Concord	38.	Colorado:	Denver
10.	Virginia:	Richmond	39.	North Dakota:	Bismarck
11.	New York:	Albany	40.	South Dakota:	Pierre
12.	North Carolina:	Raleigh	41.	Montana:	Helena
13.	Rhode Island:	Providence	42.	Washington:	Olympia
14.	Vermont:	Montpelier	43.	Idaho:	Boise
15.	Kentucky:	Frankfort	44.	Wyoming:	Cheyenne
16.	Tennessee:	Nashville	45.	Utah:	Salt Lake City
17.	Ohio:	Columbus	46.	Oklahoma:	Oklahoma City
18.	Louisiana:	Baton Rouge	47.	New Mexico:	Santa Fe
19.	Indiana:	Indianapolis	48.	Arizona:	Phoenix
20.	Mississippi:	Jackson			
21.	Illinois:	Springfield			
22.	Alabama:	Montgomery			
23.	Maine:	Augusta			
24.	Missouri:	Jefferson City			
25.	Arkansas:	Little Rock			
26.	Michigan:	Lansing			
27.	Florida:	Tallahassee			
28.	Texas:	Austin			
29.	Iowa:	Des Moines			

LESSON 15: FOR REVIEW

Write the letter of the correct answer in the space provided.

B _____ 1. During the Gilded Age,
- A. the United States witnessed the creation of an upper class based upon family titles and landed estates
- B. many of the newly rich in the United States were known for their "conspicuous consumption"
- C. the number of poor Americans had dramatically declined
- D. there was little need for social reformers to worry about drives to help the poor

D _____ 2. Which of the following was NOT true of social reformers during the Gilded Age?
- A. many of them focused on promoting the prohibition of alcohol
- B. they were criticized for not distinguishing between those worthy of being helped and those not
- C. they were accused of tampering with the natural laws of selection
- D. they no longer saw the need to establish settlement houses for the poor

A _____ 3. The test case for Jim Crow was
- A. Plessy v. Ferguson
- B. Roe v. Wade
- C. Brown v. the Board of Education of Topeka, Kansas
- D. Marbury v. Madison

B _____ 4. African Americans during the Gilded Age
- A. were no longer usually subordinate to and dependent upon white Americans
- B. were most likely to live in the South
- C. had many more opportunities for economic advancement
- D. successfully protected their right to vote

D _____ 5. Which of the following was NOT true about Jim Crow?
- A. Jim Crow was a happy black character in a song
- B. white entertainers often played Jim Crow on stage
- C. Jim Crow refers to the segregation of the races in American society
- D. Jim Crow only lasted for a few years

C _____ 6. At the turn of the century,
- A. most Americans were still Catholic
- B. Darwinism had little impact on Christianity
- C. the majority of U.S. congregations were Methodist, Baptist, or Presbyterian
- D. the social gospel emphasized the divine inspiration and inerrancy of the Bible and the sinfulness of man

B _____ 7. Dwight L. Moody
- A. held revivals in small theaters and churches
- B. was accompanied by a song leader named Ira Sankey
- C. only traveled to the South to do revivals
- D. was unwilling to use less formal gospel songs at his revivals

C _____ 8. Americans in the Gilded Age
- A. had less time for recreational activities
- B. had not yet been introduced to the circus
- C. enjoyed the first American amusement park at Coney Island
- D. no longer emphasized sports and other physical activities

A _____ 9. The most popular American spectator sport in the Gilded Age was
- A. baseball
- B. basketball
- C. football
- D. soccer

C _____ 10. The most popular American participant sport during the last quarter of the nineteenth century was
- A. wrestling
- B. tennis
- C. bicycling
- D. karate

Answer Key to the Forms, Maps, and For Review Questions in the Student Activity Book

3. Read more about the lives of Booker T. Washington and W. E. B. Du Bois. Record the information on African American forms.

4. Find and read one of Dwight L. Moody's sermons and some of Fanny Crosby's gospel songs.

Write the corresponding letter of the correct answer in the space provided.

A. Jane Addams   F. W. E. B. Du Bois
B. Caroline Astor   G. Dwight L. Moody
C. Fanny Crosby   H. James Naismith
D. Jim Crow   I. Homer Plessy
E. Charles Darwin   J. Booker T. Washington

H   1. Inventor of basketball

C   2. Most prolific composer of gospel songs in the nineteenth century

B   3. Creator of a list of four hundred prominent members of New York society

J   4. African American educator who believed that blacks could live with Jim Crow if they were given vocational training and jobs

G   5. Leader of an important urban evangelism movement during the Gilded Age

I   6. Individual who served as a test case for the legality of Jim Crow

A   7. Founder of the first American settlement house

D   8. Fictional character who became a symbol for segregation

F   9. African American who called for immediate political, economic, and social equality for black Americans

E   10. Originator of the theory of evolution

LESSON 15: FOR FURTHER STUDY

For even more interesting information about this period of history, please refer to the For Further Study answers for this lesson in the Teacher's Guide.

1. Find a copy of the list of Mrs. Astor's "Four Hundred." Does it really contain four hundred names? Is there anything similar to this list today?

2. Research the activities of the Woman's Christian Temperance Union and the Anti-Saloon League. Look for some of their printed materials — flyers, posters, banners, and cartoons.

SUMMARY OF PROJECTS AND SPECIAL ACTIVITIES

Units One and Two

READING

What biographies or nonfiction books have you read about these periods of history and who were the author(s)?

What historical fiction books have you read about these periods of history and who were the author(s)?

What magazine or Internet articles have you read about these periods of history?

FIELD TRIPS/VIRTUAL TOURS

What field trips or virtual tours have you taken to sites from these periods of history?

Which was your favorite and why?

MOVIES

What movies have you watched that are set in these time periods or what documentaries have you watched that are about persons or events from these time periods?

Which was the most interesting to you and why?

ART

What art projects have you completed that were about these time periods or were done in an artistic technique from these time periods?

NOTEBOOKS AND OTHER ACTIVITIES

Who has been highlighted in your Native American or African American notebook?

What other fun and creative activities have you done?

Answer Key to the Forms, Maps, and For Review Questions in the Student Activity Book

LESSON 16: FOR REVIEW

Write the missing word or words in the spaces provided.

1. The first official world's fair in the United States was ___the Philadelphia Centennial Exposition___, which celebrated the hundredth anniversary of the Declaration of Independence.

2. In 1893, the World's Columbian Exposition was held in ___Chicago___ to mark the four hundredth anniversary of Columbus's voyage to the New World.

3. By the 1880s, the popularity of minstrel shows was giving way to ___vaudeville___, which would remain America's most popular form of entertainment until the mid-1920s.

4. In the 1890s, a new kind of music called ___ragtime___, which featured syncopated rhythms, began to be embraced by African American and white musicians.

5. During the Gilded Age, ___realism___ and ___naturalism___ began to emerge in American literature, in contrast to the emotional romanticism of the years that preceded this period.

6. The painter of the Gilded Age known for his painting of his mother was ___James McNeill Whistler___.

7. The most dramatic American architectural development in the last quarter of the nineteenth century was the ___skyscraper___.

8. The ___Vanderbilt___ family outdid all other wealthy U.S. families of the era with their mansions and country estates, the largest being Biltmore House in Asheville, North Carolina.

9. The highly decorated exteriors of many middle-class urban homes in the Gilded Age belonged to the style of architecture referred to as ___Victorian Gothic___.

10. Young urban couples of lower-class families were often forced to live in ___boardinghouses___ near the center of town, where they shared facilities with other families in residence.

Write the corresponding letter of the correct answer in the space provided.

A. Horatio Alger
B. Edwin Booth
C. Mary Cassatt
D. George M. Cohan
E. Stephen Crane
F. Emily Dickinson
G. Victor Herbert
H. Winslow Homer
I. Henry James
J. Scott Joplin
K. Jack London
L. Frederick Remington
M. John Philip Sousa
N. Mark Twain

___H___ 1. American realist painter of outdoor life, especially the sea

___M___ 2. The "March King" who conducted the U.S. Marine band

___A___ 3. American author of rags-to-riches stories

Lesson 16: Gilded Age Culture: The Arts
©2008 Bright Ideas Press. All rights reserved.

121

All American History Volume 2 — Student Activity Book
©2008 Bright Ideas Press. All rights reserved.

122

202

All American History, Vol. II: Teacher's Guide — Section Five
©2008 Bright Ideas Press. All rights reserved.

3. Read a novel or a short story written by a realist author from the Gilded Age. Look at some of the paintings of realist painters from the era.

4. Research the life and work of Louis Sullivan, a famous American architect during the Gilded Age. What type of buildings did he design? How was he an architectural pioneer? For what did Louis Tiffany become known during this period in history? See if there are any homes in your area dating back to this period.

All American History Volume 2 — Student Activity Book
©2008 Bright Ideas Press. All rights reserved.

G _____ 4. Prolific American composer who wrote forty operettas in less than forty years

L _____ 5. American painter of cowboys, Indians, and western landscapes

J _____ 6. Popularizer of ragtime in the United States.

B _____ 7. Greatest stage actor in the United States during the Gilded Age

F _____ 8. American poet who pioneered a less formal and structured approach to poetry

K _____ 9. American realist author known for his novel Call of the Wild

N _____ 10. Perhaps the most popular American writer of the era, a master of humor and satire

C _____ 11. Leading American Impressionist of the era

I _____ 12. Novelist known for his realistic portrayals of upper-class Americans

D _____ 13. American composer who dominated Broadway musical theater at the turn of the century

E _____ 14. American realist author who wrote The Red Badge of Courage and Maggie: A Girl of the Streets

LESSON 16: FOR FURTHER STUDY

For even more interesting information about this period of history, please refer to the For Further Study answers for this lesson in the Teacher's Guide.

1. Two of the inventors showcased at the Philadelphia Centennial Exposition were Alexander Graham Bell and Thomas Edison. Read more about their lives and their inventions. Find out what George Eastman invented.

2. Listen to some of Scott Joplin's ragtime tunes, John Philip Sousa's marches, and George M. Cohan's Broadway hits. Also play some of the popular songs from the period, such as "Daisy Bell" and "My Wild Irish Rose."

Answer Key to the Forms, Maps, and For Review Questions in the Student Activity Book

UNIT 2: FINAL REVIEW

Write the corresponding letter of the correct answer in the space provided.

A. Rutherford B. Hayes
B. James A. Garfield
C. Chester A. Arthur
D. Grover Cleveland

E. Benjamin Harrison
F. William McKinley
G. Teddy Roosevelt
H. William Howard Taft
I. Woodrow Wilson

H ___ 1. Only president who also served as chief justice of the Supreme Court

B ___ 2. His assassination by an embittered office-seeker led to civil service reform

D ___ 3. First Democrat elected president after the Civil War

G ___ 4. Youngest president

A ___ 5. His disputed election in 1876 led to removal of all federal troops from the South

I ___ 6. President during World War I

C ___ 7. Member of the Stalwart faction of the Republican Party who became president upon the assassination of the incumbent who was a leader of the Half-Breed faction.

H ___ 8. Advocate of "dollar diplomacy"

F ___ 9. President during the Spanish-American War

D ___ 10. Only president elected to two nonconsecutive terms

G ___ 11. The first trustbusting president

E ___ 12. Grandson of a former president, who served when the Sherman Antitrust Act, Sherman Silver Purchase Act, and McKinley Tariff were enacted.

I ___ 13. Proponent of a "New Freedom" for the United States

G ___ 14. Advocate of carrying a "big stick" in U.S. foreign policy

D ___ 15. President during the Panic of 1893 and the four-year depression that followed

---

A. Rutherford B. Hayes
B. James A. Garfield
C. Chester A. Arthur
D. Grover Cleveland

E. Benjamin Harrison
F. William McKinley
G. Teddy Roosevelt
H. William Howard Taft
I. Woodrow Wilson

F ___ 16. His assassination by a mentally unstable anarchist at the Pan-American Exposition occurred at the turn of the century

C ___ 17. President when the Mongrel Tariff and Pendleton Act were passed by Congress

G ___ 18. Believer in a "square deal" for all Americans and winner of the Nobel Peace Prize

G ___ 19. Advocate of conservation of natural resources, a corollary to the Monroe Doctrine, and a canal in Panama

I ___ 20. President when the Seventeenth, Eighteenth, and Nineteenth Amendments were passed

Write the corresponding letter of the correct answer in the space provided.

A. William Jennings Bryan
B. Andrew Carnegie
C. Comstock Lode
D. Commodore George Dewey
E. Lt. Colonel George Custer
F. Dawes Act of 1887
G. Joseph Glidden
H. Samuel Gompers
I. Great American Desert
J. Homestead Act of 1862

K. Kettle Hill and San Juan Hill
L. Oliver Hudson Kelley
M. Ku Klux Klan
N. Major General Nelson Miles
O. William Randolph Hearst
P. John D. Rockefeller
Q. Teddy Roosevelt
R. Philippines
S. Puerto Rico
T. Sitting Bull

N ___ 1. Commander of U.S. armed forces in Cuba during the Spanish-American War

T ___ 2. Lakota chief who eventually joined Buffalo Bill's Wild West Show

J ___ 3. Promised U.S. settlers 160 acres of public land in the West if they lived on it for five years and paid a small fee

Top section (page 128)

Write T for True and F for False in the space provided.

F 1. By the end of the nineteenth century, the U.S. population had not dramatically increased.

T 2. A courting couple during the Gilded Age was required to be in sight of their parents or an adult chaperone.

T 3. Women in the late nineteenth century were often more socially active than women in previous eras.

F 4. Single women in the Gilded Age were not allowed to apply for office jobs.

F 5. Elizabeth Cady Stanton and Susan B. Anthony led the fight to prohibit women's suffrage at the turn of the century.

T 6. In rural areas of the United States, widespread poverty and sparse population had kept education relatively backward.

F 7. By 1900, a college education was available to any American who wanted to pursue it.

T 8. Perhaps the most popular of all Chautauqua speakers was William Jennings Bryan.

T 9. Isaac Singer and Elias Howe were instrumental in the development and marketing of the mechanized sewing machine.

F 10. Mail-order catalogs helped to boost the sales of small town merchants.

T 11. Men and boys in the Gilded Age slept in nightshirts and swam in sleeveless shirts and tights.

T 12. Women's fashions in the late nineteenth century continued to be inspired by European styles.

T 13. The shirtwaist and skirt became popular as a less restrictive and more versatile look for American women.

F 14. During the last quarter of the nineteenth century, Americans stopped dressing baby boys in dresses.

Bottom section (page 127)

L 4. Founder of the Grange, a political and social organization for farmers

K 5. American victory in Cuba

P 6. President of Standard Oil Company

G 7. Inventor of barbed wire, which led to the enclosure of land on the open range

R 8. Location of an insurrection led by nationalist guerillas after the Spanish-American War

M 9. Anti-African American and anti-Semitic organization

H 10. Leader of the American Federation of Labor (AFL)

I 11. The last western frontier, the Great American Plains

C 12. Nevada site of very rich silver mines

F 13. Broke up tribal lands into 160-acre plots, which were distributed among individual Indians

B 14. Industrialist who dominated the new steel industry

A 15. Three-time presidential nominee, who ran against McKinley on a platform advocating free coinage of silver

Q 16. Member of the U.S. First Volunteer Cavalry during the Spanish-American War

O 17. Proponent of yellow journalism

D 18. Commander of the U.S. naval forces that destroyed the Spanish fleet in Manila Bay

S 19. A U.S. possession in the Caribbean after 1898

E 20. American military commander who led troops massacred at Little Big Horn

Answer Key to the Forms, Maps, and For Review Questions in the Student Activity Book

F 15. At the turn of the century, medical treatment in the United States had become less dependent upon doctors, nurses, and hospitals.

F 16. By 1900 Americans had still not begun to understand the effects of germs and unclean water.

T 17. Processed cereals, one of the first foods to be promoted as a "health food," became a defining feature of many American breakfasts during the Gilded Age.

T 18. Many of the newly rich in American society were known for their "conspicuous consumption."

F 19. The Gilded Age was a period when there were no social reform movements.

T 20. The founder of Hull House, the first U.S. settlement house, was Jane Addams.

F 21. The Woman's Christian Temperance Union (WCTU) worked to ban women's suffrage.

T 22. According to the Social Darwinists, the weak were meant to perish, and strong survivors were needed to improve the human race.

F 23. In *Plessy v. Ferguson*, the Supreme Court ruled that Jim Crow was unconstitutional.

F 24. Booker T. Washington and W. E. B. Du Bois agreed on the best way for African Americans to gain equality.

F 25. At the turn of the century, most Americans were Catholic or Jewish.

F 26. Charles Darwin's theory of evolution never had an impact upon Christianity.

F 27. Dwight L. Moody held revival meetings in small rural towns and on the western frontier.

T 28. Americans in the Gilded Age had more time available for recreation because of the increasing number of home labor-saving devices.

T 29. During the last quarter of the nineteenth century, baseball was the most popular American spectator sport, and bicycling was the most popular participant sport.

T 30. Newspaper sportswriters created national sports heroes, and large stadiums began to be built in many U.S. cities during the Gilded Age.

F 31. The first world's fair in the United States did not occur until after World War II.

T 32. Theater was an important entertainment medium in the United States during the second half of the nineteenth century.

F 33. By the 1880s, the popularity of vaudeville was giving way to minstrel shows, which would remain America's most popular form of entertainment until the mid-1920s.

T 34. During the Gilded Age, a wide variety of music was popular.

F 35. John Philip Sousa became well known as the developer of a new kind of music known as ragtime.

T 36. By 1900, as many as three million phonograph records were being sold each year in the United States.

F 37. American writers and painters during the Gilded Age were known for their romantic, idealized portrayals.

T 38. Perhaps the most popular author of the era was Mark Twain.

F 39. The leading American Impressionist of the Gilded Age was James Whistler.

T 40. The most dramatic American architectural development in the last quarter of the nineteenth century was the skyscraper.

All American History, Vol. II: Teacher's Guide — Section Five

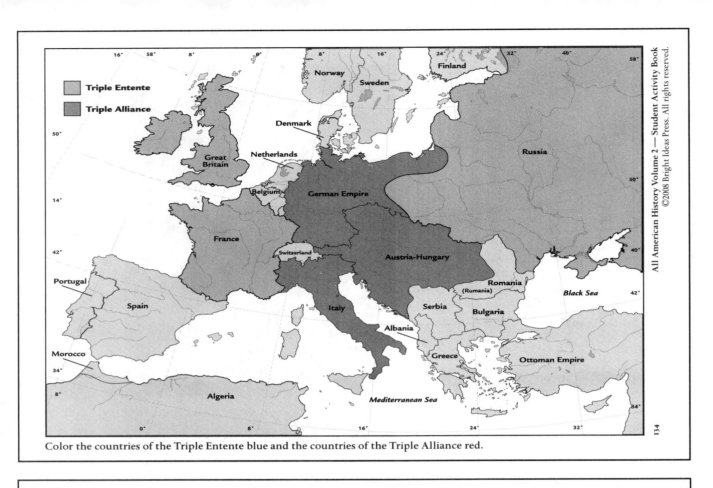

Color the countries of the Triple Entente blue and the countries of the Triple Alliance red.

134

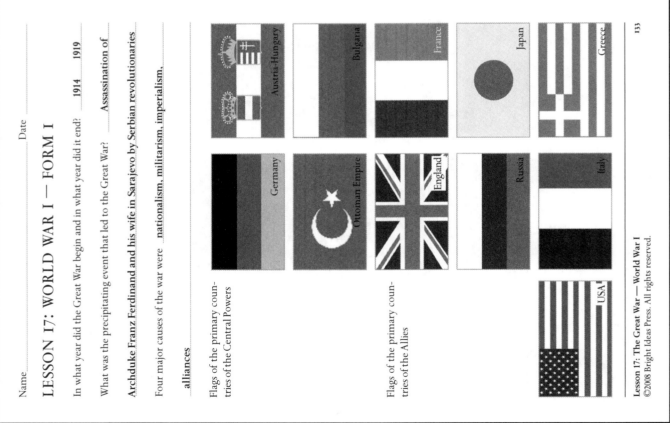

Name _____ Date _____

LESSON 17: WORLD WAR I — FORM I

In what year did the Great War begin and in what year did it end?   1914   1919

What was the precipitating event that led to the Great War?   Assassination of

Archduke Franz Ferdinand and his wife in Sarajevo by Serbian revolutionaries

Four major causes of the war were   nationalism, militarism, imperialism,

alliances

Flags of the primary countries of the Central Powers

Flags of the primary countries of the Allies

Austria-Hungary

Bulgaria

France

Japan

Greece

Germany

Ottoman Empire

England

Russia

Italy

USA

133

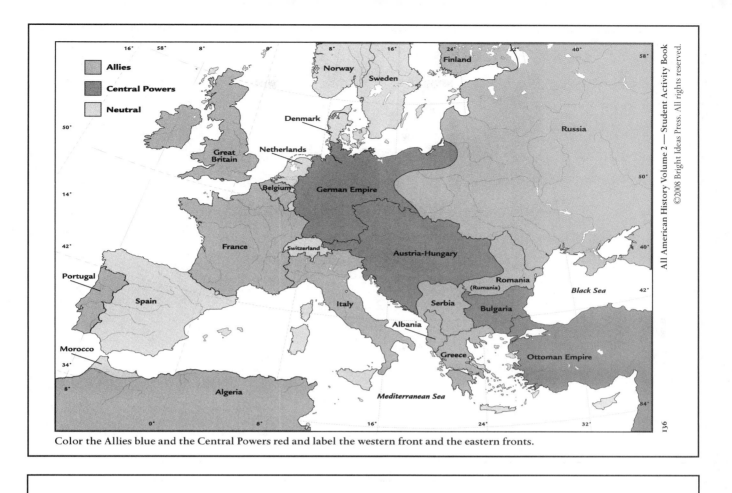

Allies
Central Powers
Neutral

Color the Allies blue and the Central Powers red and label the western front and the eastern fronts.

136

Name _____ Date _____

LESSON 17: WORLD WAR I — FORM 2

Explain what happened on the western front during the first three and a half years of the war. __The western front remained deadlocked in trench warfare.__

Explain what happened to end the fighting on the eastern front. __Following the Russian Revolution, the new Bolshevik leader, Vladimir Lenin, called for peace talks with Germany. Russia signed a peace treaty with Germany in March 1918.__

What two events led to American involvement in World War I and when did the United States enter the Great War? __Sinking of the *Lusitania*,__ __the Zimmermann note, April 6, 1917__

How did Americans help the war effort? By buying war bonds, __observing wheatless/meatless/sugarless days,__ __planting victory gardens__

President Wilson proposed a series of war aims that became known as __the Fourteen Points__

The turning point of the war was the Second Battle of __the Marne__

The armistice that ended the Great War (World War I) was signed on __November 11, 1918__

The peace conference was held at __Versailles from January to June 1919__

Some of the key individuals at the peace conference _____

Commander of the American Expeditionary Force _____

135

Answer Key to the Forms, Maps, and For Review Questions in the Student Activity Book

LESSON 17: FOR REVIEW

Write T for True and F for False in the space provided.

T _____ 1. The murder of Archduke Franz Ferdinand was plotted by a Serbian revolutionary organization known as the Black Hand.

F _____ 2. Serbia refused to agree to any of the demands sent by Austria-Hungary, making war inevitable.

T _____ 3. A complex web of alliances led all the major nations of Europe into war in less than three months' time.

F _____ 4. Austria-Hungary acted as the leader of the Central Powers.

T _____ 5. The Allies included Italy, who had been allied with Germany and Austria-Hungary before the war.

T _____ 6. Because Russia showed unexpected strength, the Central Powers were forced to fight a two-front war until 1917.

F _____ 7. In the early years of the war, the Allies succeeded in capturing several hundred miles along the western front.

T _____ 8. Poison gas, gas-propelled machine guns, and tanks were all used during the Great War.

T _____ 9. The length of the eastern front was much longer than that of the western front.

F _____ 10. The British and French succeeded in reopening the supply route to Russia that linked the Mediterranean to the Black Sea.

F _____ 11. When World War I began, most Americans pushed President Wilson to bring the United States into the war.

T _____ 12. When Germany announced the resumption of unrestricted submarine warfare in 1917, Wilson immediately broke off diplomatic relations with the German government.

F _____ 13. The first American forces arrived in Europe in the summer of 1919.

T _____ 14. Soon after Lenin took over the Russian government in late 1917, the Great War was over on the eastern front.

T _____ 15. The Second Battle of the Marne in 1918 served as the turning point of World War I for the Allies.

F _____ 16. World War I brought few changes to the map of Europe.

T _____ 17. Most of the decisions at the Versailles peace talks were made by the "Big Four."

F _____ 18. Wilson's Fourteen Points were enthusiastically embraced at Versailles, and many of them were included in the final peace treaty.

T _____ 19. A section of the Versailles treaty blamed World War I entirely on the Central Powers, especially Germany.

F _____ 20. The United States moved quickly to approve the Treaty of Versailles.

LESSON 17: FOR FURTHER STUDY

For even more interesting information about this period of history, please refer to the For Further Study answers for this lesson in the Teacher's Guide.

1. Germany had been planning for a major war for years. The name of its war plan was the Schlieffen Plan. Find out why it had this name and what the plan entailed. Discover what territory Germany had taken from France that the French were determined to recover.

2. Read more about trench warfare and the weapons used in World War I, especially poison gas. What challenges were faced by soldiers in the trenches? Look for pictures of German U-boats and find out what a zeppelin was. Who were the "Red Baron" and Eddie Rickenbacker?

3. Pick one or more of the battles of the Great War to research. Some of the major battles included Verdun, the Somme, Belleau Wood, St. Mihiel, and the Argonne. If this is an area of interest, compile a World War I Battles Notebook. There are forms in the optional forms section of the *Student Activity Book* to use to do this.

4. Find a copy of Wilson's Fourteen Points and read them. Do you think World War II would have occurred if all these points had been adopted?

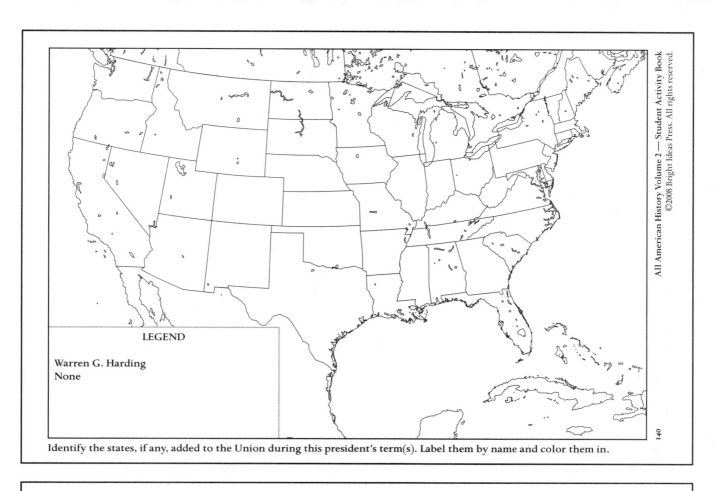

140

Identify the states, if any, added to the Union during this president's term(s). Label them by name and color them in.

LEGEND

Warren G. Harding
None

Name _____ Date _____

LESSON 18: WARREN G. HARDING

Picture of the president

Year born _____ 1865

Year died _____ 1923

In which state was he born? _____ Ohio

What jobs did he hold before becoming president? Newspaper publisher,

U.S. Senator

With what political party was this president affiliated? _____ Republican

Vice President: _____ Calvin Coolidge

What were the years of his presidency? _____ 1921 – 1923

List some significant developments during his administration _____ Signing of peace

treaties with Germany and the other Central Powers

Elimination of wartime controls and restrictions

Tax reductions

Creation of federal budget system

Increase in protective tariffs

Immigration restrictions

Scandals involving officials in Harding's administration

Answer Key to the Forms, Maps, and For Review Questions in the Student Activity Book

211

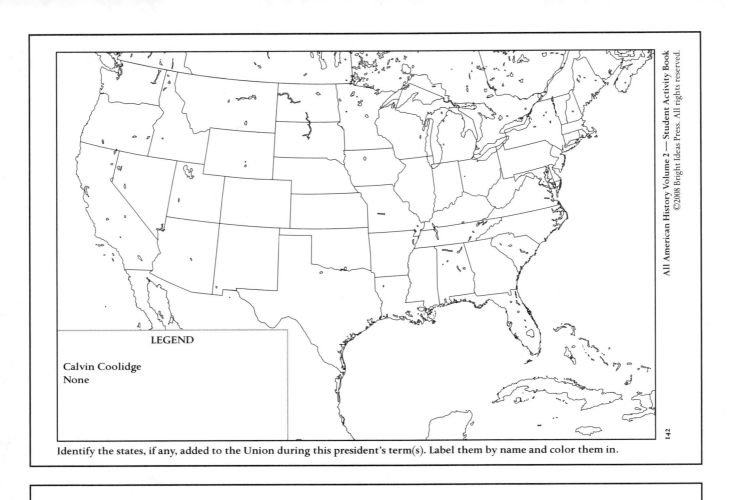

LEGEND

Calvin Coolidge
None

Identify the states, if any, added to the Union during this president's term(s). Label them by name and color them in.

142

Name _____ Date _____

LESSON 18: CALVIN COOLIDGE

Picture of the president

Year born _____ 1872 _____

Year died _____ 1933 _____

In which state was he born? _____ Vermont _____

What jobs did he hold before becoming president? _____ Governor of Massachusetts, _____

_____ Vice President _____

With what political party was this president affiliated? _____ Republican _____

Vice President: _____ None, Charles G. Dawes _____

What were the years of his presidency? _____ 1923 – 1929 _____

List some significant developments during his administration _____ Reduction in the _____

_____ national debt _____

_____ Growing speculation in the stock market (unregulated by the federal government) _____

_____ Dawes Plan (reduction in German reparations) _____

_____ More generous repayment terms for Allied war debts owed to U.S. _____

141

LESSON 18: FOR REVIEW

Write the letter of the correct answer in the space provided.

B 1. Warren G. Harding
   A. conducted a whistle-stop campaign for the presidency and won a very narrow victory
   B. believed that Wilson had usurped powers that belonged to Congress
   C. refused to sign peace treaties with Germany and the Central Powers
   D. signed laws calling for tax increases and lower protective tariffs

D 2. Which of the following is NOT true of Harding's administration?
   A. laws eliminating wartime controls and restrictions
   B. restrictions on immigration
   C. a rebound from the short postwar recession
   D. an absence of scandal and corruption

B 3. Calvin Coolidge was
   A. known as a big spender, drinker, and partygoer
   B. appreciated for his dry wit and humor
   C. criticized for his wordiness and long-windedness
   D. the first American president born after the Civil War

C 4. As president, Coolidge
   A. believed that federal power should be used to stop speculation in the stock market
   B. called for tax hikes
   C. supported high protective tariffs
   D. increased the national debt by over a million dollars

A 5. During the 1920s,
   A. the American government generally favored the interests of big business over workers' rights
   B. American labor unions rarely resorted to strikes
   C. the American Federation of Labor declined in membership
   D. the American labor movement was not investigated for communists or socialists

Lesson 18: The Roaring Twenties

C 6. In the Roaring Twenties,
   A. immigration quotas favored immigrants from southern and eastern Europe
   B. more lenient immigration laws were passed
   C. the number of Jewish and Italian immigrants was limited
   D. the execution of Sacco and Vanzetti was not controversial

A 7. The period from 1900 – 1920
   A. has often been called the golden age of agriculture in the United States
   B. brought few new technological innovations for American farmers
   C. was the beginning of the dominance of agriculture in the nation's economy
   D. was a time of low prices and declining land values for U.S. farmers

C 8. In the early 1900s, which of the following was NOT true?
   A. Americans living in urban areas often had access to horse-drawn trolleys
   B. railroads were the only feasible option available for long-distance travel
   C. travel by rail was quick, clean, and easy
   D. the U.S. railroad system was the largest, best managed transportation system in the world

B 9. Following the invention of the automobile,
   A. American factories immediately began producing practical and reliable cars
   B. Henry Ford pioneered the use of the assembly-line method of production to produce his Model T cars
   C. only the rich and adventurous were able to become car owners for more than twenty-five years
   D. Ford sold his Model T cars at prices too high for most Americans

D 10. By the turn of the century,
   A. the number of American newspapers had dramatically decreased
   B. few newspapers were interested in printing sensational stories
   C. advertising in American magazines had declined
   D. many newspapers introduced new features like recipes, puzzles, and comic strips

All American History Volume 2 — Student Activity Book

Answer Key to the Forms, Maps, and For Review Questions in the Student Activity Book

Write the corresponding letter of the correct answer in the space provided.

A. Calvin Coolidge   E. Happy Hooligan
B. Amelia Earhart   F. Charles Lindbergh
C. Henry Ford   G. A. Mitchell Palmer
D. Warren G. Harding   H. Orville and Wilbur Wright

A _____ 1. President whose campaign slogan called for Americans to "keep cool" with him

C _____ 2. Manufacturer of the new Model T automobile

D _____ 3. Associated with a "return to normalcy" in the United States

F _____ 4. Succeeded in making the first nonstop flight between New York and Paris

D _____ 5. President who died in office just as several scandals in his administration were being uncovered

H _____ 6. Flew the first heavier-than-air flight at Kitty Hawk, North Carolina

E _____ 7. Comic strip introduced at the turn of the century

A _____ 8. Known for never wasting a word and for his frugality in an age of carefree recklessness

B _____ 9. First woman to fly solo across the Atlantic

G _____ 10. Attorney general who investigated communism and socialism in the U.S. labor movement

LESSON 18: FOR FURTHER STUDY

For even more interesting information about this period of history, please refer to the For Further Study answers for this lesson in the Teacher's Guide.

1. During the 1920s, there were several attempts to bring about international disarmament and world peace. Three of these included the Washington Naval Conference (1921 – 1922), the Locarno Pact (1925), and the Kellogg-Briand Pact (1928). Discover what each of these sought to accomplish.

2. Research the Teapot Dome scandal. To what did "teapot dome" refer? Find out the details of the other scandals that occurred during Harding's administration.

3. Albert Einstein and Robert Goddard were responsible for important scientific developments during the first twenty-five years of the twentieth century. Read about the lives of these men and their accomplishments.

4. Find out who the Wobblies (the IWW) are. Look for information about the activities of "Big Bill" Haywood and Eugene V. Debs.

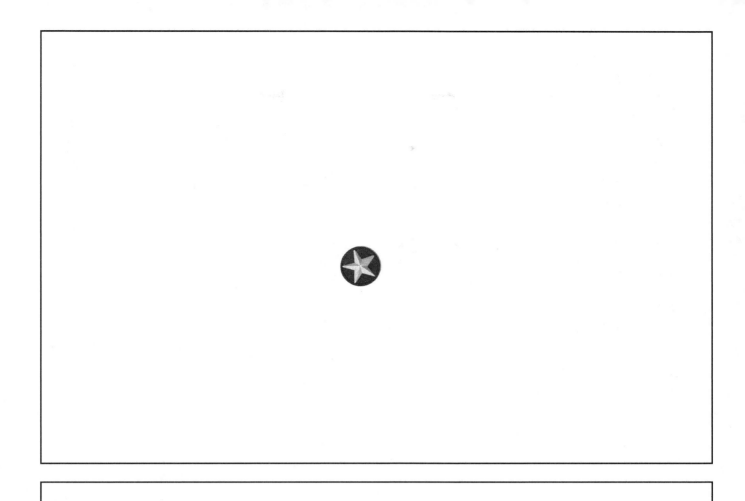

LESSONS 19 AND 21: REVIEW OF PRESIDENTS

Name _____ Date _____

Fill in the blanks with the names of the first through thirty-second presidents in order. The acrostic is provided as a tool to help you remember.

#	Acrostic	President's Name
First Set		
1.	Why:	George Washington
2.	Are:	John Adams
3.	Jeff:	Thomas Jefferson
4.	Madison:	James Madison
5.	Monty:	James Monroe
6.	and:	John Quincy Adams
7.	Jack:	Andrew Jackson
8.	Buying:	Martin van Buren
9.	Horses?:	William Henry Harrison
Second Set		
10.	Take:	John Tyler
11.	Poor:	James Polk
12.	Taylor's:	Zachary Taylor
13.	Filly:	Millard Fillmore
14.	Past:	Franklin Pierce
15.	Both:	James Buchanan
16.	Lincoln's:	Abraham Lincoln
17.	Jogging:	Andrew Johnson
18.	Goats:	Ulysses S. Grant
Third Set		
19.	Happy:	Rutherford B. Hayes
20.	Goats:	James A. Garfield
21.	Always:	Chester A. Arthur
22.	Catch:	Grover Cleveland
23.	Horses:	Benjamin Harrison
24.	Creating:	Grover Cleveland
25.	Mischief:	William McKinley

#	Acrostic	President's Name
Fourth Set		
26.	Rope:	Theodore Roosevelt
27.	The:	William Howard Taft
28.	Wild:	Woodrow Wilson
29.	Horses:	Warren G. Harding
30.	Carefully:	Calvin Coolidge
31.	Hold on:	Herbert Hoover
32.	Relentlessly:	Franklin D. Roosevelt

Lesson 19: Roaring Twenties Family Life
©2008 Bright Ideas Press. All rights reserved.

147

Answer Key to the Forms, Maps, and For Review Questions in the Student Activity Book
©2008 Bright Ideas Press. All rights reserved.

215

LESSON 19: FOR REVIEW

Write the letter of the correct answer in the space provided.

C _____ 1. In the 1920s,
- A. the U.S. divorce rate had declined
- B. American families had increased in size
- C. the infant mortality rate had declined
- D. divorce was no longer considered to be scandalous

D _____ 2. At the beginning of the twentieth century,
- A. all states granted women the right to own property
- B. most American women worked outside the home
- C. almost all states granted women an equal share in the guardianship of their children
- D. one-third of all states allowed women no claim on their earnings

B _____ 3. From 1910 until 1920,
- A. fewer than one million American women held jobs outside the home
- B. female suffragists held rallies in support of equal voting rights for women
- C. women were not allowed to hold jobs to support the war effort during the Great War
- D. the Nineteenth Amendment was not ratified

A _____ 4. During the Roaring Twenties,
- A. the growing telephone industry provided women with a new source of employment
- B. there were no women elected to Congress
- C. the number of women working outside the home declined
- D. the new model for American women was the Gibson Girl

C _____ 5. Which of the following was NOT typical of American flappers?
- A. they wore short dresses
- B. they bobbed their hair
- C. they were careful not to engage in nontraditional behavior
- D. they enjoyed driving and dancing

C _____ 6. Most American families in the 1920s
- A. abandoned listening to the radio and playing games together in the evenings
- B. were not interested in seeking advice on child care
- C. were subjected to large-scale advertising campaigns and encouraged to pay on credit
- D. refused to allow their children to participate in activities with their peers

A _____ 7. A leading American educator and advocate of Progressive education during this period was
- A. John Dewey
- B. Margaret Sanger
- C. William Jennings Bryan
- D. Clarence Birdseye

D _____ 8. The educational philosophy known as instrumentalism or pragmatism
- A. emphasized rote instruction
- B. became associated with William Jennings Bryan
- C. was not very influential after the nineteenth century
- D. focused on learning-by-doing and relating education to a child's interests

D _____ 9. At the turn of the century,
- A. few states had compulsory education laws
- B. there were significant federal efforts to maintain high educational standards in all the states
- C. American literacy rates were at an all-time low
- D. most high schools were six-year schools

B _____ 10. The Scopes trial in 1925
- A. was not well publicized at the time
- B. became known as the "monkey trial"
- C. dealt with the issue of whether creationism could be taught in a public school
- D. created a favorable public impression of Bryan and his antievolutionist arguments

A ___ 11. In the opening years of the twentieth century,
   A. most clothing still fastened with buttons
   B. American factories were still unable to manufacture clothing inexpensively
   C. few American women ordered clothing through catalogs
   D. zippers had been introduced with much fanfare

D ___ 12. Which of the following was NOT true of men's fashions in the United States during the Roaring Twenties?
   A. a hat was still a necessity
   B. fashionable young men often wore Oxford bags
   C. fewer men wore mustaches and beards than in the late nineteenth century
   D. raccoon coats were no longer popular among college men

A ___ 13. During the early years of the twentieth century,
   A. women's dresses in the the United States were becoming simpler and slightly shorter
   B. most women did not wear hats
   C. tiny waists, made possible by corsets, were no longer in style
   D. hobble skirts had been replaced by bustles

D ___ 14. By the mid-1920s, many American women
   A. were wearing longer hair
   B. still felt obligated to wear a corset
   C. refrained from wearing cosmetics
   D. wore skirts as short as knee length

C ___ 15. Children's clothing trends during the Roaring Twenties included all the following EXCEPT
   A. sailor suits for boys and girls
   B. knicker suits for boys
   C. corsets for young girls
   D. short socks for girls

D ___ 16. By the end of the 1920s,
   A. the Spanish flu epidemic was still raging in the United States
   B. training for American doctors and nurses had become more relaxed
   C. poor hygiene and sanitation were no longer a problem for most Americans
   D. a new antibiotic had been discovered

B ___ 17. The individual who discovered the importance of penicillin in medical treatment was
   A. Albert Einstein
   B. Alexander Fleming
   C. Clarence Birdseye
   D. Margaret Sanger

B ___ 18. During the Roaring Twenties,
   A. food was no longer a cultural battleground for immigrants to the United States
   B. muckrakers were asking questions about the quality of American foods
   C. few Americans faced the problem of malnutrition
   D. railroad cars and trucks had not yet become refrigerated, so fresh food could not be transported long distances

A ___ 19. The developer of a freezing process for foods was
   A. Clarence Birdseye
   B. Alexander Fleming
   C. W. K. Kellogg
   D. C. W. Post

C ___ 20. Which of the following was NOT true in the United States during the 1920s?
   A. the first hamburger stand opened
   B. the A&P and Piggly Wiggly were two leading grocery store chains
   C. candy bars had not yet been invented
   D. roadside diners were becoming common

LESSON 19: FOR FURTHER STUDY

For even more interesting information about this period of history, please refer to the For Further Study answers for this lesson in the Teacher's Guide.

1. Look for photographs of American suffragists in action during the early twentieth century. Find out for what activities Carrie Nation became famous.

2. How did the name flapper originate? The flapper subculture developed many new slang words and expressions. See if you can find out what the following mean: "bee's knees," "beeswax," "big cheese," "cat's meow," "dapper," "heebie-jeebies," "hit on all sixes," "now you're on the trolley," "putting on the Ritz," "rag-a-muffin," "the real McCoy," and "wet blanket."

Answer Key to the Forms, Maps, and For Review Questions in the Student Activity Book
©2008 Bright Ideas Press. All rights reserved.

3. Look for more information on John Dewey and Progressive education. Discuss his ideas with your family and decide what purpose(s) you think schools should serve. Should they teach only "academic" courses? Or should they offer "real-life" courses, such as vocational education and "basic living" classes (how to find a job, ways to improve your self-esteem, keys to a good marriage, etc.)?

4. Jell-O was a popular food in the 1920s. Look for the 1922 cookbook *Jell-O: America's Most Famous Dessert at Home and Everywhere* and try a recipe from it. Find out which of the following foods and drinks would have been available in the Roaring Twenties — Coca Cola, chocolate chip cookies, Kool Aid, Oreos, ice cream cones, devil's food cake, Gatorade, Girl Scout cookies, brownies, and Kraft macaroni and cheese.

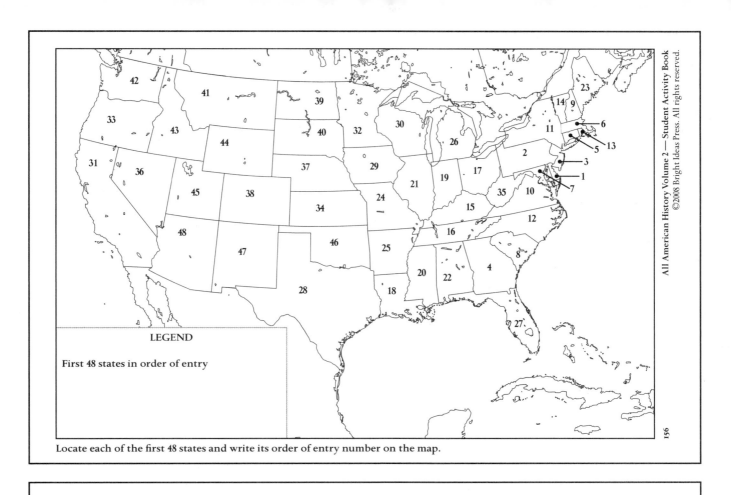

Locate each of the first 48 states and write its order of entry number on the map.

LEGEND

First 48 states in order of entry

Name _____ Date _____

LESSON 20: REVIEW OF STATES AND CAPITALS

Fill in the blanks with the names of the states for the capitals.

#	Capital City	State	#	Capital City	State
1.	Dover:	Delaware	30.	Madison:	Wisconsin
2.	Harrisburg:	Pennsylvania	31.	Sacramento:	California
3.	Trenton:	New Jersey	32.	St. Paul:	Minnesota
4.	Atlanta:	Georgia	33.	Salem:	Oregon
5.	Hartford:	Connecticut	34.	Topeka:	Kansas
6.	Boston:	Massachusetts	35.	Charleston:	West Virginia
7.	Annapolis:	Maryland	36.	Carson City:	Nevada
8.	Columbia:	South Carolina	37.	Lincoln:	Nebraska
9.	Concord:	New Hampshire	38.	Denver:	Colorado
10.	Richmond:	Virginia	39.	Bismarck:	North Dakota
11.	Albany:	New York	40.	Pierre:	South Dakota
12.	Raleigh:	North Carolina	41.	Helena:	Montana
13.	Providence:	Rhode Island	42.	Olympia:	Washington
14.	Montpelier:	Vermont	43.	Boise:	Idaho
15.	Frankfort:	Kentucky	44.	Cheyenne:	Wyoming
16.	Nashville:	Tennessee	45.	Salt Lake City:	Utah
17.	Columbus:	Ohio	46.	Oklahoma City:	Oklahoma
18.	Baton Rouge:	Louisiana	47.	Santa Fe:	New Mexico
19.	Indianapolis:	Indiana	48.	Phoenix:	Arizona
20.	Jackson:	Mississippi			
21.	Springfield:	Illinois			
22.	Montgomery:	Alabama			
23.	Augusta:	Maine			
24.	Jefferson City:	Missouri			
25.	Little Rock:	Arkansas			
26.	Lansing:	Michigan			
27.	Tallahassee:	Florida			
28.	Austin:	Texas			
29.	Des Moines:	Iowa			

Answer Key to the Forms, Maps, and For Review Questions in the Student Activity Book

LESSON 20: FOR REVIEW
Write the corresponding letter of the correct answer in the space provided.

A. Louis Armstrong
B. Al Capone
C. Enrico Caruso
D. Gertrude Ederle
E. Jack Dempsey
F. F. Scott Fitzgerald
G. Charles and Henry Greene
H. Red Grange
I. Ernest Hemingway
J. Langston Hughes
K. Al Jolson
L. J. Gresham Machen
M. Georgia O'Keeffe
N. Mary Pickford
O. Babe Ruth
P. Walter Rauschenbusch
Q. Billy Sunday
R. Rudolph Valentino
S. Benjamin Warfield
T. Frank Lloyd Wright

H   1. One of the greatest American football players of the 1920s

T   2. Most influential architect in the Chicago school

K   3. Star of *The Jazz Singer*, America's first talking movie

B   4. Famous racketeer and gangster during the Roaring Twenties

P   5. Author of *Christianity and the Social Crisis*, which accused Christians of not being concerned about the poor

N   6. Famous American actress of the early twentieth century

A   7. One of America's principal jazz musicians from New Orleans

Q   8. American evangelist who preached to large crowds in temporary tabernacles with sawdust-covered floors

E   9. Famous American boxer during the 1920s

S   10. Professor at Princeton Theological Seminary who defended orthodox Christianity

F   11. Author of *The Great Gatsby*, the quintessential work capturing the mood of the Jazz Age

R   12. Famous American actor of the early twentieth century

A. Louis Armstrong
B. Al Capone
C. Enrico Caruso
D. Gertrude Ederle
E. Jack Dempsey
F. F. Scott Fitzgerald
G. Charles and Henry Greene
H. Red Grange
I. Ernest Hemingway
J. Langston Hughes
K. Al Jolson
L. J. Gresham Machen
M. Georgia O'Keeffe
N. Mary Pickford
O. Babe Ruth
P. Walter Rauschenbusch
Q. Billy Sunday
R. Rudolph Valentino
S. Benjamin Warfield
T. Frank Lloyd Wright

G   13. Most famous in the American Craftsman style of architecture

I   14. Member of the Lost Generation who wrote *For Whom the Bell Tolls*

L   15. Author of *Christianity and Liberalism*

D   16. American long-distance swimmer known for swimming the English Channel

M   17. American artist famous during the Roaring Twenties

O   18. "Sultan of swat" who led the New York Yankees to their first World Series win

J   19. Harlem Renaissance author

C   20. Classical singer who made phonograph recordings popular in the United States

Write the missing word or words in the spaces provided.

1. **Prohibition**, referred to as the "Noble Experiment," ended with the ratification of the Twenty-first Amendment in 1933.

2. Congress passed the **Volstead Act** to enforce the Eighteenth Amendment.

LESSON 20: FOR FURTHER STUDY

For even more interesting information about this period of history, please refer to the For Further Study answers for this lesson in the Teacher's Guide.

1. Read about George Washington Carver, a famous black southern agricultural leader of this period. What crops did he encourage southern farmers to plant? Why? Record the information about Carver on an African American form. You could also fill out African American forms for any of the following that you are interested in researching — Louis Armstrong, Billie Holiday, Fats Waller, Ella Fitzgerald, and Mahalia Jackson.

2. Research the life of Billy Sunday and read one or more of his sermons.

3. See if you can find any film clips from the Roaring Twenties to view. Look for photographs of movie stars of the period and recordings of some of the popular songs. Find out why Harry Houdini was famous during this era. See if you can learn one of the dances popular in the 1920s.

4. Read about one or more of the art movements that developed during the first decades of the twentieth century — fauvism, dadaism, futurism, and cubism. Look for paintings that exemplify these movements. (Parental involvement should take place in choosing which paintings are appropriate to view.)

---

3. The name for a private club where alcoholic drinks were sold illegally was a __speakeasy__ .

4. The illegal sale and transport of alcohol became known as __bootlegging__ .

5. In the first two decades of the twentieth century, __baseball__ was the most popular spectator sport in the United States.

6. Kodak's __Brownie__ camera was the first American low-cost, easy-to-use camera.

7. Two toys introduced in the United States in 1916 were __Lincoln Logs__ and __Erector sets__ .

8. By 1908, an estimated ten thousand movie theaters, known as __nickelodeons__ , had sprung up across the United States.

9. The first full-length American movie was __Birth of a Nation__ .

10. Two dance crazes during the Roaring Twenties were the __Charleston__ and the __Shim Sham Shimmy (also, the Black Bottom and the Lindy Hop)__ .

Answer Key to the Forms, Maps, and For Review Questions in the Student Activity Book

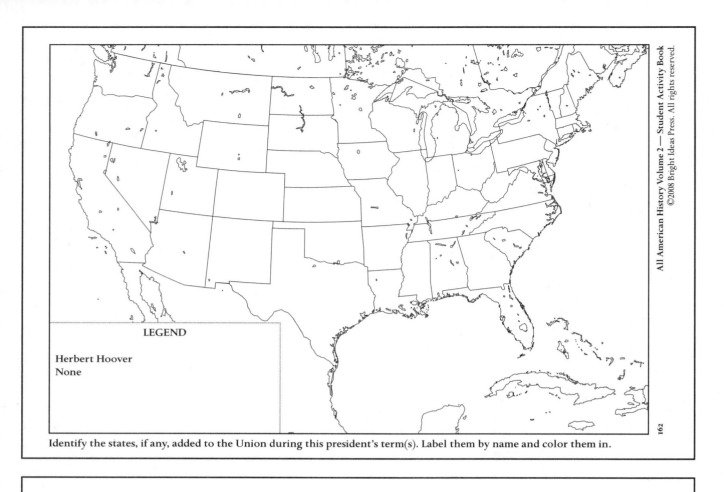

162

LEGEND

Herbert Hoover
None

Identify the states, if any, added to the Union during this president's term(s). Label them by name and color them in.

Name _____ Date _____

LESSON 21: HERBERT HOOVER

Picture of the president

Year born _____ 1874

Year died _____ 1964

In which state was he born? _____ Iowa

What jobs did he hold before becoming president? _____ Head of the Food
Administration during World War I, Secretary of Commerce

With what political party was this president affiliated? _____ Republican

Vice President: _____ Charles Curtis

What were the years of his presidency? _____ 1929 - 1933

List some significant developments during his administration _____ Stock market
crash and onset of the Great Depression

Establishment of the Reconstruction Finance Corporation (RFC)

Aid to farmers facing foreclosures

Loans to states to feed the unemployed

Hawley-Smoot Tariff (increase in tariffs on manufactured goods and farm
products)

Bonus Expeditionary Force (BEF) march on Washington, D.C.

161

Lesson 21: The Great Depression
©2008 Bright Ideas Press. All rights reserved.

All American History, Vol. II: Teacher's Guide — Section Five
©2008 Bright Ideas Press. All rights reserved.

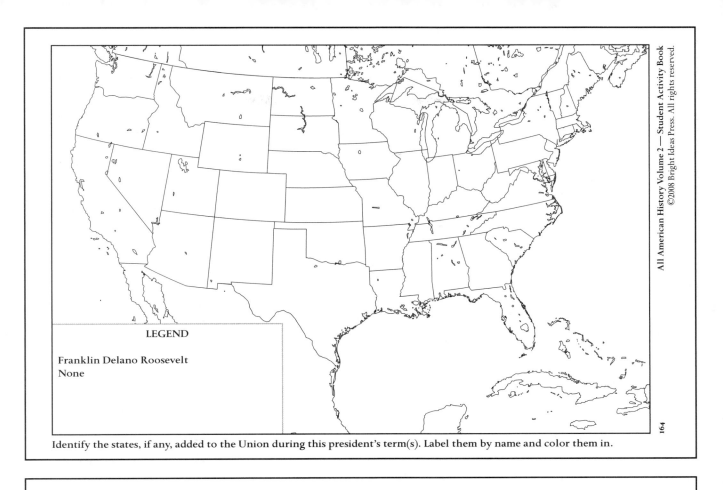

LEGEND

Franklin Delano Roosevelt
None

Identify the states, if any, added to the Union during this president's term(s). Label them by name and color them in.

Name _____ Date _____

LESSON 21: FRANKLIN DELANO ROOSEVELT

Picture of the president

Year born _____ 1882

Year died _____ 1945

In which state was he born? _____ New York

What jobs did he hold before becoming president? _____ Lawyer,
N.Y. state senator, Assistant Secretary of the Navy,
Governor of New York

With what political party was this president affiliated? _____ Democratic

Vice President: _____ John N. Garner, John N. Garner, Henry A. Wallace, Harry S. Truman

What were the years of his presidency? _____ 1933 - 1945

List some significant developments during his administration _____ Great Depression

"Bank Holiday" _____

"The New Deal" ("alphabet soup" of agencies to deal with the depression)

Social Security Act _____

Attempt at reorganizing Supreme Court _____

World War II _____

Answer Key to the Forms, Maps, and For Review Questions in the Student Activity Book
©2008 Bright Ideas Press. All rights reserved.   223

LESSON 21: FOR REVIEW

Write T for True and F for False in the space provided.

F   1. Because the U.S. stock market was regulated by the federal government in the 1920s, people were unable to manipulate huge amounts of money to their own advantage.

F   2. The period from 1927 through the summer of 1929 has been called the Big Bear Market.

T   3. On Black Thursday, October 24, 1929, a number of U.S. investors tried to sell their stock and could not find enough buyers.

F   4. When the stock market crashed in 1929, the American banking system was still very strong.

T   5. Herbert Hoover was known for his administrative abilities and humanitarian efforts.

F   6. Hoover defeated the Democratic candidate Al Smith in the 1928 election by a very slim margin.

F   7. When Hoover was elected president, most people in the United States were expecting the country to undergo an extreme financial crisis.

F   8. Soon after the stock market crash, Hoover began pushing for the passage of legislation to provide federal financial assistance to the unemployed.

T   9. The Bonus Expeditionary Force hoped to bring pressure on the U.S. Senate to pass a bill paying bonuses to World War I veterans immediately.

T   10. The American media depicted Hoover as callous and insensitive, and his name became linked to the hardships of depression life.

T   11. Perhaps no other president, except Lincoln, was as deeply loved and bitterly hated as Franklin Roosevelt.

F   12. At the beginning of his first term, Roosevelt spent six months planning for the New Deal before he began trying to get legislation passed by Congress.

T   13. The Great Depression was the worst economic collapse in American history.

F   14. The Great Depression had little effect on American farmers.

T   15. During the 1930s, major dust storms and floods occurred in the United States.

T   16. The New Deal established a variety of agencies, which became known by their initials.

F   17. Roosevelt did not succeed in getting Congress to pass a Social Security Act during his time in office.

T   18. Over time, critics of the New Deal charged that its policies were socialistic and placed too much power in the hands of the federal government.

T   19. Some of the legislation passed during the New Deal was declared unconstitutional by the U.S. Supreme Court.

T   20. The economic problems of the Great Depression were not unique to the United States.

Write the corresponding letter of the correct answer in the space provided.

A. Herbert Hoover   B. Franklin D. Roosevelt

B   1. "The only thing we have to fear is fear itself"

A   2. Bonus Expeditionary Force march on Washington, D.C.

A   3. Establishment of the Reconstruction Finance Corporation

B   4. The New Deal

A   5. "The fundamental business of the country... is on a very sound and prosperous basis."

B   6. Only president elected four times

B   7. The "First 100 Days"

A   8. President at the time of the stock market crash

B   9. Fireside chats

A   10. Hawley-Smoot Tariff

B   11. Last inauguration to occur in March

B   12. "Bank Holiday"

LESSON 21: FOR FURTHER STUDY

For even more interesting information about this period of history, please refer to the For Further Study answers for this lesson in the Teacher's Guide.

1. Learn more about the stock market. Read about the difference between bear and bull markets. Look for newspaper articles from 1929 recounting the stock market crash.

2. Read more about the march of the Bonus Expeditionary Force in Washington, D.C. How long did these protesters stay? How were they treated? Look for photographs documenting this event.

3. Draw a cartoon illustrating FDR's New Deal alphabet soup. Find out which New Deal laws were declared unconstitutional by the Supreme Court.

4. Research the life of Eleanor Roosevelt, the wife of President Roosevelt. How was she different from the first ladies who had come before her? What did she do after her husband died?

Lesson 21: The Great Depression
©2008 Bright Ideas Press. All rights reserved.

167

LESSON 22: REVIEW OF PRESIDENTS

Fill in the blanks with the names of the first through thirty-second presidents in order. The acrostic is provided as a tool to help you remember.

#	Acrostic	President's Name	#	Acrostic	President's Name
First Set			Fourth Set		
1.	Why:	George Washington	26.	Rope:	Theodore Roosevelt
2.	Are:	John Adams	27.	The:	William Howard Taft
3.	Jeff:	Thomas Jefferson	28.	Wild:	Woodrow Wilson
4.	Madison:	James Madison	29.	Horses:	Warren G. Harding
5.	Monty:	James Monroe	30.	Carefully:	Calvin Coolidge
6.	and:	John Quincy Adams	31.	Hold on:	Herbert Hoover
7.	Jack:	Andrew Jackson	32.	Relentlessly:	Franklin D. Roosevelt
8.	Buying:	Martin van Buren			
9.	Horses:	William Henry Harrison			
Second Set					
10.	Take:	John Tyler			
11.	Poor:	James Polk			
12.	Taylor's:	Zachary Taylor			
13.	Filly:	Millard Fillmore			
14.	Past:	Franklin Pierce			
15.	Both:	James Buchanan			
16.	Lincoln's:	Abraham Lincoln			
17.	Jogging:	Andrew Johnson			
18.	Goats:	Ulysses S. Grant			
Third Set					
19.	Happy:	Rutherford B. Hayes			
20.	Goats:	James A. Garfield			
21.	Always:	Chester A. Arthur			
22.	Catch:	Grover Cleveland			
23.	Horses:	Benjamin Harrison			
24.	Creating:	Grover Cleveland			
25.	Mischief:	William McKinley			

All American History, Vol. II: Teacher's Guide — Section Five

LESSON 22: FOR REVIEW

Write T for True and F for False in the space provided.

T _____ 1. During the Great Depression, many American couples delayed getting married, and the U.S. divorce rate fell.

T _____ 2. Many upper-middle-class American families still managed to live comfortably during the depression.

F _____ 3. The U.S. unemployment rate never fell below 50 percent during the depression years.

F _____ 4. The Great Depression had little impact on American education.

T _____ 5. Men's pants during the 1930s were wide and high-waisted, and the most popular men's hat was the trilby.

F _____ 6. With the onset of the Great Depression, women's skirts rose again to the knee. Bright colors were once more used in women's clothing.

T _____ 7. Many American men, women, and children could not afford to buy new clothing during the depression years.

T _____ 8. To save money, American families during the depression often neglected medical and dental care.

T _____ 9. Chocolate chip cookies, Spam, and Krispy Kreme donuts were introduced in the 1930s.

F _____ 10. The years of the Great Depression were a period of decreasing class conflict in the United States.

F _____ 11. With millions of Americans out of work, the major U.S. denominations saw a dramatic rise in church membership.

F _____ 12. With the decline of the Ku Klux Klan, tensions in U.S. race relations almost entirely disappeared.

T _____ 13. Throughout the Great Depression, the U.S. movie industry flourished.

F _____ 14. Radio listening declined among Americans during the 1930s.

Lesson 22: Great Depression Family Life and Culture
©2008 Bright Ideas Press. All rights reserved.

F _____ 15. By the 1930s, segregation was no longer being practiced in American sports.

T _____ 16. The most famous writers and journalists of New York City during the 1930s belonged to a group called the Algonquin Round Table.

T _____ 17. Penguin Books published the first paperback books during the depression years.

F _____ 18. Surrealism was no longer a significant art movement in the United States by the time of the Great Depression.

F _____ 19. The Mount Rushmore memorial was financed by private donations.

T _____ 20. Most homes built in the United States during the 1930s were smaller than those built in the years before.

Write the missing word or words in the spaces provided.

1. The most popular movie star of the 1930s was _____ **Shirley Temple** _____ .

2. The definitive cartoon of the depression was _____ **The Three Little Pigs** _____ .

3. New York Yankee _____ **Lou Gehrig** _____ set numerous major-league records before being forced into retirement because of his health.

4. The African American athlete who won four gold medals at the 1936 Olympics was _____ **Jesse Owens** _____ .

5. _____ **Monopoly** _____ was a new board game introduced during the 1930s.

All American History Volume 2 — Student Activity Book
©2008 Bright Ideas Press. All rights reserved.

Answer Key to the Forms, Maps, and For Review Questions in the Student Activity Book

LESSON 22: FOR FURTHER STUDY

For even more interesting information about this period of history, please refer to the For Further Study answers for this lesson in the Teacher's Guide.

1. John Dillinger and Bonnie and Clyde were three famous figures during the depression years. For what were they known? Read about Father Charles Coughlin. Why was he a controversial religious figure during the 1930s?

2. View *Snow White and the Seven Dwarfs*. Is it different from more recent Disney animated movies? Try some Shirley Temple films or other movies from this period. Why do you think Shirley Temple was so popular during the depression?

3. See if you can find some audio recordings of radio programs from the depression years, such as *The Shadow*, *Fibber McGee*, and *The Lone Ranger*. How is listening to a program on the radio different from viewing a program on TV? Find out who Walter Winchell and Will Rogers were, as well as the significance of Orson Welles's broadcast of *The War of the Worlds*.

4. Listen to some big band music of the swing era and look at some surrealist and regionalist paintings. Look for information about the Mount Rushmore memorial. Which presidents are included in this monument?

---

6. ___George Gershwin___, a well-known composer for the Broadway stage, also composed classical music and the folk opera *Porgy and Bess*.

7. A leading American playwright of this era was ___Eugene O'Neill___, who received a Nobel Prize in 1936.

8. A new style of popular music called ___swing___ emerged during the 1930s. It was played by big bands led by Duke Ellington, Glenn Miller, Harry James, and the Dorseys.

9. Two new dances of the 1930s were the ___Jitterbug___ and the ___Big Apple___.

10. The interest of American literature in the plight of the common man during the 1930s was epitomized by John Steinbeck's ___The Grapes of Wrath___.

11. Two American realist painters in the 1930s were Edward Hopper and Grant Wood. Wood became famous for his painting ___American Gothic___.

12. The most famous skyscraper built in this period was the ___Empire State Building___.

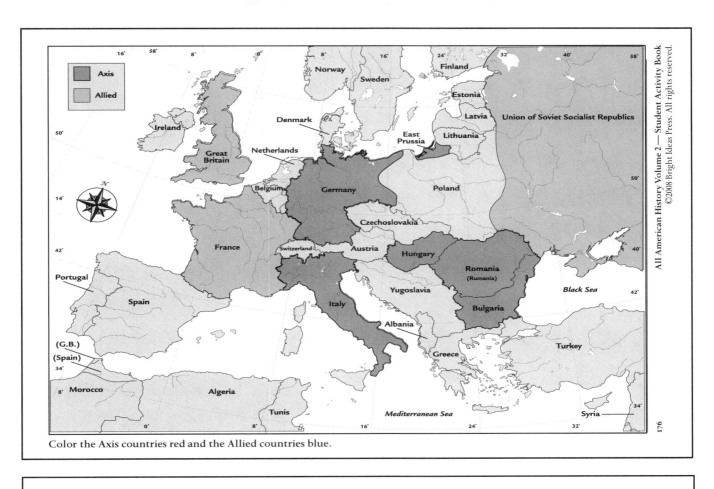

Color the Axis countries red and the Allied countries blue.

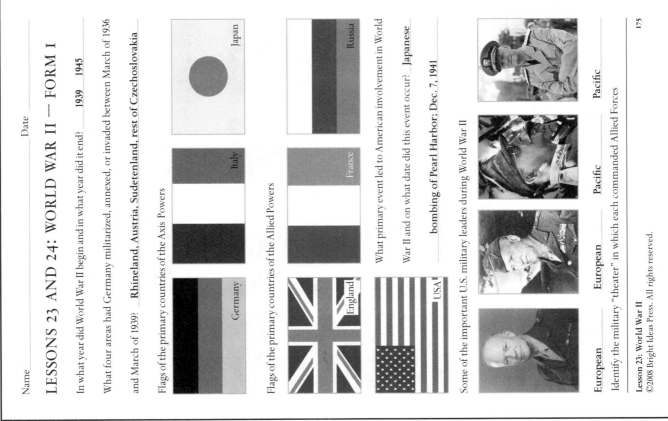

Name _____ Date _____

LESSONS 23 AND 24: WORLD WAR II — FORM I

In what year did World War II begin and in what year did it end? _____ **1939   1945**

What four areas had Germany militarized, annexed, or invaded between March of 1936

and March of 1939? _____ **Rhineland, Austria, Sudetenland, rest of Czechoslovakia**

Flags of the primary countries of the Axis Powers

Japan

Italy

Germany

Flags of the primary countries of the Allied Powers

Russia

France

England

USA

What primary event led to American involvement in World

War II and on what date did this event occur? **Japanese**

bombing of Pearl Harbor; Dec. 7, 1941

Some of the important U.S. military leaders during World War II

European   Pacific

European   Pacific

Identify the military "theater" in which each commanded Allied Forces

Answer Key to the Forms, Maps, and For Review Questions in the Student Activity Book

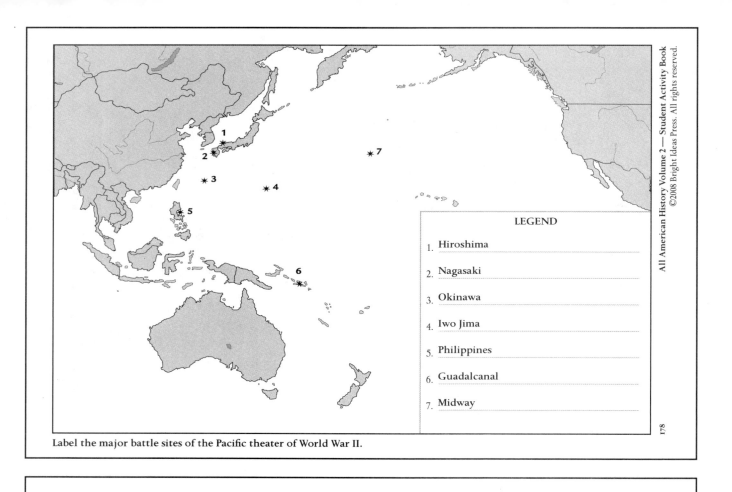

LEGEND

1. Hiroshima
2. Nagasaki
3. Okinawa
4. Iwo Jima
5. Philippines
6. Guadalcanal
7. Midway

Label the major battle sites of the Pacific theater of World War II.

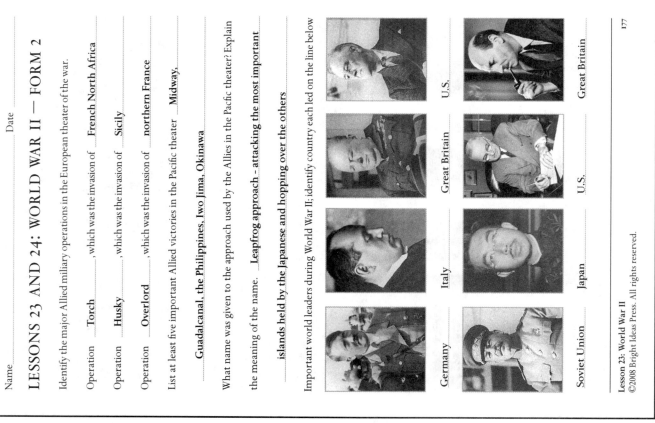

Name _____ Date _____

LESSONS 23 AND 24: WORLD WAR II — FORM 2

Identify the major Allied military operations in the European theater of the war.

Operation __Torch__, which was the invasion of __French North Africa__

Operation __Husky__, which was the invasion of __Sicily__

Operation __Overlord__, which was the invasion of __northern France__

List at least five important Allied victories in the Pacific theater __Midway,__

__Guadalcanal, the Philippines, Iwo Jima, Okinawa__

What name was given to the approach used by the Allies in the Pacific theater? Explain

the meaning of the name. __Leapfrog approach – attacking the most important__

__islands held by the Japanese and hopping over the others__

Important world leaders during World War II; identify country each led on the line below

U.S.   Great Britain

Great Britain   U.S.

Italy   Japan

Germany   Soviet Union

All American History, Vol. II: Teacher's Guide — Section Five

LESSON 23: FOR REVIEW

Write the letter of the correct answer in the space provided.

B _____ 1. The name of Franklin Roosevelt's foreign policy concerning Latin America was
    A. the Big Stick Policy
    B. the Good Neighbor Policy
    C. the Reconstruction Policy
    D. the Leap Frog Policy

B _____ 2. In 1933, the German Reichstag gave absolute government power to
    A. Benito Mussolini
    B. Adolf Hitler
    C. Francisco Franco
    D. Hirohito

C _____ 3. The German people in the 1930s were still angry about
    A. the depression gripping the world
    B. American isolationism
    C. the terms of the Versailles Treaty ending World War I
    D. the Holocaust

D _____ 4. The name of Hitler's political movement was
    A. Fascism
    B. Communism
    C. Socialism
    D. Nazism

A _____ 5. Italy's dictator during the 1930s was
    A. Benito Mussolini
    B. Adolf Hitler
    C. Francisco Franco
    D. Hirohito

D _____ 6. The political movement begun by Italy's dictator was called
    A. Socialism
    B. Nazism
    C. Communism
    D. Fascism

C _____ 7. The nation that began an assault on the Asian continent in the 1930s with an attack on Manchuria was
    A. China
    B. India
    C. Japan
    D. Vietnam

B _____ 8. General Francisco Franco came to power in the 1930s during a civil war in
    A. France
    B. Spain
    C. Italy
    D. Austria

A _____ 9. Which of the following was NOT a member of the Axis in 1937?
    A. Russia
    B. Germany
    C. Japan
    D. Italy

A _____ 10. In the United States in the 1930s, the predominant mood was
    A. isolationist
    B. militaristic
    C. imperialistic
    D. socialistic

B _____ 11. By the end of the 1930s,
    A. America's military forces ranked first in the world
    B. Germany had ignored the Versailles treaty and rebuilt its military forces
    C. Japan had not developed a naval fleet
    D. President Roosevelt encouraged American isolationism

D _____ 12. The Nazis had taken over all of the following by September 1, 1939, EXCEPT
    A. Austria
    B. the Sudetenland
    C. Poland
    D. France

Answer Key to the Forms, Maps, and For Review Questions in the Student Activity Book

B _____ 13. In 1939, the country that signed a nonaggression pact with Germany was
A. Great Britain
B. the Soviet Union
C. the United States
D. Italy

A _____ 14. Germany's "lightning war" fighting strategy was known as
A. the blitzkrieg
B. the sitzkrieg
C. the maginot
D. the anschluss

C _____ 15. By mid-1940, the country standing alone against Germany in Europe was
A. France
B. Belgium
C. Great Britain
D. Spain

D _____ 16. President Roosevelt did all of the following in 1940 – 1941 EXCEPT
A. run for an unprecedented third term
B. give a speech to Congress about four freedoms
C. issue the Atlantic Charter with Churchill
D. push for the passage of additional neutrality acts

B _____ 17. The fighting on the eastern front of the war
A. resulted in much fewer casualties than on the western front
B. involved the use of scorched-earth tactics by both sides
C. was confined primarily to the city of Leningrad
D. touched very few civilians

C _____ 18. The event bringing the United States into World War II was the bombing of
A. Manila in the Philippines
B. Miami in Florida
C. Pearl Harbor in Hawaii
D. Washington, D.C.

A _____ 19. By mid-1942, the country controlling most of Southeast Asia and a whole string of islands in the Pacific was
A. Japan
B. the United States
C. China
D. the Soviet Union

Lesson 23: World War II
©2008 Bright Ideas Press. All rights reserved.
181

D _____ 20. The Nazis defeated the Allies in
A. French North Africa
B. Sicily
C. Italy
D. none of these places

B _____ 21. The commander of Operation Overlord, which was initiated on D-Day, was
A. Douglas MacArthur
B. Dwight Eisenhower
C. George Marshall
D. Chester Nimitz

C _____ 22. By early 1945, the Allies had won a major victory in Belgium at the
A. Battle of Brussels
B. Battle of the Marne
C. Battle of the Bulge
D. Battle of Stalingrad

A _____ 23. World War II ended in Europe on May 8, a day which became known as
A. V-E Day
B. V-W Day
C. V-V Day.
D. V-J Day

B _____ 24. The Nazi reign of terror, during which as many as six million European Jews were killed, has become known as the
A. Killing Fields
B. Holocaust
C. Final Alternative
D. Star Tragedy

D _____ 25. The turning point of the war in the Pacific was the U.S. victory at
A. Pearl Harbor
B. Honolulu
C. Samoa
D. Guadalcanal

C _____ 26. The United States ended the war in the Pacific on V-J Day after
A. occupying Tokyo
B. meeting with Japan for peace negotiations
C. dropping atomic bombs on Japan
D. killing the Japanese emperor

182
All American History Volume 2 — Student Activity Book
©2008 Bright Ideas Press. All rights reserved.

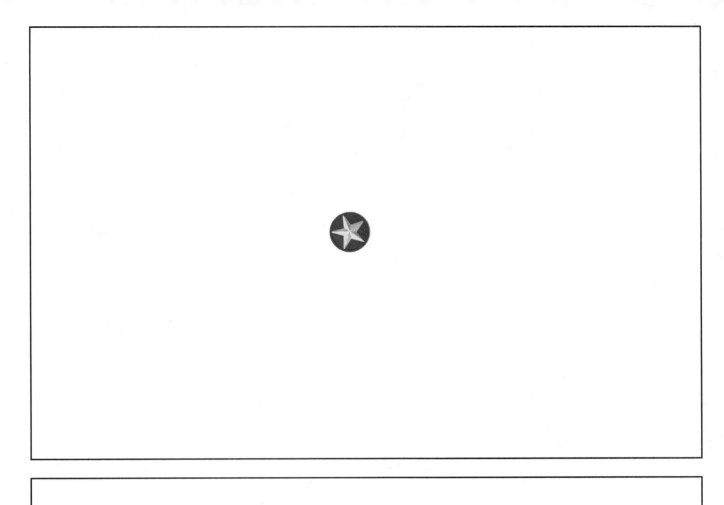

LESSON 23: FOR FURTHER STUDY

For even more interesting information about this period of history, please refer to the For Further Study answers for this lesson in the Teacher's Guide.

1. Learn more about the Japanese attack at Pearl Harbor. *On which Hawaiian island was the U.S naval base located? What was the significance of the phrase "Tora, tora, tora"? How long did the attack last? Which battleship was hit at the beginning and sank within minutes with its crew trapped inside? What role did Pearl Harbor play in the rest of the war?*

2. Several important conferences took place between Allied leaders during the war. Discover who attended the conferences at Cairo and Tehran, when they were held, and what was decided at each.

3. Find out for what Lt. Colonel James Doolittle became known during World War II, and which popular wartime movie dramatized Doolittle's story.

4. Pick one or more World War II battles to research. Some of the major battles included Dunkirk, Midway, Guadalcanal, Stalingrad, Normandy, the Bulge, Iwo Jima, and Okinawa. If this is an area of interest, compile a World War II Battles Notebook. There are forms in the optional forms section of the *Student Activity Book* to use to do this.

183

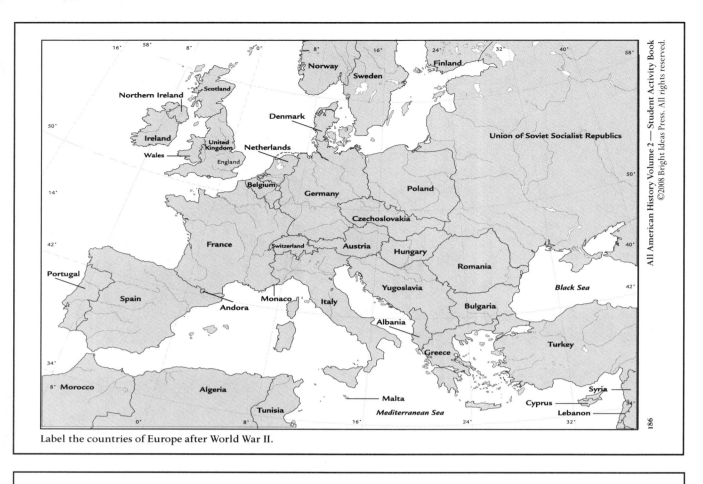

Label the countries of Europe after World War II.

186

Name _____ Date _____

LESSONS 23 AND 24: WORLD WAR II — FORM 3

How did the United States raise money to finance its involvement in the war? **Selling of war bonds and defense stamps and revenue from federal income taxes**

How did the average American family help with the war effort? **Doing without goods that were scarce; planting victory gardens; contributing to scrap drives**

In what ways did American women assist in the war effort? **Large numbers worked on assembly lines and in shipyards. Others joined the Red Cross, ran canteens for the soldiers, served as nurses' aides, drove ambulances, entertained soldiers or enlisted in special military units created for women.**

What did American children sacrifice on behalf of the war effort? **Chocolate, bubble gum, metal toys, new footballs and baseballs**

Why were Japanese Americans sent to internment camps during World War II? **Many Americans feared that Japanese Americans might be spies who might commit acts of espionage, sabotage, or treason**

Explain the types of discrimination faced by African Americans during World War II. **All branches of the U.S. military were segregated. On the home front, segregation among the races continued in transportation, eating establishments, trade unions, and defense industries.**

Date of V-E Day **May 8, 1945**   Date of V-J Day **September 2, 1945**

What made the establishment of a peace settlement following World War II difficult? **The postwar conflict between the United States and the Soviet Union**

185

LESSON 24: FOR REVIEW

Write T for True and F for False in the space provided.

F   1. When the United States entered World War II, a large number of Americans were still uncertain that the country should be involved in the fighting.

T   2. Wartime production in the United States created millions of jobs for Americans who had suffered through twelve years of the Great Depression.

F   3. U.S. farmers saw their income decline during the war years.

T   4. On several occasions during the war, President Roosevelt left the United States to attend strategic conferences with other Allied leaders.

F   5. In a secret agreement at the Yalta conference, the Soviet Union agreed not to enter the war against Japan after Germany's surrender.

F   6. Franklin Roosevelt died of a cerebral hemorrhage a week after V-E day.

T   7. Money to finance U.S. involvement in World War II was raised through the selling of war bonds and defense stamps and through federal income taxes.

T   8. Every American family during the war received a book of ration coupons.

T   9. American designers finally came into their own during World War II because Paris was under German occupation.

F   10. American women were not allowed to enlist in any type of U.S. military unit during the war.

F   11. By the beginning of World War II, the U.S. military was no longer segregated.

T   12. Executive Order 9066 called for the evacuation of some 120,000 Japanese Americans to ten relocation centers.

T   13. Japanese Americans served as linguists in the Pacific theater of the war and played a significant role in interpreting enemy documents and interrogating Japanese prisoners of war.

T   14. The U.S. Office of War declared movies to be an essential industry for propaganda and morale.

F   15. World War II did not claim as many lives as World War I.

T   16. At the end of World War II, only the United States knew how to build an atomic bomb.

Write the missing word or words in the spaces provided.

1. Franklin Roosevelt, Churchill, and Stalin were known as the **Big Three**.

2. At the **Casablanca** Conference, Roosevelt and Churchill agreed that the Allies would demand the unconditional surrender of the Axis powers and that they would establish a front in Italy to relieve German pressure on the eastern front.

3. Roosevelt met with Churchill and Stalin at the **Yalta** conference to plan the final assault on Germany and to lay plans for postwar Europe.

4. Harry Truman, Clement Attlee, and Joseph Stalin met at the **Potsdam** Conference to decide how to administer defeated Germany and to establish a post-war order.

5. **Zoot** suits for men had outrageously padded shoulders and trousers that were narrowly tapered at the ankles.

6. **Rosie the Riveter**, created by Norman Rockwell in 1943, paid tribute to American women who worked on assembly lines during the war.

7. Second-generation Japanese Americans became known as _____Nisei_____.

8. The _____United States_____ and _____the Soviet Union_____ emerged from World War II as the two most dominant countries in the world.

9. The struggle between the communist world and the noncommunist world became known as the _____Cold War_____.

10. The country of _____Germany_____ was divided into four zones and occupied by the United States, Great Britain, France, and the Soviet Union.

11. A new world peacekeeping organization, known as the _____United Nations_____, was established in San Francisco after World War II.

LESSON 24: FOR FURTHER STUDY

For even more interesting information about this period of history, please refer to the For Further Study answers for this lesson in the Teacher's Guide.

1. Look for an issue of *Look*, *The Saturday Evening Post*, *Life*, or another magazine from the World War II period. Pay special attention to the advertisements and clothing fashions, as well as other information about what life was like on the home front.

2. Find out what actions the U.S. government has taken to make restitution to the Japanese Americans sent to relocation centers during the war.

3. Discover who Anne Frank was. Read *The Hiding Place* by Corrie Ten Boom or watch the movie.

4. Research the role Hollywood played in World War II. For what was Bob Hope known in the war effort? Look for photographs of movie stars from the era. What did the expression "Kilroy was here" mean?

UNIT 3: FINAL REVIEW

Write the corresponding letter of the correct answer in the space provided.

A. Louis Armstrong
B. William Jennings Bryan
C. Calvin Coolidge
D. John Dewey
E. Dwight D. Eisenhower
F. Henry Ford
G. George Gershwin
H. Warren G. Harding
I. Ernest Hemingway
J. Herbert Hoover
K. Langston Hughes
L. Charles Lindbergh
M. Georgia O'Keeffe
N. Jack Pershing
O. Franklin Roosevelt
P. John Steinbeck
Q. Billy Sunday
R. Harry S. Truman
S. Frank Lloyd Wright
T. Orville and Wilbur Wright

J 1. President when the stock market crashed

K 2. Harlem Renaissance author

A 3. One of America's great jazz musicians from New Orleans

H 4. President who promised a "return to normalcy" and died in office just as several scandals in his administration were being uncovered

T 5. Flew the first heavier-than-air flight at Kitty Hawk, North Carolina

N 6. Commander of the American Expeditionary Force during World War I

I 7. Member of the Lost Generation who wrote *For Whom the Bell Tolls*

B 8. Democratic nominee for the presidency who also served as one of the attorneys in the Scopes trial

O 9. President during America's worst depression and worst war

F 10. Manufacturer of the Model T automobile

S 11. Most influential architect in the Chicago school

R 12. President who decided to drop the atomic bomb on Japan

D 13. Leading American educator and advocate of Progressive education

---

A. Louis Armstrong
B. William Jennings Bryan
C. Calvin Coolidge
D. John Dewey
E. Dwight D. Eisenhower
F. Henry Ford
G. George Gershwin
H. Warren G. Harding
I. Ernest Hemingway
J. Herbert Hoover
K. Langston Hughes
L. Charles Lindbergh
M. Georgia O'Keeffe
N. Jack Pershing
O. Franklin Roosevelt
P. John Steinbeck
Q. Billy Sunday
R. Harry S. Truman
S. Frank Lloyd Wright
T. Orville and Wilbur Wright

M 14. U.S. artist famous during the Roaring Twenties

E 15. General in charge of Operation Overlord (D-Day)

C 16. President known for frugal living and self-control during the Roaring Twenties

Q 17. American evangelist who preached to large crowds in temporary tabernacles with sawdust-covered floors

G 18. Well-known composer for the Broadway stage and of the folk opera *Porgy and Bess*

P 19. Author of *The Grapes of Wrath*, which epitomized the interest of American literature in the plight of the common man during the 1930s

L 20. Flew the first nonstop flight between New York and Paris

Write the corresponding letter of the correct answer in the space provided.

A. World War I   B. World War II

A 1. Treaty of Versailles

B 2. General Dwight D. Eisenhower

A 3. Assassination of Archduke Franz Ferdinand

B 4. Rosie the Riveter

Answer Key to the Forms, Maps, and For Review Questions in the Student Activity Book

Left panel (193)

A _____ 5. Woodrow Wilson

A _____ 6. Trench warfare

B _____ 7. United Nations

B _____ 8. Joseph Stalin

A _____ 9. American Expeditionary Force

B _____ 10. Axis Powers

B _____ 11. Harry S. Truman

A _____ 12. Zimmermann note

A _____ 13. Bolshevik Revolution

B _____ 14. Benito Mussolini

B _____ 15. Adolf Hitler

A _____ 16. League of Nations

B _____ 17. Lend-Lease Act

A _____ 18. General Jack Pershing

B _____ 19. Pearl Harbor

A _____ 20. *Lusitania*

B _____ 21. Winston Churchill

B _____ 22. V-E Day

A _____ 23. Central Powers

B _____ 24. Franklin D. Roosevelt

B _____ 25. Atomic bomb

Right panel (194)

Write T for True and F for False in the space provided.

F _____ 1. During the 1920s, the U.S. government generally favored the rights of workers over the interests of business.

F _____ 2. There were few labor strikes in the United States during the 1920s.

F _____ 3. U.S. immigration quotas during the 1920s heavily favored immigration from northern and eastern Europe.

F _____ 4. The golden age of American agriculture occurred during the 1920s.

T _____ 5. Henry Ford was able to offer his Model T cars at an affordable price.

T _____ 6. The Roaring Twenties witnessed a significant increase in advertising.

T _____ 7. In the 1920s, more American women worked outside the home than ever before.

T _____ 8. The prosperous U.S. economy during the Roaring Twenties contributed to a rise in educational standards.

F _____ 9. The Spanish flu epidemic did not cause a large number of deaths in the United States.

F _____ 10. Antibiotics had not been discovered until after World War II.

T _____ 11. Prohibition ended with the ratification of the Twenty-first Amendment.

F _____ 12. The Progressive movement had very little impact upon American religious beliefs.

T _____ 13. American fundamentalists developed their own Bible colleges and seminaries and took their message to the radio airwaves.

T _____ 14. Baseball was still the nation's most popular spectator sport in the 1920s.

F _____ 15. Movies did not become an important entertainment medium in the United States until the end of the Great Depression.

T _____ 16. Another name for the Roaring Twenties was the Jazz Age.

T _____ 32. The term *Nisei* refers to second-generation Japanese Americans.

F _____ 33. No Japanese Americans were allowed to serve in the military during World War II.

F _____ 34. Jews in the United States during World War II faced the same levels of discrimination as African Americans and Japanese Americans.

F _____ 35. During the war years, most Americans did not spend much money on entertainment outside their homes.

All American History Volume 2 — Student Activity Book
©2008 Bright Ideas Press. All rights reserved.

T _____ 17. Popular housing styles in the United States in the early years of the twentieth century were the American Prairie style (American Foursquare) and the Craftsman (Arts and Crafts) style.

F _____ 18. The Great Depression was not the worst economic collapse in U.S. history.

T _____ 19. The New Deal has sometimes been referred to as "alphabet soup."

T _____ 20. The economic problems of the Great Depression were faced by industrialized nations around the world.

F _____ 21. The Great Depression had little effect on U.S. education.

F _____ 22. With the onset of the depression, the skirts of American women were once again raised to above the knee.

F _____ 23. The health and nutrition of most Americans was not adversely impacted during the years of the depression.

T _____ 24. The 1930s were years of increased class conflict and turbulent race relations in the United States.

T _____ 25. Radio broadcasting came of age in the United States during the 1930s.

F _____ 26. Surrealism and realism were not important schools in American art in the 1930s.

F _____ 27. Most homes built in the United States during the depression were larger than those built in the years before.

T _____ 28. Federal agencies imposed rationing and other controls on the American people during World War II.

F _____ 29. The number of women in the U.S. workforce during World War II did not significantly increase.

T _____ 30. Millions of American women volunteered through the Red Cross and the uso during World War II.

T _____ 31. Segregation among the races existed on the home front and in the armed services during the war years.

Unit 3: Final Review

Answer Key to the Forms, Maps, and For Review Questions in the Student Activity Book

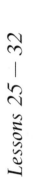

UNIT FOUR

THE COLD WAR AND BEYOND

Lessons 25 — 32

All American History, Vol. II: Teacher's Guide — Section Five

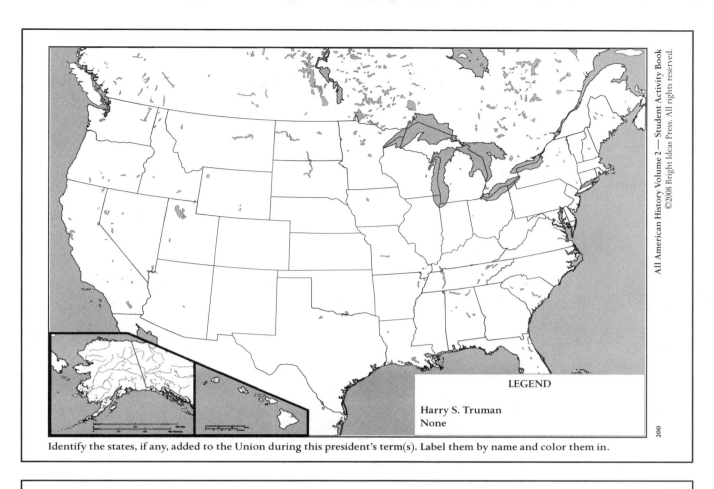

200

LEGEND

Harry S. Truman
None

Identify the states, if any, added to the Union during this president's term(s). Label them by name and color them in.

Name _____ Date _____

LESSON 25: HARRY S. TRUMAN

Picture of the president

Year born _____ 1884

Year died _____ 1972

In which state was he born? _____ Missouri

What jobs did he hold before becoming president? ___ World War I veteran,

county judge, U.S. Senator

With what political party was this president affiliated? ___ Democratic

Vice President: ___ None, Alban W. Barkley

What were the years of his presidency? _____ 1945 – 1953

List some significant developments during his administration ___ End of World War II

Truman Doctrine (strategy of containment)

Marshall Plan (program for European economic recovery)

National Security Act

"Fair Deal" (domestic reform proposals – most defeated in Congress)

Berlin blockade and airlift

Establishment of NATO

Korean War

Development of H-bomb

Sending of U.S. military advisors to Vietnam

199

Answer Key to the Forms, Maps, and For Review Questions in the Student Activity Book   241

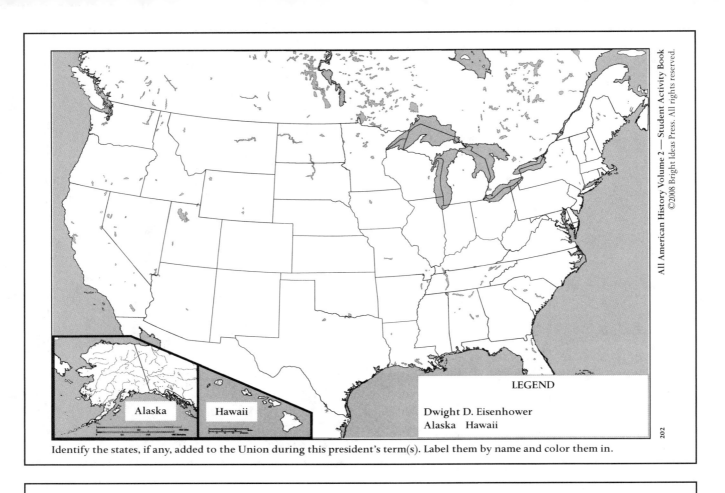

LEGEND

Dwight D. Eisenhower
Alaska   Hawaii

Alaska   Hawaii

202

Identify the states, if any, added to the Union during this president's term(s). Label them by name and color them in.

Name _____   Date _____

LESSON 25: DWIGHT D. EISENHOWER

Picture of the president

Year born ____ 1890

Year died ____ 1969

In which state was he born?   Texas

What jobs did he hold before becoming president?   Allied commander in

World War II, president of Columbia University, Supreme Commander of NATO

With what political party was this president affiliated?   Republican

Vice President: Richard M. Nixon, Richard M. Nixon

What were the years of his presidency?   1953 – 1961

List some significant developments during his administration "Modern Republicanism"

(reductions in federal government spending and goal of a balanced budget)

Construction of Saint Lawrence Seaway and interstate highways

Creation of the Dept. of Health, Education, and Welfare (HEW)

Sending of thousands of U.S. advisors to help the South Vietnamese (belief in

the "domino theory")

Eisenhower Doctrine (protection of countries in the Middle East from

communist aggression)

Lesson 25: The Beginning of the Cold War
©2008 Bright Ideas Press. All rights reserved.

201

All American History, Vol. II: Teacher's Guide — Section Five

LESSON 25: FOR REVIEW
Write the missing word or words in the spaces provided.

1. The ideological and economic conflict between the U.S. and U.S.S.R. from the end of World War II until 1989 has been called the __Cold War__.

2. In a 1946 speech in Missouri, Winston Churchill warned that __an Iron Curtain__ had descended across the continent of Europe.

3. The __Truman__ Doctrine supported the strategy of containment, the provision of military support in an attempt to restrain or halt further Soviet expansion.

4. Secretary of State __George Marshall__ proposed that all the nations of Europe join in a postwar program of mutual aid for economic recovery, assisted by American grants.

5. Between June of 1948, and May of 1949, the Western allies undertook a massive airlift to keep the western sectors of the city of __Berlin__ supplied during a Soviet blockade.

6. The United States, France, Britain, and eight other countries formed the __North Atlantic Treaty Organization (NATO)__ for mutual defense against the communists.

7. The Chinese government recognized by the United States after 1949 was the government of the Nationalist Chinese led by __Chiang Kai-shek__.

8. The head of the People's Republic of China was __Mao Zedong__.

9. When freed from Japanese control, the country of Korea was divided along the __38th__ parallel.

10. In June of 1950, __North__ Korea invaded __South__ Korea.

11. The commander of UN forces in Korea after the hostilities began was General __Douglas MacArthur__.

12. During the Korean War, President Truman held to the principle of a __limited__ war.

13. By 1950, American scientists had begun working on a __hydrogen__ bomb.

14. When the Soviet dictator Joseph Stalin died, he was replaced by __Nikita Krushchev__.

15. President Eisenhower sent military advisers to South Vietnam because of the __domino__ theory, which maintained that if one country in a region came under the influence of communists, then the others surrounding it would also fall.

LESSON 25: FOR FURTHER STUDY

For even more interesting information about this period of history, please refer to the For Further Study answers for this lesson in the Teacher's Guide.

1. Look for a copy of Winston Churchill's speech (March 5, 1945) in which he warned about the Iron Curtain descending across Europe. Also find President Eisenhower's Farewell Address to the Nation (January 17, 1961) in which he warned about the dangers of the American military-industrial complex. Read one or both of these speeches and decide how effective they were in communicating their messages.

2. Read more about the Berlin Airlift. What name did the Americans give this operation? How often did Allied planes make drops there? What type(s) of U.S. aircraft were used to make the drops?

3. Find out how many nations belong to NATO today. Is Russia a member? Where are the headquarters for NATO located? What role has NATO played in the war on terrorism?

4. Pick one or more of the battles of the Korean War to research. Some of the major battles included Inchon, Chosin Reservoir, Heartbreak Ridge, Unsan, Seoul, and Pork Chop Hill. If this is an area of interest, compile a Korean War Battles Notebook. There are forms in the optional forms section of the *Student Activity Book* to use to do this.

---

16. The ___Eisenhower___ Doctrine recommended the use of American forces to protect countries in the Middle East against communist aggression.

Write the corresponding letter of the correct answer in the space provided.

A. Harry S. Truman   B. Dwight D. Eisenhower

B 1. A popular American war general and hero

A 2. President when the fighting in Korea began

A 3. Rugged individual known for the saying "the buck stops here"

B 4. Called his legislative program Modern Republicanism

B 5. Warned the country of the dangers of the military-industrial complex

A 6. Winner of one of the biggest upsets in American political history

B 7. Supreme Commander of NATO

B 8. Called for a reduction in federal government spending and saw a small surplus in federal government revenues

A 9. Chairman of a wartime Senate investigating committee that saved the United States billions of dollars

B 10. Approved construction of interstate highways and the Saint Lawrence Seaway

A 11. Signed into law the National Security Act, which reorganized U.S. armed forces and foreign policy structure

A 12. Developed a domestic reform program called the "Fair Deal"

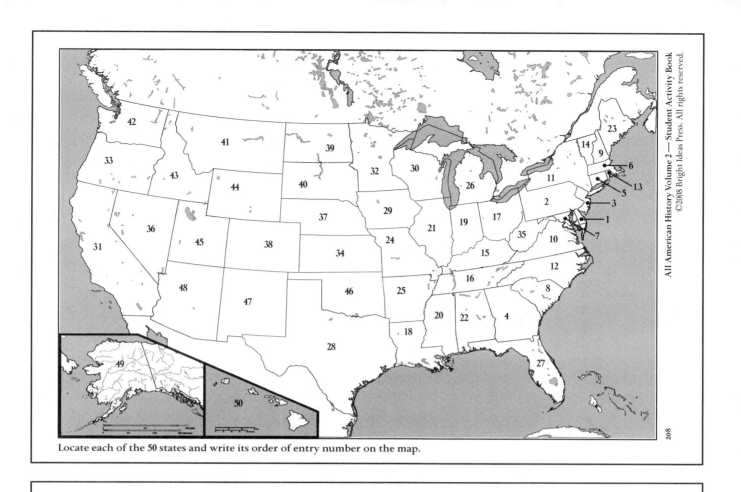

Locate each of the 50 states and write its order of entry number on the map.

Name _____ Date _____

LESSONS 26 & 28: REVIEW STATES AND CAPITALS

Fill in the blanks with the names of the state capitals.

#	State	Capital City
1.	Delaware:	Dover
2.	Pennsylvania:	Harrisburg
3.	New Jersey:	Trenton
4.	Georgia:	Atlanta
5.	Connecticut:	Hartford
6.	Massachusetts:	Boston
7.	Maryland:	Annapolis
8.	South Carolina:	Columbia
9.	New Hampshire:	Concord
10.	Virginia:	Richmond
11.	New York:	Albany
12.	North Carolina:	Raleigh
13.	Rhode Island:	Providence
14.	Vermont:	Montpelier
15.	Kentucky:	Frankfort
16.	Tennessee:	Nashville
17.	Ohio:	Columbus
18.	Louisiana:	Baton Rouge
19.	Indiana:	Indianapolis
20.	Mississippi:	Jackson
21.	Illinois:	Springfield
22.	Alabama:	Montgomery
23.	Maine:	Augusta
24.	Missouri:	Jefferson City
25.	Arkansas:	Little Rock
26.	Michigan:	Lansing
27.	Florida:	Tallahassee
28.	Texas:	Austin
29.	Iowa:	Des Moines

#	State	Capital City
30.	Wisconsin:	Madison
31.	California:	Sacramento
32.	Minnesota:	St. Paul
33.	Oregon:	Salem
34.	Kansas:	Topeka
35.	West Virginia:	Charleston
36.	Nevada:	Carson City
37.	Nebraska:	Lincoln
38.	Colorado:	Denver
39.	North Dakota:	Bismarck
40.	South Dakota:	Pierre
41.	Montana:	Helena
42.	Washington:	Olympia
43.	Idaho:	Boise
44.	Wyoming:	Cheyenne
45.	Utah:	Salt Lake City
46.	Oklahoma:	Oklahoma City
47.	New Mexico:	Santa Fe
48.	Arizona:	Phoenix
49.	Alaska:	Juneau
50.	Hawaii:	Honolulu

Answer Key to the Forms, Maps, and For Review Questions in the Student Activity Book

LESSON 26: FOR REVIEW

Write T for True and F for False in the space provided.

F _____ 1. During the 1950s, the U.S. economy hovered near a depression once again.

F _____ 2. Veterans returning from World War II struggled to buy a house and get a college education.

F _____ 3. The Taft-Hartley Act of 1947 was a pro-union law.

T _____ 4. At the end of World War II, the U.S. farm economy faced the challenge of overproduction.

T _____ 5. During Eisenhower's administration, a law was passed providing for the construction of an American interstate highway system.

F _____ 6. The United States was the first nation to launch a satellite to orbit the earth.

T _____ 7. The popularity of radio faded with the advent of television.

T _____ 8. UNIVAC I was the first computer developed for nonmilitary use.

F _____ 9. The period after World War II saw a decline in births in the United States.

F _____ 10. In the 1950s, most American women wanted to have one or two children, and divorce had become quite common.

T _____ 11. Dr. Benjamin Spock's *Common Sense Book of Baby and Child Care* was a best-seller following World War II.

T _____ 12. In 1946, about three million American women left the workforce.

F _____ 13. The 1954 Supreme Court decision *Brown v. Board of Education of Topeka, Kansas,* ruled that racially segregated schools were constitutional.

T _____ 14. After the launch of *Sputnik,* there was a push in the United States to spend more money to raise American academic standards.

T _____ 15. Rudolf Flesch promoted the phonics-first method of reading instruction in his book, *Why Johnny Can't Read.*

F _____ 16. Dr. James Conant's study of American high schools called for an emphasis on vocational instruction and promoted small high schools.

F _____ 17. American women in the 1950s discarded their poodle skirts for miniskirts.

T _____ 18. With American men. the "Organization Man" look was popular, as were blue jeans for American children.

T _____ 19. In the 1950s, Americans were thankful for penicillin and the polio vaccine.

T _____ 20. The 1950s have been called the casserole decade.

T _____ 21. The first McDonald's opened in San Bernardino, California, in 1955.

LESSON 26: FOR FURTHER STUDY

For even more interesting information about this period of history, please refer to the For Further Study answers for this lesson in the Teacher's Guide.

1. Look for photographs of cars from the 1950s. How did they differ from today's cars? What was the Edsel?

2. Discover who Wernher von Braun and the Army Redstone Arsenal team were. For what did Chuck Yeager become known in 1947?

3. Read some excerpts from Dr. Benjamin Spock's *Common Sense Book of Baby and Child Care.* See if you agree with his philosophy.

4. Find out the significance of Linda Brown and Elizabeth Eckford. Record the information on African American forms.

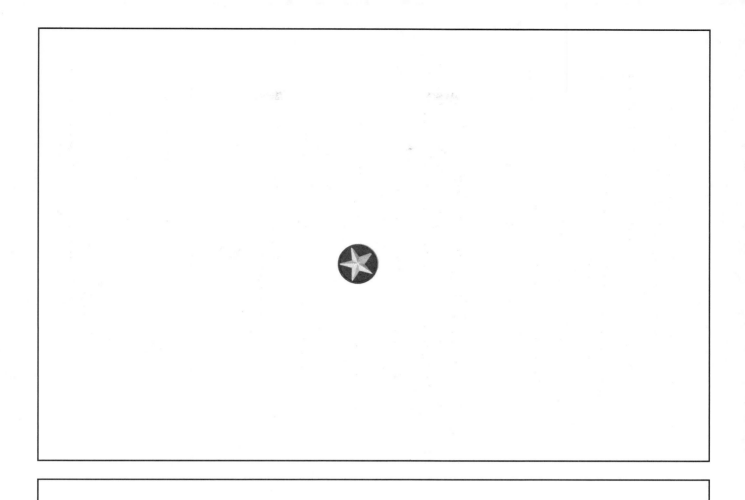

Name _____ Date _____

LESSON 27: REVIEW OF PRESIDENTS

Fill in the blanks with the names of the first through thirty-second presidents in order. The acrostic is provided as a tool to help you remember.

#	Acrostic	President's Name	#	Acrostic	President's Name
First Set				*Fourth Set*	
1.	Why:	George Washington	26.	Rope:	Theodore Roosevelt
2.	Are:	John Adams	27.	The:	William Howard Taft
3.	Jeff:	Thomas Jefferson	28.	Wild:	Woodrow Wilson
4.	Madison:	James Madison	29.	Horses:	Warren G. Harding
5.	Monty:	James Monroe	30.	Carefully:	Calvin Coolidge
6.	and:	John Quincy Adams	31.	Hold on:	Herbert Hoover
7.	Jack:	Andrew Jackson	32.	Relentlessly:	Franklin D. Roosevelt
8.	Buying:	Martin van Buren			
9.	Horses?:	William Henry Harrison			
Second Set					
10.	Take:	John Tyler			
11.	Poor:	James Polk			
12.	Taylor's:	Zachary Taylor			
13.	Filly:	Millard Fillmore			
14.	Past:	Franklin Pierce			
15.	Both:	James Buchanan			
16.	Lincoln's:	Abraham Lincoln			
17.	Jogging:	Andrew Johnson			
18.	Goats:	Ulysses S. Grant			
Third Set					
19.	Happy:	Rutherford B. Hayes			
20.	Goats:	James A. Garfield			
21.	Always:	Chester A. Arthur			
22.	Catch:	Grover Cleveland			
23.	Horses:	Benjamin Harrison			
24.	Creating:	Grover Cleveland			
25.	Mischief:	William McKinley			

Lesson 27: Society and Culture During the Early Cold War Years
©2008 Bright Ideas Press. All rights reserved.

211

LESSON 27: FOR REVIEW

Write T for True and F for False in the space provided.

T   1. During the late 1940s and early 1950s, there was an anticommunist frenzy in the United States.

F   2. The Alger Hiss and Rosenberg cases dealt with discrimination against blacks.

F   3. The Republican senator who waged a four-year campaign in the early 1950s to find communists in the government and entertainment industry was Ronald Reagan.

T   4. President Truman desegregated the military in 1948.

F   5. The famous black boycott of buses in Montgomery, Alabama, was triggered by the shooting of Rosa Parks by a white bus driver.

T   6. The Ku Klux Klan experienced another revival in the 1950s.

F   7. The civil rights bill passed by Congress during Eisenhower's administration offered great encouragement to African Americans.

F   8. Evangelicals did not hold to the inerrancy of the Bible and believed that fundamentalists had gone too far in isolating themselves from society and culture.

F   9. Billy Sunday was a famous evangelist preaching to record-breaking crowds in the 1950s.

T   10. During the 1950s, there was a major upswing in church membership in the United States, and religion was seen by many as an indicator of non-communism.

T   11. In the early years of the Cold War, many Christian colleges and seminaries began to reflect liberal biblical scholarship, and a growing ecumenical movement emerged.

T   12. The first Barbie doll appeared in 1959, and Mr. Potato Head became the first kids' toy advertised on television.

T   13. The building of highways in the 1950s led to the creation of shopping malls, which profoundly changed Americans' shopping and leisure habits.

F   14. Television was not introduced in the United States until the 1960s.

T   15. Early TV shows were broadcast live on one of three major networks—NBC, ABC, and CBS.

T   16. Very quickly American TV began to be influenced by its advertising sponsors.

T   17. American movies during the 1950s capitalized on a growing trend toward youthful rebelliousness and alienation.

F   18. As television became more available, fewer Americans were interested in following sports.

Write the corresponding letter of the correct answer in the space provided.

A. Billy Graham   H. Richard Nixon
B. Martha Graham   I. Harold John Ockenga
C. Bill Haley   J. Jackson Pollock
D. Alger Hiss   K. Elvis Presley
E. Jack Kerouac   L. Jackie Robinson
F. Martin Luther King, Jr.   M. Julius Rosenberg
G. Jasper Johns   N. Wilma Rudolph

B   1. American dancer who influenced dancers worldwide in the 1950s

J   2. Abstract expressionist artist

N   3. African American athlete who became the first U.S. woman to win three gold medals in an Olympics game

K   4. King of American rock 'n' roll who had fourteen consecutive million-selling records.

A   5. American evangelist who preached to record-breaking crowds in his crusades.

M   6. American executed after being convicted of selling atomic secrets to the Soviet government

C   7. Pioneer of rock 'n' roll music, known for "Rock Around the Clock"

D ____ 8. American former state department official accused of passing U.S. secret documents to the Russians

L ____ 9. First African American baseball player in the American major leagues

E ____ 10. Most prolific of the beat authors

H ____ 11. U.S. congressman who captured American attention with his questioning of Alger Hiss

I ____ 12. A leading evangelical leader during the 1950s

G ____ 13. One of the American artists leading the reaction against abstract expressionism

F ____ 14. Founded the Southern Christian Leadership Conference (SCLC) to help African Americans in their fight for civil rights

LESSON 27: FOR FURTHER STUDY

For even more interesting information about this period of history, please refer to the For Further Study answers for this lesson in the Teacher's Guide.

1. Investigate the strategy used by Dr. Martin Luther King, Jr., in leading the civil rights movement in the United States. What leader's ideas influenced his thinking? Fill out an African American form on Martin Luther King, Jr. Read about the lives of Ralph Abernathy and Coretta King and fill out African American forms for them.

2. Learn more about Billy Graham and the Billy Graham Evangelistic Association. Whom did Graham choose to succeed him in his ministry?

3. Listen to some of Elvis Presley's records from the 1950s. Why do you think Elvis is still an important American phenomenon, even after he has been dead for so many years?

4. Discover what Levittown is. See if you can find pictures of it. Look for the words to Peter Seeger's recording of the song, "Little Boxes on the Hillside." What is the meaning of this song?

Name _____ Date _____

LESSON 28: JOHN F. KENNEDY

Picture of the president

Year born _____ 1917 _____

Year died _____ 1963 _____

In which state was he born? _____ Massachusetts _____

What jobs did he hold before becoming president? _____ Service in U.S. Navy (World War II), U.S. Representative, U.S. Senator, Pulitzer Prize-winning author _____

With what political party was this president affiliated? _____ Democratic _____

Vice President: _____ Lyndon B. Johnson _____

What were the years of his presidency? _____ 1961 – 1963 _____

List some significant developments during his administration _____ "New Frontier" _____

Development of the Peace Corps _____

Challenge to put a man on the moon by the end of the 1960s _____

23rd Amendment _____

Bay of Pigs invasion, Cuban missile crisis _____

Building of the Berlin Wall _____

"Undeclared" war in Vietnam _____

Kennedy's assassination in Dallas _____

217

Lesson 28: The Sixties and Seventies
©2008 Bright Ideas Press. All rights reserved.

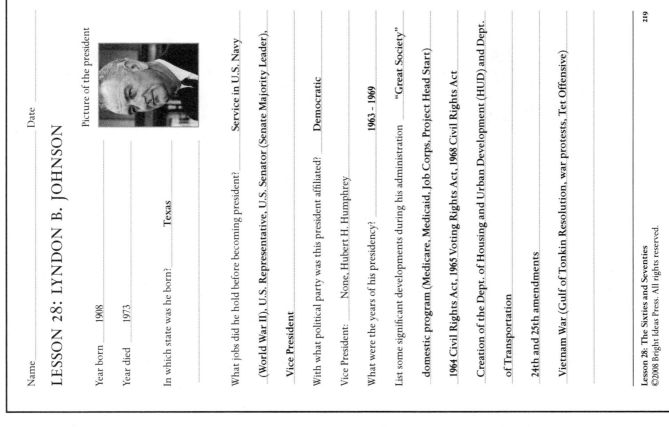

Name _____ Date _____

LESSON 28: LYNDON B. JOHNSON

Picture of the president

Year born ___1908___

Year died ___1973___

In which state was he born? ___Texas___

What jobs did he hold before becoming president? ___Service in U.S. Navy (World War II), U.S. Representative, U.S. Senator (Senate Majority Leader).___

Vice President

With what political party was this president affiliated? ___Democratic___

Vice President: ___None, Hubert H. Humphrey___

What were the years of his presidency? ___1963 – 1969___

List some significant developments during his administration ___"Great Society" domestic program (Medicare, Medicaid, Job Corps, Project Head Start)___

___1964 Civil Rights Act, 1965 Voting Rights Act, 1968 Civil Rights Act___

___Creation of the Dept. of Housing and Urban Development (HUD) and Dept. of Transportation___

___24th and 25th amendments___

___Vietnam War (Gulf of Tonkin Resolution, war protests, Tet Offensive)___

Lesson 28: The Sixties and Seventies
©2008 Bright Ideas Press. All rights reserved.

219

Answer Key to the Forms, Maps, and For Review Questions in the Student Activity Book
©2008 Bright Ideas Press. All rights reserved.

251

Name _____   Date _____

LESSON 28: RICHARD M. NIXON

Picture of the president

Year born _____ 1913

Year died _____ 1994

In which state was he born? _____ California

What jobs did he hold before becoming president? _____ Service in U.S. Navy

_____ (World War II), U.S. Representative, U.S. Senator, Vice President

With what political party was this president affiliated? _____ Republican

Vice President: _____ Spiro Agnew, Gerald R. Ford

What were the years of his presidency? _____ 1969 – 1974

List some significant developments during his administration _____ "New Federalism"

_____ (revenue sharing plan and reforms in federal tax laws)

Rising inflation, rising unemployment

26th Amendment

Watergate break-in/Senate investigation/Nixon's resignation

"Vietnamization," Paris Peace Accords calling for withdrawal of U.S. troops

from Vietnam

Presidential visits to the Soviet Union and Communist China; signing of the

Salt I Treaty with Soviets

Nixon Doctrine (U.S. withdrawal from many overseas troop commitments)

221

Lesson 28: The Sixties and Seventies

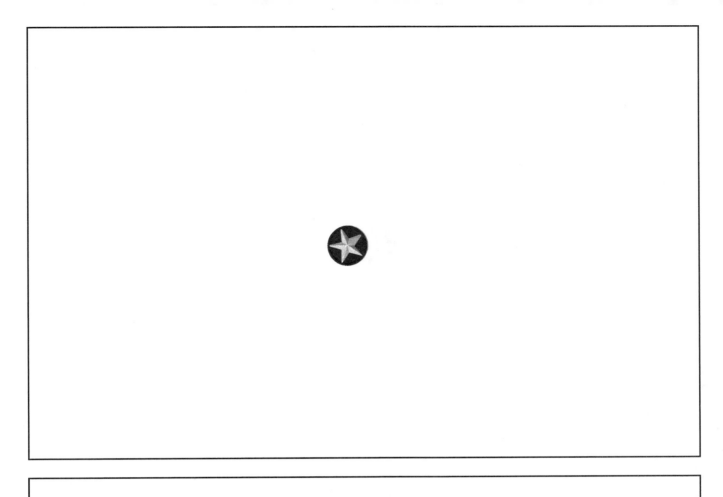

Name _____ Date _____

LESSON 28: GERALD R. FORD

Picture of the president

Year born ___1913___

Year died ___2006___

In which state was he born? ___Michigan___

What jobs did he hold before becoming president? ___Service in U.S. Navy___

___(World War II), lawyer, U.S. Representative (House Minority Leader),___

___Vice President___

With what political party was this president affiliated? ___Republican___

Vice President: ___Nelson Rockefeller___

What were the years of his presidency? ___1974 - 1977___

List some significant developments during his administration ___Presidential pardon of___

___Richard Nixon___

___61 presidential vetoes in an attempt to hold down government spending and___

___to protect the powers of the presidency___

___Recession, rapid inflation, high unemployment___

___Reuniting of Vietnam under communist rule; fall of Laos and Cambodia___

___to the communists___

223

Lesson 28: The Sixties and Seventies

Name _____ Date _____

LESSON 28: JAMES E. CARTER

Picture of the president

Year born ___ 1924 ___

Year died ___ N/A ___

In which state was he born? ___ Georgia ___

What jobs did he hold before becoming president? ___ U.S. naval officer, ___

Governor of Georgia

With what political party was this president affiliated? ___ Democratic ___

Vice President: ___ Walter Mondale ___

What were the years of his presidency? ___ 1977 – 1981 ___

List some significant developments during his administration ___ Soaring inflation ___

and fuel crisis

Creation of Dept. of Energy; division of Dept. of Health, Education and

Welfare into Dept. of Education and Dept. of Health and Human Services

Salt II Treaty negotiations; Soviet invasion of Afghanistan

U.S. boycott of Moscow Summer Olympics

Carter Doctrine

Camp David Accords (Egyptian-Israeli peace agreement)

American hostage crisis in Iran

225

254

All American History, Vol. II: Teacher's Guide — Section Five

LESSON 28: FOR REVIEW

Write the letter of the correct answer in the space provided.

D _____ 1. Which of the following was NOT true about John F. Kennedy?
A. he wrote a Pulitzer Prize-winning book
B. his domestic program became known as the New Frontier
C. he issued a challenge to the space program to put a man on the moon by the end of the decade
D. he served two terms in office

C _____ 2. The Twenty-third Amendment
A. gave the right to vote to eighteen-year-olds
B. changed the date for the presidential inauguration
C. gave residents of the District of Columbia the right to vote in presidential elections
D. clarified the line of succession to the presidency

A _____ 3. Lyndon B. Johnson
A. was highly successful in getting Congress to approve many of Kennedy's social programs
B. had not held an elected office before becoming vice president
C. vetoed any civil rights legislation sent to him
D. led the United States to victory in Vietnam

B _____ 4. The Twenty-fourth Amendment
A. gave residents of the District of Columbia the right to vote in presidential elections
B. outlawed poll taxes
C. prohibited racial discrimination in any businesses serving the public
D. gave the right to vote to eighteen-year-olds

B _____ 5. The Twenty-fifth Amendment
A. outlawed poll taxes
B. clarified the line of succession to the presidency
C. changed the date for the presidential inauguration
D. gave residents of the District of Columbia the right to vote in presidential elections

D _____ 6. Richard M. Nixon
A. proposed domestic reforms that he called New Republicanism
B. inherited a booming economy
C. vetoed a proposal calling for revenue sharing
D. resigned in August of 1974 because he faced almost certain impeachment

C _____ 7. The Twenty-sixth Amendment
A. changed the date for the presidential election
B. prohibited racial discrimination in any businesses serving the public
C. gave the right to vote to eighteen-year-olds
D. outlawed poll taxes

A _____ 8. As president, Gerald Ford
A. saw his popularity drop sharply when he pardoned Nixon
B. worked well with the Republican-controlled Congress
C. was helped by a recovering economy
D. vetoed only one bill sent to him by Congress

D _____ 9. In the 1976 presidential race,
A. Ford defeated Carter in a close election
B. Ford pointed to his success in eliminating inflation
C. Carter was a nationally known figure and Washington insider
D. Carter charged that Ford had mismanaged the economy

B _____ 10. Jimmy Carter
A. persuaded Congress to pass almost all of his domestic proposals
B. appointed record numbers of women, African Americans, and Latinos
C. succeeded in curbing inflation
D. enjoyed high approval ratings throughout his time in office

C _____ 11. Which of the following was NOT true about U.S. relations with Cuba in the 1960s?
A. the Bay of Pigs invasion was an attempt by Cuban rebels, trained by the CIA, to overthrow Fidel Castro
B. the United States discovered that the Soviet Union was installing missiles in Cuba
C. a second invasion supported by the United States succeeded in overthrowing Castro
D. President Kennedy ordered a blockade of Cuba during the missile crisis there

Answer Key to the Forms, Maps, and For Review Questions in the Student Activity Book

B _____ 12. The Soviet Union
    A. was not interested in occupying the city of Berlin
    B. increased its military strength in Berlin and moved to increase its control of the border
    C. refused to meet with the United States to discuss the status of Berlin
    D. discouraged the building of a wall between East and West Berlin

B _____ 13. Fighting conditions in Vietnam included all of the following EXCEPT
    A. a tropical monsoon climate
    B. clear fronts and lines of battle
    C. dangers of guerilla warfare
    D. a corrupt, unstable South Vietnamese government

A _____ 14. During Johnson's administration
    A. the first U.S. combat troops were sent to South Vietnam
    B. the Gulf of Tonkin Resolution limited the president's authority to fight the Vietnam War
    C. American support for the Vietnam War grew
    D. the Tet offensive was a tremendous military success for the North Vietnamese

D _____ 15. In the second half of the 1960s,
    A. the U.S. draft was discontinued
    B. American TV refused to display war images from Vietnam
    C. the North Vietnamese refused to begin peace talks
    D. large student demonstrations against the Vietnam War took place

A _____ 16. President Nixon
    A. initiated a policy known as Vietnamization
    B. halted all U.S. bombing in Vietnam and the surrounding region in 1971
    C. saw American support of the war increase
    D. failed to convince negotiators in Paris to reach a peace agreement

D _____ 17. In the 1970s,
    A. Vietnam was reunited under a democratic government
    B. South Vietnamese refugees were not allowed to enter the United States
    C. all draft dodgers and deserters were prosecuted and given long prison sentences
    D. South Vietnam, Laos, and Cambodia all fell to the communists

D _____ 18. During his presidency, Richard Nixon
    A. refused to negotiate or trade with communist China
    B. formulated a doctrine that called for an increase in U.S. overseas troop commitments
    C. refused to visit the Soviet Union
    D. pursued policies with the Soviet Union that led to détente

B _____ 19. In Carter's administration,
    A. the Salt II Treaty was ratified by the Senate
    B. the Soviet Union invaded Afghanistan
    C. the president formulated a doctrine bearing his name that stated that the United States would not resist Soviet aggression in the Persian Gulf area
    D. the American grain embargo against the Soviets pleased American farmers

C _____ 20. President Carter
    A. was unsuccessful in arranging a meeting between Sadat and Begin at Camp David
    B. prevented the deposed Iranian shah from entering the United States for medical treatments
    C. refused to meet the Iranian revolutionaries' demands after their seizure of American hostages
    D. authorized a successful rescue mission to free the American hostages in Iran

Write the corresponding letter of the correct answer in the space provided.

A. John F. Kennedy   C. Richard M. Nixon
B. Lyndon B. Johnson   D. Gerald R. Ford
                  E. James E. Carter

B _____ 1. War on poverty

C _____ 2. Watergate

A _____ 3. Assassinated in Dallas, Texas

D _____ 4. Only person to serve as both president and vice president without being elected to the office

LESSON 28: FOR FURTHER STUDY

For even more interesting information about this period of history, please refer to the For Further Study answers for this lesson in the Teacher's Guide.

1. Look for footage from the Kennedy/Nixon TV debates, Kennedy's inaugural address, and Kennedy's assassination and funeral. Learn more about his wife Jacqueline's renovation of the White House. What were the findings of the Warren Commission concerning Kennedy's assassination?

2. Learn more about the Vietnam War. If this is an area of interest, compile a Vietnam War Battles Notebook. There are forms in the optional forms section of the *Student Activity Book* to use to do this. What happened at Kent State University in 1970? Who was William Calley and what happened to him? What were the Pentagon Papers? Who was Daniel Ellsberg?

3. Why did federal officials investigate Vice President Spiro Agnew? What evidence did they uncover? What role did the Twenty-fifth Amendment play in the events that followed? Find out what the Saturday Night Massacre was. What role did Carl Bernstein and Bob Woodward play in Watergate? What role did Chuck Colson play in Watergate? What has Colson done since serving in the Nixon White House?

4. Research the terms of the new treaties negotiated between the United States and Panama in 1977. Why were some Americans opposed to these treaties?

232

   A   5. "Ask not what your country can do for you; ask what you can do for your country"

   E   6. Self-proclaimed "man of the people" who eliminated some of the ceremonial trappings of the presidency

   D   7. Pardoned Richard Nixon

   B   8. Great Society

   C   9. New Federalism

   B   10. Twenty-fourth and Twenty-fifth Amendments

   E   11. Appointed record numbers of women, African Americans, and Latinos

   A   12. Twenty-third Amendment

   A   13. Bay of Pigs invasion and Cuban missile crisis

   C   14. Twenty-sixth Amendment

   C   15. Trips to the Soviet Union and communist China

   D   16. Vetoed sixty-one bills in an attempt to hold down government spending and protect the powers of the presidency

   A   17. Building of the Berlin Wall

   E   18. Salt II Treaty

   A   19. New Frontier

   E   20. Camp David Accords

   B   21. Three civil rights laws

   E   22. Iranian hostage crisis

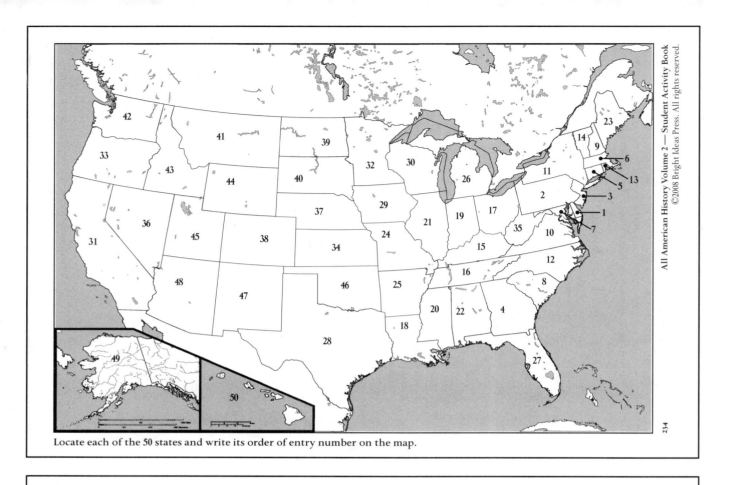

Locate each of the 50 states and write its order of entry number on the map.

234

Name _____ Date _____

LESSON 29: REVIEW OF STATES AND CAPITALS

Fill in the blanks with the names of the states.

#	Capital City	State	#	Capital City	State
1.	Dover:	Delaware	30.	Madison:	Wisconsin
2.	Harrisburg:	Pennsylvania	31.	Sacramento:	California
3.	Trenton:	New Jersey	32.	St. Paul:	Minnesota
4.	Atlanta:	Georgia	33.	Salem:	Oregon
5.	Hartford:	Connecticut	34.	Topeka:	Kansas
6.	Boston:	Massachusetts	35.	Charleston:	West Virginia
7.	Annapolis:	Maryland	36.	Carson City:	Nevada
8.	Columbia:	South Carolina	37.	Lincoln:	Nebraska
9.	Concord:	New Hampshire	38.	Denver:	Colorado
10.	Richmond:	Virginia	39.	Bismarck:	North Dakota
11.	Albany:	New York	40.	Pierre:	South Dakota
12.	Raleigh:	North Carolina	41.	Helena:	Montana
13.	Providence:	Rhode Island	42.	Olympia:	Washington
14.	Montpelier:	Vermont	43.	Boise:	Idaho
15.	Frankfort:	Kentucky	44.	Cheyenne:	Wyoming
16.	Nashville:	Tennessee	45.	Salt Lake City:	Utah
17.	Columbus:	Ohio	46.	Oklahoma City:	Oklahoma
18.	Baton Rouge:	Louisiana	47.	Santa Fe:	New Mexico
19.	Indianapolis:	Indiana	48.	Phoenix:	Arizona
20.	Jackson:	Mississippi	49.	Juneau:	Alaska
21.	Springfield:	Illinois	50.	Honolulu:	Hawaii
22.	Montgomery:	Alabama			
23.	Augusta:	Maine			
24.	Jefferson City:	Missouri			
25.	Little Rock:	Arkansas			
26.	Lansing:	Michigan			
27.	Tallahassee:	Florida			
28.	Austin:	Texas			
29.	Des Moines:	Iowa			

233

All American History, Vol. II: Teacher's Guide — Section Five

LESSON 29: FOR REVIEW

Write the letter of the correct answer in the space provided.

A 1. Which of the following was NOT true of the U.S. economy during the 1970s?
  A. budget deficits led to the government's printing less money
  B. the condition of simultaneously high inflation and high unemployment was called stagflation
  C. President Carter hoped to slow down inflation rates by establishing voluntary wage and price controls
  D. Carter called for increased government spending

C 2. In the 1960s and 1970s,
  A. American employers emphasized benefit plans for their employees, as well as full-time employment
  B. younger American workers were impressed by the strength of labor unions and eager to join one
  C. American union membership grew among African Americans, Mexican Americans, and women
  D. César Chávez fought to improve labor conditions for U.S. urban women

3. C 3. During this period in American history,
  A. there continued to be many restrictions on southern and eastern European immigration
  B. an immigration quota system was established
  C. increasing numbers of immigrants arrived from Asia, Latin America, and the Caribbean
  D. immigration slowed dramatically

B 4. U.S. agriculture during the 1960s and 1970s
  A. experienced a decline in crop production
  B. was primarily in the hands of large agribusiness firms
  C. received no assistance from the federal government
  D. witnessed a significant increase in the number of Americans living on farms

C 5. Because of the 1973 oil crisis,
  A. the U.S. government banned all exports to the Middle East
  B. Volkswagens and Toyotas became less popular
  C. American carmakers were forced to begin designing cars that took less gas
  D. U.S. forces in the Middle East were attacked by OPEC nations

Lesson 29: The Economy and Family Life During the Sixties and Seventies
©2008 Bright Ideas Press. All rights reserved.
235

B 6. The American space program during this period accomplished all of the following EXCEPT
  A. sending Americans to the moon
  B. avoiding any major accidents and human loss of life
  C. exploring Mars, Jupiter, and several other planets with unmanned space probes
  D. flying Mercury, Gemini, and Apollo programs

D 7. Which of the following did NOT appear in the 1960s and 1970s?
  A. microprocessors
  B. VCRs
  C. Atari games
  D. the Internet

A 8. One of the first mass-produced personal computers, the Apple II was designed by Stephen Wozniak and
  A. Steven Jobs
  B. Buzz Aldrin
  C. Bill Gates
  D. John Glenn

B 9. Microsoft Corporation was started by Paul Allen and
  A. John Glenn
  B. Bill Gates
  C. Steven Jobs
  D. Gloria Steinem

B 10. The author of *The Feminine Mystique*, which sparked a national debate on the role of women, was
  A. Gloria Steinem
  B. Betty Friedan
  C. Phyllis Schlafly
  D. Jane Fonda

D 11. The Women's Liberation Movement called for all of the following EXCEPT
  A. easier divorce laws
  B. abortion on demand
  C. women not confining themselves to the roles of housewives
  D. reversal of the *Roe v. Wade* Supreme Court decision

All American History Volume 2 — Student Activity Book
©2008 Bright Ideas Press. All rights reserved.
236

Answer Key to the Forms, Maps, and For Review Questions in the Student Activity Book
©2008 Bright Ideas Press. All rights reserved.

259

D _____ 12. The Equal Rights Amendment was
  A. not passed by the U.S. Senate
  B. finally ratified in 1978 and added to the Constitution
  C. criticized by liberal Democrats
  D. not approved by three-fourths of the state legislatures within the specified time period

C _____ 13. By the end of the 1970s,
  A. only a small percentage of American women were attending college
  B. large numbers of American women were finding high-paying jobs
  C. the rising divorce rate was forcing more and more women into low-income jobs
  D. no steps had been taken to end discrimination against women in American colleges

A _____ 14. Which of the following was NOT true of American teens during the 1960s and 1970s?
  A. they had less freedom than in previous years
  B. they played an influential role in the establishment of fashion trends and fads
  C. they experienced rising delinquency rates and increasing problems with drug and alcohol abuse
  D. they were 70 million strong due to the post-World War II baby boom

C _____ 15. American public schools by the early 1970s
  A. were free from racial tensions
  B. still enjoyed the opportunity for prayer during the school day
  C. were confronted with forced integration and busing
  D. had eliminated the teaching of phonics

A _____ 16. Women's fashion during much of the 1960s
  A. was influenced first by Jackie Kennedy and then by Twiggy
  B. emphasized modest, conservative outfits
  C. had not yet introduced jogging or warm-up suits
  D. encouraged women not to wear jeans

B _____ 17. In the late 1960s and 1970s,
  A. long, straight hair for women was no longer stylish
  B. many African American women began choosing Afro hairstyles
  C. psychedelic designs in fabrics had not yet been invented
  D. the popularity of miniskirts had led to a decline in the wearing of jeans among American women

D _____ 18. Men's clothing in this era included all of the following EXCEPT
  A. Nehru jackets
  B. polyester leisure suits
  C. double-breasted sports jackets
  D. zoot suits

A _____ 19. Many American children and teens in the 1970s
  A. wore bell bottoms
  B. knew nothing about designer labels
  C. had not yet been introduced to tie-dyed shirts
  D. attended schools that had strict dress codes

B _____ 20. During these two decades,
  A. cigarette manufacturers were not required to put warning labels on their packages and in their ads
  B. a significant health movement had begun to develop among baby boomers
  C. organ transplants were not yet available
  D. scientists were still struggling to understand the structure of the DNA molecule

LESSON 29: FOR FURTHER STUDY

For even more interesting information about this period of history, please refer to the For Further Study answers for this lesson in the Teacher's Guide.

1. Discover what happened at Three Mile Island in 1979. When was the first Earth Day? What books did Rachel Carson and Ralph Nader write that made them famous?

2. Find pictures of cars from the 1960s and 1970s. How did they differ from the cars of today? Look for pictures of U.S. Mercury, Gemini, and Apollo spacecraft. Read about the moonwalks taken by American astronauts.

3. Read about the life of Bill Gates. What has he done in the years since he made his millions?

4. Research *Engel v. Vitale* (1962), *Wallace v. Jaffree* (1985), *Lee v. Weisman* (1992), and *Santa FE ISD v. Doe* (2000). What was the significance of the ruling by the Supreme Court in each of these cases?

LESSONS 30 AND 31: REVIEW OF PRESIDENTS

Name _____ Date _____

Fill in the blanks with the names of the first through forty-third presidents in order. The acrostic is provided as a tool to help you remember.

#	Acrostic	President's Name
First Set		
1.	Why:	George Washington
2.	Are:	John Adams
3.	Jeff:	Thomas Jefferson
4.	Madison:	James Madison
5.	Monty:	James Monroe
6.	and:	John Quincy Adams
7.	Jack:	Andrew Jackson
8.	Buying:	Martin van Buren
9.	Horses?:	William Henry Harrison
Second Set		
10.	Take:	John Tyler
11.	Poor:	James Polk
12.	Taylor's:	Zachary Taylor
13.	Filly:	Millard Fillmore
14.	Past:	Franklin Pierce
15.	Both:	James Buchanan
16.	Lincoln's:	Abraham Lincoln
17.	Jogging:	Andrew Johnson
18.	Goats:	Ulysses S. Grant
Third Set		
19.	Happy:	Rutherford B. Hayes
20.	Goats:	James A. Garfield
21.	Always:	Chester A. Arthur
22.	Catch:	Grover Cleveland
23.	Horses:	Benjamin Harrison
24.	Creating:	Grover Cleveland
25.	Mischief:	William McKinley

#	Acrostic	President's Name
Fourth Set		
26.	Rope:	Theodore Roosevelt
27.	The:	William Howard Taft
28.	Wild:	Woodrow Wilson
29.	Horses:	Warren G. Harding
30.	Carefully:	Calvin Coolidge
31.	Hold on:	Herbert Hoover
32.	Relentlessly:	Franklin D. Roosevelt
Fifth Set		
33.	The:	Harry S. Truman
34.	Elephant:	Dwight D. Eisenhower
35.	Knows:	John F. Kennedy
36.	John:	Lyndon B. Johnson
37.	Never:	Richard M. Nixon
38.	Follows:	Gerald R. Ford
39.	Cows:	James E. Carter
40.	Racing:	Ronald W. Reagan
41.	Buffalos and:	George H. W. Bush
42.	Chasing:	William J. Clinton
43.	Bears:	George W. Bush

239

Answer Key to the Forms, Maps, and For Review Questions in the Student Activity Book

LESSON 30: FOR REVIEW
Write T for True and F for False in the space provided.

F ___ 1. In the 1960s, there emerged a counterculture of hippies that supported the Vietnam War, a crackdown on drugs, and a return to parental goals and lifestyles.

T ___ 2. The hundred-year fight for civil rights by African Americans reached a peak in the 1960s.

T ___ 3. Supreme Court decisions in the late 1960s and early 1970s called for the immediate desegregation of segregated public schools and upheld busing to achieve racial balance.

F ___ 4. Malcolm X consistently supported King's advocacy of nonviolent protests.

F ___ 5. The number of African Americans in Congress decreased during this period.

T ___ 6. Native Americans began to assert themselves in the courts and in violent protests.

F ___ 7. The Jesus People had little influence on the contemporary evangelical Christian movement.

T ___ 8. A growing number of American young people in the 1960s turned to mystic Eastern religions.

F ___ 9. Pentecostalism was a dying movement by the 1960s.

T ___ 10. Parachurch groups, like Campus Crusade for Christ and InterVarsity Christian Fellowship, reached out to millions of American college students in the 1960s and 1970s.

T ___ 11. The first professional football championship game, later to be called the Super Bowl, was played in 1967 between the Green Bay Packers and the Kansas City Chiefs.

T ___ 12. By the 1970s, American television had begun branching out into more controversial programming.

F ___ 13. American literature during this period did not really reflect what was going on in the political arena and with the youthful counterculture.

F ___ 14. American art in the 1960s and 1970s was either romantic or impressionist in style.

Write the missing word or words in the spaces provided.

1. The pinnacle of the hippie movement seemed to be at the Woodstock Festival in New York state in 1969.

2. ___ James Meredith ___ became the first black student to enroll in the University of Mississippi, and three hundred federal troops were needed to put down the riots that followed his enrollment.

3. Martin Luther King, Jr., gave his famous "I Have a Dream" speech during the 1963 March on Washington.

4. Two African American groups more radical in their approach to the civil rights movement than King were the Black Panthers and the Black Muslims .

5. ___ Andrew Young ___ became the first African American voted into the House of Representatives from the deep South since 1898.

2. Find out more details concerning the 1960 sit-in at the Woolworth's in Greensboro, North Carolina, and the 1963 Birmingham demonstrations.

3. For what did the X in Malcolm X stand? What happened to Malcolm X? Fill out an African American form on Malcolm X.

4. Discover the significance of Patricia Hearst and the Symbionese Liberation Army (SLA).

---

6. One of the most publicized American Indian protests during this period occurred at **Wounded Knee, South Dakota**.

7. The establishment of a San Francisco mission known as the Living Room ushered in the **Jesus People** movement.

8. **Reverend Sun Myung Moon** attracted hundreds of young followers and established the Unification Church.

9. The Moral Majority was established by **Jerry Falwell** during the 1970s.

10. The huge success of the British rock group, **the Beatles**, in 1965 caused the popular music business to mushroom.

11. **Andy Warhol**, a leading name in pop art, printed multiple images of comic strips and silk-screen reproductions of everyday images.

12. Perhaps one of the most influential architects of the 1960s was **I. M. Pei**.

LESSON 30: FOR FURTHER STUDY

For even more interesting information about this period of history, please refer to the For Further Study answers for this lesson in the Teacher's Guide.

1. Read about the lives of Thurgood Marshall and Medgar Evers. For what are they remembered? Fill out African American forms on Marshall and Evers.

Answer Key to the Forms, Maps, and For Review Questions in the Student Activity Book

Name _____ Date _____

LESSON 31: RONALD W. REAGAN

Picture of the president

Year born _____ 1911

Year died _____ 2004

In which state was he born? _____ Illinois

What jobs did he hold before becoming president? _____ Actor, Governor of California

With what political party was this president affiliated? _____ Republican

Vice President: _____ George H. W. Bush, George H. W. Bush

What were the years of his presidency? _____ 1981 – 1989

List some significant developments during his administration _____ Attempted presidential

assassination (unsuccessful)

High inflation, high unemployment, high interest rates, high fuel prices

(supply-side economics)

Creation of the Dept. of Veterans Affairs

Reductions in federal welfare and unemployment programs

Large increase in national defense spending

Eventual economic recovery but still record-level federal budget deficits

Reagan Doctrine (U.S. support to insurgent groups battling communist

governments)

Soviet *glasnost*, nuclear arms treaty with the Soviet Union, invasion of Grenada

245

Lesson 31: The End of the Cold War and Beyond
©2008 Bright Ideas Press. All rights reserved.

Name _____ Date _____

LESSON 31: GEORGE H. W. BUSH

Picture of the president

Year born _____ 1924 _____

Year died _____ N/A _____

In which state was he born? _____ Massachusetts _____

What jobs did he hold before becoming president? _____ U.S. naval pilot (World War II),

Texas oil businessman, U.S. Representative, U.S. ambassador to the UN, chief

of U.S. liaison office in China, chairman of the National Republican

Committee, CIA Director, Vice President

With what political party was this president affiliated? _____ Republican _____

Vice President: _____ J. Danforth Quayle _____

What were the years of his presidency? _____ 1989 – 1993 _____

List some significant developments during his administration _____ Huge federal

budget deficits; tax increase (breaking of a campaign promise); 2-year recession

Transitioning of U.S. economy from manufacturing to service base with many

job losses

27th Amendment

Fall of the Iron Curtain (Berlin Wall); breakup of the Soviet Union into

independent republics; improved U.S.–Soviet trade relations

Overthrow of Noriega in Panama; Operation Desert Storm

Lesson 31: The End of the Cold War and Beyond

247

Name _____ Date _____

LESSON 31: WILLIAM J. CLINTON

Picture of the president

Year born ____1946____

Year died ____N/A____

In which state was he born? ____Arkansas____

What jobs did he hold before becoming president? ____Lawyer,____
____Governor of Arkansas____

With what political party was this president affiliated? ____Democratic____

Vice President: ____Albert Gore, Jr., Albert Gore, Jr.____

What were the years of his presidency? ____1993 - 2001____

List some significant developments during his administration ____First balanced____
____federal budget in decades; decline in inflation and unemployment____
____Attempt (unsuccessful) to reform U.S. healthcare system____
____Republican "Contract with America" (welfare reform, increased military____
____funding, cut in capital gains taxes, balanced budget amendment)____
____Presidential impeachment____
____U.S. peacekeeping troops in Bosnia____

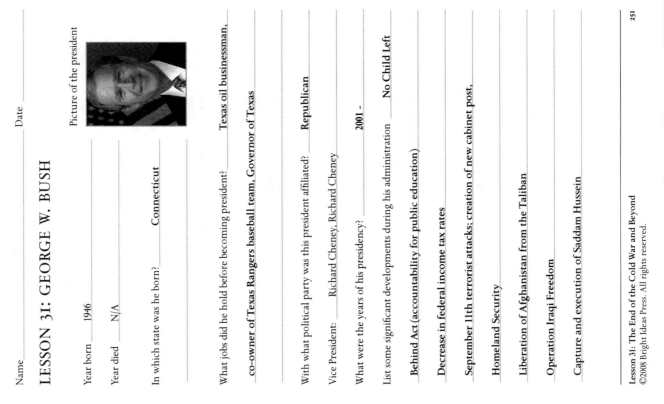

Name _____ Date _____

LESSON 31: GEORGE W. BUSH

Picture of the president

Year born _____ 1946

Year died _____ N/A

In which state was he born? _____ Connecticut

What jobs did he hold before becoming president? _____ Texas oil businessman,
co-owner of Texas Rangers baseball team, Governor of Texas

With what political party was this president affiliated? _____ Republican

Vice President: _____ Richard Cheney, Richard Cheney

What were the years of his presidency? _____ 2001 –

List some significant developments during his administration _____ No Child Left
Behind Act (accountability for public education)

Decrease in federal income tax rates

September 11th terrorist attacks; creation of new cabinet post,

Homeland Security

Liberation of Afghanistan from the Taliban

Operation Iraqi Freedom

Capture and execution of Saddam Hussein

Lesson 31: The End of the Cold War and Beyond
©2008 Bright Ideas Press. All rights reserved.

251

Write T for True and F for False in the space provided.

T ____ 1. Ronald Reagan was known as the "Teflon" president.

T ____ 2. The keystone of Reagan's economic program was supply-side economics.

F ____ 3. By the end of Reagan's time in office, unemployment and inflation rates had risen.

F ____ 4. President Reagan believed that income tax cuts were responsible for harming the U.S. economy.

F ____ 5. The Cold War had ended before Reagan was elected president.

F ____ 6. Reagan refused to give support to groups in Latin America and Africa who were battling communist governments.

T ____ 7. Gorbachev and Reagan signed a treaty leading to a reduction in Soviet and U.S. nuclear arms.

F ____ 8. In 1981, Reagan was assassinated by John Hinckley, Jr.

F ____ 9. George H. W. Bush was a successful Texas oil man, who had very little previous government experience before his election to the presidency.

T ____ 10. When George H. W. Bush became president, the U.S. government was seriously in debt, and the U.S. economy was transitioning from a manu-facturing base to a service base.

T ____ 11. During George H. W. Bush's administration, the Berlin Wall came down, and the Soviet Union broke up into independent republics.

F ____ 12. George H. W. Bush refused to send U.S. troops to Panama to overthrow the dictatorship of General Manuel Noriega.

T ____ 13. Saddam Hussein invaded Kuwait in 1990 and threatened to take over Saudi Arabia in order to control 20 percent of the world's oil resources.

T ____ 14. Bill Clinton was the first Democratic president since Franklin Roosevelt elected to a second term in office.

LESSON 31: FOR REVIEW
Write the corresponding letter of the correct answer in the space provided.

A. Ronald Reagan   C. Bill Clinton
B. George H. W. Bush D. George W. Bush

A ____ 1. Survived a 1981 assassination attempt

B ____ 2. Led the United States to victory in Operation Desert Storm

A ____ 3. Ordered invasion of the Caribbean island of Grenada in 1983

D ____ 4. Served six years as governor of Texas

A ____ 5. Became the oldest man ever elected U.S. president

B ____ 6. Broke a 1988 presidential campaign promise by signing a federal tax increase

C ____ 7. Appointed more minorities and women to his cabinet than any other pres-ident

D ____ 8. Declared a war on terrorism after the September 11 terrorist attacks

D ____ 9. Succeeded in capturing Saddam Hussein

B ____ 10. Ordered American troops into Panama to overthrow the dictatorship of Noriega

C ____ 11. Second president to be impeached

C ____ 12. Appointed his wife to head a major committee that sought to reform health care

A ____ 13. Promoted supply-side economics

D ____ 14. Ran for president as a "compassionate conservative"

D ____ 15. Launched Operation Iraqi Freedom

F____ 15. At the time Clinton became president, the attention of the United States had shifted from domestic issues to foreign affairs.

F____ 16. The Republicans were unsuccessful in pushing through any of the proposals in their Contract with America.

F____ 17. George W. Bush was elected president in 2000 with a large majority in the Electoral College.

T____ 18. As governor of Texas, George W. Bush was known for emphasizing the principles of limited government and personal responsibility.

F____ 19. The terrorist attacks of September 11 had little bearing on U.S. foreign affairs during George W. Bush's presidency.

T____ 20. Bush ordered the invasion of Iraq in 2003 because he believed that it was necessary to disarm Saddam Hussein's weapons of mass destruction.

LESSON 31: FOR FURTHER STUDY

For even more interesting information about this period of history, please refer to the For Further Study answers for this lesson in the Teacher's Guide.

1. Read about the Iran-Contra affair. What role did Oliver North play?

2. Find out what NAFTA is and why it is significant.

3. Research the ratification of the Twenty-seventh Amendment. What was unique about this amendment?

4. What happened in Waco, Texas, in April of 1993 and in Oklahoma City in April of 1995? Discover how these two events were connected. Research the activities of Theodore Kaczynski. Determine what the right-wing militia movement of this era believed and what actions they took.

255

Lesson 31: The End of the Cold War and Beyond
©2008 Bright Ideas Press. All rights reserved.

Answer Key to the Forms, Maps, and For Review Questions in the Student Activity Book
©2008 Bright Ideas Press. All rights reserved.

269

SUMMARY OF PROJECTS AND SPECIAL ACTIVITIES

Name _____ Date _____

Units Three and Four

READING

What biographies or nonfiction books have you read about these periods of history and who were the author(s)? _____

What historical fiction books have you read about these periods of history and who were the author(s)? _____

What magazine or Internet articles have you read about these periods of history? _____

FIELD TRIPS/VIRTUAL TOURS

What field trips or virtual tours have you taken to sites from these periods of history? _____

Which was your favorite and why? _____

MOVIES

What movies have you watched that are set in these time periods or what documentaries have you watched that are about persons or events from these time periods? _____

Which was the most interesting to you and why? _____

ART

What art projects have you completed that were about these time periods or were done in an artistic technique from these time periods? _____

NOTEBOOKS AND OTHER ACTIVITIES

Who has been highlighted in your Native American or African American notebook? _____

What other fun and creative activities have you done? _____

LESSON 32: FOR REVIEW

Write the letter of the correct answer in the space provided.

C _____ 1. Which of the following was NOT true of American businesses in the 1980s and 1990s?

A. corporations gained stratospheric profits

B. businessmen succeeded in pushing for government deregulation

C. there were few corporate mergers or takeovers

D. a new breed of American billionaire, personified by Donald Trump, emerged

B _____ 2. The U.S. stock market

A. shrank during the 1980s

B. went into a free fall on Black Monday in October of 1987

C. experienced record lows fifty-five times in the first eight months of 1987

D. never recovered from the 1980s

D _____ 3. American savings and loan associations

A. have never been subject to restrictive regulations

B. obtained most of their funds from the federal government

C. failed to attract many customers in the 1980s

D. underwent a crisis in the 1980s that required federal assistance

B _____ 4. During the 1980s and 1990s,

A. the United States experienced an increase in the number of jobs in heavy industries

B. the technology of computers created new fortunes and new communities

C. many new factories opened in the industrial heartland of America

D. the Texas oil boom continued without an end in sight

A _____ 5. Which of the following was true of organized labor in the 1980s and 1990s?

A. union members represented a shrinking share of the workforce

B. more and more American workers held blue-collar factory jobs

C. the gap between the wages of skilled and unskilled workers narrowed

D. the number of strikes in the United States dramatically increased

---

A _____ 6. Which of the following was NOT true of American agriculture in the 1980s and 1990s?

A. the U.S. government never broke with the farm policies of the New Deal

B. the bottom fell out of land and food prices, leading to farm foreclosures and bankruptcies

C. American agriculture was increasingly becoming an agribusiness

D. new trends, such as organic farming and genetic engineering, emerged

A _____ 7. By the 1990s,

A. the interstate highway system had almost been completed

B. minivans had not yet been introduced

C. American auto sales were higher than Japanese auto sales

D. the best-selling cars in the United States were Chryslers and Fords

D _____ 8. The American space program

A. decided to scuttle the space shuttle program in 1980

B. received strong public support in the early 1980s

C. has never faced tragic accidents or loss of human lives

D. sent the first American woman into space in the early 1980s

B _____ 9. During the last two decades of the twentieth century,

A. the World Wide Web failed to capture the American imagination

B. computers became common in offices, schools, banks, and homes

C. computer prices continued to climb

D. Apple was the only large computer company

C _____ 10. In the 1980s and 1990s,

A. the proportion of nuclear families was rising

B. the number of children living in single-parent homes was declining

C. the divorce rate had tripled since the 1960s

D. there was little controversy over the definition of marriage and the family

D _____ 11. American women in the 1980s and 1990s

A. had achieved their goal of equal pay for equal work

B. failed to rise to prominence in fields closed to women

C. very rarely earned college degrees

D. saw an improvement in their wages, although usually not equal pay for equal work

---

Answer Key to the Forms, Maps, and For Review Questions in the Student Activity Book

3. The largest single religious group in the United States at the end of the twentieth century was **Roman Catholicism**. Numerically, the fastest growing religion was **Islam**.

4. Mainline denominations in the United States became increasingly divided into **liberal** and **conservative** factions over issues such as the morality of abortion and various sexual orientations.

5. The founder of the Christian Coalition was **Pat Robertson**.

6. **Dr. James Dobson**, founder of Focus on the Family, used his radio audience to generate floods of mail and phone calls for conservative Christian causes.

7. In the 1980 presidential election, the majority of evangelical Christian voters aligned themselves with the **Republican** political party.

8. The author of the best-selling nonfiction work in the twentieth century (*The Purpose-Driven Life*) is **Rick Warren**.

9. The most coveted consumers in the 1980s and 1990s were American **teenagers**.

10. The best-selling American record album of all time was *Thriller*.

B   12. The first woman appointed to the U.S. Supreme Court was
    A. Geraldine Ferraro
    B. Sandra Day O'Connor
    C. Hillary Clinton
    D. Gloria Steinem

D   13. Which of the following was NOT true of American education during this period?
    A. the issue of school violence became more prominent
    B. school vouchers were suggested as a way to improve education
    C. widespread discipline problems and racial tensions continued
    D. the number of families homeschooling their children declined

A   14. In the final two decades of the twentieth century,
    A. clothing with designer labels was popular among both men and women
    B. almost all offices still had a very formal dress code
    C. most Americans were uninterested in buying exercise clothing
    D. black was no longer a popular color for clothing

C   15. The American music industry during this period
    A. was not yet affected by MTV
    B. faced few copyright issues
    C. was revolutionized by the introduction of compact discs
    D. offered less variety to its listeners

Write the missing word or words in the spaces provided.

1. During the 1980s and 1990s, **AIDS** was considered to be an epidemic for the first time.

2. In 1997, a lamb named **Dolly** was cloned from a single cell of an adult sheep in Scotland.

Lesson 32: Economics, Family Life, and Culture During the Eighties and Nineties

All American History, Vol. II: Teacher's Guide — Section Five

LESSON 32: FOR FURTHER STUDY

For even more interesting information about this period of history, please refer to the For Further Study answers for this lesson in the Teacher's Guide.

1. Discover the significance of Rodney King and the 1995 Million Man March. Read about the lives of Jesse Jackson and Ben Carson and fill out African American forms for them.

2. Find out the meaning of the following financial terms — junk bonds, corporate raids, and insider trading. Learn what the Y2K bug was.

3. Read about Christa McAuliffe, who died in the *Challenger* space shuttle explosion. Why was McAuliffe chosen to fly on this mission? What did she hope to accomplish on the flight? Why did the shuttle explode?

4. Learn who founded the Parents Music Resource Center and why it was founded. Determine who started CNN and why its launching was significant.

Lesson 32: Economics, Family Life, and Culture During the Eighties and Nineties
©2008 Bright Ideas Press. All rights reserved.

Answer Key to the Forms, Maps, and For Review Questions in the Student Activity Book

UNIT 4: FINAL REVIEW

Write the corresponding letter of the correct answer in the space provided.

A. Harry S. Truman
B. Dwight D. Eisenhower
C. John F. Kennedy
D. Lyndon B. Johnson
E. Richard M. Nixon
F. Gerald R. Ford
G. James E. Carter
H. Ronald W. Reagan
I. George H. W. Bush
J. William J. Clinton
K. George W. Bush

E _____ 1. Watergate
A _____ 2. Korean War
A _____ 3. Fair Deal
J _____ 4. Second president impeached
C _____ 5. Building of the Berlin Wall
G _____ 6. Iranian hostage crisis
C _____ 7. Bay of Pigs invasion and Cuban missile crisis
B _____ 8. Modern Republicanism
D _____ 9. War on Poverty
H _____ 10. Survivor of an assassination attempt
I _____ 11. Operation Desert Storm
B _____ 12. Approval of construction of interstate highways
D _____ 13. Gulf of Tonkin Resolution
K _____ 14. Capture of Saddam Hussein
A _____ 15. Berlin Airlift
K _____ 16. September 11th

A. Harry S. Truman
B. Dwight D. Eisenhower
C. John F. Kennedy
D. Lyndon B. Johnson
E. Richard M. Nixon
F. Gerald R. Ford
G. James E. Carter
H. Ronald W. Reagan
I. George H. W. Bush
J. William J. Clinton
K. George W. Bush

C _____ 17. Assassination in Dallas
H _____ 18. Supply-side economics
H _____ 19. Oldest man elected president
B _____ 20. Warning about the "military-industrial complex"
D _____ 21. Great Society
K _____ 22. Operation Iraqi Freedom
F _____ 23. Pardon of Richard Nixon
G _____ 24. Camp David Accords
E _____ 25. Vietnamization
C _____ 26. New Frontier
I _____ 27. Tearing down of the Berlin Wall
G _____ 28. Self-proclaimed "man of the people" who eliminated some of the ceremonial trappings of the presidency
E _____ 29. Only president to resign from office
K _____ 30. Compassionate conservative

Write the corresponding letter of the correct answer in the space provided.

A. Neil Armstrong
B. James Coleman
C. James Conant
D. Betty Friedan
E. Berry Gordy
F. Billy Graham
G. Alger Hiss
H. Jack Kerouac
I. Malcolm X
J. Martin Luther King, Jr.
K. George Marshall
L. Douglas MacArthur
M. Christa McAuliffe
N. Sandra Day O'Connor
O. I. M. Pei
P. Jackson Pollock
Q. Jackie Robinson
R. Julius Rosenberg
S. Benjamin Spock
T. Andy Warhol

Q ___ 1. First African American professional baseball player

G ___ 2. Former American state department official accused of passing U.S. secret documents to the Russians

H ___ 3. Most prolific of the beat authors

J ___ 4. Founder of the SCLC and leader of many nonviolent civil rights demonstrations

P ___ 5. Abstract expressionist artist

L ___ 6. Commander of UN forces during the Korean War

A ___ 7. First man on the moon

S ___ 8. Author of the best-selling *Common Sense Book of Baby and Child Care*

R ___ 9. American executed after being convicted of selling atomic secrets to the Soviet government

F ___ 10. Well-known American evangelist during the second half of the twentieth century who preached to record-breaking crowds in his crusades

D ___ 11. Author of *The Feminine Mystique*

C ___ 12. Conducted a study of American high schools in the 1950s that called for the teaching of foreign languages and meeting the needs of academically talented students

A. Neil Armstrong
B. James Coleman
C. James Conant
D. Betty Friedan
E. Berry Gordy
F. Billy Graham
G. Alger Hiss
H. Jack Kerouac
I. Malcolm X
J. Martin Luther King, Jr.
K. George Marshall
L. Douglas MacArthur
M. Christa McAuliffe
N. Sandra Day O'Connor
O. I. M. Pei
P. Jackson Pollock
Q. Jackie Robinson
R. Julius Rosenberg
S. Benjamin Spock
T. Andy Warhol

M ___ 13. American teacher who died in the *Challenger* explosion

T ___ 14. Leading American pop artist who printed multiple images of comic strips and silk-screen reproductions of everyday images

O ___ 15. Influential American architect in the last decades of the twentieth century

B ___ 16. Author of a 1960s landmark study entitled *Equality of Educational Opportunity*, which led the way to forced integration and busing

K ___ 17. Secretary of state who proposed that all the nations of Europe join in a post-war program of mutual aid for economic recovery

I ___ 18. Leader of the Black Muslims, who preached that African Americans should liberate themselves through violent revolution

E ___ 19. Founder of the Motown Record Company

N ___ 20. First woman to serve on the U.S. Supreme Court

Write T for True and F for False in the space provided.

F ___ 1. The Korean War caused the U.S. economy to be depressed during the early 1950s.

T ___ 2. The Taft-Hartley Act in 1947 weakened American labor.

T ___ 3. The American farm economy faced the challenge of overproduction following World War II.

Answer Key to the Forms, Maps, and For Review Questions in the Student Activity Book   275

F _____ 20. The Equal Rights Amendment is the Twenty-seventh Amendment to the Constitution.

F _____ 21. A rule of thumb in fashion has been that skirts often become longer in times of prosperity and shorter in times of economic instability.

T _____ 22. Some of the largest corporate takeovers in history occurred in the United States during the 1980s.

T _____ 23. A crisis occurred in the U.S. savings and loan industry in the 1980s.

T _____ 24. During the last two decades of the twentieth century, the United States witnessed a large decline in heavy industry and a shift toward the creation of jobs in lower-paying service industries.

F _____ 25. In the 1980s, American auto sales surpassed Japanese auto sales.

T _____ 26. The Internet changed the way Americans did their business and banking and how they communicated with one another.

F _____ 27. The issue of school violence became less troubling in the 1990s.

T _____ 28. The cost of a college education continued to accelerate dramatically in the last decades of the twentieth century.

F _____ 29. By the turn of the century, the United States had become a religiously homogenous nation.

T _____ 30. In the 1990s, it was possible to read entire books online, and mega bookstores were responsible for driving many smaller bookstores out of business.

T _____ 4. The Soviet Union was the first nation to launch a satellite that orbited the earth.

F _____ 5. The U.S. baby boom reached its height in the 1970s.

T _____ 6. The Supreme Court in *Brown v. Board of Education of Topeka, Kansas*, ruled that racially segregated schools were unconstitutional.

F _____ 7. The ladies' fashion industry in the United States in the 1950s did not prosper.

T _____ 8. The 1950s brought the first polio vaccine and the first laser.

F _____ 9. Casseroles had not been invented in the 1950s.

F _____ 10. During the 1950s, anticommunist fears were a thing of the past in the United States.

F _____ 11. Joseph McCarthy's Senate committee investigations from 1950 through 1954 were not very controversial.

T _____ 12. Following Rosa Park's arrest, Martin Luther King, Jr., led a bus boycott in Montgomery, Alabama, that lasted thirteen months.

F _____ 13. Bill Haley and the Comets pioneered a new sound in music called hip-hop.

T _____ 14. In the late 1950s, Elvis Presley became famous as the king of rock.

F _____ 15. Stagflation was the condition of simultaneously low inflation and low unemployment.

F _____ 16. Membership in U.S. labor unions rose steadily following World War II.

T _____ 17. By 1980, the number of Americans living on farms was less than 3 percent of the population.

T _____ 18. VCRs, video game consoles, and personal computers appeared as mass market consumer products during the last two decades of the twentieth century.

F _____ 19. The National Organization for Women promoted a traditional, conservative approach to the roles of women.

Section Six

OPTIONAL FORMS

All American History, Vol II: Teacher's Guide — Section Six —Optional Timeline Form

Name_____ Date _____

NATIVE AMERICAN TRIBE

Name of the tribe _____

In what region of the United States did this tribe live? _____

Pictures of important tribal leaders

<table>
<tr><td>Paste image here</td><td>Paste image here</td><td>Paste image here</td></tr>
</table>

What explorer(s) or colonist(s) interracted with this tribe?_____

_____

_____

Were relations friendly? _____

What kind of food did this tribe eat? _____

_____

What language did they speak? _____

_____

Write about this tribe's religious customs, transportation methods, and recreation.

_____

_____

_____

_____

Name_____ Date _____

TRIBAL LIFE

Draw some pictures based on your research.

Man in tribal clothing

Woman in tribal clothing

Draw a picture of typical tribal housing and some tribal tools or weapons.

Name_____ Date _____

NATIVE AMERICAN

Picture of this individual

Name_____

_____

Year born _____

Year died _____

Tribe into which he or she was born _____

What job or jobs did this person hold?_____

_____

Explain about the type of obstacles he or she needed to overcome _____

_____

_____

_____

_____

_____

_____

_____

_____

_____

Name_____ Date _____

Explain the role that this individual played in the history of the United States.

_____

_____

_____

_____

_____

_____

Locate a picture of a significant event or place from this individual's life, photocopy it, and paste it here. Or draw a scene if no picture is available.

Name_____ Date _____

AFRICAN AMERICAN

Name_____

Picture of this individual

_____

<table>
<tr><td></td><td>Paste
image
here</td></tr>
</table>

Year born _____

Year died _____

State in which he or she was born _____

What job or jobs did this person hold?_____

_____

Explain about the type of obstacles he or she needed to overcome _____

_____

_____

_____

_____

_____

_____

_____

_____

_____

_____

Name_____ Date _____

Explain the role that this individual played in the history of the United States.

_____

_____

_____

_____

_____

_____

Locate a picture of a significant event or place from this individual's life, photocopy it, and paste it here. Or draw a scene if no picture is available.

Name _____ Date _____

UNITED STATES PRESIDENT

Name of the president _____

Picture of the president

_____

Year born _____

Year died _____

Paste
image
here

What political party was this president affiliated with?

_____

What jobs did he hold before becoming president?

_____

Picture of vice president

Paste
image
here

What state was he born in? _____

List some significant developments in domestic policy during his administration

_____

_____

_____

_____

_____

_____

_____

Identify the states, if any, added to the Union during this president's term(s). Label them by name and color them in.

All American History, Vol II: Teacher's Guide — Section Six

Name_____ Date _____

CIVIL WAR BATTLE

Name of the battle? _____

Date(s) of the battle _____

Location of the battle _____

Pictures of some of the key
individuals in this battle

| Paste image here | Paste image here |
| Paste image here | Paste image here | Paste image here |

What was the purpose of this battle? _____

_____

List any other important facts about this battle _____

_____

_____

How was this battle significant to the Civil War?_____

_____

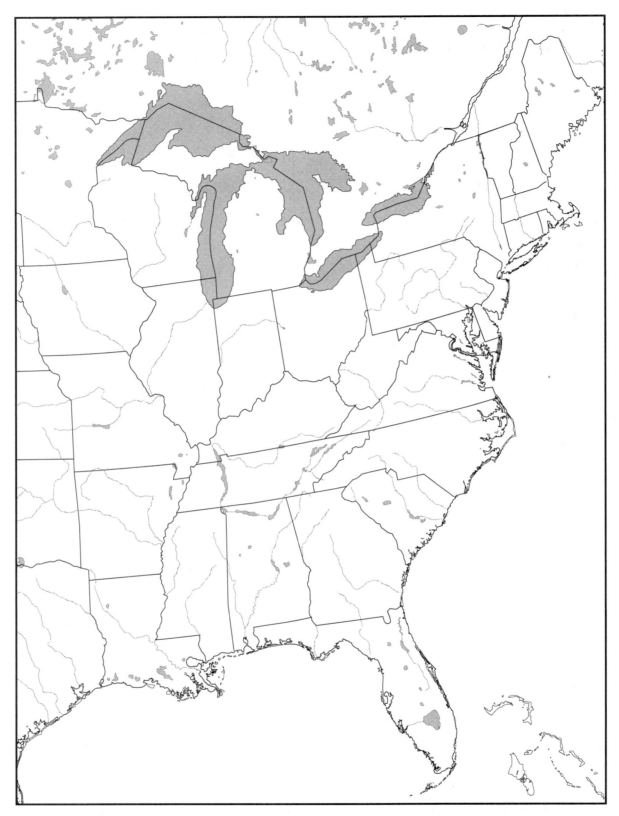

Locate and label your chosen Civil War battle on the map.

All American History, Vol II: Teacher's Guide — Section Six

Name_____ Date _____

WORLD WAR I BATTLE

Name of the battle? _____

Date(s) of the battle _____

Location of the battle _____

Pictures of some of the key
individuals in this battle

Paste image here	Paste image here

Paste image here	Paste image here	Paste image here

What was the purpose of this battle? _____

_____

List any other important facts about this battle _____

_____

_____

How was this battle significant to World War I? _____

_____

Locate and label your chosen World War I battle on the map.

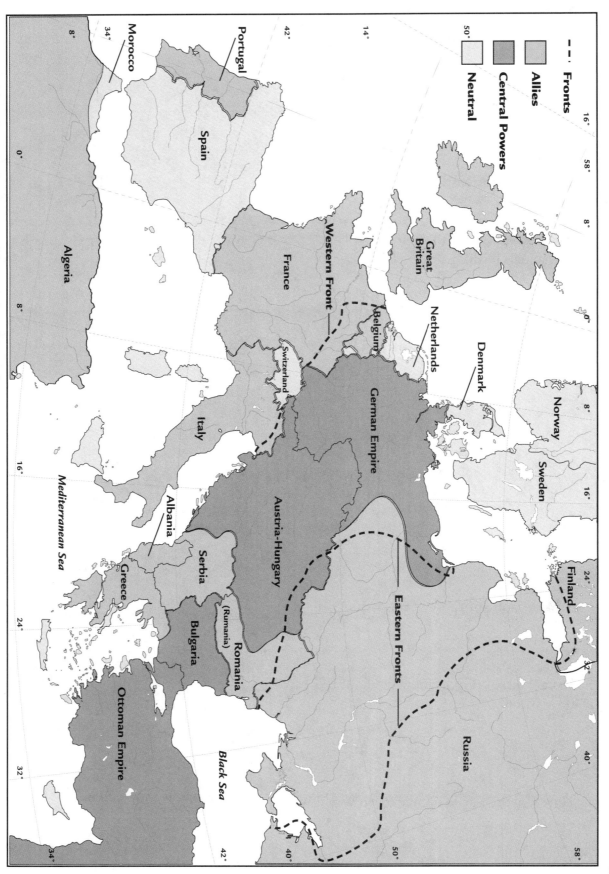

Legend:
- Fronts
- Allies
- Central Powers
- Neutral

50°

16°
58°
8°
0°

14°

42°

Morocco
34°
8°

Portugal
Spain
0°

Great Britain
8°

Western Front
France
Netherlands
Belgium
Denmark
Norway
Sweden
16°

German Empire
Switzerland
Italy
Algeria
8°

Albania
Austria-Hungary
Eastern Fronts
Finland
24°

Mediterranean Sea
16°

Greece
Serbia
(Rumania)
Romania
Russia
32°

Bulgaria
Black Sea
40°

Ottoman Empire
24°

32°

40°
42°
50°
58°
34°

All American History, Vol II: Teacher's Guide — Section Six

Name_____ Date _____

WORLD WAR II EUROPEAN BATTLE

Name of the battle? _____

Date(s) of the battle _____

Location of the battle _____

Pictures of some of the key
individuals in this battle

Paste image here		Paste image here
Paste image here	Paste image here	Paste image here

What was the purpose of this battle? _____

_____

_____

List any other important facts about this battle _____

_____

_____

How was this battle significant to World War II? _____

_____

Locate and label your chosen World War II European battle.

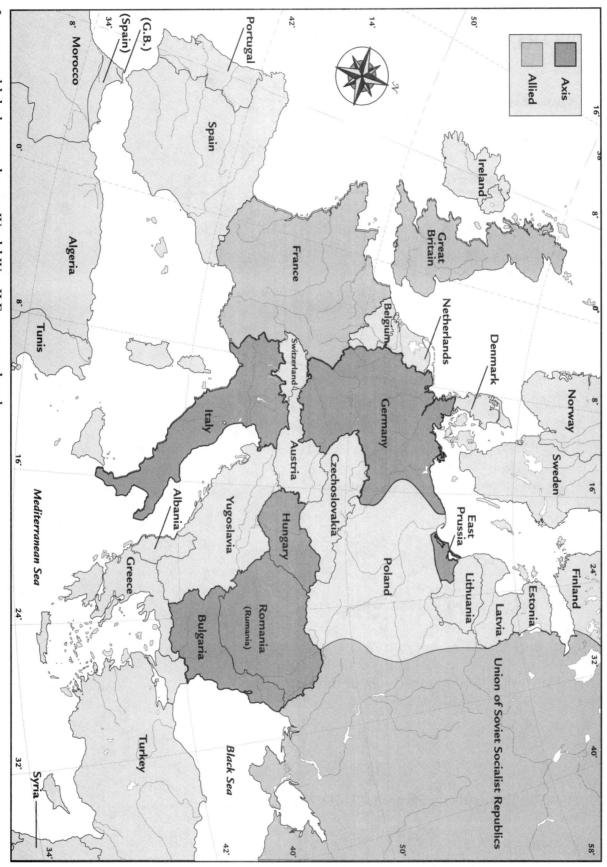

Legend:
- Axis
- Allied

Morocco
8°
34°
(G.B.) (Spain)
(Spain)
Portugal
42°
14°
50°
N
16°
38°
Ireland
8°
Spain
France
Great Britain
Belgium
Netherlands
Denmark
Norway
Germany
Sweden
8°
0°
Algeria
Switzerland
Austria
Czechoslovakia
East Prussia
8°
Tunis
Italy
Yugoslavia
Hungary
Poland
Lithuania
Latvia
Estonia
Finland
16°
24°
16°
Albania
Romania (Rumania)
Mediterranean Sea
Greece
Bulgaria
Union of Soviet Socialist Republics
32°
24°
Black Sea
Turkey
40°
32°
Syria
34°
42°
40°
50°
58°

Name_____ Date _____

WORLD WAR II PACIFIC BATTLE

Name of the battle? _____

Date(s) of the battle _____

Location of the battle _____

Pictures of some of the key individuals in this battle

Paste image here	Paste image here

Paste image here	Paste image here	Paste image here

What was the purpose of this battle? _____

_____

List any other important facts about this battle. _____

_____

_____

How was this battle significant to World War II? _____

_____

Locate and label your chosen World War II Pacific battle.

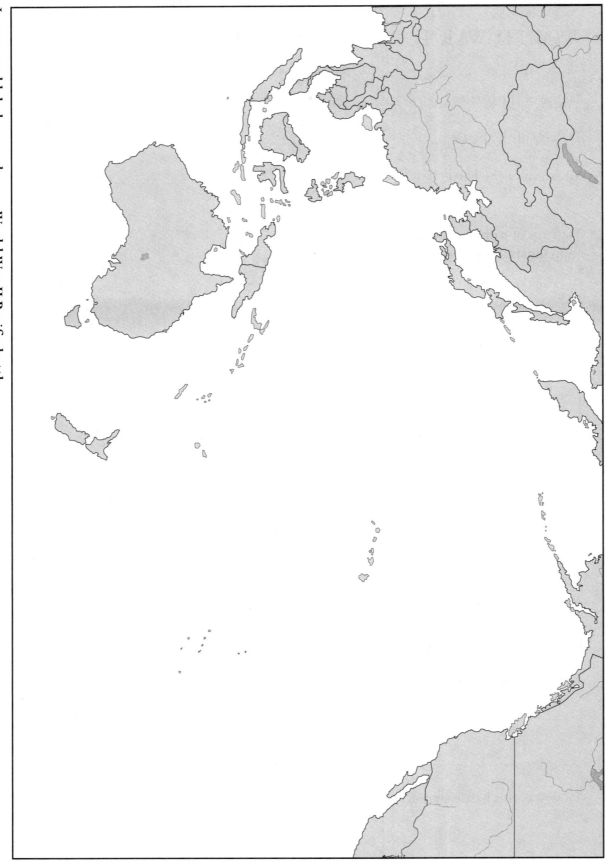

All American History, Vol II: Teacher's Guide — Section Six

Name_____ Date _____

KOREAN WAR BATTLE

Name of the battle? _____

Date(s) of the battle _____

Location of the battle _____

Pictures of some of the key individuals in this battle

	Paste image here	Paste image here
Paste image here	Paste image here	Paste image here

What was the purpose of this battle? _____

_____

List any other important facts about this battle. _____

_____

_____

How was this battle significant to the Korean War?_____

_____

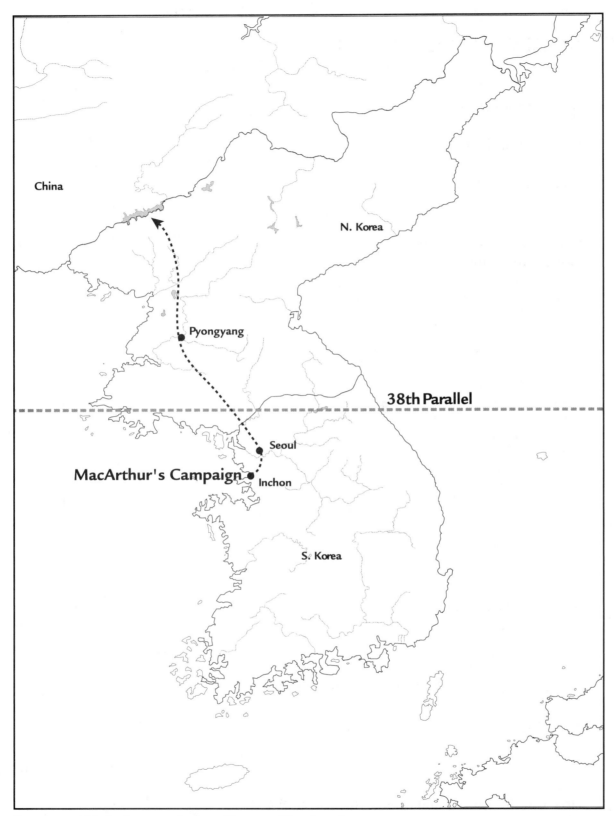

China

N. Korea

Pyongyang

38th Parallel

MacArthur's Campaign

Seoul

Inchon

S. Korea

Locate and label your chosen Korean War battle.

Name_____ Date _____

VIETNAM WAR BATTLE

Name of the battle? _____

Date(s) of the battle _____

Location of the battle _____

Pictures of some of the key
individuals in this battle

Paste image here

Paste image here

Paste image here

Paste image here

Paste image here

What was the purpose of this battle? _____

_____

List any other important facts about this battle. _____

_____

_____

How was this battle significant to the Vietnam War?_____

_____

Section Seven

IMAGES FOR REQUIRED FORMS

Starting at the right, cut images out of each column from the bottom up.

The thin black line between some images indicates the last of the images for one unit and the first of the next unit.

Abraham Lincoln	Frederick Douglass	Brigadier General Pierre Beauregard	Brigadier General Joseph Johnston
James Buchanan	Harriet Beecher Stowe	Jefferson Davis	Brigadier General Irvin McDowell
Franklin Pierce	William Lloyd Garrison	Abraham Lincoln	General Winfield Scott
Millard Fillmore	Dred Scott	John Brown	General Ulysses S. Grant
Zachary Taylor	Harriet Tubman	Sojourner Truth	General Robert E. Lee

Starting at the right, cut images out of each column from the bottom up.

The thin black line between some images indicates the last of the images for one unit
and the first of the next unit.

Admiral David Farragut	Major General William Rosecrans	Ulysses S. Grant	Benjamin Harrison
Clara Barton	Major General George Meade	Andrew Johnson	Grover Cleveland
General Albert Sidney Johnston	Major General Ambrose Burnside	Brigadier General John Hood	Chester A. Arthur
Major General George McClellan	Major General J.E.B. Stuart	General William Tecumseh Sherman	James A. Garfield
Major General Thomas "Stonewall" Jackson	Major General John Pope	General Braxton Bragg	Rutherford B. Hayes

All American History, Vol. II: Teacher's Guide — Section Seven

Starting at the right, cut images out of each column from the bottom up.

The thin black line between some images indicates the last of the images for one unit and the first of the next unit.

Admiral Pascual Cervera	Woodrow Wilson	Calvin Coolidge	General Douglas MacArthur
Colonel Theodore Roosevelt	General Jack Pershing	Warren G. Harding	General George Patton
Admiral George Dewey	Woodrow Wilson	Vittorio Orlando	General Dwight Eisenhower
Enrique de Lome	William Howard Taft	Georges Clemenceau	Franklin Delano Roosevelt
William McKinley	Theodore Roosevelt	David Lloyd-George	Herbert Hoover

Starting at the right, cut images out of each column from the bottom up.

The thin black line between some images indicates the last of the images for one unit and the first of the next unit.

Franklin Delano Roosevelt	Harry S. Truman	Gerald R. Ford	George W. Bush
Winston Churchill	Clement Attlee	Richard M. Nixon	William J. Clinton
Benito Mussolini	Harry S. Truman	Lyndon B. Johnson	George H.W. Bush
Adolf Hitler	Emperor Hirohito	John F. Kennedy	Ronald W. Reagan
Admiral Chester Nimitz	Joseph Stalin	Dwight D. Eisenhower	James E. Carter

Weak
Presidential
Leadership

1

Compromise
of
1850

2

Kansas-Nebraska
Act of
1854

3

Formation of
the Republican
Party

4

The
Dred Scott
Case

5

Election of 1860
and the
Confederacy

6

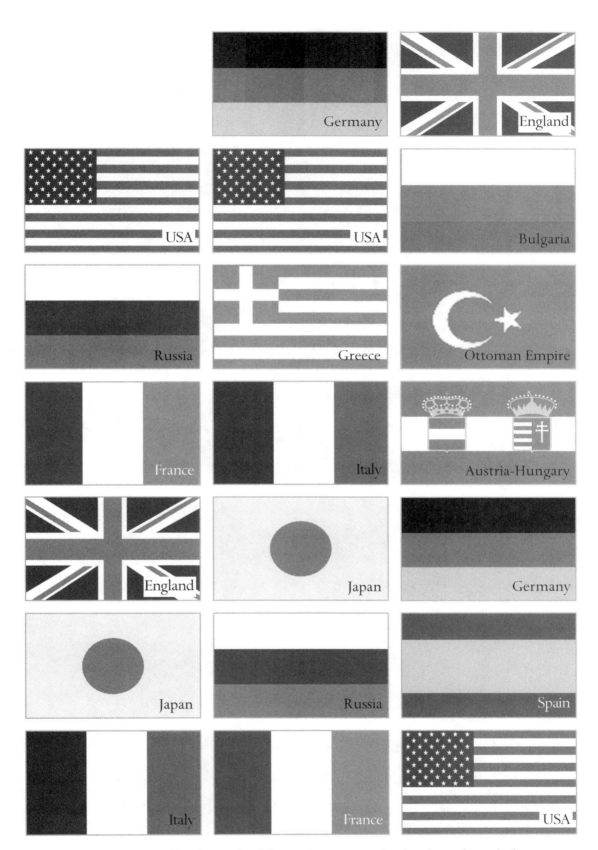

Starting at the right, cut images out of each column from the bottom up.

Appendix

SELECT BIBLIOGRAPHY

UNIT ONE

Baker, Jeffrey. *Strike the Tent*. Garden City: Doubleday, 1970.

Bender, David. *Reconstruction: Opposing Views*. San Diego: Greenhaven Press, 1995.

Brewer, Paul. *The American Civil War*. Austin: Raintree Steck-Vaughn, 1999.

Brooks, Victor. *Civil War Forts*. Philadelphia: Chelsea House, 2000.

Brown, Fern G. *Franklin Pierce: 14th President of the United States*. Ada: Garrett Educational Corporation, 1989.

Bunting, Eve. *The Blue and the Gray*. New York: Scholastic, 1996.

Carter, Alden. *The Civil War*. New York: Franklin Watts, 1992.

Chang, Ina. *A Separate Battle — Women and the Civil War*. New York: Lodestar Books, 1991.

Clinton, Catherine. *Hold the Flag High*. New York: Harper Collins, 2005.

Coddon, Karin. *Runaway Slaves*. San Diego: Greenhaven Press, 2004.

Collins, David R. *James Buchanan: 15th President of the United States*. Ada: Garrett Educational Corporation, 1990.

Collins, David R. *Zachary Taylor: 12th President of the United States*. Ada: Garrett Educational Corporation, 1989.

Cooper, Jason. *Gettysburg*. Vero Beach: Rourke Corporation, Inc., 1999.

Cox, Clinton. *Undying Glory*. New York: Scholastic, 1991.

D'Aulaire, Ingri and Edgar Parin. *Abraham Lincoln*. Garden City: Doubleday, 1957.

Ellis, Keith. *The American Civil War*. New York: Putnam, 1971.

Fritz, Jean. *Just a Few Words, Mr. Lincoln*. New York: Grosset and Dunlap, 1993.

Gay, Kathlyn and Martin. *Civil War: Voices from the Past*. New York: Henry Holt and Company, 1995.

Goldston, Robert. *The Coming of the Civil War*. New York: Macmillan, 1972.

Graves, Charles P. *Robert E. Lee: Hero of the South*. New York: Chelsea House, 1991.

Graves, Kerry. *The Civil War: America Goes to War*. Mankato: Capstone Press, 2001.

Hakim, Joy. *Liberty for All?* New York: Oxford University Press, 1994.

Hakim, Joy. *Reconstruction and Reform*. New York: Oxford University Press, 1994.

Hakim, Joy. *War, Terrible War*. New York: Oxford University Press, 1994.

Haskins, Jim. *The Day Fort Sumter Was Fired On*. New York: Scholastic, 1995.

Heinrich, Ann. *The Emancipation Proclamation*. Minneapolis: Compass Point Books, 2002.

Ito, Tom. *Mysterious Deaths: Abraham Lincoln*. San Diego: Lucent Books, 1997.

Jakoubek, Robert E. *Harriet Beecher Stowe*. New York: Chelsea House Publishers, 1989.

Kallen, Stuart. *The Civil War and Reconstruction*. New York: Abdo and Daughters, 1990.

Kent, Zachary. *Encyclopedia of Presidents: Andrew Johnson*. Chicago: Childrens Press, 1989.

Kent, Zachary. *Encyclopedia of Presidents: Ulysses S. Grant*. Chicago: Childrens Press, 1989.

King, David C. *American Kids in History: Civil War Days*. New York: John Wiley and Sons, 1999.

Law, Kevin J. *Millard Fillmore: 13th President of the United States*. Ada: Garrett Educational Corporation, 1990.

Lester, Julius. *To Be a Slave*. New York: Dial, 1968.

Lewin, Ted. *Red Legs: A Drummer Boy of the Civil War*. New York: Harper Collins, 2000.

Lilley, Stephen R. *Fighters Against American Slavery*. San Diego: Lucent Books, 1999.

MacDonald, John. *Great Battles of the Civil War*. New York: Macmillan Publishing Company, 1988.

McGovern, Ann. *If You Grew Up with Abraham Lincoln*. New York: Scholastic Books, 1966.

McLoone, Margo. *Frederick Douglass*. Mankato: Bridgestone Books, 1997,

McLoone, Margo. *Sojourner Truth*. Mankato: Bridgestone Books, 1997.

Malone, Mary. *Dorothea L. Dix: Hospital Founder*. New York: Chelsea House, 1991.

Moore, Kay. *If You Lived at the Time of the Civil War*. New York: Scholastic, 1994.

Nofi, Albert. *The Underground Railroad and the Civil War*. Philadelphia: Chelsea House, 2000.

O'Shei, Tim. *Ulysses. S. Grant: Military Leader and President*. New York: Chelsea House, 2001.

Ray, Delia. *A Nation Torn*. New York: Lodestar, 1990.

Ray, Delia. *Behind the Blue and the Gray*. New York: Lodestar, 1991.

Reef, Catherine. *Civil War Soldiers*. New York: Twenty First Century Books, 1993.

Roberts, Russell. *The Civil War: Lincoln and the Abolition of Slavery*. San Diego: Lucent Books, 2000.

Sandak, Cass. *The Lincolns*. New York: Crestwood House, 1992.

Savage. Douglas. *The Civil War in the West*. Philadelphia: Chelsea House, 2000.

Savage, Douglas. *Civil War Medicine*. Philadelphia: Chelsea House, 2000.

Savage, Douglas. *Ironclads and Blockades in the Civil War*. Philadelphia: Chelsea House, 2000.

Savage, Douglas. *Rangers, Jayhawkers, and Bushwhackers in the Civil War*. Philadelphia: Chelsea House, 2000.

Savage, Douglas. *The Soldier's Life in the Civil War*. Philadelphia: Chelsea House, 2000.

Savage, Douglas. *Women in the Civil War*. Philadelphia: Chelsea House, 2000.

Sinnott, Susan. *Charley Waters Goes to Gettysburg*. Brookfield: Millbrook Press, 2000.

Smith, Carter. *1863: The Crucial Year: A Sourcebook on the Civil War*. Brookfield: The Millbrook Press, 1993.

Steele, Christy. *A Confederate Girl: The Diary of Carrie Berry (1864)*. Mankato: Blue Earth Books, 2000.

Stevens, Rita. *Andrew Johnson: 17th President of the United States*. Ada: Garret Educational Corporation, 1989.

Tracey, Patrick Austin. *Military Leaders of the Civil War*. New York: Facts on File, 1993.

Weiner, Eric. *The Civil War: Facts America*. New York: Smithmark Publishers, Inc., 1992.

UNIT TWO

Alter, Judith. *Growing Up in the Old West*. New York: Franklin Watts, 1989.

Auchincloss, Louis. *The Vanderbilt Era: Profiles of a Gilded Age*. New York: Macmillan Publishing Company, 1989.

Bachrach, Deborah. *The Spanish-American War*. San Diego: Lucent Books, 1991.

Beckner, Chrisanne. *100 African-Americans Who Shaped American History*. San Mateo: Bluewood Books, 1995.

Blay, John S. *After the Civil War: A Pictorial Profile of America from 1865 to 1900*. New York: Bonanza Books, 1960.

Boni, Margaret Bradford. *Songs of the Gilded Age*. New York: Golden Press, 1960.

Brown, Fern G. *James A. Garfield: 20th President of the United States*. Asa: Garrett Educational Corporation, 1990.

Carlson, Laurie. *Westward Ho! An Activity Guide to the Wild West*. Chicago: Chicago Review Press, Inc., 1996.

Carter, Alden. *The Spanish-American War*. New York: Franklin Watts, 1992.

Casey, Jane Clark. *Encyclopedia of Presidents: William Howard Taft*. Chicago: Childrens Press, 1989.

Clinton, Susan. *The Story of Susan B. Anthony*. Chicago: Childrens Press, 1986.

Collins, David R. *Grover Cleveland: 22nd and 24th Presidents of the United States*. Ada: Garrett Educational Corporation, 1988.

Collins, David R. *William McKinley: 25th President of the United States*. Ada: Garrett Educational Corporation, 1990.

Fritz, Jean. *You Want Women to Vote, Lizzie Stanton?* New York: G. P. Putnam's Sons, 1995.

Gay, Kathlyn and Martin. *Voices from the Past: Spanish-American War*. New York: Henry Holt and Company, 1995.

George, Charles. *Life Under the Jim Crow Laws*. San Diego: Lucent Books, 2000.

Gibbons, Gail. *Yippee Yay! A Book about Cowboys and Cowgirls*. Boston: Little, Brown, and Company, 1998.

Glubok, Shirley. *The Art of America in the Gilded Age*. New York: Macmillan Publishing Company, 1974.

Goble, Paul and Dorothy. *Red Hawk's Account of Custer's Last Battle*. New York: Pantheon Books, 1969.

Goldman, David J. *Presidential Losers*. Minneapolis: Lerner Publications Company. 2004.

Graves, Kerry A. *America Goes to War: The Spanish-American War*. Mankato: Capstone Books, 2001.

Greenwood, Janette. *The Gilded Age: A History in Documents*. New York: Oxford University Press, 2000.

Hakim, Joy. *The New Nation*. New York: Oxford University Press, 1993.

Hitchcock, H. Wiley. *Music in the United States: A Historical Introduction*. Englewood Cliffs: Prentice-Hall, Inc, 1969.

Jarnow, Jesse. *America's Big Businesses in the Late 1800s: Oil, Steel, and Railroads*. New York: The Rosen Publishing Group. 2004.

Kalman, Bobbie. *Life in the Old West: Wagon Train*. New York: Crabtree Publishing Company, 1999.

Kent, Zachary. *Andrew Johnson: 17th President of the United States*. Chicago: Childrens Press, 1989.

King, David C. *American Kids in History: Pioneer Days*. New York: John Wiley and Sons, Inc., 1997.

King, David C. *Wild West Days*. New York: John Wiley and Sons, Inc., 1998.

Kingsbury, Robert. *The Assassination of James A. Garfield*. New York: The Rosen Publishing Company, 2002.

Kraft, Betsy Harvey. *Theodore Roosevelt: Champion of the American Spirit*. New York: Clarion Books, 2003.

Lewis, Arnold. *American Country Houses of the Gilded Age*. Toronto: Dover Publications, Inc., 1982.

Lickteig, Mary J. *Amelia Bloomer*. Mankato: Capstone Books, 1998.

McLerran, Alice. *The Ghost Dance*. New York: Clarion Books, 1995.

Matthews, Leonard J. *The Wild West in American History: Railroaders*. Vero Beach: Rourke Publications, Inc., 1989.

Merrill, Marlene Deahl. *Growing Up in Boston's Gilded Age: The Journal of Alice Stone Blackwell (1872–1874)*. Yale University Press, 1990.

Mitchell, Barbara. *The Wizard of Sound: A Story about Thomas Edison*. Minneapolis: Carolrhoda Books, 1991.

Reef, Catherine. *Buffalo Soldiers*. New York: 21st Century Books, 1993.

Robbins, Neal E. *Rutherford B. Hayes: 19th President of the United States*. Ada: Garrett Educational Corporation, 1989.

Ross, Stewart. *Fact or Fiction: Cowboys*. Brookfield: Copper Beech Books, 1995.

Segall, Grant. *John D. Rockefeller: Anointed with Oil*. New York: Oxford University Press, 2001.

Stein, R. Conrad. *Cornerstones of Freedom: Ellis Island*. Chicago: Childrens Press, 1992.

Stevens, Rita. *Benjamin Harrison: 23rd President of the United States*. Ada: Garrett Educational Corporation, 1989.

Stevens, Rita. *Chester A. Arthur: 21st President of the United States*. Ada: Garrett Educational Corporation, 1989.

Thrasher, Thomas. *Gunfighters*. San Diego: Lucent Books, 2000.

Venezia, Mike. *John Philip Sousa*. New York: Childrens Press, 1998.

Walker, Robert. *Everyday Life in the Age of Enterprise: 1865 – 1900*. New York: G. P. Putnam's Sons, 1967.

Wallner, Alexandra. *Laura Ingalls Wilder*. New York: Scholastic, 1997.

Weisberger, Bernard A. *Reaching for Empire (1890–1901)*. New York: Time, Inc., 1965.

Wright, David. *P. T. Barnum*. Austin: Raintree Steck-Vaughn, 1995.

Wukovits, John. *Annie Oakley*. Philadelphia: Chelsea House, 1997.

Wukovits, John. *Jesse James*. Philadelphia: Chelsea House, 1997.

UNIT THREE

Aaseng, Nathan. *Twentieth-Century Inventors*. New York: Facts on File, 1991.

Adler, David. *Lou Gehrig: The Luckiest Man*. San Diego: Harcourt Brace, 1997.

Ambrose, Stephen E. *The Good Fight: How World War II Was Won*. New York: Atheneum Book, 2001.

Bankston, John. *Shirley Temple*. Hockessin: Mitchell Lane Publishers, 2004.

Blassingame, Wyatt. *Franklin D. Roosevelt, Four Times President*. Champaign: Garrard Publishing, 1966.

Canadeo, Anne. *Warren G. Harding: 29th President of the United States*. Ada: Garrett Educational Corporation, 1990.

Collins, David. *Woodrow Wilson: 28th President of the United States*. Ada: Garrett Educational Corporation, 1989.

Cwiklik, Robert. *Albert Einstein and the Theory of Relativity*. Brookfiled: Millbrook Press, 1993.

Dewey, Anne. *Robert Goddard, Space Pioneer*. Boston: Little Brown, 1962.

Downey, Matthew. *The Twentieth Century: The Progressive Era and the First World War (1900–1918)*. New York: Macmillan, 1992.

Downey, Matthew. *The Twentieth Century: The Roaring Twenties and Unsettled Peace (1919–1929)*. New York: Macmillan, 1992.

Downey, Matthew. *The Twentieth Century: The Great Depression and World War II (1930–1945)*. New York: Macmillan, 1992.

Falkof, Lucile. *William Howard Taft: 27th President of the United States*. Ada: Garrett Educational Corporation, 1990.

Gaff, Jackie. *20th Century Art (1900–1910): New Ways of Seeing*. Milwaukee: Gareth Stevens Publishing, 2000.

Gaff, Jackie. *20th Century Art (1910–1920): The Birth of Abstract Art*. Milwaukee: Gareth Stevens Publishing, 2000.

Gaff, Jackie. *20th Century Art (1920–1940): Realism and Surrealism*. Milwaukee: Gareth Stevens Publishing, 2000.

Gay, Kathlyn and Martin. *Voices from the Past: World War II*. New York: Henry Holt and Company, 1995.

George, Charles. *Life Under the Jim Crow Laws*. San Diego: Lucent Books, 2000.

Gourley, Catherine. *Welcome to Molly's World—Growing Up in World War Two America*. Middleton: Pleasant Company Publications, 1999.

Graves, Charles. *Annie Oakley, the Shooting Star*. New York: Chelsea Juniors, 1991.

Hanson, Erica. *A Cultural History of the United States through the Decades: the 1920s*. San Diego: Lucent Books, 1999.

Hanson, Ole Steen. *The War in the Trenches*. New York: Raintree Steck-Vaughn, 2001.

Hitchcock, H. Wiley. *Music in the United States: A Historical Introduction*. Englewood Cliffs: Prentice-Hall, Inc., 1969.

Holford, David M. *United States Presidents: Herbert Hoover*. Berkeley Heights: Enslow Publishers, Inc., 1999.

Hopkinson, Deborah. *Pearl Harbor*. New York: Dillon Press, 1991.

Kallen, Stuart A. *World War II: The War at Home*. San Diego: Lucent Books, 2000.

King, David C. *American Kids in History: World War II Days*. New York: John Wiley and Sons, Inc., 2000.

Krull, Kathleen. *America Remembers World War II: V Is for Victory*. New York: Alfred A. Knopf, 1995.

Levinson, Nancy Smiler. *Turn of the Century: Our Nation One Hundred Years Ago*. New York: Lonestar Books, 1994.

Malone, Mary. *Will Rogers: Cowboy Philosopher*. Springfield: Enslow Publishers, 1996.

Maltby, Richard. *Popular Culture in the Twentieth Century*. London: Andromeda Oxford Limited, 1988.

Marshall, Richard. *Great Events of the Twentieth Century: How They Changed Our Lives*. Pleasantville: Reader's Digest Association, 1977.

Meehan, Elizabeth. *Twentieth-Century American Writers*. San Diego: Lucent Books. 2000.

Mitchell, Barbara. *America, I Hear You*. Minneapolis: Carolrhoda Books, 1987.

Mitchell, Barbara. *Click! A Story about George Eastman*. Minneapolis: Carolrhoda Books, 1986.

Mitchell, Barbara. *"Good Morning, Mr. President"—A Story about Carl Sandburg*. Minneapolis: Carolrhoda Books, 1988.

Mitchell, Barbara. *We'll Race You, Henry Ford*. Minneapolis: Carolrhoda Books, 1986.

Montgomery, Elizabeth Rider. *Alexander Graham Bell: Man of Sound*. Champaign: Garrard Publishing Company, 1963.

Montgomery, Elizabeth Rider. *Henry Ford: Automotive Pioneer*. Champaign: Garrard Publishing Company, 1969.

Montgomery, Elizabeth Rider. *Walt Disney: Master of Make Believe*. Champaign: Garrard Publishing Company, 1971.

Murphy, Wendy. *Frank Lloyd Wright*. Englewood Cliffs: Silver Burdett Press., 1990.

Peacock, John. *Twentieth Century Fashion*. New York: Thames and Hudson, 1993.

Polikoff, Barbara. *Herbert C. Hoover, 31st President of the United States*. Ada: Garrett Educational Corporation, 1990.

Press, Petra. *A Cultural History of the United States through the Decades: the 1930s*. San Diego: Lucent Books, 1999.

Preston, Diana. *Remember the Lusitania!* New York: Walker and Company, 2003.

Rollin, Lucy. *Twentieth Century Teen Culture by the Decades*. Westport: Greenwood Press, 1999.

Ross, Stewart. *Causes and Consequences of World War I*. Austin: Raintree Steck-Vaughn, 1998.

Sagan, Miriam. *Women's Suffrage*. San Diego: Lucent Books, 1995.

Sandak, Cass. *The Franklin Roosevelts*. New York: Crestwood House, 1992.

Sandak, Cass. *The Theodore Roosevelts*. New York: Crestwood House, 1991.

Sinnott, Susan. *Doing Our Part: American Women on the Home Front During World War II*. New York: Franklin Watts, 1995.

Sobol, Donald. *The Wright Brothers at Kitty Hawk*. New York: Thomas Nelson, 1961.

Sommerville, Donald. *World War I: History of Warfare*. Austin: Raintree Steck-Vaughn, 1999.

Stein, R. Conrad. *World at War: The Holocaust*. Chicago: Childrens Press, 1986.

Stevens, Rita. *Calvin Coolidge: 30th President of the United States*. Ada: Garrett Educational Corporation, 1990.

Tames, Richard. *The Eventful Century: The Way We Lived*. Pleasantville: the Reader's Digest Association, Inc., 1999.

Tanenhaus, Sam. *Louis Armstrong*. New York: Chelsea House, 1989.

Traylor, Myrna E. *20th- Century America: Time Life Student Library*. Richmond: Time-Life Education, Inc., 1999.

Uschan, Michael V. *A Cultural History of the United States through the Decades: the 1910s*. San Diego: Lucent Books, 1999.

Uschan, Michael V. *A Cultural History of the United States through the Decades: the 1940s*. San Diego: Lucent Books, 1999.

Wade, Linda. *Warren G. Harding: 29th President of the United States*. Chicago: Children's Press, 1989.

Wong, Adam. *A Cultural History of the United States through the Decades: the 1900s*. San Diego: Lucent Books, 1999.

Younkin, Paula. *Spirit of St.Louis*. New York: Crestwood House, 1994.

UNIT FOUR

Aaseng, Nathan. *Twentieth-Century Inventors*. New York: Facts on File, 1991.

Adler, David. *A Picture Book of Martin Luther King, Jr.* New York: Holiday House, 1989.

Anger, David. *Robert A. M. Stern*. Minneapolis: Capstone Press, 1996.

Barbour, Scott. *Lyndon B. Johnson*. San Diego: Greenhaven Press, 2001.

Billings, Charlene. *Christa McAuliffe, Pioneer Space Teacher*. Hillside: Enslow Publishers, 1986.

Buell, Tonya. *Terrorist Attacks: The Crash of United Flight 93 on September 11, 2001*. New York: The Rosen Publishing Group, 2003.

Collins, David. *Gerald R. Ford: 38th President of the United States*. Ada: Garrett Educational Corporation, 1990.

Collins, David. *Harry S. Truman: 33rd President of the United States*. Ada: Garrett Educational Corporation, 1989.

Collins, David. *William Jefferson Clinton: 42nd President of the United States*. Ada: Garrett Educational Corporation, 1995.

Downey, Matthew. *The Twentieth Century: Postwar Prosperity and the Cold War (1946–1963)*. New York: Macmillan, 1992.

Downey, Matthew. *The Twentieth Century: The Civil Rights Movement to the Vietnam Era (1964–1975)*. New York: Macmillan, 1992.

Downey, Matthew. *The Twentieth Century: Baby Boomers and the New Conservatism (1976–1991)*. New York: Macmillan, 1992.

Ellis, Rafaela. *Dwight D. Eisenhower: 34th President of the United States*. Ada: Garrett Educational Corporation, 1989.

Epstein, Dan. *20th Century Pop Culture: The 50s*. Philadelphia: Chelsea House Publishers, 2001.

Epstein, Dan. *20th Century Pop Culture: The 60s*. Philadelphia: Chelsea House Publishers, 2001.

Epstein, Dan. *20th Century Pop Culture: The 70s*. Philadelphia: Chelsea House Publishers, 2001.

Epstein, Dan. *20th Century Pop Culture: The 80s*. Philadelphia: Chelsea House Publishers, 2001.

Epstein, Dan. *20th Century Pop Culture: The 90s*. Philadelphia: Chelsea House Publishers, 2001.

Falkof, Lucille. *John F. Kennedy: 35th President of the United States*. Ada: Garrett Educational Corporation, 1988.

Falkof, Lucille. *Lyndon B. Johnson: 36th President of the United States*. Ada: Garrett Educational Corporation, 1989.

Fremon, David K. *The Watergate Scandal in American History*. Springfield: Enslow Publishers, Inc., 1009.

Gard, Carolyn. *Terrorist Attacks: The Attack on the Pentagon on September 11, 2001*. New York: The Rosen Publishing Group, 2003.

Gath, Jackie. *20th Century Art (1940–1960): Emotion and Expression*. Milwaukee: Gareth Stevens Publishing, 2000.

Gath, Jackie. *20th Century Art (1960–1980): Experiments and New Directions*. Milwaukee: Gareth Stevens Publishing, 2000.

Gath, Jackie. *20th Century Art (1980–2000): New Media, New Messages*. Milwaukee: Gareth Stevens Publishing, 2000.

George, Charles. *Life Under the Jim Crow Laws*. San Diego: Lucent Books, 2000.

Graham, Billy. *Just as I Am: the Autobiography of Billy Graham*. San Francisco: Harper, 1997.

Green, Robert Green. *George W. Bush: Business Executive and U.S. President*. Chicago: Ferguson Publishing Company, 2000.

Hamilton, John. *War on Terrorism: Operation Noble Eagle*. Edina: Abdo and Daughters, 2002.

Hay, Jeff. *Richard M. Nixon*. San Diego: Greenhaven Press, 2001.

Hitchcock, H. Wiley. *Music in the United States: A Historical Introduction*. Englewood Cliffs: Prentice-Hall, Inc., 1969.

Holland, Gini. *A Cultural History of the United States through the Decades: the 1960s*. San Diego: Lucent Books, 1999.

Howard, Todd. *William J. Clinton*. San Diego: Greenhaven Press, 2001.

Italia, Bob. *Bill Clinton: 42nd President of the United States*. Edina: Abdo and Daughters, 1993.

Kallen, Stuart. *A Cultural History of the United States through the Decades: the 1950s*. San Diego: Lucent Books, 1999.

Kallen, Stuart. *A Cultural History of the United States through the Decades: the 1980s*. San Diego: Lucent Books, 1999.

Kallen, Stuart. *A Cultural History of the United States through the Decades: the 1990s*. San Diego: Lucent Books, 1999.

King, Dexter Scott. *Growing Up King*. New York: Warner Books, 2003.

Levinson, Nancy Smiler. *Turn of the Century: Our Nation One Hundred Years Ago*. New York: Lonestar Books, 1994.

McKown, Robin. *Eleanor Roosevelt's World*. New York: Grosset and Dunlap, 1964.

Maltby, Richard. *Popular Culture in the Twentieth Century*. London: Andromeda Oxford Limited, 1988.

Marquez, Heron. *George W. Bush*. Minneapolis: Lerner Publications, 2006.

Marsh, Carole. *The Day That Was Different—September 11, 2001 (When America Was Attacked by Terrorists)*. New York: Gallopade International, 2001.

Marshall, Richard. *Great Events of the Twentieth Century: How They Changed Our Lives*. Pleasantville: Reader's Digest Association, 1977.

Meehan, Elizabeth. *Twentieth-Century American Writers*. San Diego: Lucent Books, 2000.

Peacock, John. *Twentieth Century Fashion*. New York: Thames and Hudson, 1993.

Randolph, Sallie. *Gerald R. Ford President*. New York: Walker and Company, 1987.

Rediger, Pat. *Great African Americans in Civil Rights*. New York: Crabtree Publishing Company, 1996.

Richman, Daniel. *James E. Carter: 39th President of the United States*. Ada: Garrett Educational Corporation, 1989.

Robinson, Sharon. *Promises to Keep: How Jackie Robinson Changed America*. New York: Scholastic Press, 2004.

Rollin, Lucy. *Twentieth Century Teen Culture by the Decades*. Westport: Greenwood Press, 1999.

Sandak, Cass. *The Lyndon Johnsons*. New York: Crestwood House, 1993.

Sandak, Cass. *The Kennedys*. New York: Crestwood House, 1991.

Sandak, Cass. *The Nixons*. New York: Crestwood House, 1992.

Sandak, Cass. *The Reagans*. New York: Crestwood House, 1993.

Sandak, Cass. *The Tafts*. New York: Crestwood House, 1993.

Sandak, Cass. *The Trumans*. New York: Crestwood House, 1992.

Steffof, Rebecca. *George H. W. Bush: 41st President of the United States*. Ada: Garrett Educational Corporation, 1990.

Steffof, Rebecca. *Richard M. Nixon: 37th President of the United States*. Ada: Garrett Educational Corporation, 1990.

Stein, R. Conrad. *The Story of the Assassination of John F. Kennedy*. Chicago: Childrens Press, 1985.

Steins, Richard. *The Postwar Years: The Cold War and the Atomic Age (1950–1959)*. New York: Henry Holt and Company, 1993.

Stewart, Gail. *A Cultural History of the United States through the Decades: 1970s*. San Diego: Lucent Books, 1999.

Tames, Richard. *The Eventful Century: The Way We Lived*. Pleasantville: the Reader's Digest Association, Inc., 1999.

Thomson, Virgil. *American Music Since 1910*. New York: Holt, Rinehart, and Winston. 1970.

Torr, James D. *Ronald Reagan*. San Diego: Greenhaven Press, 2001.

Traylor, Myrna E. *20th-Century America: Time Life Student Library*. Richmond: Time-Life Education, Inc., 1999.

Wheeler, Jill C. *War on Terrorism: America's Leaders*. Edina: Abdo and Daughters, 2002.

Wheeler, Jill C. *War on Terrorism: September 11, 2001—The Day that Changed America*. Edina: Abdo and Daughters, 2002.

Wheeler, Jill C. *War on Terrorism: George W. Bush*. Edina: Abdo and Daughters, 2002.

Woodson, Jacqueline. *Martin Luther King, Jr. and His Birthday*. Englewood Cliffs: Silver Press, 1990.

ALSO AVAILABLE FROM
BRIGHT IDEAS PRESS...

All American History by Celeste W. Rakes
Containing hundreds of images and dozens of maps, *All American History* is a complete year's curriculum for students in grades 5 – 8 when combined with the Student Activity Book and Teacher's Guide (yet adaptable for younger and older students).

There are 32 weekly lessons, and each lesson contains three sections examining the atmosphere in which the event occurred, the event itself, and the impact this event had on the future of America.

- Vol. I Student Reader—
  ISBN: 1-892427-12-5
- Vol. I Student Activity Book—
  ISBN: 1-892427-11-7
- Vol. I Teacher's Guide—
  ISBN: 1-892427-10-9

The Mystery of History Volumes I & II by Linda Hobar
This award-winning series provides a historically accurate, Bible-centered approach to learning world history. The completely chronological lessons shed new light on who walked the earth when, as well as on where important Bible figures fit into secular history. Grades 4 – 8, yet easily adaptable.

- Volume I: Creation to the Resurrection—
  ISBN: 1-892427-04-4
- Volume II: The Early Church & the
  Middle Ages—ISBN: 1-892427-06-0

CHRISTIAN KIDS EXPLORE... SERIES

Christian Kids Explore Biology by Stephanie Redmond
One of Cathy Duffy's 100 Top Picks! Elementary biology that is both classical and hands-on. Conversational style and organized layout make teaching a pleasure.

- ISBN: 1-892427-05-2

Christian Kids Explore Earth & Space by Stephanie Redmond
Another exciting book in this award-winning series! Author Redmond is back with more great lessons, activities, and ideas.

- ISBN: 1-892427-19-2

Christian Kids Explore Chemistry
by Robert W. Ridlon, Jr., and Elizabeth J. Ridlon
Authors Robert and Elizabeth Ridlon team up for 30 lessons, unit wrap-ups, and even coloring pages all about the fascinating world of chemistry.

- ISBN: 1-892427-18-4

Christian Kids Explore Physics
NEW!
by Robert W. Ridlon, Jr., and Elizabeth J. Ridlon
Both college professors and creation scientists, the Ridlons offer their depth of knowledge about science and scripture.

- ISBN: 1-892427-20-6

FOR ORDERING INFORMATION, CALL 877.492.8081 OR
VISIT WWW.BRIGHTIDEASPRESS.COM